Sex and the Cthulhu Mythos

THE HIPPOCAMPUS PRESS LIBRARY OF CRITICISM

S. T. Joshi, *Primal Sources: Essays on H. P. Lovecraft* (2003)
S. T. Joshi and David E. Schultz, *An H. P. Lovecraft Encyclopedia* (2004)
Robert H. Waugh, *The Monster in the Mirror: Looking for H. P. Lovecraft* (2006)
Mara Kirk Hart and S. T. Joshi, eds., *Lovecraft's New York Circle: The Kalem Club, 1924-1927* (2006)
Kenneth W. Faig, Jr., *The Unknown Lovecraft* (2009)
S. T. Joshi, ed., *A Weird Writer in our Midst: Early Criticism of H. P. Lovecraft* (2010)
Robert H. Waugh, *A Monster of Voices: Speaking for H. P. Lovecraft* (2011)
S. T. Joshi and David E. Schultz, eds., *An Epicure in the Terrible: A Centennial Anthology of Essays in Honor of H. P. Lovecraft* (2011)
Steven J. Mariconda, *H. P. Lovecraft: Art, Artifact, and Reality* (2013)
S. T. Joshi, *Unutterable Horror: A History of Supernatural Fiction* (2014)
S. T. Joshi, *Lovecraft and a World in Transition: Collected Essays on H. P. Lovecraft* (2014)
Lovecraft Annual (2007–)
Dead Reckonings (2007–)

SEX
and the Cthulhu Mythos

Bobby Derie

Hippocampus Press
New York

Copyright © 2014 by Bobby Derie.

Published by Hippocampus Press
P.O. Box 641, New York, NY 10156.
http://www.hippocampuspress.com

All rights reserved.
No part of this work may be reproduced in any form or by any means without the written permission of the publisher.

Archival material by Gahan Wilson from *Playboy* magazine. Copyright © 1973 by Playboy. Reprinted by permission. All rights reserved.

Cover design by Barbara Briggs Silbert.
Hippocampus Press logo designed by Anastasia Damianakos.

First Edition
1 3 5 7 9 8 6 4 2

ISBN13: 978-1-61498-088-9

Contents

Introduction 9
1. Sex and Lovecraft 13
   Lovecraft and Love..14
   Views on Sex 15
   Views on Love and Relationships 23
   Views on Eroticism and Pornography 28
   The Shadow of Syphilis 34
   Views on Gender and Homosexuality 38
   Views on Miscegenation 48
   Mrs. H. P. Lovecraft..53
2. Sex and the Lovecraft Mythos 57
   Precursors and Influences 58
      "The Great God Pan" (1890) 61
      "Novel of the Black Seal" (1895) 63
      "The White People" (1904)..64
   Analyses 65
      "Facts concerning the Late Arthur Jermyn and His Family" (1920) 70
      "The Outsider" (1921) 73
      "The Lurking Fear" (1922)...73
      "The Rats in the Walls" (1923)..75
      "The Unnamable" (1923) 77
      "The Horror at Red Hook" (1925) 78
      The Dream-Quest of Unknown Kadath (1926-27) 79
      The Case of Charles Dexter Ward (1927) 80
      "The Dunwich Horror" (1928)...81
      "The Shadow over Innsmouth" (1931) 85
      "The Dreams in the Witch House" (1932) 90
      "The Thing on the Doorstep" (1933)..91
      "Supernatural Horror in Literature" (1927; revised 1933) 97
   Collaborations 99
      "Poetry and the Gods" (with Anna Helen Crofts) (1920) 99

    "Ashes" (with C. M. Eddy, Jr.) (1924) 100
    "The Loved Dead" (with C. M. Eddy, Jr.) (1924) 100
    "The Last Test" (with Adolphe de Castro) (1927) 101
    "The Curse of Yig" (with Zealia Bishop) (1928) 102
    "The Mound" (with Zealia Bishop) (1929–30) 103
    "Medusa's Coil" (with Zealia Bishop) (1930) 104
    "The Man of Stone" (with Hazel Heald) (1932) 106
    "The Horror in the Burying-Ground" (with Hazel Heald) (1933/35).... 106
Themes and Parallels...107
  Sexual Symbolism in Lovecraft.. 107
  Weird Sex... 109
  The Lure of the Forbidden 110
  Forbidden Knowledge, Personal Transformation 111
  Miscegenation and Mis-generation.. 112
The Role of Women 113
  The Unseen Mothers 115
  The Wise Woman.. 117
  The Anti-Gothic Heroine 118
  Lovecraft's Slatterns 119
  Rape in the Lovecraft Mythos 120
  Searching for Shub-Niggurath 121
Asexual Aliens 124
Homosexual Interpretation 128

3. Sex and the Cthulhu Mythos.. **131**
New Developments 132
  Family Trees of the Gods.. 134
  Naming the Unnamable 136
  The *Necronomicon* as Pornography.. 137
  Body Horror.. 140
    Pregnancy 141
    The Tentacle as a Sexual Symbol.. 142
  Alien Heats.. 153
  Parody.. 156
Lovecraft as a Sexual Character 157
Gender, Sexuality, and Mythos Writers 159
Key Works and Authors 162
  Robert E. Howard.. 164
  Clark Ashton Smith... 171
  Robert Bloch 176
  August Derleth.. 179

Ramsey Campbell 188
Richard A. Lupoff 195
Peter H. Cannon 196
Brian McNaughton 198
Robert M. Price 205
W. H. Pugmire 210
Caitlín R. Kiernan 214
Edward Lee 218
Alan Moore 223
Cthulhu Sex Magazine (1998-2007) 228
Eldritch Blue: Love & Sex in the Cthulhu Mythos (2004) 229
Cthulhurotica (2010) 231
Whispers in Darkness: Lovecraftian Erotica (2011) 233
Other Authors and Works of Note 234
Sex and Mythos Poetry 238
Mythos Ebook Erotica 239

4. Beyond Cthulhurotica 243
  Sex and the Lovecraftian Occult 244
    Background 245
    Kenneth Grant 248
    Michael Bertiaux 252
    Simon 253
    Phil Hine 254
    Donald Tyson 256
    Asenath Mason 258
  Sex and the Mythos in Art 260
  Sex and the Mythos in Comics 263
  Sex and the Mythos in Japanese Manga and Anime 271
  Sex and the Mythos Cinema 273
  The Mythos and Rule 34 284
    Discussion 285
    Fanfiction 285
    Fanart 286
    Webcomics 287

Afterword 289
Works Cited 291
Suggested Further Reading 301
Index 305

Introduction

Any warning I might give to readers about the contents of this study will no doubt pale in comparison to what they themselves will picture given the title; I can only say that it is both more and less perverse than you may imagine. Writing this essay has found me following in the footsteps of Lovecraft's fictional scholars, tracking down esoteric, occult, and obscene works and forcing myself to read and consider them. In walking in the shadow of earlier writers who have assayed the topic, I have been forced to re-examine what I thought I knew of the Mythos and the assumptions I had made of Lovecraft and his fiction; and I believe that this has deepened my understanding and appreciation for the man, his work, and all that came after. I do not ask that readers agree with my analsyses or conclusions, but only that they keep an open mind and give due consideration to the material.

There has been academic interest on the role of sex and gender in the weird fiction of H. P. Lovecraft, and the sexuality of Lovecraft himself, since his earliest biographies. Less has been published about Lovecraft's use of sex in his stories, and scarcely anything has been written of the sexually aware and explicit Cthulhu Mythos stories that came after Lovecraft. Work on all three subjects is sporadic and scattered, often in obscure fanzines and literary journals, addressed piecemeal in reviews and critiques. This book draws together these disparate bits of scholarship and adds to the store in an effort to present a comprehensive view of Lovecraft, his weird fiction, and the Cthulhu Mythos with regard to sex.

The first section of this book, "Sex and Lovecraft," examines the sexuality and views of H. P. Lovecraft. A shelf's worth of biographies, commentaries, and collected letters has laid bare much of Lovecraft's personal and professional life; this chapter focuses only on those areas of relevant interest: his personal thoughts on love and sex, his sexual education and attitudes, etc. Lovecraft the sexual entity is worthy of study for two reasons: the insight it gives into his fiction, and the elements of his personal life that have been used in stories that feature Lovecraft (or his family) as characters.

The second section, "Sex and the Lovecraft Mythos," deals with sexuality and gender in Lovecraft's corpus of weird fiction. Of particular interest are his literary influences and the themes he developed and expressed through his own stories and his revisions. The Lovecraft Mythos remains the well from which most later Mythos authors draw to create their own pastiches and additions to the Cthulhu Mythos, and it is important to understand the foundation stories to truly appreciate and understand the works of those who followed Lovecraft.

The third section, "Sex and the Cthulhu Mythos," examines the development of sexuality and gender in Mythos stories outside the body of Lovecraft's fiction. Attention is given to the most prominent, influential, and seminal works and authors, particularly the adult or erotic anthologies that are important milestones in collecting such fiction and presenting some literary insight into the creation of sexually explicit Mythos stories.

The fourth section, "Beyond Cthulhurotica," is a brief discourse on sexual Mythos material in other media. As the Mythos has expanded into film, comics, and manga, on the Internet, and the literature of the occult, so has there been a discernible undercurrent of sexually cognizant Mythos materials in those new forms.

A Note on Sources and Citations

Many of the original articles and creative works cited by authorities on Lovecraft and the Mythos are scarce and somewhat obscure, as are a few of the more ephemeral sources that combine the Mythos and adult content. Where possible, I have tracked down the original fanzines and publications for citation; where this has not been possible, because of rarity or cost, I have resorted to reprints or simply pointed the reader in the proper direction. Any italics, ellipses not in brackets, and alternate or incorrect spellings are quoted exactly as they appear in the text.

For brevity and in keeping with established tradition, a code for multi-volume works like Lovecraft's *Selected Letters* will be used in place of the standard method of citation. The following abbreviations are used:

CC Lovecraft, *The Call of Cthulhu and Other Weird Stories* (1999)
CF Smith, *The Collected Fantasies of Clark Ashton Smith* (5 vols.)

CrC	Lovecraft et al., *The Crawling Chaos and Others* (2011)
DWH	Lovecraft, *The Dreams in the Witch House and Other Weird Stories* (2004)
ES	Lovecraft and Derleth, *Essential Solitude* (2008)
HM	Lovecraft et al., *The Horror in the Museum and Other Revisions* (1989)
LJM	Lovecraft, *Letters to James F. Morton* (2011)
LR	Cannon, *Lovecraft Remembered* (1998)
LRB	Lovecraft, *Letters to Robert Bloch* (1993)
LRK	Lovecraft, *Letters to Rheinhart Kleiner* (2005)
LSLS	Lovecraft, *Letters to Samuel Loveman & Vincent Starrett* (1994)
MC	Lovecraft et al., *Medusa's Coil and Others* (2012)
MF	Lovecraft and Howard, *A Means to Freedom* (2009)
OFF	Lovecraft, *O Fortunate Floridian* (2007)
REH	Howard, *The Collected Letters of Robert E. Howard* (3 vols.)
TD	Lovecraft, *The Thing on the Doorstep and Other Weird Stories* (2001)

Thanks and appreciation to Andrew Heston, Carrie Cuinn, Dan Harms, François Launet, Jess Gulbranson, Justine Geoffrey, Katha Pollitt, Kevin L. O'Brien, Matthew Carpenter, Robert M. Price, Scott R. Jones, and S. T. Joshi for all their help and support.

1. Sex and Lovecraft

The study of Lovecraft's life and beliefs is grounded in three purposes: the greater understanding of his fiction, the mining of his materials for new works, and the interest elicited in the reader about the author. More than seventy years after his death, Howard Phillips Lovecraft the man has passed from living memory, but lives on through his fiction, his letters, and the recollections of others. Scholarship into Lovecraft's sexuality, sex life, relationships, and his attitudes and beliefs toward gender, sex in literature, and sexuality in life has been sporadic, but is an important and often overlooked element in understanding the Lovecraft Mythos, and through that the greater Cthulhu Mythos that arose after his death.

This chapter is not an attempt to analyze Lovecraft's character, but to summarize and organize what is known of his life and beliefs, through his own accounts, those of his friends, and especially his former wife Sonia. The focus will begin on his own views and sexual education, as expressed through his letters and supported by the statements of those that knew him. This chapter will finish with a few issues of particular attention in Lovecraft scholarship—the fact that Lovecraft's father died of syphilis; his gender prejudice, particularly with regard to women and homosexuals; and his views on miscegenation. These subjects are relevant not only as some of the most controversial elements of Lovecraft's character, but for their impact (real or perceived) on his fiction and the adult-oriented Cthulhu Mythos fiction that followed. They will provide a transition to discussing "Sex and the Lovecraft Mythos."

The tenth chapter of L. Sprague de Camp's *Lovecraft: A Biography* (1975), entitled "Bashful Lover," is basically a prototype of this chapter. De Camp was the first to refer to and quote extensively from Lovecraft's letters in an attempt to understand his sexual orientation, views, and life. The material was controversial at the time, and one can see in the beginning of chapter 14 in Frank Belknap Long's *Howard Phillips Lovecraft: Dreamer on the Nightside* (1975) an effort to counter or correct de Camp's claims—*Dreamer* having been written and published in haste by Long in response to reading some manuscript chapters of de Camp's biography. The two main flaws of both chapters are a lack of information, since more letters and anecdotes have come to light since 1975, and biases in trying to interpret Lovecraft's personality—or, in Long's case, in an effort to salvage his reputation. While I endeavor to do better, no doubt a future commenter will observe the same basic mistakes in this work. Readers are advised to consider the material in this chapter with that in mind.

Lovecraft and Love

The trouble began with Winfield Townsley Scott, who in "His Own Most Fantastic Creation: Howard Phillips Lovecraft" summed up Lovecraft's sexuality:

> His stories are sexless and one supposes the man was nearly so, all but mothered into impotency. One can say that almost all of his adult relationships were homosexual, if the word is intended in the blandest sense: there is no sign of strong sexual impulse of any kind. He was "not at ease" with women. His marriage was a mistake and a quick failure. He was disturbed by even mildly sexual writing. When he bought pulps at Douglass Dana's Old College Book Shop, at the foot of College Street, he tore off the more lurid covers lest friends misunderstand his interests. (*LR* 26)

Scott's essay first appeared in Arkham House's *Marginalia* (1944) and was later revised and included in his own collection *Exiles and Fabrications* (1961); it was most recently reprinted in *Lovecraft Remembered* (1998) and has thus influenced over five decades of Lovecraft scholarship. There was good reason for this, because it contained much important original research on the facts of Lovecraft's life, that of his parents and family, and personal communications with Lovecraft's former wife; but in the past several decades a much more complete picture of Lovecraft's personal life has emerged that disabuses many of Townley's notions of Lovecraft as sexless or impotent, either in his fiction or as a man.

By his own admissions and the recollections of others, Lovecraft rarely discussed sex, particularly racy or spicy stories. This sometimes made him the odd man out in the crowd at Kalem Club meetings in New York, as Sonia attested:

when the boys and HPL used to meet in his (Sam Loveman's) studio room on Clinton Street, when I was not there—whether they did it on purpose or to tease him, they would open a conversation re sex, knowing that Lovecraft did not like to listen to such stories [. . .] (Everts)

Sonia's account is in keeping with the letters of another Kalem Club member, George W. Kirk, who records that at least a few times sex became a focus for conversation (Hart and Joshi 28, 33). One in particular is of especial interest: "One was a homo, one an avowed fetishist, one quite nothing where sex is concerned, and your GW with whom you are usually acquainted" (Hart and Joshi 28). George Kirk is "GW." It is tempting to assign these sexual identities from among known Kalemites, perhaps Loveman ("homo"), Morton ("fetishist"), and Lovecraft ("quite nothing"), but this is mere speculation on my part. Frank Belknap Long, for instance, is cited as saying that "Morton [. . .] would never have mentioned sex in conversation," though this seems strange given what we know of Morton's past participation in a "free love" group and such (Cannon 1997, 23).

However, Lovecraft did talk about sex in his letters. In 1919, for example, he began a conversation by correspondence with fellow writer Rheinhart Kleiner on sex (SL 1.88), and George Kirk recalls talking with Lovecraft about "certain aspects of the sex" during a long autumn walk in New York (Hart and Joshi 65). It is these few published letters and recollections that give some insight into the most personal life of a most private gentleman and provides some direct statements of Lovecraft's views on love, sex, marriage, and eroticism in art and literature. Lovecraft, like all human beings, continued to refine and re-evaluate his opinions over time, and as related in his letters (SL 1.122), fiction, and actions, his views on sex, eroticism, and human relationships continued to change and develop throughout his life. The most notable example of such a change is his relationship with Sonia H. Greene, who in 1924 would become his wife.

Views on Sex

In a 1924 letter to Frank Belknap Long, Lovecraft described his initial sexual education:

> When I was six or seven I was of course curious about the allusions which I did not understand in adult books, and about the prohibitions imposed by elders upon my conversation. Being of a scientifick and investigative cast, I

naturally followed up the mysteries step by step in encyclopedias and other books—for with my temper no one dared seriously restrict my reading. Ending with the medical books of my physician-uncle, I knew everything there is to be known about the anatomy and physiology of reproduction in both sexes before I was eight years old; after which curiosity was of course impossible. The entire subject had become merely a tedious detail of animal biology [. . .] (SL 1.304)

A decade later, in a letter to J. Vernon Shea, Lovecraft offered a slightly different take on this story:

In the matter of the justly celebrated "Facts of life" I didn't wait for oral information, but exhausted the entire subject in the medical section of the family library (to which I had access, although I wasn't especially loquacious about this side of my reading) when I was 8 years old—through Quain's Anatomy (fully illustrated & diagrammed), Dunglinson's Physiology, &c. &c. This was because of curiosity & perplexity concerning the strange reticences & embarrassments of adult speech, & the oddly inexplicable allusions & situations in standard literature. The result was the very opposite of what parents generally fear—for instead of giving me an abnormal & precocious interest in sex (as *unsatisfied* curiosity might have done), it virtually killed my interest in the subject. The whole matter was reduced to prosaic mechanism—a mechanism which I rather despised or at least thought non-glamourous because of its purely animal nature & separation from such things as intellect & beauty—& all the drama was taken out of it. When the kids talked or acted dirtily I could have told them more than they tried to tell me [. . .] (SL 4.355–56)

The two passages differ in exact details, but the essential story told in each letter is consistent and in keeping with Lovecraft's materialist view of the universe. Curiosity satisfied, Lovecraft appears to have had little actual interest in pursuing further knowledge of sex, as he stated in a letter to Kleiner in 1919: "Of course I am unfamiliar with amatory phenomena save through cursory reading" (SL 1.88). According to Everts, Lovecraft's ex-wife Sonia confided that "Lovecraft purchased and read thoroughly all subject matter he could obtain regarding marriage, sex and the duties of a husband in the connubial bed" (Everts). The depth and nature of Lovecraft's reading in this area is unknown, but there were plentiful available works that Lovecraft might have stumbled across in his normal reading of literary and scientific materials, plus whatever he might have gotten from his friends, and a few possibilities in particular deserve attention.

Everts suggests as a possible source for such materials Lovecraft's friend and correspondent James Ferdinand Morton. "Mortonius," as Lovecraft nicknamed him, was well-versed in sexual matters, had written some explicit erotic poetry, and even dabbled in a free love group in the early 1900s (Everts), but by the 1920s was getting old, lonely, and "of late a believer in matrimony, and proposes about once a week to the ornate Mme. Greene" (SL 1.178). Whether Lovecraft consulted Morton or any of his other friends is unknown. Aside from Morton, at least two of his fellow Kalemites may have supplied materials: the booksellers George Kirk and Samuel Loveman. Kirk's letters from the period indicate that he dealt somewhat in under-the-counter materials and would have at least been able to direct Lovecraft to a good lending library for sexology materials.

Lovecraft does mention several times in his letters then-current "sexologists" and writers on sex, marriage, and relationships such as Bertrand Russell, Sigmund Freud, Auguste Forel, Richard von Krafft-Ebing, and in particular Havelock Ellis (SL 3.70-72, 106; 4.298, 5.164). Another possible source of material was Lovecraft's revision client, the Rev. David Van Bush, a public lecturer of popular psychology, clergyman, and poet. During the course of their business relationship, Bush published such works as *Practical Psychology and Sex Life* (1922) and *Psychology of Sex: How to Love and Marry* (1924)—the latter issued the same year as Lovecraft and Sonia were married. It is impossible to know whether Lovecraft read either of these books, much less revised any part of them for the author. Though he was certainly engaging in "Bush work" (as he liked to put it) during the period, this appears to have been mostly poetry. (Joshi 2010, 405-9).

Lovecraft recognized Freud's eminence in psychology and the value of his work and those of his successors such as Alfred Adler (SL 1.134). It is not clear how much of Freud's work he actually read (Joshi 2010, 469-70), but he obviously did not care for all Freud's theories, particularly concerning dreams and psychosexual development. (OFF 246). Lovecraft refers in his letters to Havelock Ellis, Krafft-Ebing, et al., but he never mentions when exactly he read them, or what specific works of theirs he read, except in one instance. Lovecraft first names a group of sexologists in a 1929 letter to Woodburn Harris, and in the same letter he mentions by title Ellis's *Little Essays in Love & Virtue* (1922) (SL 3.60). If it was the only work by Ellis that Lovecraft read, he might have done so shortly before his marriage, when he was studying to be a husband. The continued reference to Ellis's writings as late as 1935 suggests that they had some impact on Lovecraft, or at least that he continued to see Ellis as an authority (SL 5.164). It is possible that Lovecraft did not read the sexologists, but only mentioned known and significant authorities; regrettably, the specific terminology and ideas Lovecraft uses are too general to trace definitively back to individual authors. Whatever the case, the impact of Lovecraft's academic reading on his conception and perception of sex appears to have fed into his generally materialist line of thought. Lovecraft was at least conversant enough to recognize and discuss sadism, homosexuality, pedophilia, necrophilia, and incest with correspondents like Robert E. Howard and August Derleth when the subjects arose, and he appeared to give them roots in both biological and psychological causes.

Aside from academic works, Lovecraft certainly read other literature that might have influenced his thoughts on love and sex. Winfield Townley Scott, taking a cue from Sonia's memoir (Davis 1992, 23-24), suggests *The Private Papers of Henry Ryecroft* (1903) by George Gissing as a major influence on Lovecraft, noting: "There is no love in Ryecroft's life" (LR 24-25).

Sonia also claims that Lovecraft invoked the almost-marriage of Edgar Allan Poe and Sarah Helen Whitman (Davis 1992, 27)—though later, after his marriage, he would write disparagingly of "the maundering love-letters of Poe & Mrs. Whitman" (SL 3.65). S. T. Joshi has speculated on which version of the *Arabian Nights* a young Lovecraft might have read: "Interestingly, in light of Lovecraft's later racial views, several tales speak with outrage about sexual encounters between black men and Islamic women" (Joshi 2010, 31). Ultimately, however, Lovecraft himself gives little indication on the matter in his letters, and very little can be said definitively on this line, except with regard to Greco-Roman classical literature and culture:

> As to the limited value of eroticism when divested of its romantic aura—certainly the process ceases to be anything worthy of *primary* exploitation in life & art, as we may easily see by noting how secondary it was in the great human classics of antiquity. (SL 3.68)

Lovecraft was a classicist, and the literature of the ancient world abounds in material on the subjects of love and sex, from the quaint to the explicit, and Lovecraft cited classical sources at times when talking about sex. He even went so far as to include the gods Hymen ("Lovecraft on Love," 245) and Priapus (SL 1.308) at times in his writing on love and sex, though of course these were never intended for publication. There was considerable classical material dealing with adult themes available to scholars and laymen, including Boccaccio's *Decameron*, which Lovecraft owned (SL 3.109), Ovid's *Ars Amatoria* (SL 3.266, 4.285), and the more scatological poems of Jonathan Swift (SL 1.306, 3.109).

1. Sex and Lovecraft

Whatever his reading, Lovecraft's personal experience with physical affection was very likely limited almost entirely to his brief period of cohabitation while he was married. According to his wife, "He shunned promiscuous association with women before his marriage" (Davis 1969). She also noted Lovecraft's lack of personal displays of affection very early in their courtship:

> His continued enthusiasm the next day was so genuine and sincere that in appreciation I surprised and shocked him right then and there by kissing him. He was so flustered that he blushed, then he turned pale. When I chaffed him about it he said he had not been kissed since he was a very small child and that he was never kissed by any woman, not even by his mother or aunts, since he grew to manhood, and that he would probably never be kissed again. (But I fooled him.) (Davis 1992, 19)

This anecdote, told in its entirety, is remarkable both as the origin of the revision "The Horror at Martin's Beach" (1922) and as one of the few genuinely romantic stories concerning Lovecraft.

It is known that on their honeymoon night, the couple stayed up reconstructing the typescript of "Under the Pyramids" (ghostwritten for Harry Houdini, published in 1924), which had been lost the night before they were married (Davis 1992, 12). Sonia spoke rarely of their sex life, and Lovecraft not at all in his published letters. The most she said about it in print was: "As a married man, he was an adequately excellent lover, but refused to show his feelings in the presence of others," and "One way of expressions of H. P.'s was to wrap his 'pinkey' finger around mine and say, 'Umph!'" (Davis 1969). Everts goes on to greater length about Lovecraft's reticence and sexual ability, based on conversations with Sonia:

> This inhibition was clarified when I spoke with Sonia and tape-recorded our conversation—HPL never once made any sexual overtures to his wife—she, Sonia, always had to make the overtures for their sexual relations, however, as she stated to me, HPL had read up on his husbandly duty, and he was more than adequate in his performance. [. . .] He did, however, make the statement that if a man cannot be or is not married at the greatest height of his sex-desire, which in his case, he said was at age 19, he became somewhat unappreciative of it after he passed thirty. I was somewhat shocked but held my peace. (Everts)

Lovecraft's general lack of interest in sex, whether on account of age, personal quirk, or some combination thereof, is not an unusual observation for his wife to have made. Lovecraft mentioned it himself (*SL* 5.163), and it would make sense if he were speaking somewhat from personal experience when he addressed youthful ardor in "Lovecraft on Love":

> Youth brings with it certain erogenous and imaginative stimuli bound up in the tactile phenomena of slender, virginally-postured bodies and visual imagery of classical aesthetic contours symbolizing a kind of freshness and Springtime immaturity which is very beautiful but which has nothing to do with domestic love. [. . .] No conservative man or woman expects such extraordinary physical exaltation except for a brief period in extreme youth [. . .]. Love in extreme youth is more a matter of physiology, than psychology and wholly independent of the mature middle age. Since in most cases of youth, love has been imperfect or unsatisfactory, in later life there comes a wholesome craving for another chance to find true love which maturity alone seems capable of fashioning and keeping unimpaired without expecting to thrill with the physical exaltation which is the rightful heritage of Springtime youth only. (245)

Lovecraft recognized this aspect of himself and may have combined self-observation with his racial views in describing "our savage blond forefathers as erotically sluggish & extremely chaste" (SL 3.65). An apt description of Lovecraft himself—as he wrote in a letter to J. Vernon Shea in 1931: "In these transitional days the luckiest persons are those of sluggish eroticism who can cast aside the whole muddled business & watch the squirming of the primitive majority with ironic detachment" (SL 3.425).

In spite of his disdain for "the undisguised animalism of youth" ("Lovecraft on Love," 245), Lovecraft also recognized the "originally motivating eroticism" (SL 3.66) or "element of biological eroticism" (SL 4.356) that might form the basis of a relationship was necessary at the beginning.

In 1927, Lovecraft and August Derleth debated birth control. Although Derleth's side of the correspondence is lost, we can read something of it from Lovecraft's counterarguments: "And remember that birth control is no more artificial & contrary to Nature than the peace-policies & sentimental coddling of the weak which overpopulates the world and makes it necessary" (ES 78). Lovecraft was definitely in favor of birth control, citing no personal preference or experience but rather general, rational issues regarding overpopulation and practicability, with a solid dose of racialism or class-divide thrown in:

> There is no use at all in expecting the tastefully-living but non-wealthy middle-class citizen not to practice birth control. As long as he knows he never can bring up ten children decently, he is going to stick to one or two or three & see that they *are* brought up decently. For him the matter is an intensely practical one, no matter what he may think in vague theory. The better classes, then, are outside the argument. With them birth control is an accomplished fact, & it will always be so. Meanwhile, since the reproduction of good blood

is so artificially cut off, shall we allow bad blood to multiply unchecked through ignorance, till the spawn of weak & unfit stock forms the bulk of our population? My answer is emphatically *no!* To hell with principle—our first duty is to save the fundamental biological quality of the race! (ES 78)

By all accounts, after the failure of his marriage Lovecraft returned once more to a chaste existence. He remained friends with Sonia, but their relationship was no longer a physical one, on any level, as Sonia discovered when she returned from Europe to visit him:

When Howard and I parted for the night I said "Howard, won't you kiss me goodnight?" His reply was, "No, it's better not to." [The next evening] In parting for the night, I no longer asked for a kiss. I'd learned my lesson well. [. . .] I had hoped (perhaps it was wish-thinking) that my "embrace" would make him not only a great *genius* but also a lover and husband. While the genius developed and broke through its chrysalis, the lover and husband receded into the background until they became apparitions that finally vanished. (Davis 1992, 23, 27)

Lovecraft is not known to have engaged in another physical or romantic relationship. If there is any final indication that he retained some physical desire but chose not to act on it out of principle or practicality, it may have been expressed in a letter to R. H. Barlow in 1936: "We'd all *like* to kiss pretty girls to our dying day—but we know damn well that it would be only a repellent and sordid mockery except with the very few women who really have affection for us when we are young" (SL 5.314-15).

Lovecraft's mental views on sex in the last years of his life are given in another letter to Barlow in 1935 and represent a sort of culmination of his beliefs on the place of sex in human nature and society.

Sex? [. . .][1] That it serves as a kind of stimulus to all other kinds of human activity is very probable; but this of course involves sublimated, etheralised, & tenuously associative forms of it which have nothing in common with the

---

1. Immediately before the quoted section, Lovecraft had given a table with "13 divisions of the basic ego-urge," and to which the section in ellipses refers; I have removed the list for the sake of clarity. The relevant section of the table is:

Instinct	Intelligible Emotion	Application
Reproduction	Eroticism	Sex, Religion (in part), Love (in part)
Parentalism	Tenderness	Love (mainly)

Those interested should compare the contents of this letter to Lovecraft's essay "Some Causes of Self-Immolation" (1931).

cheap wenching of the rabble & of the Greenwich-Village type of decadent pseudo-intelligentsia. Of its *specific* figuring in art—as apart from the general way in which it adds force to the force of other urges—I am extremely skeptical. The Freudians confuse its frequent choice (by a decadent modernity) as *subject-matter* with its supposed function as an ingredient of the whole aesthetic process. It is scarcely necessary to point out that the feverish overemphasis on sex in the western world since 1920 is a factitious & essentially temporary phenomenon incident to suddenly changed philosophic perspectives & a decadent, transitional social order. We may assume from the start that sex is a very strong instinct for whose natural & adequate expression every social order should provide as a matter of course, & that in earlier phases of society it has been dealt with in dozens of different ways—wise & unwise, productive of results varying from reasonable harmony (Republican Rome before B.C. 150) to unspeakable hideousness & disgustingness (India since the Middle Ages; parts of Africa & Polynesia). In our own specific case, the preceding age employed three factors no longer capable of use in the regulation & canalization of eroticism—(a) religious & mystically ethical pressure, (b) prudential expediency base don the incurability of venereal diseases & absence of birth-control methods, & (c) an hypocritical attitude involving curious dualities of standard. Western civilization came to rely on these things as its sole defence against the disastrous hypertrophy of sex, just as it relied on various temporary factors (absence of effective transportation & destructive apparatus) as a defence against the disastrous hypertrophy of pugnacity as exemplified in warfare. As a result, the *real* reasons—aesthetic & social in the higher sense—for regulating & canalizing sex were totally neglected. Then came the age of scientific rationalism—& the bottom dropped out of all the old defences. Result— the licence of the "jazz age" & the popularity of ol' Doc Sigmund. But such complete disorganization is not likely to endure indefinitely. (OFF 246-48)

Brought together here are Lovecraft's acceptance of sex as a driving need and aesthetic utility, his rose-tinted admiration of the classical world contrasted plainly with his xenophobia concerning other cultures, an outright disdain for Edwardian and religious mores and censorship against sexuality, and finally disapproval of the flaunting of sexuality in the decadent Roaring Twenties, the theories of Sigmund Freud, and the "pseudo-intelligentsia" encountered during his time in New York City. These are all subjects he had addressed before in different contexts, but never quite combined into a single thesis: not only an acknowledgment of the sexual urge, but the importance of controlling and channeling ("canalising") those impulses. Having established this basis, the end of Lovecraft's mini-essay on the subject looks to the future and what future society might or will do in this regard:

In the course of time, reason & taste will be brought to bear upon this as upon other subjects. The erotic instincts of man will be gauged anthropologically & zoölogically, & solvable problems connected with them (e.g. sex-expression among adolescents, conceivably solvable through trial marriages of non-economic basis) will be separate from those problems (desire for polygamy despite conflicting desire for the psychology of monogamy; unreciprocated desire of the aging for young & beautiful partners, &c.) which are probably incapable of solution. The actual urges of the race will be correlated scientifically with the yearning for limitation established by nature & aesthetic tradition—at the same time the growth of philosophy on a sounder basis will perhaps restore man's once fairly established realization that some instincts must always be curbed in the interest of other & more basically important ones. Thus with a new & accepted code whereby natural & harmonious erotic expression will be vastly facilitated, it may reasonably be expected that a great deal of morbid attention will eventually be withdrawn from the whole subject of sex. (OFF 248)

This second extract includes several hints of Lovecraft's more personal experiences and beliefs with regard to sex. The "non-economic basis" for trial marriages was likely inspired in part by the economic difficulties that Lovecraft blamed for the failure of his own marriage; the reference to polygamy may refer to his friend Morton's views on "free love"; and the "unreciprocated desire of the aging" is an aspect that reoccurs several times in his writings on love. It is notable, however, that Lovecraft only speaks of sex and eroticism here, the physical desire to have sex and sexual unions—not the emotion of love, or of relationships based on love.

Views on Love and Relationships

In 1971 Sonia Davis submitted an essay to August Derleth, "The Psychic Phenominon [sic] of Love," which contained a rare excerpt from one of Lovecraft's 1922 letters to Sonia. Derleth published the letter as "Lovecraft on Love" in the Winter 1971 issue of the *Arkham Collector*. On the original manuscript by Sonia is a note: "It was Lovecraft's part of this letter that I believe made me fall in love with him; but he did not carry out his own dictum; time and place, and reversion of some of his thoughts and expressions did not bode for happiness" (Joshi 2010, 497).

The four pages of text are our earliest glimpse at Lovecraft's meditations on romantic love between a man and a woman. The letter shows many attitudes toward emotional or romantic love, erotic attraction, and relationships that Lovecraft would continue to evince at other points in his life, and others that he would subsequently abandon. Many of the assertions in "Lovecraft on Love" would prove to be a point in his marriage with Sonia, but what is really remarkable is that this letter shows Lovecraft at a point when he believes in love, and one often entwined with, though not dependent upon, sexual intimacy and physical closeness to the object of affection.

> Love is generally linked with subsidiary conditions such as pride, admiration, eroticism, intellectual congeniality, &c., and in practice it may be taken for granted that all other things being equal, the possessor generally prefers to have the object close at hand, although a purely ethereal and imaginative force such as real love is sometimes independent of time, space or corporeal existence. True love thrives equally well in presence or in absence, proving that the force is an exalted and imaginative one, and directed toward the most permanent spiritual and aesthetically responsive part of the personality. It need not disavow a parallel erotic appreciation but it inwardly eclipses and transcends it. (242)

The latter would be a major sticking-point in Lovecraft and Sonia's marriage, as Sonia would relate:

> For the next several months we again lived in letters only. He was perfectly willing and even satisfied to live this way, but not I. I began urging a legal separation, in fact, divorce. But during this period of time he tried every method he could devise to persuade me how much he appreciated me and that divorce would cause him great unhappiness; and that a gentleman does not divorce his wife unless he has cause, and that he has no cause for doing so. [. . .] Then he would tell me of a very happy couple whom he knew, where the wife lived with her parents, in Virginia, while the husband lived elsewhere for reasons of illness, and that their marriage was kept intact through letters. (Davis 1992, 21)

Letters after the failure of his marriage show a Lovecraft who believed love was only a "thorough illusion as envisaged by medievalists & Victorians," a mere social construct with no grounding in reality (SL 3.65-74). In a letter to Elizabeth Toldridge in 1930 he claimed:

> Since the pioneering work of Freud & the still more analytical work of his successors—Pavlov, Jung, Adler, Watson, &c. &c. &c. we have come to see that there is no such thing as "love" in any unified, permanent, or important sense; & recognize that the earlier notions of such matters were due to sheer lack of scientific knowledge & to certain well-defined poetic or religio-mystical

delusions. To speak of the "immortality" or cosmic significance of anything as mythical & illusory as "love", is today essentially meaningless. (SL 3.134-35)

Again, Lovecraft appeals to science to resolve a human mystery. Where once he turned to books on anatomy to educate himself on the physical reality of sex, he likewise turned to psychologists, historians, and sexologists to educate himself on modern love and relationships, to dismiss any petty superstitions or beguiling mysteries that might linger about the subject for him. After his marriage, he wrote as a man with both book learning and practical experience; in a 1934 letter to J. Vernon Shea he wrote:

> I didn't slop over in youthful romance, since I didn't believe—& still don't—in the existence of sentimental "love" as a definite, powerful, or persistent human emotion. I have always regarded marriage as composed of friendly regard, mental congeniality, social foresight, & practical advantage; to which *at first* the element of biological eroticism is added. (SL 4.356)

The echoes of "Lovecraft on Love" can still be clearly seen here—mental or intellectual congeniality being a prominent and recurring element—but the Lovecraft of 1934 has refined and revised his opinion of love and marriage.

The Woodburn Harris letter of 9 November 1929 totals 70 pages; the truncated version in *Selected Letters* has been edited down to 27 pages, a third of which comprise an essay on sex and relationships. Among the subjects discussed are Lovecraft's views on marriage, in particular the foundations of the institution of marriage, its perceived decline, and the apparent rise of promiscuity during his own lifetime, which he predicted would lead to its eventual abolition (SL 3.58-85). While this letter is a valuable record, Lovecraft evinced views stated to derive from the scientific, medical, psychological, and historical literature, and it is probably best not to try to read deeper personal meaning into them. For instance, in consider the following passage:

> [. . .] females, in the absence of the male, experience desires & frustrations just as intense as those of the isolated male—hence the savage sourness of old maids, the looseness of modern spinsters, & the infidelity or tendency thereto of wives left alone by their husbands for more than a week or two. (cf. Ellis, Fielding, Collins, Overstreet, Forel, &c.) (SL 3.72)

Lovecraft lived for many years with his two aunts (both of whom were divorced or widowed for many years) and a widowed mother who lived apart from her husband for five years before his death; and he himself once attempted a long-distance relationship with his wife. There has been no intimation in Lovecraft's letters or in the recollections of others I have read that any of them were promiscuous; and given the citation of academic authorities, it is probable that Lovecraft is not speaking directly from personal experience, but only expounding on generalities based on his reading. Further, it would have been directly contrary to what he had intimated of his own sexuality as an "isolated male." Another possibly misleading passage reads: "[. . .] impossibility of inducing men to live erotically with women over forty except under compulsion of strong aesthetic & ethical obligations which vanish with the economic independence & relinquished chastity of the modern female" (SL 3.69).

Lovecraft's wife Sonia was forty-one years old at the time of their marriage and financially independent. Finances were an issue for the Lovecrafts during the marriage, as he was unable to obtain regular employment and was forced to rely on his wife's income, a small allowance from his aunts, and a little money from revision work. In 1931 he wrote: "My one venture into matrimony ended in the divorce-court for reasons 98% financial" (SL 3.261–62). The matter of age in this passage, however, need not imply any slight toward Sonia or a sexual problem between the couple, but actually ties back into beliefs laid out in "Lovecraft on Love" and his expectations for a relationship: "At forty or fifty the more mental and deeply seated affection is a far more appropriate subject for sentimental interest and rhetorical celebration than in the undisguised animalism of youth" (244–45).

It is also just conceivable that Lovecraft owes something of this opinion to the first chapter of David Van Bush's *Practical Psychology and Sex Life* (1922; revised 1927), which includes sections entitled "Women at Forty" and "Women More Attractive at Forty" that expound on the sexual drive of older women.

For all that he talked about love and affection, Sonia states that Lovecraft had great difficulty in expressing such emotions to her, either in word or deed. Sonia wrote:

> H. P. was inarticulate in expressions of love except to his mother and to his aunts, to whom he expressed himself quite vigorously; to all others, it was expressed by deep appreciation only. (Davis 1969)

> I believe he loved me as much as it was possible for a temperament like his to love. He never mentioned the word *love*. He would say instead "My dear, you don't know how much I appreciate you." I tried to understand him and was grateful for any crumbs from his lips that fell my way. (Davis 1992, 15)

"No, my dear," he would say, "if you leave me, I shall never marry again. You do not realize how much I appreciate you." (Davis 1992, 22)

Joshi attributes Lovecraft's "extreme restraint in displays of affection" to his sexual repression and general upbringing (Joshi 1996, 37). Whatever the case, already separated, Lovecraft and Sonia did eventually proceed through the divorce process, under the fictitious grounds that Sonia had deserted her husband. Lovecraft failed to sign the final decree, and he and Sonia remained legally married until Lovecraft's death. Sonia, who had remarried some years later, was understandably very upset when she learned of this later in her life (Joshi 2010, 727). Biographers and friends of Lovecraft were generally critical of the marriage—the differences of age, financial position, ethnicity (Sonia was a Ukrainian emigrant of Jewish descent), and disposition are substantial hurdles for any couple to overcome. The best that can be said is that there was a mutual attraction between the two: for a time at least, Lovecraft was in love. In a 1924 letter to Frank Belknap Long, about a month before his marriage, he wrote: "One who so values love, shou'd realize that there are only two genuine kinds of it: matrimonial and parental" (*SL* 1.292). This expression neatly encapsulates the entirety of Lovecraft's personal experience on the matter, even if it is far from the last word he ever uttered on the subject.

There has been some supposition that Lovecraft had relationships with, or at least was enamored with or the subject of unrequited affections by, different women. For the most part there is little evidence to support any substantial romantic relationship outside of his marriage.

The most prominent candidate is Winifred Virginia Jackson, a noted poet of the amateur press whom Lovecraft corresponded with. He also wrote an effusive review of her poetry and even collaborated with her on two pieces of fiction, "The Green Meadow" (composed 1919) and "The Crawling Chaos" (composed 1920). George Wetzel and R. Alain Everts make the case for their romance in *Winifred Virginia Jackson, Lovecraft's Lost Romance* (1970), and it is covered well in Joshi's *I Am Providence* (2010). Their correspondence ends abruptly in 1921, the same year Sonia met Lovecraft at the National Amateur Press Association convention in Boston, which Jackson also attended—according to Everts, Sonia claims she "stole" Lovecraft from Jackson, so perhaps that explains it. If Lovecraft was enamored with Jackson, perhaps he discovered her former marriage to a black man named Horace Jordan, or that she was involved in an affair with noted Harlem Renaissance poet and critic William Stanley Braithwaite, either of which would probably have curbed his affections.

The only other possibility of note is Hazel Heald, a revision client whom Muriel Eddy believed held a torch for Lovecraft and even invited him to her home for dinner (Eddy and Eddy 23-26). If this was not simply an artifact of Eddy's wistful recollection, then Lovecraft recorded no reciprocal feelings in his letters and nothing came of it.

Views on Eroticism and Pornography

In his correspondence with Kleiner, Lovecraft's initial reaction to eroticism is concise and negative: "Eroticism belongs to a lower order of instincts, and is an animal rather than nobly human quality" (SL 1.106). However, the question forced a bit of introspection, and a later letter greatly expanded on and revised the answer, culminating in a reversal of his original opinion:

> I have opposed eroticism for several reasons, (a) because of the acknowledged repulsiveness of direct erotic manifestations, as felt by all races and cultures and expressed in reticence to a greater or less degree, (b) because the obvious kinship of erotic instincts to the crudest and earliest neural phenomena of organic nature, rather than to the phenomena resulting from complex and advanced development (i.e., purely intellectual phenomena), (c) because of the apparent connexion betwixt ages of erotic interest and national decadence, and (d) because so far as I could judge erotic interests are overrated; being in truth mere trifles which engross crude minds when more worthy interests are lacking. It was my theory that eroticism would diminish if thinkers would awake and turn to really important phenomena. Such, in brief, were the bases of my opinions; but perusal of representative realistic works without prejudice leads me to attempt a revaluation [. . .] thus I am coming to be convinced that the erotic instinct is in the majority of mankind far stronger than I could ever imagine without wide reading and observation; that it relentlessly clutches the average person—even of the thinking classes—to a degree which makes its overthrow by higher interests impossible. Probably my recommendation of dismissing it by displacement by purely imaginative and cosmic interests is an absurdity based on ignorance of its extent and intensity. (SL 1.129)

> Much as a delicate mind may grow nauseated at the bestiality of mankind, that same mind cannot deny what it discovers to exist—and surely romance is no more crude than the analogous phenomenon of hunger. All, then, that we must ask, is a more refined and artistic treatment of the erotic motive. From

what I have heard, the fault of Saxon eroticism is its morbidness, which no doubt results from a social system which seeks to banish it, and which therefore only makes it the more obnoxious when it breaks out. [. . .] This seems to be the idea adumbrated by Nietzsche and other realists—to remove morbid erotic interest by removing the prejudices and inhibitions which make it doubly strong. It is quite possible that the net amount of vulgarism would thus be decreased rather than increased; surely, the decrease in hypocrisy would make for a gain in wholesomeness . . . Thus have I changed my views on what I formerly censured. (SL 1.130)

Several additional letters exhibit similar artistic and literary sentiments: "'tis of no use to omit mention of cheats and pimps and rakes and whores where the subject calls for 'em" (SL 1.282)—a fact Lovecraft himself proved in a letter to Frank Belknap Long which included a long and somewhat bawdy poem. "The Pathetic History of Sir Wilful Wildrake" (c. 1921) was dedicated to Rheinhart Kleiner and very probably was a direct result of their conversations about sex (SL 1.306); this is reinforced by the fact that Lovecraft addressed a 1921 letter to Kleiner as "Sir Wilful Wildrake, Bt." (SL 1.131).

While admissible to the sometime necessity of sexual content, Lovecraft had a dislike of those who revel in the subject unnecessarily—"I look upon this sort of writing as a mere prying survey of the lowest part of life" (SL 1.282)—and possessed a distinct distaste for pornography, as mentioned again to Long:

> There's nothing beautiful or artistick about it, any more than the idealization of certain ultimate digestive processes would be; and its only value is extrinsick—as a necessity in the detail'd and realistick depiction of mankind in psychological fiction. I am undogmatick enough to affirm that it hath no interest in itself, and that its apparent interest among the young is wholly factitious, and deriv'd from that curiosity which false education and unwise reticence impart. (SL 1.304)

What actual pornography Lovecraft might have been exposed to is a matter for conjecture. Certainly he was at least aware of a few literary or artistic depictions of adult nature such as *Venus in Furs* (1870) by Sacher-Masoch or *Justine* (1791) by the Marquis de Sade, though he claims not to have read them ("Letters to Lee McBride White" 33-34); classical poets like Catullus he definitely had read; and he was aware of the existence of the more lurid pulp magazines like *Snappy Stories* (SL 3.106-8; MF 884), the latter of which Lovecraft might have been referring to when he wrote to Maurice W. Moe in 1931: "One might be highly grateful to be rid of the ugly and worthless pornography which might otherwise clutter up the low-grade stationery shops" (SL 5.266). Even so, Lovecraft was aware enough of the existence of pornography and was able to recommend a few private suppliers of "curiosa" in New York, Falstaff Press and the Esoterika Biblion Society, when asked by a correspondent ("Letters to Lee McBride White" 34). He may have heard of these dealers through his bookseller friend George Kirk, who had dealings in erotic and banned literature according to his letters printed in *Lovecraft's New York Circle* (2006), though Kirk never mentions Falstaff Press or its owners, or anyone connected to the Esoterika Biblion as far as I could determine. This may in part be due to the time gap involved: Kirk's letters in that volume end in 1927, and Lovecraft's letter is dated 1933. Another possibility is that Lovecraft ran across one of the advertisements Falstaff Publications ran in pulp magazines in the early 1930s.

Lovecraft was not affronted by mere nudity in artwork, though he did have a few choice words about the covers of *Weird Tales*: "I have no objection to the nude in art—in fact, the human figure is as worthy a type of subject matter as any other object of beauty in the visible world. But I don't see what the hell Mrs. Brundage's undressed ladies have to do with weird fiction!" (SL 5.304). As well as the interiors:

> As you remark, the mania for undraped ladies in the "art" department has come to be an unmitigated nuisance—especially since they are lavishly supplied where the text explicitly calls for something else. You'll recall that Rankin made ample-bosomed wenches of my *male* orgiasts in the Louisiana swamp scene of "Cthulhu!" I suppose Wright thinks the custom has a sales value. (ES 176)

Margaret Brundage was an illustrator that provided most of the covers for *Weird Tales* between 1933 and 1938, which often featured provocative nude female figures (Joshi 2010, 876). There is a recurrent legend that Lovecraft would tear the covers off the more garish and offensive pulps, possibly dating back to this snippet: "When he bought pulps at Douglass Dana's Old Corner Book Shop, at the foot of College Street, he tore off the most lurid covers lest friends misunderstand his interests" (Scott, 1961). The anecdote was perpetuated in part by stories such as Fritz Leiber's "The Terror from the Depths" (1976). Joshi reports that the rumor is untrue: Lovecraft's complete collection of *Weird Tales*, covers intact, resides at the John Hay Library (Joshi 2010, 876-77).

Lovecraft continued to be prudish throughout his life, as attested by his wife, and disliked to speak openly about sex, a fact that Samuel Loveman and his friends in New York reportedly ribbed him about. According to Sonia, "they would open up a conversation re sex, knowing that Lovecraft did not like to listen to such stories" and "the very word *sex* seemed to upset him" (Everts). With her, however, Lovecraft was somewhat more open and intimate, at least in private: "Lovecraft took pride in telling me that he was born on the mattress on which we both slept. This, I believe, he told no one but me" (Everts). This prudishness was at least in part in keeping with Lovecraft's innate conservative nature, and a response to the "new morals" of the day. Sexual promiscuity and sexual thought were on the rise in the 20s and 30s, and Lovecraft saw this as part of the degeneration of the modern world:

> If the dog-&-bitch promiscuity of the earliest "new moralists" could be excused on the ground that our normal disgust is only "old fashioned prejudice", it is not remarkable that nauseous & abnormal sodomy should make an equal claim. Next will come incest—people will clamour for "warmer, freer, more wholesome" relations betwixt brothers & sisters, parents & children—& finally bestiality ... the frantic maenad & the black goat of the Sabbat.... will be justified & praised as something "honest" & "progressive". Who shall define the absolute validity of our disgust at any or all of these "new freedoms" present & future? What is the line betwixt "irrational & archaic prejudice" & a sound aesthetic standard? Echo alone answers. Unlike you, I find that most sexual letting down is also accompanied by a corresponding letdown in other spheres—honour, general taste in living, &c. It is also undeniable that a loosening of erotic standards has a strong connexion with the decay of nations & cultures. But what is to come, will come. (ES 553)

For all that he was personally prudish about sex and disliked talking about it for its own sake, Lovecraft did talk about sex from a scientific or artistic perspective. As evidenced in his letters, as the subject came up, he proved willing and able to discuss it, particularly where it concerned literary interests, such as certain of his letters to J. Vernon Shea (such as SL 3.425 and 4.234-35), Clark Ashton Smith (*SL* 2.50), R. H. Barlow (OFF 246-48), and August Derleth, to the latter of whom he wrote: "for although I detest all sexual irregularities *in life itself*, as violations of a certain harmony which seems to me inseparable from high-grade living, I have a scientific approval of perfect realism in the *artistic delineation of life*" (ES 542).

Censorship was an issue Lovecraft and his friends also faced. In 1924, an issue of *Weird Tales* featuring the Eddy/Lovecraft revision "The Loved Dead" was banned in Indiana, which led to several later Lovecraft stories being rejected as too gruesome (Joshi and Schultz, 156), and that same year in the *Oracle,* an amateur publication, both Sonia and Lovecraft commented on censorship, with Lovecraft writing:

> Not many of us, even in this age, have any marked leaning toward public pornography; so that we would generally welcome any agency calculated to banish offences against good taste. But when we come to reflect on the problem of enforcement, and perceive how absurdly any censorship places us into the hands of dogmatic and arbitrary officials with Puritan illusions and no true knowledge of life or literary values, we have to acknowledge that absolute liberty is the lesser evil. The literature of today, with its conscientious striving toward sincerity, must necessarily contain large amounts of matter repugnant to those who hold the hypocritical nineteenth-cenutry view of the world. It need not be vulgarly presented, but it cannot be excluded if art is to express life. (Joshi 2010, 482)

In a pair of letters to August Derleth in 1929, Lovecraft is "neutral" on the issue:

> The whole problem of censorship is a highly complex one—so much so that I am still frankly neutral concerning it. I don't think the abstract right to suppress a book ought to be wholly abrogated by the government, yet it is obvious that some means must be provided to distinguish between authentic art—or science—& commercial pornography if the process is to be other than ridiculous. (ES 178)

> The question of literary censorship need not really be connected with anything so basic as a nation's moral code. It concerns, rather, a nation's custom or technique in applying its moral code. As I have said before, I don't think any genuine work of art ought to be censored—yet commercial pornography would certainly become a very ungraceful nuisance if not constantly discouraged. It seems to me that very few works of major art have ever been permanently suppressed—so that the "problem of censorship" is really a far less important matter than most of the eager younger generation at present imagine. (ES 186)

By the next year, Lovecraft had apparently made up his mind and presented a particularly cogent and forceful argument against censorship to Maurice W. Moe. Part of the groundwork he lays out to Moe is an "offhand list" of "the whole field of erotic literature and iconography as defined and reprobated by the Victorian maiden-aunt class":

1) Impersonal and serious descriptions of erotic scenes, relationships, motivations, and consequences in real life.
2) Poetic—and other aesthetic—exaltations of erotic feelings.
3) Satirical glimpses of the erotic realities underlying non-erotic pretences and exteriors.
4) Artificial descriptions or symbols designed to stimulate erotic feelings, yet without a well-proportioned grounding in life and art.
5) Corporeal nudity in pictorial or sartorial art.
6) Erotic subject matter operating through the medium of wit and humour.
7) Free discussion of philosophic and scientific issues involving sex. (SL 3.105-6)

Lovecraft picked apart each point, in accordance with his reading and philosophy. His greatest ire is for Victorians—"We don't have to be told nowadays that the whole structure of Victorian art and thought and sexual morality was based upon a tragic sham" (SL 3.103); those for whom pornography was an end in itself, rather than subservient to artistic purpose—"They are not genuine art, and may therefore be ranked as just so much waste material" (SL 3.107); and finally for those that would not permit frank and scientific discussion of sex:

> Point #7, on the other hand, is not *debatable at all*. No full-witted adult outside the Popish church or the vestigial backwoods of Georgia and Tennessee could wish to limit the sober scientific investigation of any subject whatsoever [. . .] A puritan who would limit the discussion and study of any phase of biology is simply outside civilization—outside any argument which can take place among civilized men in 1929 or 1930. (SL 3.109)

If there is any doubt left as to Lovecraft's opinion against censorship while retaining his dislike for pornography, he stated it even more clearly in a following letter to Moe in 1931:

> Now we know again, as we did in the sane days before Victoria, that *no subject exists which cannot be seriously treated in literature*. There are no exceptions—indeed, there could be no exceptions according to any soundly impersonal and universal view of the organic history of the planet. [. . .] Even now I have no use for a fellow who simply sets out to violate people's inherited sensibilities for no adequate reason—such swine as you'll see listed in book-catalogues under the euphemism of "curiosa"—but in my intellectual maturity I refuse to commit the blunder of confusing these leprous scavengers with honest men whose affronts to convention are merely incidents in a sincere and praiseworthy struggle to interpret or symbolise life as it is. (SL 3.264)

This, as a final point with regard to Lovecraft's views on love, sex, and eroticism, brings us full circle to where his self-education in human sexuality began. Lovecraft, discussing sex in his first few letters to Kleiner in 1919, is a young man of little experience or erudition in sex—how different from the Lovecraft of 1924, contemplating marriage and apparently "reading up" on husbandly duties, who warned off a young Frank Belknap Long from pornography; or the old hand of 1929-31 explaining the basics of life with Woodburn Harris and arguing against censorship of sex with Moe, or suggesting adult bookdealers to White in 1933.

The Shadow of Syphilis

"Winfield Lovecraft died, the death certificate states, 'in an advanced stage of general paresis'" (*LR* 11). So innocently began yet another popular rumor about Lovecraft, thanks once more to the meticulous research of Winfield Townley Scott. Winfield Scott Lovecraft, the father of Howard Phillips Lovecraft, was a commercial traveler who very likely contracted syphilis from a sexual contact preceding his marriage. The disease reached an advanced stage (tertiary syphilis would account for all his known symptoms), which required Winfield Lovecraft to be hospitalized in 1893, where he remained until his death in 1898 (Faig 46-50; McNamara 14-17; Joshi 2010, 21-13).

One of Winfield Lovecraft's symptoms was periodic violent hallucinations. There are few extant records of Winfield's hallucinatory episodes, of which two were recorded, and this is a version of the most popular:

> According to one anecdote, Winfield had to be placed under restraint while on a business trip to Chicago and returned to Providence. De Camp relates: "Alone in his hotel room, he suddenly began crying out that the chambermaid had insulted him and that his wife was being assaulted on the floor above." (Faig 51)

L. Sprague de Camp's *Lovecraft: A Biography* takes this anecdote from Arthur S. Koki's "H. P. Lovecraft: An Introduction to His Life and Writings" (1962); the ultimate source is Winfield Lovecraft's medical records at Butler Hospital (Joshi 2010, 21).

The second hallucination comes directly from Winfield's medical record, which was discovered at Butler Hospital by Prof. John McInnis and published in *Lovecraft Studies* No. 24 with annotations by M. Eileen

McNamara, M.D. This episode is very similar in character to the first, but was recorded after Winfield was committed to the hospital:

> Violent and noisy—especially so tonight; hallucinations and delusions of a most distressing character—says three men—one a negro—in the room above trying to do violence to his wife; shrieks wildly at them to desist in their attempts and calls to his friends to go to his aid [. . .] (McNamara 15)

Family anecdotes as related to Sonia by Lovecraft's aunt Annie Gamwell suggest that the family was aware of the nature of Winfield Lovecraft's condition "and the adventures with prostitutes and women on his lengthy adventures that gave him his affliction" (Everts). Sonia herself seems to have been of the opinion that Winfield Lovecraft "took his pleasures wherever he could find them" (Davis 1969). Both of Lovecraft's parents had died by the time he met Sonia, so any of her observations cannot be taken as fact. It is likely she was just repeating family gossip, but then again she might not have learned of Winfield Lovecraft's disease until after Lovecraft was dead, when Winfield Townley Scott revealed it.

There is no evidence that Lovecraft himself was aware of the true source of his father's illness; if he was aware, then he deliberately lied to conceal such knowledge even in his letters (Joshi 2010, 25–26). Joshi avers that even if Lovecraft did know the truth of his father's illness, he "is under no obligation to be wholly candid about such a delicate matter even to close friends or correspondents" (Joshi 2010, 26). There is a similar case in Lovecraft's letters to support this possibility: in 1936 he misrepresented his aunt Annie Gamwell's diagnosis of breast cancer and mastectomy as a case of the grippe to several of his correspondents. (*OFF* 321, 326n1; *ES* 727n3; *LJM* 372, 382n1).

The suggestion that Lovecraft himself suffered congenital syphilis was advanced in print by David H. Keller, M.D. in his essay "Shadows over Lovecraft" (1948)—a study of Lovecraft's medical history, published in *Fantasy Commentator*. Keller was a psychologist who specialized in sexology, author of the ten-volume *Sexual Education Series* (1928) for Charles Atlas, and editor of the science magazine *Sexology* (1933–38) among many other credits. Keller was also a pulp writer of science, fantasy, and fiction, a contemporary of Lovecraft sometimes noted for the sexual bondage and sadism in his works such as in "Binding Deluxe" (*Marvel Tales*, May 1934).

Keller was rebutted by Kenneth Sterling, M.D., again in the pages of *Fantasy Commentator*, in 1951 (Faig 49). Robert M. Price notes that neither Drs. Keller nor Sterling are perfectly objective; Keller may have intended the article as a stab at Derleth, who was heavily promoting Lovecraft's material at the time, and Sterling collaborated with Lovecraft on "In The Walls of Eryx" (1936) and was eager to defend Lovecraft (Price 1988, 25).

Some still gave the idea that Lovecraft had congenital syphilis credit in the following decades, probably helped by reports that his aunt Annie Gamwell had told Sonia they "could not have children" (Everts). In 1975, Willis Conover in his otherwise excellent *Lovecraft at Last* attempted to refute the idea that Winfield Lovecraft even had syphilis (xxii–xxiii). Even as late as 1996 in her essay "H. P. Lovecraft and the Great Heresies," which was first printed in *Raritan* and later reprinted in the collection *The Secret Life of Puppets* (2001), Victoria Nelson contends Winfield Lovecraft's illness affected his son's fiction:

> We may wonder if actual memories or overheard stories of Winfield Scott Lovecraft's death from syphilis, the sexually transmitted disease whose physical marks were lesions, eruptions, tubercles, bubos, and gummas of the most horrific sort, may have impressed themselves on his sensitive son. Whether or not Lovecraft's father's neurosyphilitic psychosis manifested such bodily symptoms as well, an avid lay reader—as Lovecraft was, in a wide range of subjects—who looked up "paresis" in the medical textbooks of the early twentieth century would have encountered graphic photographs of real-life deformities the horrific magnitude of which most certainly defies description. It is hard not to believe, viewing these anonymous and pathetic images of suffering, that one has located the originals of Lovecraft's pustulating horrors. (Nelson 2001, 117)

Nelson's view is difficult to take at face value, since Lovecraft is not known to have ever visited his father after Winfield's hospitalization[2] and in his letters never gives an accurate description of Winfield Lovecraft's illness; however, it is illustrative of the general form and reasoning behind such claims.

The matter was put to rest by Robert M. Price, who gained access to Lovecraft's medical records, which included a negative Wasserman test. Price's article "Did Lovecraft Have Syphillis?" was published in *Crypt of Cthulhu* in 1988 and is almost the final word on the matter. Faig takes the

---

2. A mention of Lovecraft visiting with Winfield Lovecraft after he was hospitalized is made in the introduction to the *Necronomicon: The Book of Dead Names* (1978). This introduction so skillfully weaves together fact and fiction that some mistook it as fact, but as with the rest of the book it is a hoax; see Wilson's "The *Necronomicon*, the Origin of a Spoof" (1984).

trouble to note that a Wasserman test may be negative when the infection is dormant, but that the fact remains the possibility that Lovecraft had congenital syphilis is remote (Faig 49, 76). Despite this data, speculation that Lovecraft inherited syphilis from his father—or at least, was aware of the possibility—has long been an object of consideration in Lovecraft studies, and sometimes still crops up. Maurice Lévy best stated the reason behind the abiding and continued interest in Lovecraft's possible congenital syphilis in "The Horror of Heredity":

> What is important to emphasize is this horror of familial antecedents in Lovecraft, of the secret taint that, in precise cases, reactivates sleeping tendencies, suddenly brings out certain traits, and transforms—in the most material sense of the term—the characters. These obsessive images, which seem to be imposed so strongly on the author, are too numerous and too carefully articulated to be explained away as simple literary effect. Can we from now on completely avoid imputing them to the more or less clear consciousness that Lovecraft had of his own heredity? Everything centers, in sum, on the crucial problem of corrupted blood. And this child of a paretic perhaps had some legitimate reasons for giving way to an anguished reverie on the ever possible perturbation of hereditary patrimony and the regrettable transmission of acquired characteristics. (Lévy 78)

Whether his mother, Sarah Susan Lovecraft, contracted syphilis from her husband is also unknown, but more likely. Since her husband died in 1898 and the connection between paresis and syphilis was not known until 1911, Susie Lovecraft may not have known for certain the nature of her husband's ailment for some time. What effect this knowledge had on her, or on her treatment of her son, is pure conjecture on the part of most biographies (Joshi 2010, 132). Certainly, Susie and Lovecraft shared a strong and strange relationship, the details of which are better covered by Kenneth Faig, Jr.'s essay "The Parents of H. P. Lovecraft" and S. T. Joshi's biographies of Lovecraft.

The most bizarre and possibly misleading comment about the relationship between mother and son comes again from Winfield Townley Scott: "The psychiatrist's record takes note of an Oedipus complex, a 'psycho-sexual contact' with the son, but observes that the effects of such a complex are usually more important on the son than on the mother, and does not pursue the point" (*LR* 16). In interpreting this statement, Joshi argues cogently against the likelihood of any sort of abuse (Joshi 2010, 305–6). There is no evidence to support such a claim in Lovecraft's letters, and it becomes particularly unlikely if his wife Sonia was correct and that

Susie Lovecraft was a "touch-me-not" (Davis 1969) and that Lovecraft had not seen much physical affection as a youth (Davis 1992, 19). Susie Lovecraft was obsessed with her only child, but probably not in a sexual way. Stanley C. Sargent made a little more of the factoid in his essay "Howard Phillips Whateley, An Observation," first published in *The Fantastic World of H. P. Lovecraft* (1999) and then revised for the release of Sargent's second Cthulhu Mythos collection, *The Taint of Lovecraft*: "If Lovecraft were aware of his mother's abnormal "psycho-sexual contact" with him, it might explain the special abhorrence Lovecraft the author demonstrated for inbreeding and incest as demonstrated in several of his tales" (Sargent 158).[3]

Views on Gender and Homosexuality

For a complete discussion of Lovecraft and his views on sex, it is necessary to discuss some issues of gender, homosexuality, and gender identity—mainly to lay bare and examine his own prejudices with regard to gender and homosexuals as expressed in his letters, but also to address depictions or suggestions of his own gender identity that have seen print. Lovecraft's views on gender tie in to his views on love and sex, and the discussion here also lays the foundations for later discussion about Lovecraft's use of gender, particularly in "The Thing on the Doorstep" (1933).

As with his views on sex and love, Lovecraft's views on gender and homosexuality were not constants throughout his life, but evolved over the years. In a 1923 letter he answered a comment by Frank Belknap Long with:

> I do not agree with you regarding the Merit of the Female Mind. In my opinion, 'tis not only not more imaginative than that of Men, but vastly less so; so that I can scarce think of any really Powerful phantastical Vision, which is not of Masculine Origin. Females are in Truth much given to affected Baby Lisping, but there is nothing of truly childlike Oneiroscopy in it. They are by Nature literal, prosaic, and commonplace, given to dull realistick Details and practical Things, and incapable alike of vigorous artistick Creation and genuine, first-hand appreciation. 'Tis foolish to draw generalities from the few Exceptions which by Reason of the singularity attract Notice, where a vilely democratical Society chains down the Men to commercial Pursuits, leaving the mediocre Female Train to achieve literary Distinction merely by Default, or for

---

3. See also T. R. Livesey, "Lovecraft's Mother's Bed," *Redux: A Journal of Reflection* No. 2 (May 2007). Mailing 138 of the Esoteric Order of Dagon Amateur Press Association.

Want of Competition. When, in the near Course of the Revolutions of Society, American females shall themselves be given over to Business, and depriv'd of their present deceptive advantage, you will perceive how inferior the mass of them are, in aesthetick Matters, to the Male part of Humanity. (SL 1.238)

Lovecraft's early chauvinistic opinions on women are strange given that he was raised primarily by his mother and aunts and had first-hand acquaintance with female amateur writers, including young Dorothy Roberts, a writer and poet he otherwise held of great promise "despite her unfortunate failure to belong to the superior gender" (SL 1.254). Later in life Lovecraft evinced much less of a sexist attitude toward women, at least with regard to the accomplishments of female writers such as those discussed in his essay "Supernatural Horror in Literature."

At least late in his life, Lovecraft was relatively egalitarian in his views of the treatment of women under the law. A long drawn-out discussion with Robert E. Howard in 1935 over an incident of the mistreatment of a woman by police officers wended its way in turns through discussions of chivalry, rape, and violence against women, Maj. Gen. Butler's infamous General Order 28, and other examples and finally resolved itself when Lovecraft admitted: 'Rest assured that I do *not* condone the rough handling of any weak person, male or female, by a strong person or crowd of strong persons—unless (as was *not* so in the cited case) some definite and extreme social necessity [. . .] exists" (MF 884).

With regard to the biological equality of women, which he spoke of in a 1934 letter to R. H. Barlow, Lovecraft was of the same mind:

> Biologically a female line is just as important as a male one—the fact that titles & estates descend through the male lines being merely an arbitrary custom of economic & sociological origin. Among many races—notably the American Indians—descent & inheritance are always reckoned in the female line. (OFF 115)

Evidence of Lovecraft's change in opinion can also be seen in a 1934 letter to Clark Ashton Smith, at a time in life when his marriage and divorce was long behind him:

> It so happens that the last few generations have witnessed profound changes of thought and custom through the progress of human knowledge and mechanical technology; and some of these changes have undeniably tended toward the breakdown of traditional inhibitions. Absence of religious restraints has operated adversely on those lacking aesthetic standards and practical sense, while the multiplication of material luxuries [. . .] has certainly promoted a trace of softness and effeminacy in the race. On the other hand, I do not regard the rise of

woman as a bad sign. Rather do I fancy that her traditional subordination was itself an artificial and undesirable condition based on Oriental influences. Our virile Teutonic ancestors did not think their wives unworthy to follow them into battle, or scorn to dream of winged Valkyries bearing them to Valhalla. The feminine mind does not cover the same territory as the masculine, but is probably little if any inferior in total quality. To expect it to remain perpetually in the background in a realistic state of society is futile—despite the most feverish efforts of Nazis and Fascisti. However—it will be some time before women are sufficiently freed from past influences to form an active factor in national life. By the time they do gain influence, they will have lost many of the emotional characteristics which now impair their powers of judgment. Many qualities commonly regarded as innate—in races, classes, and sexes alike—are in reality results of habitual and imperceptible conditioning. (SL 5.64)

I am reminded of a few lines Lovecraft famously wrote of his mother, which perhaps presaged the general shift in his opinions on women as equals or near-equals: "She was a person of unusual charm and force of character, accomplished in literature and the fine arts; a French scholar, musician, and painter in oils. I shall not again be likely to meet with a mind so thoroughly admirable" (SL 1.134).

A breakdown of societal norms and upswing of women's position in society was characteristic of the time in which Lovecraft lived, from the success of the women's suffrage movement in 1919 through the flapper era and the growing population of women in the workforce. It is difficult to say exactly how Lovecraft handled this on a personal level, but one incident in particular from Lovecraft's marriage with Sonia is illustrative: "At this time the aunts gently but firmly informed me that neither they nor Howard could afford to have Howard's wife work for a living in Providence. That was that. I now knew where we all stood. Pride preferred to suffer in silence; both theirs and mine" (Davis 1992, 20).

Lovecraft is silent in this account, but the result is that when confronted with the social and financial decision between the genteel poverty in which his family lifed after his grandfather's death and the sacrifice of social standing and adaptation to the financial reality of a single woman supporting him and his household, Lovecraft by inaction accepted the former.

The focus on the female as a negative is present in Lovecraft's thoughts and language—"effeminacy" being the specific symptom of a decayed race, the loss of male traits and behaviors and the gaining of feminine softness a characteristic of degeneracy; a view that may be an outgrowth or part of Lovecraft's racial views. In 1931 he wrote: "these masculine qualities happen [. . .] to constitute *our* particular main standard" (SL 3.278). If this was a typical view for Lovecraft, then the degeneration of a race noted for its masculine qualities would very likely mean the loss of those qualities—emasculation or effeminacy.

In his published letters Lovecraft has relatively few direct mentions of homosexuality. The clearest explanation of his beliefs with regard to homosexuality is expressed in a 1933 letter to August Derleth:

> So far as the case of homosexualism goes, the primary & vital objection against it is that it is naturally (physically & instinctively—not merely 'morally' or aesthetically) repugnant to the overwhelming bulk of mankind—including all cultures except the few (the ancient Orient, Persia, post-Homeric Greece) in which strongly inculcated artificial traditions have temporarily overcome nature. There's nothing 'moral' in the adverse feeling. For instance—I hate both physically normal adultery (which is contemptible sneaking treachery) & paederasty—but while I might enjoy (physically) or be tempted toward adultery, I simply *could not* consider the abnormal state without physical nausea. Even excessive psychological sentimentality betwixt members of the same sex has for the average healthy person a repulsion varying from a sense of the ridiculous to a feeling of disgust [. . .] (ES 545-46)

Lovecraft viewed homosexuality as a perversion (a typical medical and psychological view of the period) and regarded as a sexual crime, like adultery or pedophila, admitting at least that he enjoys heterosexual intercourse. It is also an example of his tendency toward hypocrisy: for all that he rails against "excessive psychological sentimentality" he had many close friendships with other men.

Lovecraft's earliest reference to actual homosexuals concerns his meeting Gordon Hatfield and Hart Crane, recorded in a 1924 letter. The comments are jovial, but generally derogatory: "Have you seen that precious sissy that I met in Cleveland? [. . .] When I saw that marcelled what is it I don't know whether to kiss it or kill it! [. . .] It didn't like me and Galpin—too horrid, rough and mannish for it!" (SL 1.280-82). S. T. Joshi suggests Hatfield may have been the first openly homosexual individual Lovecraft ever met, which would go some way toward explaining his reaction—although if that was the case, Lovecraft's opinion appears entirely based on "sissy" (feminine, perhaps "camp gay") behavior (Joshi 2010, 427). A subsequent letter on the encounter with Hatfield replaces the neuter "it" with the equally sexless "creature," but the primary focus of the sexually derogatory comments in these letters is on Lovecraft's belief in the effeminate nature of homosexual men. Lovecraft wrote to Frank Belknap Long: "Alfredus never spoke a harsh word to the creature, but I suppose he couldn't conceal the contempt of an ultra-masculine personality for such attenuated exquisiteness." (SL 1.291).

Lovecraft had a much better reaction to Crane: "Then too, Galpin unmistakably liked Crane [. . .] Crane has at least the external appearance and actions of a man, and for that much Alfredus respected him" (SL 1.292). Joshi suggests Lovecraft did not know Hart Crane was a homosexual, which is why he fared better in Lovecraft's letters than Hatfield (Joshi 2010, 427). Conversely, Frank Belknap Long reportedly confided in Peter Cannon that "Howard and the rest knew of it, but that didn't affect their friendship with Crane" (Cannon 1997, 33). Reading Lovecraft's letters, the matter is unclear; for example, in a 1923 letter to Samuel Loveman he wrote: "And so the delectable Crane is now wallowing in the underworld of N.Y.? Good idea, your going there, but don't get in his Bohemian, near-Oscar-Wilde sort of circles! Gawd, how I hate that swinish Heliogabalan type!" (LSLS 18). The references to Heliogabalus and Oscar Wilde may be interpreted either as examples of specific homosexuals, or of sensual excess and sexual decadence in general; the latter is probably most likely the meaning intended, but the former cannot be ruled out. It is entirely possible Lovecraft was unable to recognize homosexuals who were not openly effete—and even then, he later found out that not all effete males are homosexuals. Whether he was aware of Hart Crane's homosexuality or not, Crane's masculine appearance and behavior apparently saved him from Lovecraft's jibes. Whatever the case, there is no other hint of Crane's sexuality in Lovecraft's other letters, nor in the few volumes of Crane's letters is it mentioned Lovecraft ever insulted him in that regard. More tellingly, Lovecraft is not known to have identified any of his homosexual friends such as Samuel Loveman or R. H. Barlow as such.

Later references to homosexuality are more general and do not refer to any specific individuals or current examples, but appear to be drawn from literature, classical studies, and the emerging psychological and sexologist literature on the subject. One letter to J. Vernon Shea goes into some depth, connecting the idea of gender identity with sexual identity:

> I guess it is true that homosexuality is a rare theme for novels—partly because public attention was seldom called to it (except briefly during the Wilde period) until a decade ago, & partly because any literary use of it always incurs the peril of legal censorship. As a matter of fact—although of course I always knew

that paederasty was a disgusting custom of many ancient nations—I never heard of homosexuality as an actual instinct till I was over thirty ... which beats your record! It is possible, I think that this perversion occurs more frequently in some periods than in others—owing to obscure biological & psychological causes. Decadent ages—when psychology is unsettled—seem to favour it. Of course—in ancient times the extent of the practice of paederasty (as a custom which most simply accepted blindly, without any special inclination) cannot be taken as any measure of the extent of actual psychological perversion. Another thing—many nowadays overlook the fact that there are always distinctly *effeminate* types which are most distinctly *not homosexual*. I don't know how psychology explains them, but we all know the sort of damned sissy who plays with girls & who—when he grows up—is a chronic "cake-eater", hanging around girls, doting on dances, acquiring certain feminine mannerisms, intonations, & tastes, & yet *never* having even the slightest perversion of erotic inclinations. (SL 4.234-35)

Lovecraft's comment "I never heard of homosexuality as an actual instinct till I was over thirty" is clarified in another letter: "I was middle-aged & married before I ever knew there was such a thing as *instinctive* homosexuality—though I suppose there must be dozens of Haldeman-Julius booklets about the matter now" (SL 4.356). Emanuel Haldeman-Julius was a publisher of cheap pamphlets, the "Little Blue Book" series, which included reprints of Arthur Machen and classic literature as well as frank discussion of atheism, socialism, marriage, and sexuality such as Little Blue Book No. 692, *Homo-Sexual Life* by William J. Fielding (1921). Lovecraft was a fan of the little blue books (ES 99) as well as the *Haldeman-Julius Weekly*, in which he had a letter printed in 1923 (LSLS 14, 37-40). It is possible that Lovecraft was first exposed to the notion of instinctive homosexuality while studying up to be a husband—several sexologists addressed the homosexuality in their works, including Havelock Ellis and J. A. Symonds's *Sexual Inversions* (1897). Reading in the same area is also the probable source of Lovecraft's choice of determining homosexuality a "psychological perversion"—at that time, the leading literature described it exactly as such.

Lovecraft wrote little about homosexuality among women—though he was certainly aware of the concept of lesbianism, as he mentions it in passing with regard to a literary work in a 1931 letter to R. H. Barlow (OFF 91). As with male homosexuality, Lovecraft confused sexual identity with gender identity, as when he wrote in 1933: "There are too, undoubtedly, many masculine women whose masculine manners & outlook are equally free from actual homosexuality" (SL 4.235). Possibly supporting this idea is an anecdote from Rheinhart Kleiner's "A Memoir of Lovecraft" (1949):

> George Kirk once told me a story of an excursion made by Lovecraft and himself to some similar locality. Stopping at a rural refreshment stand, they beheld two sturdy women hikers, attired in breeches and with all accessories, not an unusual sight today, also in quest of refreshment. One of them of a particularly virile and commanding type strode aggressively past Kirk and Lovecraft. "Well," commented Lovecraft, "at least, you can't say *she's* effeminate!" (LR 203)

There have been some who have questioned whether Lovecraft himself was a closeted homosexual or confused as to his gender. There is basically no evidence for either position. L. Sprague de Camp in *Lovecraft: A Biography* summarizes the general gist of these comments:

> Others have surmised that he might have been a homosexual or at least a latent one. They have cited his indifference to heterosexual relationships; the lack of women in his stories, whose leading characters are often a single male narrator and one close male friend; and his many friendships with younger men, some of whom either were overt homosexuals or had tendencies in that direction. (De Camp 1975, 189)

Most of these points are spurious and subjective, but all the better illustrate the basic ignorance behind many of these claims. Yes, Lovecraft was generally "indifferent"—but to any and all romance; he never gave any indication of considering or desiring a homosexual relationship, and at least for the brief period of cohabitation in his marriage performed heterosexual intercourse. Lovecraft did have many close male friends, some of whom were younger (Barlow), some older (Morton), and some his own age (Loveman). Some of them, notably R. H. Barlow and Samuel Loveman, were homosexual, but that in no way implies Lovecraft was as well. With regard to Lovecraft's fiction, I deal with those arguments in depth in the next chapter; suffice it to say that the male-protagonist-and-friend is a formula popularized by Sir Arthur Conan Doyle's Sherlock Holmes stories, the female population in Lovecraft's stories is not grossly disproportionate considering the fiction of the period, and that attempting to divine personality traits of authors from their fiction is never definitive.

The best, or at least the most all-encompassing of arguments concerning the possibility of Lovecraft's sexuality was made by Stanley C. Sargent during an interview with Peter A. Worthy. This long passage combines everything from Robert M. Price's "Homosexual Panic in 'The Outsider'" (1982) to Sargent's own "The Black Brat of Dunwich" (1997):

I felt convinced the author had gone through the same situation I was going through, the abject horror of recognizing you are gay in a very anti-gay world. [. . .] I tried to find an alternative reason for Lovecraft considering himself such an extreme "outsider," but I discovered no plausible other reason for such an extreme feeling of being an isolated monster. I didn't really care a whit about Lovecraft's sexual orientation (I am not trying to claim him as one of "us"), so at the time it occurred to me that I might be projecting a bit. Yet, as I read more about Lovecraft's life, I began to see that all the ingredients were there. [. . .]

His upbringing with a dominant, overly protective mother (who dressed him as a girl for the first few years of his life) and the nearly total absence of a father is the classic formula for a male child being gay. Although he declared his distaste for homosexuals, in particular effeminate males, he was often described as effeminate himself. Plus he was a close friend with Samuel Loveman for many years and Loveman was hardly in the closet about his activities. Finally, I can come up with no other logical explanation for Lovecraft's close relationship with the teenage Barlow during the last years of his life, to the point of making Barlow his literary executor. [. . .]

It all makes even more sense if you interpret "The Dunwich Horror" as an autobiographical cloaked confession of his dilemma. Wilbur obviously represents Lovecraft, all the way down to Lovecraft believing his own appearance was "hideous" (again, thanks to mom), and I believe the twin brother was a symbol of the homosexual desires Lovecraft so desperately tried to suppress. No one could see the monster and it was essentially so evil that it had to be contained. Yet it kept growing and even Wilbur feared it would someday break out (read "come out") and destroy the world (Lovecraft's little conservative world). That thought terrified him as being gay went against everything he believed in; it must have been awful for him. He surely married Sonia, a mother figure, in hope of changing his orientation, a very common and futile mistake. If he didn't confess his problem to her, she undoubtedly guessed and was sympathetic. ("Stanley C. Sargent," 1997)

There has been some speculation on Lovecraft's gender identity by critics. For example, Joel Pace writes: "Given this background, Lovecraft's later homophobia can be seen as his means of self-definition to correspond to his scripted gender role while distancing himself from the early liminal space he occupied" (108). This "background" consists entirely from anecdotes and a few photographs of Lovecraft's early childhood. As a very young boy Lovecraft went unbreeched, and his mother Susie—who is said by Sonia to have wanted a daughter—had him in gowns and grew his hair out into long, girlish locks until about the age of six; and he had a tendency to insist at that young age "I'm a little girl!" (Joshi 2010, 65–66). Such an outburst may make slightly more context given Lovecraft's extremely young age, and the possible innocent encouragement of his mother: "My mother innocently helped to swell my self-esteem by recording all my 'cute' childish sayings, and I began to make these 'naïve' remarks *on purpose* to draw attention" (LRK 66). Long locks and going unbreeched were fairly typical practices for children of Lovecraft's age at those times, and probably should not be used as examples of gender identity issues. After his hair was shorn and he began to wear pants, there is no material in his letters or biography to suggest that Lovecraft had any questions or issues with his gender.

Suggestions of homosexuality are based mainly on Lovecraft's lack of interest in women and close friendships with men, some of whom (R. H. Barlow, Samuel Loveman, etc.) were homosexuals, bolstered by remembrances such as: "He was not at ease with the other sex and was only at his best when with a few chosen male friends" (LR 13). J. Vernon Shea gives a good example of such an argument:

> Some would-be psychiatrists, learning of H.P.L.'s detestation of perverts (he cold-shouldered Hart Crane in Cleveland and was railing against Oscar Wilde as late as the thirties), learning of Lovecraft's forays into the night and his encouragement of young male writers, might suspect that all this covers up an unconscious urge in that direction [. . .] But they would be wrong. There is not an iota of evidence to support such a suspicion. (12)

In fact, Lovecraft apparently had very little sexual drive of any sort, and he was very diffident toward women, as his friend Rheinhart Kleiner observed:

> I cannot pretend to offer any inside information regarding Lovecraft's attitude toward women, even the most charming of them. He treated them all with a formal politeness which did not have a touch of gallantry in it. Some of our livelier damsels were at first inclined to resent this aloofness of the man from Providence and probably felt somewhat slighted at his indifference to them. But that was the natural, unaffected Lovecraft, and nothing could be done about it. (LR 162)

Zealia Brown Reed Bishop, one of Lovecraft's clients, initially wished to write romance stories under his tutelage, but Lovecraft disabused her of the notion: "Briefly, I soon learned under this strict teaching that I dared not write contemporary love stories which would invite such criticism as:

'No gentleman would dare kiss a girl in that fashion'; 'No gentleman would think of knocking on a lady's bedroom door even at a house party'" (*LR* 267). Bishop's brief memoir of Lovecraft, "H. P. Lovecraft: A Pupil's View," contains many errors, but these quotations ring true for Lovecraft.

While there is no solid evidence that Lovecraft was a homosexual (which is to say, there is no written account or a proof of a homosexual affair or admission involving Lovecraft), it remains for many that lack of interest in women is tied to an interest in men, particularly when coupled with unmasculine behavior. No proof is sufficient to remove the suspicions of those who choose to read a homosexual subtext into accounts of Lovecraft's life. That he married a woman and had sexual relations with her, or that he was derisive to homosexuals in his letters, is insufficient or even considered proof for those determined to believe; certainly, some homosexual men have attempted to conform to heteronormative behavior by engaging in heterosexual marriages and sexual relationships, or to hide themselves or voice self-disgust by loudly deriding homosexuals.

Consider for example this anecdote related by Kleiner:

> Lovecraft did not sleep away from his home until after his thirtieth birthday [. . .] But it was certainly very early in the course of our friendship that he came to the Broadway Central Hotel in New York for an amateur-press-association convention, and that he and I shared the same bed for one night. [. . .] The point I wish to make has to do with Lovecraft's sleeping habit, which consisted of a long night-shirt, reaching almost to his ankles. I believed this article of apparel had long been relegated by modern folk to the attic, even at that time, but its use by Lovecraft certainly indicated his love of the old and the orthodox. Lovecraft had already grown on me considerably by that time, and his frequent letters were received more gladly and read more carefully than the daily newspaper at my door. (*LR* 197)

Most will probably read this innocent paragraph of two male friends chastely sharing a bed out of economic need; others consider it a veiled allusion to a homosexual encounter and may pick up the fact that this incident occurred after Lovecraft turned thirty (echoing his earlier statement "I never heard of homosexuality as an actual instinct till I was over thirty"), suggesting it might even have been his first. This illustrates how such subtexts may be found in Lovecraft's life by those who choose to do so. Similarly, Robert M. Price in his article "Homosexual Panic in 'The Outsider'" demonstrates how homosexual themes might be read in some of Lovecraft's fiction, and is at pains to explain:

J. Vernon Shea and others have suggested that Lovecraft was himself gay, at least a "latent homosexual". This, of course, is not impossible, but neither is it particularly likely (though, ultimately, who cares?). Even the present article does not really count as evidence for Lovecraft's homosexuality, since "The Outsider"'s vivid parallel to "homosexual panic" notwithstanding, Lovecraft seems never to have undergone this crisis. (Price 1982)

Perhaps further demonstrating the difficulty of reading Lovecraft's sexual identity from his fiction, the following is an excerpt from a letter that Eileen McNamara M.D. wrote in response to Price's article:

What is it that Lovecraft sensed about himself that he detested, that he hid from others and himself? I think that it is entirely plausible that it was homosexual desires, given his view of the prototypical woman in his life as engulfing and dominating. However, the story gives us no clue, and the repressed wish may also, or in addition, have been matricide or incest. (Price 1983)

Winfield Townley Scott made the most cogent observation: "One can say that almost all his adult relationships were homosexual, if the word is intended in its blandest sense" (*LR* 26).

Views on Miscegenation

Lovecraft's letters, poetry, and fiction give proof of his xenophobia, which was manifested in prejudicial attitudes against different cultures and peoples that in his mind threatened his own culture; a belief in racialism, the segregation of humanity into distinct races and the necessity of maintaining their separatism, to preserve that culture; and his belief that the Nordic/Aryan group, of which he considered himself a member, and its associated culture was obviously superior to all others. Where these beliefs intersect with the matter of sex—and so fall under the purview of this essay—is the matter of miscegenation. Because of its impact on his fiction and his life, Lovecraft's views on this subject are important to understand. He makes his opinion very clear in a letter to James F. Morton in 1930:

The real problem is the quadroon & octoroon—& still lighter shades. Theirs is a sorry tragedy, but they will have to find a special place. What we can do is discourage the increase of their numbers by placing the heaviest possible penalties on miscegenation, & arousing as much public sentiment as possible against lax customs & attitudes—especially in the inland South—at present favouring the melancholy & disgusting phenomenon. (LJM 255)

Lovecraft's thoughts on miscegenation should be understood in the context of his broader philosophy and development. This is addressed extensively by S. T. Joshi in *H. P. Lovecraft: The Decline of the West* (1990), but in brief many of Lovecraft's views on race and miscegenation were endemic to the society of the United States, inculcated in Lovecraft at an early age, and persisted throughout his life. While Lovecraft used racialist scientific research to attempt and support his arguments, the tide of evidence turned against his racial theories, and he ceased to use them to express his views to his more open-minded friends, though he never entirely gave them up.

Lovecraft's beliefs in miscegenation were present at an early age. Lovecraft's earliest explicit racialist document was a poem, "De Triumpho Naturae: The Triumph of Nature over Northern Ignorance" (1905), dedicated to William Benjamin Smith, author of *The Color Line: A Brief in Behalf of the Unborn* (1905), and described "The savage black, the ape-resembling beast" (Joshi 2010, 110-12). The libel of blacks resembling apes is a recurring hallmark of American racial thought, and Lovecraft made such comments repeatedly throughout his life: in a 1917 letter to Rheinhart Kleiner he says: "The negro is obviously a link betwixt apedom & man; though all species do not show equal affinity to the beast." (LRK 111); a 1926 letter to Frank Belknap Long refers to blacks as "childlike half-gorillas" (SL 2.68); two 1931 letters to Robert E. Howard describe blacks as "very primitive and apelike" and "gorilla-like" (MF 140, 183); and similar comments are made in others letters. Lovecraft's fullest calculated expression in this line is in a 1933 letter to Robert Bloch:

> In the matter of the inferior races, however—negro & australoid—I think an absolute colour-line is justified. These stock definitely depart from the norm of homo sapiens in the direction of lower animal forms, & there is no more reasons for considering them our equals than there is for considering certain other primitive stem-offshoots (like the extinct Neanderthals) our equals. Any substantial infusion of African, Australian Blackfellow, Melanesia, or black southern Hindoo blood into another stock means the definite lowering of the latter's biological status; hence it ought to be avoided at any cost. (LRB 39)

These statements provide some context for understanding something of Lovecraft's thoughts behind miscegenation, particularly with regard to his fiction. Beyond any intrinsic or culturally instilled bigotry that came from his upbringing in the race-conscious 1890s and 1900s, there is also an intimation of evolutionary thought, implying that scientific racism played a large role in his prejudice, or at least was used to augment and support it. In his letters, Lovecraft references certain anthropological sources that appeared to support his views, such as in this passage from a 1923 letter to Frank Belknap Long:

> I know the tendency is to give a separate classification to the Neanderthal–Piltdown-Heidelberg type—using the flashy word "Eoanthropus"—but in truth this creature was probably as much a man as a gorilla. Many anthropologists have detected both negroid and gorilla resemblances in these "dawn" skulls, and to my mind it's a safe bet that they were exceedingly low, hairy negroes existing perhaps 400,000 years ago and having perhaps the rudiments of a guttural language. (SL 1.258)

Eoanthrupus dawsoni, the scientific name attributed to the Piltdown Man hoax, was widely accepted as a "missing link" until exposed as a forgery in 1953. The Piltdown Man is referred to in Lovecraft's writings, notably "Dagon" and "The Rats in the Walls."

The focus on evolutionary development, racial theories, and the descent of humankind from a common ancestor with apes appears to be the common element of Lovecraft's "scientific" support of his views, as further expressed in a 1934 letter to Natalie Wooley: "Of the complete biological inferiority of the negro there can be no question—he has anatomical features consistently varying from those of other stocks, & always in the direction of the lower primates" (SL 5.77). As Bennet Lovett-Graff notes in "Primate Geniture in H. P. Lovecraft's 'Arthur Jermyn,'" this line of argument owes much to Thomas Henry Huxley's *Evidence as to Man's Place in Nature* (1863), which concludes that man and apes are descended from a common ancestor—Lovecraft is known to have read Huxley, and mentioned him several times in his letters. Lovett-Graff may also have pointed out an answer to a minor mystery in Joshi's *I Am Providence*: "Lovecraft retained to the end of his days a belief in the biological inferiority of blacks and also of Australian aborigines, although it is not clear why he singled out this latter group" (Joshi 2010, 936).

Lovecraft's racism in this regard is quite candid and particular. He writes that "the Australian blackfellow" is "a race being nearly as far below the negro as the negro is below the full human."—and this despite, as far as is known, Lovecraft never met an Australian aborigine (*LJM* 252). Lovett-

1. Sex and Lovecraft

Graff suggests a possible answer to the mystery in one of Lovecraft's letters: "Equally inferior—& perhaps even more so—is the Australian black stock, which differs widely from the real negro. This race has other stigmata of primitiveness—such as great Neanderthaloid eyebrow-ridges" (SL 5.78). The last comment, as Lovett-Graff points out, is a reference back to Huxley's "race-based conclusion that the Neanderthal skull most closely resembles that of contemporary Australians" (Lovett-Graff 1997b, 383). In another letter, Lovecraft refers to Sir Arthur Keith as follows: "He now doubts *whether we have any common ancestor with negroes & australoids*, & believes the Australians are descended from the Java pithecanthropus" (*LJM* 306; see also MF 482). Here we can see that Lovecraft's selection of flawed anthropological scholarship was probably responsible for his affected disdain of Australian aborigines, or at least its reinforcement.

Lovecraft mentions in places other authors known for their racialist ideas, such as Arthur Schopenhauer and Ernst Haeckel, who also made claims that blacks were more closely related to apes and argued against miscegenation, but he does not directly mention their beliefs or the works that advocated such views, so it is difficult to say how much influence they had on him in this regard. These evolutionary theories, the typical effort to differentiate humankind into different races based on ethnicity and phenotype, and the prominent rise of the eugenics movement in the early 1900s were all different streams of intellectual thought of which Lovecraft was certainly very aware, and they certainly colored or reinforced his views (SL 4.75–76).

Whereas some of Lovecraft's other views appeared to change with time, his belief in the biological inferiority of blacks remained throughout his life (Joshi 2010, 110–14), and his views on miscegenation likewise did not substantially change. Compare these two excerpts from his letters, written in 1919 and 1933 respectively:

> The whole U. S. negro question is very simple. (1) *Certainly* the negro is vastly the biological inferior of the Caucasian. (2) Therefore if racial amalgamation were to occur, the net level of American civilization would perceptibly fall, as in such mongrel nations as Mexico—& several South American near-republics. (3) Amalgamation would undoubtedly take place if prejudice were eradicated, beginning with the lowest grades of Jews & Italians & eventually working upward until the whole county would be poisoned, & its culture & progress stunted. (4) Therefore the much-abused "colour line" is a self-protective measure of the white American people to keep the blood of their descendants

pure, & the institutions & greatness of their country unimpaired. The colour line *must be maintained* in spite of the ranting & preaching of fanatical & ill-informed philanthropists. The genius of a few individuals is never an index of collective racial capacity. In spite of all the Booker Washingtons & Dunbars we can see that the negro as a whole has never made any progress or founded any culture. We cannot judge a man sociologically by this own individual qualities; we have the future to think of. Two persons of different races, though equal mentally & physically, may have a vitally different sociological value, *because one will certainly produce an incalculably better type of descendants than the other.* (LRK 155)

As for the negro question—I think that intermarriage ought to be banned in view of the vast number of blacks in the country. Illicit miscegenation by the white male is bad enough, heaven knows—but at least the hybrid offspring is kept below a definite colour-line & kept from vitiating the main stock. Nothing but pain & disaster can come from the mingling of black & white, & the law ought to aid in checking this criminal folly. Granting the negro his full due, he is not the sort of material which can mix successfully into the fabric of a civilized Caucasian nation. Isolated cases of high-grade hybrids prove nothing. It is easy to see the ultimate result of the wholesale pollution of highly evolved blood by definitely inferior strains. (SL 4.230)

A substantial part of the real fear that Lovecraft felt with regard to miscegenation was the potential destruction of his own "Nordic" race:

Concerning heredity in general—it is curious how a dark strain will persistently crop out among a blond stock, whereas a blond strain is completely lost among a dark stock. This proves that the dark type is by far the more basic and normal in the species, and that the Nordic is the product of an exceptional and tenuous specialization—whose results are insecurely lodged in the race, and always ready to be overthrown by any influence favouring the original arrangement. (SL 3.412)

While not speaking directly of miscegenation here—elsewhere he addresses the "dark strain" more specifically as "brunets"—this passage makes clear Lovecraft's concern that the "race" he considered as his own was a tenuous product, a beleaguered minority that might be irrevocably diluted and lost, as much of the antiquarian architecture Lovecraft loved were gradually lost to progress, replaced by newer structures that were ugly in his eyes.

Lovecraft's prejudice against miscegenation also extended in part to other nationalities and ethnicities, though without the attestation and support of pseudo-scientific racialist theories. While not seeking to deny or downplay this aspect of his beliefs, the strictly hereditary biological argument is much less prominent when discussing miscegenation than the anthropological and "colour-line" arguments Lovecraft put forth, and he used other arguments. Lovecraft still appeared to be against any miscegenation between "whites" and "non-whites." For example, he once voiced his disgust for an "Oriental love" tale:

> "Pilgrims in Love", by De Lysle Ferrée Cass, is contemptibly disgusting, unspeakably nauseating. Mr. G. W. S., of Chicago, has written that Cass "diplomatically handles a very difficult subject—Oriental love".
>
> We do not care for subjects so near allied to vulgarity, however "diplomatically" they maybe be "handled". Of such "Oriental love" we may speak in the words of the lazy but ingenious schoolboy, who when asked by his tutor to describe the reign of Caligula, replied "that the less said about it the better." (*Uncollected Letters* 3)

Mrs. H. P. Lovecraft

S. T. Joshi provides an excellent biography of H. P. Lovecraft's wife Sonia and a detailed account of their courtship, marriage, separation, and divorce in *I Am Providence* (2010). However, this was not the end of Sonia's relationship with Lovecraft, and as she has provided some of the critical anecdotes and material regarding Lovecraft's intimate thoughts on love and sex, I think it is relevant to briefly address some of what happened after their divorce.

With their marriage irrevocably over, Lovecraft rarely spoke to his correspondents of having ever been married, and eventually the two drifted out of touch so that at the end of his life and even some time afterwards many of Lovecraft's friends were generally ignorant of any details pertaining to his wife. The original version of Winfield Townley Scott's "His Own Most Fantastic Creation: Howard Phillips Lovecraft" printed in *Marginalia* (1944) depends heavily on Lovecraft's letters and recollections of his friends for details of his marriage. Scott notes the deficiency prominently:

> It is very difficult—and so I think I shall not bury this somewhat footnote-ish aside in an actual footnote but, without apology, keep it up here in larger print—to write of Lovecraft's marriage. This is principally because the former Mrs. Lovecraft is inaccessible; one hears that she is remarried and that she is probably living out west, but even old friends of Lovecraft who knew his wife are unable to establish communication with her because they are denied, by

her relatives, knowledge of her present name and whereabouts. To write of the marriage from others' reminiscences and speculations is under the circumstances certainly permissible, and is certainly embarrassing. One can only hope, in view of Lovecraft's increasing fame and the consequent importance of his biography and of the need for fairness all around, that this one woman who ever lived intimately with him will tell her story. Until then, one can only piece the story together from the fragments offered by outsiders—*human* outsiders! (Scott 1944, 321)

On finally making contact with Sonia Davis, Scott reworked the piece. The revised essay is the version in Scott's *Exiles and Fabrications* (1961) and in Peter Cannon's *Lovecraft Remembered* (1998). With Scott's help, she published a memoir, "Howard Phillips Lovecraft as His Wife Remembers Him," in the 22 August 1948 issue of the *Providence Sunday Journal*, and again in *Books at Brown* (1949). August Derleth edited the piece further and published it as "Lovecraft as I Knew Him" in *Something about Cats and Other Pieces* (1949); it would not be reprinted in its original form until 1985, as a pamphlet from Necronomicon Press entitled *The Private Life of H. P. Lovecraft*, which was later revised and reissued in 1992 (Davis, 1992). Comparison between the different versions shows that the main editing of Sonia's manuscript in "Lovecraft as I Knew Him" was to put her entries in something like chronological order, but some data was lost in the restructuring and rephrasing. Comparing the text with *The Private Life of H. P. Lovecraft* reveals these editorial remainders, which are mostly trivial. For example, when Lovecraft cites a married couple who live through letters, the fact that the couple in question lives in Virginia is included in *Private Life* but omitted from "As I Knew Him."

Dorothy Litersky's biography *Derleth: Hawk ... and Dove* contains a questionable episode about when Sonia and Derleth met in New York:

> Sonia was very startled when August told her he had copies of H. P. L.'s letters containing a detailed description of Sonia's life with Lovecraft. He forbade her to quote H. P. L.'s letters without his and Wandrei's approval. His action was not without an unfortunate reprisal, for subsequently Sonia burned most of Lovecraft's letters to her, another invaluable source of information about his personal and romantic life, destroyed for posterity. (Litersky 137)

Litersky cites as her sources letters from August Derleth to Robert Barlow (23 October 1947) and Ray Bradbury (21 November 1947). Sonia's own account adds little detail and does not give her reason for burning the letters or the date she did so:

1. Sex and Lovecraft 55

> I had a trunkful of his letters which he had written me throughout the years but before leaving New York for California I took them to a field and set a match to them. I now have only the one in the *Rainbow* and one which I received from him after I returned from Europe. But there are still about a dozen picture postal cards that he sent me before our marriage, during and afterward. Some are still of interest. (Davis 1992, 24)

In *The Normal Lovecraft* (1973), Gerry de la Ree's article "When Sonia Sizzled" contains the contents or excerpts from three of Sonia's letters to Samuel Loveman from the period 1947–49 and one letter from Derleth to Sonia. These letters confirm a few of Litersky's claims, as when Derleth wrote:

> I hope you are not going ahead regardless of our stipulations to arrange for publication of anything containing writings of any kind, letters or otherwise, of H. P. Lovecraft, thus making it necessary for us to enjoin publication and sale, and to bring suit, which we will certainly do if any manuscript containing works of Lovecraft does not pass through our office for the executor's permission. [. . .] You will be interested to know that we now have in Lovecraft's own letters to his aunts a complete and detailed account of how things went during his entire married life. (de la Ree 29)

In spite of their differences, some sort of peace was reached, considering that in later years Arkham House did publish "Lovecraft as I Knew Him" (1949) and "Memories of Lovecraft: I" (1969). By Derleth's own account he met and spoke with Sonia while in Los Angeles in 1953, as revealed in a letter to *Haunted*:

> Apropos your piece on Lovecraft, the question of Lovecraft and sex had been bothering me for some time, especially in view of his violent reaction against Oscar Wilde as a person, however much he admired his work; so in 1953 when I was in Los Angeles, I asked Sonia Davis—the ex-Mrs. Lovecraft—rather bluntly about Lovecraft's sexual adequacy. She assured me that he has been entirely adequate sexually, and since she impressed me as a well-sexed woman, not easily satisfied, I concluded that Lovecraft's "aversion" was very probably nothing more than a kind of Puritanism—that is, it was something "gentleman" don't discuss, and so on. I don't think it ought, in the light of this, to be called "extreme aversion." (Russell 114)

In addition to her memoir, Sonia continued to communicate sporadically with friends and fans until shortly before her death. Sonia wrote to Muriel Eddy in 1967 after Derleth had published some of C. M. Eddy Jr.'s work in *The Dark Brotherhood and Other Pieces* (1966), which contain three of Eddy's stories revised by Lovecraft. This exchange lasted until Muriel was informed of Sonia's death in 1972 (Eddy and Eddy 29). In 1974 a Lovecraft scholar named R. Alain Everts published a final few details based on his interviews with Sonia in articles for the fanzines *Nyctalops* and *The Outsider*, one of which is used here: "Howard Phillips Lovecraft and Sex" (Everts).

Everts is a pseudonym for Randal Alan Kirsch. In 1968, while a student, Everts traveled around the country interviewing individuals who had known or been associated with H. P. Lovecraft in life, including his former wife Sonia. The tapes of these interviews, and other materials he collected from them, were to be turned over to the John Hay Library at Brown University, which held the bulk of Lovecraft's papers after his death. Everts did not turn over all these materials to Brown, and the university was forced to pursue legal means to reclaim them (*Brown University vs. Kirsch*). "Howard Phillips Lovecraft and Sex," published in 1974, obviously uses as its source material some of these taped interviews and materials. Other publications likely drawn from these materials is *Alcestis* (1985), an unbound holograph of a manuscript purported to be a collaboration between Lovecraft and Sonia.

The attraction of Sonia to Lovecraft fans and scholars was her unique relationship with Lovecraft, and the insights that only a wife and lover could give of his life and character. Some pressed too hard; Derleth's characteristic pushiness and perceived ownership of the Lovecraft copyrights; the holocaust of letters that certainly many scholars have bitterly resented; and we will perhaps never know all that Everts heard or obtained from Sonia. The bits and pieces that remain in her letters and remembrances still provide crucial insight into Lovecraft found nowhere else, and the efforts that fans and scholars went through to obtain these snippets prove at least the strong and continued interest in sex and H. P. Lovecraft.

2. Sex and the Lovecraft Mythos

> As for copulating with Cthulhu, the thought of catching unspeakable alien STDs scares me more than anything Lovecraft ever wrote. (Gonce and Harms 118)
>
> You should be so lucky as to last for the incubation period of any earthly disease if you have sex with Cthulhu! ("alt.sex.cthulhu FAQ")

There are two understandings to be gained by examining the Lovecraft Mythos in terms of sexual elements, gender roles, and love: a greater knowledge and appreciation of the Lovecraft Mythos itself, and a thorough familiarity with the fiction that serves as the foundation for development and adaptation of the Cthulhu Mythos by later authors. This chapter focuses primarily on Lovecraft's own approach to such material in his fiction, but readers should keep in mind that these stories form a kind of *Corpus Hermeticum* for weird authors, and the presence of sexuality and relationships in these stories, whether overt or subtextual, has implications beyond the story.

This chapter begins with a brief overview of Lovecraft's immediate precursors and influences in fiction, with respect to how their approach and treatment of sexuality and relationships is evident in the Lovecraft Mythos, with particular emphasis on Arthur Machen. Following is a literary analysis of Lovecraft's weird fiction, with respect to its sexual content, gender roles, and relationships. Finally, this chapter will conclude with an identification and discussion of the disparate common plot elements with regard to sex in the Lovecraft Mythos, with special regard to how these themes developed over the course of Lovecraft's life and fiction, and a look at sex in Mythos poetry and e-book erotica.

Not all of Lovecraft's literary output was weird fiction. He wrote many nonfiction essays, poetry, the occasional non-weird fiction, and at least one short play. For the purposes of this essay I consider only his weird fiction, including Lovecraft's substantial revisions, and the essay "Supernatural Horror in Literature" as part of the Lovecraft Mythos. This distinction allows the inclusion of many of Lovecraft's stories that have no direct tie to the popular conception of the Cthulhu Mythos (that is, no mention of Yog-Sothoth, the *Necronomicon*, etc.), but are nevertheless works of weird fiction, and thus provide a more complete picture of Lovecraft's work as a whole. Likewise, for the purposes of this essay I have left out stories whose sole possible claim to inclusion is having the word "orgy" or the like somewhere in the text, such as in the Eddy/Lovecraft revision "Deaf, Dumb, and Blind" (1924). The use of such terms is undoubtedly meant to hark back to antiquarian concepts of pagan religion, rather than a specific reference to group sex, and so have nothing to add to an understanding of how Lovecraft used sex, love, and gender in his work.

With regard to sex, love, and gender and Lovecraft's works outside of the Lovecraft Mythos, there are a few items of note: the mildly bawdy poem "The Pathetick History of Sir Wilful Wildrake," in the style of Jonathan Swift; a series of seduction poems written on behalf of Alfred Galpin and published in the *Tryout*; the weird poem "The Bride of the Sea" (1916); the comedic short story "Sweet Ermengarde; or, The Heart of a Country Girl" (c. 1919-21); and *Alfredo; a Tragedy* (1918), a play dealing with romance. None of these, however, had much if any impact on later authors, so the focus of this chapter is on his weird fiction.

Precursors and Influences

In creating the Lovecraft Mythos, Lovecraft drew on many previous works, including weird and fantastic stories that contained sexual elements and themes. However, the sexual text and subtext in most of these literary influences do not shine through in the majority of Lovecraft's fiction. It is difficult, for example, to draw a line of descent for adult ideas from the bawdier *Arabian Nights* through *Vathek* (1786) to the *Necronomicon*, or to label the Lovecraft Mythos as reflecting the implicit sexual horror of the Gothic tradition exemplified in Mary Shelley's *Frankenstein* (1818) and Bram Stoker's *Dracula* (1897). Even in contemporary weird fiction that strongly influenced Lovecraft, he eschewed any romantic element: Lovecraft derided the last half of Merritt's *The Moon Pool* (1919) specifically because it went from a weird yarn into a sappy romantic adventure (SL 4.406-7). Of all Lovecraft's precursors, the most important in terms of this essay, the ones with the greatest or at least most apparent influence in terms of sex, are Edgar Allan Poe and Arthur Machen.

Edgar Allan Poe was the early American master of the macabre, one of Lovecraft's idols and a critical influence on his fiction. Of Poe's tales, "Ligeia" (1838) and "The Fall of the House of Usher" (1839) are likely to have influenced Lovecraft's use of sex and gender. From "The Fall of the House of Usher" in particular Lovecraft derived elements like the twin narrative structure, one generational and one in present time, which is apparent in several stories; the metaphor of the ancestral manse, often in neglect or ruined, which reflects the state of the family; and the families themselves, of old stock and with few if any branches. Bennet Lovett-Graff goes so far as to classify "Facts concerning the Late Arthur Jermyn and His Family" (1920), "The Lurking Fear" (1922), and "The Rats in the Walls" (1923) as a sort of unplanned trilogy based on similar themes derived from Poe, and differentiates them with "The Shadow over Innsmouth" (1931), written after Lovecraft returned from New York and the failure of his marriage (Lovett-Graff 1997b, 373; Lovett-Graff 1997a).

A more immediate influence is the Welsh mystic Arthur Machen. Lovecraft's fiction, particularly "The Dunwich Horror," is so invested with Arthur Machen's ideas, concepts, and names that several of Machen's stories—notably "The Great God Pan" (1890), "Novel of the Black Seal" (1895), and "The White People" (1904)—are sometimes considered part of the wider Cthulhu Mythos. Other Machen stories that feature implications of illicit sex, pornography, etc. are "The Bright Boy" (1936) and "The Children of the Pool" (1936), but these were published relatively late and have little discernible influence on later Mythos tales.

These stories of Machen include subtle insinuations of rape, the degeneracy associated with sex and vice, secret and pagan worship of a primeval and sensual nature, the prejudice against children born of foreign fathers or of illegitimate birth, the horrors of science unlocking the secrets of life that separate man from animal, and the terrible implication of diabolic cross-breeding between unsuspecting humans and ancient races, or even incarnate forces of nature. The recurring figure of the faun or satyr in Machen's work contains dual aspects—that of the classical pagan fertility figure, and that of the demonic Satan-figure crafted by later Christian authors, aspects of which are present in Shub-Niggurath, the Goat with a Thousand Young. Because of how directly these three stories tie in to the Mythos, they will be addressed here in brief.

It is important, in examining these three stories of Machen, to remember their time and context—the tail end of the Victorian era, a period when the merest mention of sex was a taboo that flourished behind closed doors, when the first sexologists began their scholarly research on the subject, which to the general public was too shocking even to be hinted at obliquely in word or text. The circumstances of "The Great God Pan"'s publication put it in rare company in the Yellow Nineties: the first edition was issued from The Bodley Head and featured illustrations by Audrey Beardsley, both infamous for their work with the *Yellow Book* (1894-97). It was to this atmosphere and association that in 1890, when H. P. Lovecraft was born into the world, Machen's "The Great God Pan" was also born. Public opinion in England considered Machen's story almost an obscenity—"It is an incoherent nightmare of sex and the supposed horrible mysteries behind it," as the *Westminster Gazette* famously had it (Machen 2001, xxii). Machen's reputation in this regard was probably not improved by the printing of his translation of a censored French version of *The Memoirs of Jacques Casanova de Seingelt* into English in 1894, though otherwise his contact with Decadents like Oscar Wilde was very slight. Perhaps as continued evidence of Machen's reputation, some later editions of the pornographic novel *The Amatory Experience of a Surgeon* (1881) contain an introduction by an "A. Machen." This is generally considered a spurious addition to American editions of the work printed in the late 1920s or early 1930s, though publishers failed to specify exactly when and where such things were printed. However, this date would approximately coincide with the reprintings of Machen's works by Knopf in the early-to-mid-1920s, as well as the private printing of Machen's translation of the mildly obscene work *Fantastic Tales or the Way to Attain* by Béroalde de Verville (1923).

The obfuscation that Machen employed, the teasing suggestions he relied on to address his subject, would prove to be a substantial tool to Lovecraft in his own fiction; for the exact same method used to explore one forbidden subject could be effectively used in others, and it was one Lovecraft much admired. In his essay "Supernatural Horror in Literature" Lovecraft wrote: "No one could begin to describe the cumulative suspense and ultimate horror with which every paragraph abounds without following fully the precise order in which Mr. Machen unfolds his gradual hints and revelations" (Lovecraft 2000, 63).

Where Lovecraft disagreed with Machen was the reason behind his focus on the taboo:

What Machen probably likes about perverted and forbidden things is their departure from and hostility to the commonplace. To him—whose imagination is not cosmic—they represent what Pegana and the River Yann represent to Dunsany, whose imagination is cosmic. People whose minds are—like Machen's—steeped in the orthodox myths of religion, naturally find a poignant fascination in the conception of things which religion brands with outlawry and horror. Such people take the artificial and obsolete concept of "sin" seriously, and find it full of dark allurement. On the other hand, people like myself, with realistic and scientific point of view, see no charm or mystery whatever in things banned by religious mythology. We recognize the primitiveness and meaninglessness of the religious attitude, and in consequence find no element of attractive defiance or significant escape in those things which happen to contravene it. [. . .] The filth and perversion which to Machen's obsoletely orthodox mind meant defiances of the universe's foundations, mean to us only a rather prosaic and unfortunate species of organic maladjustment—no more frightful, and no more interesting, than a headache, a fit of colic, or an ulcer on the big toe. (SL 4.4)

"The Great God Pan" (1890)

The most openly sexual of any of Machen's stories, each of the eight episodes of "The Great God Pan" are rife with the intimation of relationships and sexual activities—but never more than an intimation, until the final confession. Throughout the story readers must interpret the evidence and make their own conclusions, filling in details from their own imaginations. On top of the merely carnal sins hinted at are suggestions of more otherworldly terror, and it is this supernatural aspect that connects "The Great God Pan" with "The Dunwich Horror."

Central to the novel is the idea that a young woman—appropriately enough named Mary—becomes aware of a supernatural world beyond normal human perception; as her adoptive father Dr. Raymond calls it, "she has seen the Great God Pan." The process effectively destroys her mind—but nine months later she gives birth to a daughter, Helen. The conception here is almost a parody of the visitation to the Virgin Mary by the Holy Spirit, which in Christian belief resulted in the birth of Jesus. As noted in the text, "ET DIABOLUS INCARNATUS EST. ET HOMO FACTUS EST" ("And the devil was made flesh. And a human was made") (Machen 2001, 14) is a direct parody or inversion of the line from the Nicene Creed, "ET INCARNATUS EST DE SPIRITU SANCTO EX MARIA VIRGINE ET HOMO FACTUS EST" ("And became incarnate by the Holy Spirit in the Virgin Mary and was made man"). As if to cement her inappropriate parentage, Helen is described as "of a very different type from the inhabitants of the village; her skin was a pale, clear olive, and her features were strongly marked, and of a somewhat foreign character" (Machen 2001, 10).

In her life, Helen drives people to ruin. As a child she was spied in the woods "playing on the grass with a 'strange naked man'" (Machen 2001, 11)—later suggested to be a faun or satyr—and later brought a female friend with her into the woods, with the result:

> her mother heard a noise which sounded like suppressed weeping in the girl's room, and on going in found her lying, half undressed, upon the bed, evidently in the greatest distress. As soon as she saw her mother, she exclaimed, "Ah mother, mother, why did you let me go to the forest with Helen?" (Machen 2001, 13)

Less direct are the tales of men, suggested to have been her lovers, who are driven to take their own lives after visiting with her, and the husbands whom she ruined in a manner they could not speak of. Confronted with her crimes, Helen commits suicide, and her accuser watches her body undergo a terrible transformation, changing from "sex to sex [. . .] descend to the beasts whence it ascended" (Machen 2001, 46), breaking all boundaries separating human from animal, undoing in moments the work of evolution in her death throes:

> for one instant I saw a Form, shaped in dimness before me, which I will not farther describe. But the symbol of this form may be seen in ancient sculptures, and in paintings which survived beneath the lava, too foul to be spoken of . . . as a horrible and unspeakable shape, neither man nor beast, was changed into human form, there came finally death. (Machen 2001, 46–47)

This passage, and others like it in *Thesaurus Incantatus* (1888) and *Dog and Duck* (1924), show Machen was aware of the sexually explicit antiquities discovered in the ruins of Pompeii and Herculaneum, such as the erotic statue *Pan and She-Goat*. Due to sensibilities of the time, these kinds of erotic discoveries were hidden or locked away in the Secret Museum of Naples, the Secretum of the British Museum, and private collections.

The basic plot of this tale—from the otherworldly conception to the bizarre transformative death—is a clear influence on "The Dunwich Horror," with the goatish, half-human Wilbur Whateley taking the place of Helen Vaughan, and also "The Curse of Yig." The figure of Pan in this story, as a doppelgänger of the Holy Ghost that impregnated the Virgin Mary, is typical of Lovecraft's later entities—a plot device, and an ambiguous, mysterious figure whom readers clothe with their own imagination. Pan is not a character in the story, and he never appears in a single scene (the point may be argued that Pan does appear as the "naked man" with whom Helen is playing in the woods, but the character is never named as such, and so is still open to interpretation) and is not even visually described—but from outside the narrative he still manages, through Helen Vaughan, to be the primary catalyst of the tale. Without Pan there is no story—and Pan's only definitive act is impregnation. If one were to leave out the final deathbed transformation of Helen Vaughan, there is nothing directly supernatural in the story up to the very end; Helen may be read as the illegitimate child of Mary and Dr. Raymond—the result of a somewhat inappropriate relationship, given their respective ages and Mary's relationship as Raymond's foster child—and to a Victorian audience reading "The Great God Pan" as a serial, it would almost seem a child conceived in sin, born to sin—until the final episode, which would transform it from a lurid-for-the-times thriller with a mad scientist to supernatural horror.

The figure of Pan as used in "The Great God Pan" directly or indirectly inspired at least three of Lovecraft's entities: Yog-Sothoth, who fathered Wilbur Whateley in "The Dunwich Horror," and who serves much the same purpose as Pan in that story; Shub-Niggurath through the epithet "The Black Goat of the Woods with a Thousand Young," which first appeared in "The Last Test" (1927) and may refer to the classical half-man, half-goat form; and finally Yig, the "half-human father of serpents" (CrC 173) from "The Curse of Yig," who again assumes a similar function to Pan—the "half-human" descriptor possibly used to emphasize the connection.

"Novel of the Black Seal" (1895)

Machen's "Novel of the Black Seal" is one of the embedded episodes in his novel *The Three Impostors; or, The Transmutations*, and is primarily regarded as a key entry in his "Little People" mythos—a set of mostly unconnected tales that take as part of their premise the idea that a stunted, primitive, troglodytic race once inhabited the British Isles ... and still does, in lonely and far-off wild places and underground, as strange survivals. What "Novel of the Black Seal" adds to the concept is the possibility of interbreeding between that race and human beings, and to a lesser extent the use of rape to achieve this interbreeding and the idea that powers or memories of this race may be passed on to the hybrid offspring.

The first hint is Jervase Cradock's appearance, which shows a foreign character "with black hair and black eyes and an olive skin" (Machen 2001, 153), and is rapidly confirmed with the details of his birth, though none of the locals think much odd about it:

> I did know his father, Thomas Cradock, well, and a very fine workman he was too, indeed. He got something wrong with his lungs owing to working in the wet woods, and never got over it, and went off quite sudden like. And they do say as how Mrs. Cradock was quite off her head; anyhow, she was found by Mr. Hillyer, Ty Coch, all crouched up on the Grey Hills, over there, crying and weeping like a lost soul. And Jervase, he was born about eight months afterwards [...] (Machen 2001, 153-54)

The idea is tied together with old legendry of changelings, children replaced with "a thin and wizened creature, with sallow skin and black, piercing eyes, the child of another race" (Machen 2001, 165). More important than his mere physical appearance, Jervase Cradock has inherited something of the knowledge and attributes of the "Little People." While not scientific in the manner of eugenics, the tale stands as a literary predecessor in many ways to "The Shadow over Innsmouth" and "The Curse of Yig."

"The White People" (1904)

The influence of "The White People" on the Lovecraft Mythos is immediate and apparent; Lovecraft directly lifted the "Aklo letters" for use in "The Dunwich Horror," and there is much speculation that the Dôls of "The White People" became the Dholes of "Through the Gates of the Silver Key" (1934). Lovecraft ranks it first among weird stories in "Supernatural Horror in Literature." In the context of this essay, however, "The White People" is difficult. It is the most ambiguous of the three Machen tales addressed here, written from the perspective of a girl-child who yet maintains a sort of innocence, and is the most circumspect with regard to love and sex. Some of the tales-within-tales of "The White People" have a definite *Arabian Nights* quality, complete with bowdlerized naughty bits. The most suggestive is the story of the Lady Avelin, a secret sorceress or priestess who used a magical image as a lover; and that of a poor girl who married a prince, but was stolen away on her wedding night by "a tall, black man, with a dreadful face" (Machen 2001, 77). In the context of medieval folklore, this would have been understood as the devil, a Caucasian with black skin rather than a person of African descent or other ethnicity. The Black Man in the context as God of Witches appears in Margaret Murray's *The Witch-Cult in Western Europe* (1921), which Lovecraft read. Lovecraft would later recast the Black Man as Nyarlathotep in "The Dreams in the Witch House" (1932).

Some of that material did find its way into the Lovecraft Mythos. The Black Man of "The White People," for example, reappears in *The Case of Charles Dexter Ward* (1927), "The Dreams in the Witch House," and "The Man of Stone" (1932). More important is how the story affected Lovecraft, and how his understanding of it tied it together, as he explained in a 1931 letter to J. Vernon Shea, with Machen's other tales:

> I. The image found in the woods was that of two entities locked in a monstrous & obscene embrace—from which, had they been living things would have been born a Thing of non-human horror . . . . . like Helen Vaughn in *The Great God Pan*, or the boy in *The Black Seal*. II. On account of a sympathetic action like that described in the prologue, the now-adolescent child—though without contact with any creative elements—became pregnant with a Horror, to whose birth (knowing what she did of dark tradition) she could not look forward without a stark frenzy far beyond the fear of mere disgrace. Thus she killed herself. If she had not, a nameless hybrid abnormality of daemoniac paternity would have been loosed upon the world. There seems to be very little question about the correctness of this interpretation, since several small allusions toward the end—especially regarding the girl's age & the nature of the image—join with earlier allusions to sketch the implications. (SL 3.438–39)

Part of the ending may be lost on modern readers, since it was hinted at very indirectly, culminating in the line "She had poisoned herself—in time" (Machen 2001, 97); this may be read as an attempted pharmaceutical abortion gone awry or a suicide to avoid dishonor; the critical idea is that the girl—still young but now of age to bear children—had only a limited duration in which to act, and did so.

Analyses

The most obvious problem in analyzing Lovecraft's fiction is the lack of overt sexual material. Victoria Nelson's summary is typical:

> Lovecraft is not the sort of writer, or person, to look at his own stories and say: "Aha! My male creatures are always horribly deformed below the waist,

they worship great phallic monoliths dripping with green liquid, and there is never a whisper of sex in my stories! I wonder if there is a connection?" Lovecraft's awareness of the displacement of sexuality in his fictions—like Poe's of his obsessive sex-death nexus—seems nonexistent and consequently untransformed. (Nelson 2001, 136)

The details are inaccurate, but the idea is common: there is no sex in the Lovecraft Mythos. This is not entirely the case, because while sex is never in the forefront of the Lovecraft Mythos, the results of sex are the basis of several Lovecraft stories. A minority of critics have countered with arguments of their own. A passage from David E. Schultz's "On 'The Loved Dead,'" where he counters a claim by Colin Wilson that "Lovecraft himself was too much of a puritan to allow a sexual element to intrude into his stories", is exemplative of the counterview:

> Furthermore, several of Lovecraft's stories do have sexual elements, so Lovecraft was perfectly capable of the treatment given the theme in "The Loved Dead." While Lovecraft would never write a bedroom scene in his stories, he would describe with horror the results of the coupling of hideous alien creatures with humans (which most would consider to be bestiality). Lavinia Whateley's intercourse with Yog-Sothoth in "The Dunwich Horror" occurs offstage, but the hideous results capture the basic emotion of the horror story—the realization that something unknown has intruded upon the normal and the familiar. The same could be said of "The Shadow over Innsmouth," in which the decaying seaport is populated by the hybrid offspring of the town's original human inhabitants and the amphibian creatures from the South Seas. (Price 1990, 57)

This apparent contradiction has been recognized by many writers who emphasize or attempt to explicate various aspects of Lovecraft's treatment (or apparent lack thereof) of sex, gender, and love in his Mythos. In analyzing and criticizing the Lovecraft Mythos, many authors look at Lovecraft himself, using what letters and biographical information are available. Given the generally negative portrayal of Lovecraft's attitudes with regard to sex, many of these critiques paint Lovecraft and his fiction as somewhat misogynistic or misanthropic. For example, Bennett Lovett-Graff and Barton Levi St. Armand both evince the idea that Lovecraft had disgust for the sexual act and by extension organic life. An illustrative passage from St. Armand:

> In Lovecraft's fictional universe [. . .] life is a festering disease that, given its contagious sexual properties, must be contained and endured. This may ac-

2. Sex and the Lovecraft Mythos

count for the often-noted fact of Lovecraft's seeming asexuality and the asexual nature of his works in general. The individual solution remains chastity and continence, but the force of attraction is often too great even for the stoic—as Lovecraft himself discovered when he suddenly married Sonia Haft Greene [...] The gods themselves are not immune to desire, since Lovecraft's works (in particular, "The Dunwich Horror") deal repeatedly with cosmic monsters spawning and breeding uncontrollably, using human females only as convenient vessels for their cosmic lust, ostensibly as a means of reclaiming a lost domain. Zeus descends not as a shower of gold but as a color out of space [...] (St. Armand 65)

Such an interpretation of Lovecraft is understandable, but assumes that Lovecraft's views with regard to sex were both simple and unchanging. In a similar vein, *The H. P. Lovecraft Companion* notes that "Lovecraft himself was so lukewarm on the subject of human sexuality that he would never have consciously invested his fiction with it" (Shreffler 12), and in "The Genetics of Horror: Sex and Racism in H. P. Lovecraft's Fiction" Bruce Lord writes:

> It is doubtful that Lovecraft ever consciously realised that his tales were ever dealing with the subject of sex to any real degree. Instead, sexuality lurks behind more immediately threatening horrors in Lovecraft's fiction (the degeneration and monsters that the unpredictability of sexuality produces), horrors Lovecraft was likely not to look any further past while conceiving or reviewing his writing. Put more poetically, sex can be found in the shadow of the monster. (Lord)

I believe both miss the possibility that Lovecraft as an author was keenly aware of the sexual activity both implied and neglected in his stories. Lovecraft avoided depicting actual copulation in his stories, not simply out of propriety and his dislike of outright eroticism (not to mention editorial limitations of the era), but because it served no artistic purpose: "And if he refused all sexual allusions in his work, it was first and foremost because he felt such allusions had no place in his aesthetic universe" (Houellebecq 59).

Further, Lovecraft was writing for a grown-up audience, and there is more than a hint of satirical, adult humor in his stories when appropriate. In "The Dunwich Horror" rural promiscuity is such a part of the background for the tale that Dr. Armitage remarks, "Shew them Arthur Machen's Great God Pan and they'll think it a common Dunwich scandal!" (*TD* 221). It would have been quite understandable for Lovecraft, who was so familiar with "The Great God Pan" and its reputation, to deliberately play with the memorable sexual elements of the story.

The lack of romance in the Lovecraft Mythos is mostly attributable to a paucity of female characters and a lack of interest in writing romance on Lovecraft's part. The lack of homosexuals in his fiction is more understandable in that generally homophobic era, since Lovecraft's attitude toward homosexuals probably precluded his use of them. Where there are prominent female characters in Lovecraft's stories and revisions they are generally in romantic relationships (married or being courted). Exceptions exist, like Lavinia Whateley, whose lack of a proper husband is a salient detail of the plot. It is likely, given his lack of personal relationships and his dislike of romanticism in fiction, and particularly in light of his views on the essential inconsequence of romantic love in the cosmic scheme, that Lovecraft simply chose not to address a subject that he had little personal experience in and which did not pertain to what he wished to write.

The H. P. Lovecraft Companion also suggests that in Lovecraft's fiction "the sexual dimension is forced upon his characters" (Shreffler 12). This is a point worth considering—to what degree did Lovecraft define his characters, from a sexual standpoint, and to what degree do the readers define the sexuality of the characters based on their own nature and understanding? Inevitably, both the intention of the author and the conception of the reader must strike a balance, so that while all read the same words, readers come away with different understandings of what they mean and imply, but a few things can be objectively noted.

It is obvious that Lovecraft had a general heteronormative bias in his fiction, with no overt homosexuals, bisexuals, etc. of any sort with the possible exception of Aesnath Waite in "The Thing on the Doorstep." Lovecraft probably deliberately avoided romantic entanglements (and indeed, any personal relationship with other human beings) that were not directly relevant to the plot of the story, but those relationships that exist are fairly traditional, with a focus on courtship and marriage. The "mechanics" of sex are never addressed, and so the details of that aspect of their lives remain perpetually off the page. Thus I do not think it correct to say that Lovecraft forces a sexual dimension on his characters when discussing "The Dunwich Horror" or "The Thing on the Doorstep"—all his characters in all his stories have what Lovecraft probably considered the appropriate sexual dimension for their background and role.

Shreffler writes that Lovecraft's "disinclination to write about women" was probably a result of "his lack of experience with women. After all, it is fairly difficult to write about something to which one has had little exposure and that one simply does not understand" (30). There is both truth and error in this statement: Lovecraft was raised primarily by his mother and his aunts, and probably knew his female relatives better than many men by the time he was thirty, but he did generally lack (as far as we know) girlfriends and romantic social contacts before his courtship and marriage to Sonia. In re-reading Lovecraft's stories with the specific focus of this essay in mind, I am reminded of a passage Lovecraft wrote in a 1931 letter to J. Vernon Shea:

> I never thought pre-marital experience worth the attendant ignominiousness, & doubt very much if I was the loser thereby. Indeed, I can't see any difference in the work I did before marriage & that I did during a matrimonial period of some years—none of my stylistic transitions corresponding in the least to any change in biological status. (SL 3.425)

I would argue that this is not true, as Lovecraft's post-marriage fiction is considerably different from his earlier work, and though this development was likely due more to Lovecraft's increased socialization and exposure to new people and new ideas than simply to losing his virginity, the latter should not be discounted completely. Whether or not Lovecraft was aware of it, there is a difference in both content and language apparent in his stories of and before 1924 (when he married), and during and after 1926 (when Lovecraft and Sonia separated). While never sexually explicit in his writing, tales like "The Curse of Yig" (1928), "The Dunwich Horror" (1928), and "The Shadow over Innsmouth" (1931) feature more prominently the products of sexual congress with supernatural beings, and do so with language that more directly addresses such relations than any of his previous fiction. Several stories after his marriage feature women in more important roles than previously—most notably "The Thing on the Doorstep" (1933). The fact that female characters are featured more prominently in some of Lovecraft's later work, particularly his revisions, may also be attributable to the fact that several of his most notable clients during this period were women, including Zealia Brown-Reed Bishop and Hazel Heald. While it is too much to say that the events of his marriage influenced all his later fiction, there is general consensus among Lovecraft scholars that the period of his marriage and habitation in New York City was a significant one for Lovecraft personally, and that it informed his later writing, and his marriage was a part of that.

For the purposes of this essay, I assume the reader is generally familiar with the texts of Lovecraft's fiction, and so I will not summarize each story but focus on analysis, criticism, and commentary. The texts referenced are the most recent corrected texts available, for the most part the Penguin Classic editions. After Lovecraft's death, August Derleth and others wove original weird stories around fragments of Lovecraft's writing and ideas. Derleth's are the most famous and are collected in *The Watchers out of Time and Others* (1974), which includes the short novel *The Lurker at the Threshold* (1945). These posthumous collaborations by Derleth and others may contain some fragment of text from Lovecraft and carry his name in the byline, but they are part of the expanded Cthulhu Mythos and are addressed in the next chapter where appropriate.

"Facts concerning the Late Arthur Jermyn and His Family" (1920)

"Arthur Jermyn" is a tale of hereditary degeneration, family secrets, and a case of bestiality that is essentially thinly veiled miscegenation. While sex and love are never the focus of the story, the continuing generations of the Jermyns are perpetuated by sexual action, and the ultimate horror of the story only works because each succeeding member continues the line, until it concludes with the unfortunate and eponymous Arthur Jermyn. Yet this is not a typical story of generations: the biological action is flawed. The initial union of Sir Wade Jermyn and the Ape Princess produces a half-breed son, but the successive generations do not dilute or diminish the genetic contribution of the Ape Princess (as simple Mendelian inheritance would suggest); instead, it grows more intensive until it finds full expression in the sensitive and artistic Arthur Jermyn:

> Most of the Jermyns had possessed a subtly odd and repellent cast, but Arthur's case was very striking. It is hard to say just what he resembled, but his expression, his facial angle, and the length of his arms gave a thrill of repulsion to those who met him for the first time. (CC 18)

The "facial angle" is a reference to anthropometry invented by Pieter Camper in 1790 and used here to suggest that Arthur Jermyn more resembled an ape than a human being; Camper's theories were later appropriated by racialists, so it also carries the implication that Jermyn, at least in his skull, more closely resembled a black man than a white man, though it is not clear if Lovecraft exactly intended this since, as Lovett-Graff states:

> It should be noted that by Lovecraft's era, the facial angle index had been discarded, even by some of the most vociferous racists (Gobineau 108-10). Lovecraft's mention of it in the tale thus suggests one of three possibilities: his own belief in the facial angle index; his use of it to evoke a thrill of fear from his less well-informed readers; or his mistaken use of the term for the then popular belief in craniometry (the measurement, often race-based, of skull shape and capacity, a science in which Lovecraft did believe). (Lovett-Graff 1997b, 384)

The ignorant neighbors of the Jermyns attribute the bulk of the deformations and behaviors of the succeeding generation to mismarriage with lower-class folk—music hall dancers, entertainers, gypsies, and foreigners. It is impossible to determine if Lovecraft actually intended for the genetic contribution of succeeding wives to worsen the Jermyn bloodlines, or merely to serve as indicators of the family's lowering social status and false flags to stave off the hinted-at great revelation.

The hereditary degeneration of the Jermyns is based on a single misalliance (reminiscent in many ways of the Jukes and Kallikak studies, which attempted to trace criminality or "feeble-mindness" back to a single pairing) that spawned generations of the clan descending the social and evolutionary scales. "Arthur Jermyn" is not a moral tale against miscegenation or bestiality, however—it is an effort to evoke personal horror in the reader, by suggesting that they too may succumb to ancestral degeneration, for modern science in Lovecraft's time had already discovered evidence of the common ancestry of man and apes. In his notes on the story, Joshi makes the argument:

> What Lovecraft appears to be suggesting is that the inhabitants of the primeval African city of "white apes" are not only the "missing link" between ape and human but also *the ultimate source for all white civilization*. The entire white race is derived from this primal race in Africa, a race that had corrupted itself by intermingling with apes. This is the only explanation for the narrator's opening statement, "If we knew what we are, we should do as Sir Arthur Jermyn did [i.e., commit suicide]": we may not have a white ape in our immediate ancestry, but we are all the products of an ultimate miscegenation. (CC 365)

Compare with Lévy:

> Doubtless it is easy to accept in the abstract the truth taught by naturalists— that man is descended from monkeys. It is, however, more difficult to learn

without losing one's head that one's grandmother was a chimp—even though white and advanced.... (77)

Anthropological evidence of Lovecraft's day showed that all humanity ultimately has a hominid somewhere in its ancestry, but the argument agrees with Lovecraft's own beliefs as expressed in his letters. In line with Joshi's comment, if the city of hybrid "white apes" were the ultimate source of humanity, it might explain why the genetic inheritance of the Jermyns did not dilute—the Ape Princess represented the original race and, on exposure the tenuous features of humanity, developed by millennia of evolution, succumbed. As Lovecraft put it elsewhere: "the Nordic is the product of an exceptional and tenuous specialization—whose results are insecurely lodged in the race, and always ready to be overthrown by any influence favouring the original arrangement" (SL 3.412).

The genealogical narrative of "Arthur Jermyn" is primarily patrilineal (assisted by the fact that only male heirs survive), and the female characters of the line are faceless and nameless. As a female unnatural ancestor entity, the Ape Princess is exceptional in the Lovecraft Mythos. In "The Curse of Yig" and "The Dunwich Horror," the entities are implicitly male through epithet ("father of serpents" for Yig, "Father" by Wilbur Whateley's twin) and action (impregnating human females); only in "The Shadow over Innsmouth" do we come across another case where the ultimate source of degeneration is a female ancestor.

The lost city in the jungle and its inhabitants—"white ape of some unknown species, less hairy than any recorded variety, and infinitely nearer mankind—quite shockingly so" (CC 22-23)—are strongly reminiscent of the city of Opar and its inhabitants in the Tarzan novels of Edgar Rice Burroughs, particularly as featured in *The Return of Tarzan* (1913). In Burroughs's Opar the inhabitants of the ancient city possess "white skins—neither in color nor feature was there a trace of the negroid about them" and just as clearly interbreed with the local ape population, resulting in a race of "short, stocky men [...] their arms long and muscular," who are prey to fits of violent madness; all attributes shared by several of the Jermyn descendents of the Ape Princess. Lovecraft wrote approvingly of Edgar Rice Burroughs in a 1914 letter to the *All-Story Weekly* (Lovecraft 1986, 1-4); in later letters was more critical of Burroughs—"His stuff is really almost juvenile—with all the cheap & unconvincing stock devices of commercial quantity-production" (LRK 231), but he was familiar with his work. It is possible he wrote "Arthur Jermyn" in part either as a deliberate "take-that" or homage to Burroughs. For more on the influence of Burroughs on Lovecraft, see William Fulwiler's "E. R. B. and H. P. L." (1992).

"The Outsider" (1921)

Objectively, "The Outsider" has no explicit sexual material and almost no gender content. However the construction of the narrative is such that the story lends itself to analysis from different viewpoints, and these different "faces" of "The Outsider" (as they were termed by Dirk W. Mosig) provide additional ways to read and interpret the story. Two of these faces are relevant with respect to this essay: the Outsider as homosexual, and the Outsider as female. There is no indication that Lovecraft intended either interpretation, but the narrative is sufficiently open to allow others to read such interpretations into their views. Readers interested in exploring these faces should consult Robert M. Price's "Homosexual Panic in 'The Outsider'" (1982) and Mollie L. Burleson's "The Outsider: A Woman?" (1990), respectively.

"The Lurking Fear" (1922)

Another tale of hereditary degeneration, "The Lurking Fear" follows a similar though more subtle tack than "Arthur Jermyn," with a greater emphasis placed on breeding out-of-class, and later actual incest and inbreeding to a literally inhuman degree. Again, sex is not present in the story, but silently drives the generational narrative, until the consequences literally burst forth in the final section; and the unspoken carnality is implied to be incest, though this is never directly addressed.

The extent of mental and physical degradation is much greater in "The Lurking Fear" than in "Arthur Jermyn." Whereas it took an ape matriarch and four generations of gradually more marked change to proceed from the purely human Wade to the near-ape Arthur Jermyn, the Martenses of "The Lurking Fear" degenerated to an apparently subsentient cannibalistic simian clan in something less than 250 years. By the time of the main story the clan had, without a recent ape ancestor, become something more animalistic than Arthur Jermyn: "a filthy whitish gorilla thing with sharp yellow fangs and matted fur. It was the ultimate product of mammalian degeneration; the frightful outcome of isolated spawning, multiplication, and cannibal nutrition above and below ground" (*DWH* 81).

Nor is the backslip of evolution unique to the Martense clan. Lovecraft is at pains throughout the story to dehumanize the local mountain folk with whom the Martenses had interbred, before their seclusion led them to inbreeding: "Simple animals they were, gently descending the evolutionary scale because of their unfortunate ancestry and stultifying isolation" (*DWH* 69).

The effect plays on and enhances the more sensational aspects of a certain stereotype—the reclusive hill-dwellers of the Appalachians, tracing their ancestry back to old pioneer families, cut off by geography and given to poverty, ignorance, feuding, and inbreeding. The libel was commonly applied in Lovecraft's time, and the image remains in use today. Indeed, Lovecraft used it more than once in his stories—most notably in "Beyond the Wall of Sleep" (1919). The Martenses, then, are a reclusive and degenerate family within an already degenerate and reclusive population marked as "simple animals"—of course, by this point the Martense clan had literally become animals.

What really marks "The Lurking Fear" as different from "Arthur Jermyn" is the fervent fertility of the Martense clan. Unlike the lines of Usher and Jermyn, which had "put forth no branches," the descendants of Gerrit Martense were numerous—and here is one of the paramount horrors experienced by the unnamed narrator:

> from that opening beneath the chimney a burst of multitudinous and leprous life—a loathsome night-spawned flood of organic corruption [. . .] Seething, stewing, surging, bubbling like serpents' slime it rolled up and out of that yawning hole, spreading like a septic contagion and streaming from the cellar at every point of egress [. . .] (*DWH* 80)

The terror and disgust experienced from a single example of physical degeneration is multiplied by the vast numbers involved. There are many ways to read and interpret this scene—a response to the crowded streets of New York City, with their immigrant hordes; an early effort to demonize the frightful fecundity of organic life, which finally found expression in the Goat with a Thousand Young; some poetic souls might even see it as a sort of inversion of the stagnant House of Usher, with the Martense mansion literally birthing a vast new flood of darkling life. One such interpretation proceeds as follows:

> With a certain paranoiac gusto, a far from concealed disgust with sexuality and reproduction overwhelms Lovecraft's description of this birthing of "lep-

rous life" and "organic corruption" from this subterranean hole. From where once the warmth of a chimney issued, there now bubbles forth the products of the overheated libidinal lusts of the Martense family. In this frightening image of overflowing life, Lovecraft taps a common image of eugenicist thought, which held the reproductive capacity of America's degenerate populations (i.e., non-white, immigrant, criminal, and poor) as a threat to America's better stock. From the unrestrained sexuality of those reduced by isolation to interbreeding, and then inbreeding, Lovecraft paints a horrific portrait of the plethoric vitality of degeneration. (Lovett-Graff 1995, 336)

Lovecraft's disinclination to address sex kept him from even using the word "incest" in the story to describe the Martenses' relations, relying instead on implication.

The story was originally serialized over four issues of the slightly risqué humor magazine *Home Brew* (1923), and bore illustrations by Clark Ashton Smith. In his notes, Joshi adds as an aside: "Smith had a bit of fun with these illustrations, drawing trees and vegetation in the shape of male and female genitalia" (*DWH* 412). It was Lovecraft who suggested Smith submit his art for the magazine; they were the first drawings that Smith ever published (Smith 2003, 67). Given the nature of the magazine and the illustrations, it is likely they were accepted in good fun.

"The Rats in the Walls" (1923)

In his essay "Supernatural Horror in Literature," Lovecraft asserts of "The Fall of the House of Usher" that the story "displays an abnormally linked trinity of entities at the end of a long and isolated family history—a brother, his twin sister, and their incredibly ancient house all sharing a single soul and meeting one common dissolution at the same moment" (Lovecraft 2000, 45).

Of the three early tales that trace hereditary degeneration and atavism, "The Rats in the Walls" most strongly reflects this idea in Lovecraft's own work. When Walter de la Poer murders his family, the house is almost destroyed; and when the last Delapore arrives, the house is a ruin. It is the resurrection of the house that prompts the resurrection of the ancient evil it—and the line—were built on, and the return of the spirit of the de la Poers in the last Delapore. The story also includes many other direct and indirect references to E. A. Poe, including the family name—de la Po*er* (*CC* 381–84).

Both "Arthur Jermyn" and "The Lurking Fear" sketch a relatively swift degeneration over a few generations—never more than a few hundred years from the first sexual transgression to the finish of the line. "The Rats in the Walls," by contrast, traces a history that leads back through the whole history of England, and into prehistory. In this story, physical degeneration is not apparent on the living Delapores—there are no literal white apes—but what the Jermyns and Martenses did by accident or seclusion without awareness of the consequences, the de la Poers/Delapores deliberately instigated or continued with an apparent aim to achieve what had claimed the Jermyns or Martenses by chance. The evidence lies in the ruins beneath the foundation of the Priory—the literal roots of the family tree—and shows hereditary degeneration on a scale greater than in "Arthur Jermyn" or "The Lurking Fear":

> some of the skeleton things must have descended as quadrupeds through the last twenty or more generations. [. . .] The quadruped things—with their occasional recruits from the biped class—had been kept in stone pens [. . .] There had been great herds of them, evidently fattened on the coarse vegetables whose remains could be found as a sort of poisonous ensilage at the bottom of huge stone bins older than Rome. I knew now why my ancestors had had such excessive gardens—would to heaven I could forget! The purpose of the herds I did not have to ask. (CC 106)

Here, the implication is that the cult that interbred with the de la Poer line had bred human beings, or a race close to human beings, toward a specific purpose—just as a farmer might attempt to breed fatter pigs. The addition of cannibalism gives grim purpose to the procedure, but the strong but silent implication is that this was something possible—that there was nothing special about humans, above other animals, that made them immune to that kind of treatment and selective breeding. It is a stark and materialist moral.

In this story, more than in "Arthur Jermyn" and "The Lurking Fear," the dark stain of the line appears to be primarily mental or moral degeneration—the inner cult within the family, continuing loathsome rites. As the anecdote of Lady Margaret Trevor shows, it was possible for members that married into the family to contribute to the de la Poer line; and, as the fate of Mary de la Poer shows, it was possible for women to inherit the family traits as well. This cult was based on that of Cybele, the Magna Mater "whose dark worship was once vainly forbidden to Roman citizens" (CC 92), and her consort Attis or Atys. Priests of Cybele and Attis, the *galli*, ritually castrated themselves in honor of their deities, and Roman citizens were prohibited from becoming *galli* because of this practice until the time of the Emperor Claudius. According to Joshi, Lovecraft probably learned about the worship of Cybele and Attis from Sir James George Frazer's seminal work, *The Golden Bough* (two volumes, 1890, twelve volumes: 1906–15), and the ninth edition of the *Encyclopaedia Britannica* (1901), which Lovecraft owned and contained sufficient details of Cybele/Attis worship that Lovecraft would have known of the self-castration aspect (Lovecraft 1997, 42). The best overall review of Cybele/Attis in "Rats" is probably Fred Blosser's "The Sign of the Magna Mater" (1997).

"The Rats in the Walls" does not paint an accurate picture of Cybele's worship—in fact, it presents a (possibly deliberate) sexual paradox. In antiquity, the main repellent aspect of the religion was the practice of self-castration by the priests of Cybele/Attis—naturally, this appears to directly contravene the idea of a continuous biological line of priests through the patrilineal de la Poers. Further, the reference one character in the story makes to Catullus—Gaius Valerius Catullus was a poet of ancient Rome; his surviving poetry is still read and studied by classicists, particularly for his admiration of the female poet Sappho of Lesbos. Catullus 63 is a 93-line poem about Attis, and his self-castration as an act of faith to become one Cybele's *galli*. It is surely the poem being referenced in the story, and it reinforces the idea of a self-castrating priesthood (Lovecraft 1997, 42). If, as it seems apparent, Lovecraft was aware of this aspect of Cybele/Attis worship, it is possible he crafted the paradox on purpose as an in-joke for the more widely read readers who would have realized the possible contradiction.

"The Unnamable" (1923)

Bestiality is an uncommon theme in the Lovecraft Mythos, and Lovecraft's use of it is generally limited to humans mating with the not-quite-human, such as the white apes of "Arthur Jermyn" or the Deep Ones of "The Shadow over Innsmouth." An exception occurs in "The Unnamable," where Lovecraft takes as a starting point an obscure historical record and elaborates on it to illustrate a philosophical point of weird fiction. The central account that spurs the action in the story reads: "he told of the beast that had brought forth what was more than beast but less than man—the thing with the blemished eye—and of the screaming drunken wretch that they hanged for having such an eye" (*DWH* 85). This is a simplification and re-telling of a footnote in Massachusetts legendry, an account recorded in Lovecraft's family copy of Cotton Mather's *Magnalia Christi Americana* (1702):

> At the southward there was a beast, which brought forth a creature which might pretend to something of an human shape. Now, the people minded that the *monster* had a blemish in one eye, much like what a profligate fellow in the town was known to have. This fellow was hereupon examined; and upon his examination, confess'd his infandous Bestialities; for which he was deservedly executed. (*DWH* 415)

The result is not quite a trial run for "The Dunwich Horror," though there are bare similarities, since the hybrid is hidden away from the world until its keeper dies, and then goes on a rampage. It is appropriate to the story that we never know what animal birthed the creature or get a clear look at the result, but piecemeal descriptions of the human-animal hybrid bring to mind a creature similar to the Minotaur of Greek legend.

"The Horror at Red Hook" (1925)

Lovecraft borrowed from articles in the *Encyclopaedia Britannica* for this story, as a result of which "Red Hook" contains a tremendous mishmash of legendry. While many of the entities involved (Lilith, Ashtaroth, the Magna Mater, incubi, succubi, fauns, satyrs, aegipans, etc.) have some sexual aspect to their individual mythologies, their use here generally disregards or does not make overt use of those aspects (*DWH* 422).

The plot of the story is confused, but features a sort of double wedding. Aged scholar of the occult and cult leader Robert Sudyam is married to a young kinswoman, Cornelia Garritsen; the couple is apparently murdered by an inhuman creature on their honeymoon cruise, and Suydam's corpse and Cornelia's blood are transported to a hellish cavern beneath the New York City neighborhood of Red Hook by members of Suydam's cult for a further ritual. The corpse of Sudyam, bathed in his bride's blood and re-animated, is presented there to "the naked, tittering, phosphorescent" Lilith (*DWH* 134), whose limbs are bathed in the blood of children, with the words "Lilith, Great Lilith, behold the Bridegroom!" (*DWH* 133). If this is supposed to be an infernal mockery of a wedding in the same way that a Black Mass is a mockery of the Catholic Mass, it apparently fails, but the text never gives us sufficient insight into what is going on to say for sure.

Near the end of the story, however, is one of the few passages of implied rape in Lovecraft's fiction:

[. . .] solitary prisoners in a state of complete idiocy were found chained, including four mothers with infants of disturbingly strange appearance. These infants died soon after exposure to the light; a circumstance which the doctors thought rather merciful. Nobody but Malone, among those who inspected them, remembered the somber question of old Delrio: "*An sint unquam daemons incubi et succubae, et an ex tali congressu proles nasci queat?*" (*DWH* 135)

The quotation is from the 1603 text *Disquisitionum Magicarum Libri Sex* (Six Books of Disquisions on Magic) by Martin Anton Del Rio, by way of the article on "Demonology" in the *Encyclopaedia Britannica*, and translates to: "Have there ever been demons, incubi and succubae, and from such a union can offspring be born?" (*DWH* 430). The passage, along with the idiot mothers and the Latin quotation, are all highly reminiscent of Machen's "The Great God Pan."

The Dream-Quest of Unknown Kadath (1926–27)

This short novel of the Dreamlands, completed by Lovecraft in early 1927 but not published until after his death, owes much to the fantasies of Lord Dunsany and carries a mythological tone. A critical element of *The Dream-Quest of Unknown Kadath* is that the gods of earth were apt to breed demigods: "It is known that in disguise the younger among the Great Ones often espouse the daughters of men, so that around the borders of the cold waste wherein stands Kadath the peasants must all bear their blood" (*DWH* 161).

Readers probably need not look farther than classical Greco-Roman mythology for the origin of the god-blooded described here, though of course there are many possible sources of inspiration, including Nathaniel Hawthorne's *The Marble Faun* (1860). It is further noted these demigods "might inherit little memories" from their god-blood, an aspect that probably derives in part from Jervase Cradock in "Novel of the Black Seal," Irvin S. Cobb's "Fishhead" (1911), or even Lord Dunsany's "The Bride of the Man-Horse" (1911), and which is very close (intentionally or not) to Carl Jung's concept of racial memory. Lovecraft was familiar with the general concept of racial memory, but doubted the factual basis of it (*MF* 183–84, 207).

The Case of Charles Dexter Ward (1927)

The sexual action in *The Case of Charles Dexter Ward* serves as part of an elaborate genealogical sorcery, whereby the unnaturally youthful-looking wizard Joseph Curwen, in anticipation of his own death, conspires to marry and conceive a family line so that in time an heir will be born to resurrect him from the dead. The story shares many familiar plot details with other Lovecraft works, such as a search for a missing ancestor as in "The Shadow over Innsmouth," and a scholarly elder sorcerer who marries a young woman of good social standing such as "The Horror at Red Hook" (*TD* 389).

As a plot-mechanism, the spell or ritual Curwen performs serves several functions, but arguably the most important is that it explains the close physical resemblance between the two, a resolution of the hackneyed device of having 'twins' in a story. As with Arthur Jermyn and the unnamed narrator in "The Shadow over Innsmouth," Charles Dexter Ward, though separated by generations, is or becomes the physical embodiment of his aberrant ancestor—and as in those other stories, the unusual resemblance establishes the relationship between Curwen and Ward as both a natural (genealogical) and unnatural (sorcerous) compulsion, which leads to a culminating conflict that destroys Ward.

Eliza Tillinghast, the wife of Joseph Curwen and great-great-great-grandmother to Charles Dexter Ward, is the most significant of the minor female characters in the novel, as the matriarch of Curwen's lineage and the means to bring his spell to fruition. Lovecraft paints a portrait of Eliza as Ward would have seen her through his genealogical researches—a bright young woman of good family in reduced circumstances, well educated for domestic life by the standards of the time, and forced to break off an engagement to a passionate young man to marry an older gentleman at the insistence of her father. She served dutifully as a wife and mother until her husband's death, then—again at the insistence of her father—reverts to her maiden name and lives the rest of her days a widow in his house. At the very least, Eliza Tillinghast does not come across as another nameless female antecedent. While never given voice in the novel, she is a catalyst for action, both violent and sexual—the violent in that her one-time husband, Joseph Curwen, died at the hands of the town's political and social elite, and the sexual in that Eliza gave birth and started the family line that led down to Charles Dexter Ward.

"The Dunwich Horror" (1928)

One of the core stories of the Lovecraft Mythos and the basis of an entire cycle of stories in the larger Cthulhu Mythos, "The Dunwich Horror" is definitely an homage to and is sometimes considered a pastiche of "The Great God Pan" and "The White People" (Price 1995, ix–x). Others have come very close to this same conclusion:

> One senses that the eroticism in "The Dunwich Horror" is very much like that of the Victorian and Edwardian periods in general, as these periods in history were characterized by a staid moral rectitude on the surface but boiled enough underneath to leave behind works like Frank Harris's *My Secret Life*. (Shreffler 12)

Lovecraft even calls out to Machen in the story:

> "Inbreeding?" Armitage muttered half-aloud to himself. "Great God, what simpletons! Shew them Arthur Machen's Great God Pan and they'll think it a common Dunwich scandal! But what thing—what cursed shapeless influence on or off this three-dimensioned earth—was Wilbur Whateley's father? Born on Candlemas—nine months after May-Eve of 1912, when the talk about the queer earth noises reached clear to Arkham—What walked on the mountains that May-Night? What Roodmas horror fastened itself on the world in half-human flesh and blood?" (*TD* 221)

James Arthur Anderson in *Out of the Shadows* (2011) attempted a structuralist approach to understanding the Lovecraft Mythos, and constructed a Greimas square for the sexual ethics of "The Dunwich Horror" from the perspective of the Dunwich residents, where incest is the default or normal state and non-incestuous relationships are abnormal. By Anderson's reckoning, the Whateley twins are still taboo because they are *not* the product of inbreeding.

Here again is traced the conception, life, and final destruction of the half-human offspring of a supernatural entity—"as close to eroticism as anything Lovecraft wrote" (Shreffler 12). Another prominent influence on "The Dunwich Horror" is the obscure novel *The Thing in the Woods* (1924) by Harper Williams, as discovered by S. T. Joshi and noted by Robert M. Price in the introduction to *Tales out of Dunwich* (2005). Elements of Williams's novel in "The Dunwich Horror" include an albino mother, pregnant by an unknown father, who gives birth to a set of monstrous twins later suspected of matricide.

Lovecraft did much more with the story than merely recapitulate; he continued to develop several of the elements he had introduced in his previous stories. The residents of Dunwich, for example, are a rural folk in the mode of the squatters from "The Lurking Fear," but even more degenerate (and promiscuous):

> They have come to form a race by themselves, with the well-defined mental and physical stigmata of degeneracy and inbreeding. The average of their intelligence is woefully low, whilst their annals reek of overt viciousness and of half-hidden murders, incests, and deeds of almost unnamable violence and perversity. (*TD* 208)

Among this degenerate race lives an even more degenerate family, the Whateleys—abhorred even by the Dunwich folk for rumors of black magic. Unlike the Martenses, Jermyns, or Delapores, this is only one branch of a sprawling family tree, some of which are degenerate, some of which are "undecayed," and others are in-between. The branch, however, still follows the same general idea: there is a generational narrative (Old Whateley, his daughter Lavinia, and her children), miscegenation or perversity that corrupts the line, and the ultimate destruction of the family. The doom of the Whateleys is somewhat inspired by "The Fall of the House of Usher": the decayed Whateley residence in Dunwich reflects the habits and nature of the family and continues to do so throughout the story, for when Lavinia gives birth, the house expands and is rebuilt, even as the humans are crowded out of it by the unseen twin—and when the last partly human descendant of the degenerate Whateley branch is destroyed, the house is destroyed with it.

Unlike the young, beautiful Mary of "The Great God Pan," Lavinia is described as "a somewhat deformed albino woman of thirty-five," "slatternly, crinkly-haired," and with "misproportioned arms." There are two possible definitions for the word "slatternly" in the context given here: dirty and unkempt, or promiscuous. It is more likely that Lovecraft intended it to mean "unkempt," since the rest of the sentence describes Lavinia's appearance—but given Lovecraft's description of the general promiscuity in Dunwich, he could have intended either meaning, or perhaps wished to evoke both definitions.

The Whateleys were given to going unclothed to ceremonies or revels ("orgies" in Lovecraft's parlance) atop Sentinel Hill on certain nights, and on that hill Lavinia Whateley conceived and gave birth:

Lavinia Whately had no known husband, but according to the custom of the region made no attempt to disavow the child; concerning the other side of whose ancestry the country folk might—and did—speculate as widely as they chose. On the contrary, she seemed strangely proud of the dark, goatish-looking infant who formed such a contrast to her own sickly and pink-eyed albinism [. . .] (TD 210)

The descriptions of Wilbur Whateley—particularly his dark coloring and "dark, almost Latin eyes"—immediately bring to mind the descriptions of both Jervase Cradock from "Novel of the Black Seal" and Helen Vaughan from "The Great God Pan"; and the goatish aspect is a transparent reference to the typical satyr-figure. Despite being referred to as "Lavinny's black brat," there is no indication that the Dunwich locals thought of Wilbur Whateley as the product of literal miscegenation—and, if Dr. Armitage's comments are true, the general suspicion is that Wilbur Whateley was the product of inbreeding between Lavinia and her father (TD 221). Wilbur Whateley grows quickly to mental and physical maturity, tremendous in size and strength, but it is not until his death and final disintegration that his full form is laid bare:

> Above the waist it was semi-anthropomorphic; though its chest [. . .] had the leathery, reticulated hide of a crocodile or alligator. The back was piebald with yellow and black, and dimly suggested the squamous covering of certain snakes. Below the waist, though, it was the worst; for here all human resemblance left off and sheer phantasy began. The skin was thickly covered with coarse black fur, and from the abdomen a score of long greenish-grey tentacles with red sucking mouths protruded limply. Their arrangement was odd, and seemed to follow the symmetries of some cosmic geometry unknown to earth or the solar system. On each of the hips, deep set in a kind of pinkish, ciliated orbit, was what seemed to be a rudimentary eye; whilst in lieu of a tail there depended a kind of trunk or feeler with purple annular markings, and with many evidences of being an undeveloped mouth or throat. The limbs, save for their black fur, roughly resembled the hind legs of prehistoric earth's giant saurians; and terminated in ridgy-veined pads that were neither hooves nor claws. (TD 223-24)

Wilbur Whateley is a fabulous creature like nothing out of common myth—though with the black fur, goatish face, and the shape of his legs he has the general outlines of a satyr—and it is left up to the imagination of the reader what the purpose of the greenish-gray tentacles may have been. The death scene is quick, with little evidence of Wilbur's existence, similar to the remains of Helen Vaughan. So as to leave no guess at his nature,

Lovecraft appends: "He had taken somewhat after his unknown father" (*TD* 225). An important distinction between "The Dunwich Horror" and Machen's "The Great God Pan" or "Novel of the Black Seal," or his own "Arthur Jermyn" and "The Curse of Yig," is that here, the revelation of Wilbur's true form is not the real climax of the story: it is the setup. The true and final revelation (or confirmation of what the reader has already guessed), at which Lovecraft hints throughout the whole story, and which the undecayed Whateley kin had guessed earlier than the rest of the Dunwich folks, goes back to the origin of Wilbur Whateley in Lavinia's womb: "*It was his twin brother, but it looked more like the father than he did*" (*TD* 245).

Like Pan, Wilbur Whateley's "father" Yog-Sothoth does not make a direct appearance in the story, even when invoked by his spawn. Lovecraft spends more time on the nature of the impregnating entity than Machen ever does, relating Yog-Sothoth to Cthulhu and some of his other creations, to establish Yog-Sothoth (who would have been new to most readers) within the Lovecraft Mythos, since in contrast to Pan, Lovecraft could not rely on readers' immediately grasping the implications of the entity. As with all myths and stories, a degree of sexual symbolism can sometimes be read into Yog-Sothoth's function as described in "The Dunwich Horror." "Yog-Sothoth knows the gate. Yog-Sothoth is the gate. Yog-Sothoth is the key and guardian of the gate" (*TD* 220) is particularly poignant: if the "gate" is understood as a metaphor for the vagina, then the "key" may be understood as a phallus and the "guardian of the gate" perhaps the hymen; under this interpretation, Yog-Sothoth may literally be considered to birth Lovecraft's other extradimensional entities into their reality.

One comment from the *Necronomicon*—in the largest passage of that book Lovecraft ever included in his stories—is the line: "but of their semblance can no man know, *saving only in the features of those They have begotten on mankind*; and of those are there many sorts, differing in likeness from man's truest eidolon to that shape without sight or substance which is *Them*" (*TD* 220). The passage reproduces the logic of *The Dream-Quest of Unknown Kadath* and is sufficiently vague on detail that it can be applied not only to the Whateley twins, but to the half-human spawn of Yig from "The Curse of Yig." No other Lovecraft stories make explicit use of half-human hybrids fathered by entities from outside, but this story more than any other clearly establishes not only the possibility but the pattern of such characters in Lovecraftian fiction.

Of the few female characters in "The Dunwich Horror," the most prominent and important is Lavinia Whateley. Her event of greatest importance appears off the page "we do not see the conception scene, we do not know if it amounts to cosmic rape. Possibly not; she does do apparently willing homage later, upon Sentinel Hill" (Burleson 1992, 24). Critics have recognized the basic inversion of the conception and death of Christ in "The Dunwich Horror." Where "The Great God Pan" depicts an immaculate conception as unholy, Lovecraft's homage takes the reversal a step or two further—the virginal Mary replaced by the slatternly Lavinia, Golgotha by Sentinel Hill, scripture by the *Necronomicon*, and the Holy Spirit by Yog-Sothoth. There is no reason given in the story that the conception of the Whateley twins should be any less immaculate—but it is curious that this view is practically absent from the literature; the basic assumption is that Lavinia did have some form of intercourse with Yog-Sothoth to get with child.

Unlike Mary of "The Great God Pan," Lavinia survives the supernatural conception and birth alive and with mind intact, and unlike many previous Lovecraft matrons she is neither nameless or faceless. She is decidedly rural, with only a partial education from her wizardly father, "fond of wild and grandiose day-dreams," but proud of having borne her child. Yet Lavinia's end is a sad one: as her purpose has been served and Wilbur grows beyond her understanding, she is brushed aside. "Through all the years Wilbur had treated his half-deformed albino mother with a growing contempt, finally forbidding her to go to the hills with him on May-Eve and Hallowmass" (*TD* 217–18). Burleson best captures Lavinia's place in "The Dunwich Horror" and her place in its inevitable continuations later in the Cthulhu Mythos when he writes: "there will be other Lavinias, and other wizards like old Whateley to arrange such monstrous procreations" (Burleson 2002, 207).

"The Shadow over Innsmouth" (1931)

The only story of Lovecraft's to be published separately during his lifetime (as an error-riddled book by Visionary Publishing in 1936), "The Shadow over Innsmouth" is in many ways the culmination of different streams of Lovecraftian thought, marrying the genealogical horror and physical atavism or degeneration of such earlier tales as "Arthur Jermyn," "The Lurking Fear," and "The Rats in the Walls" with the alien miscegenation evident in his later stories "The Dunwich Horror" and "The Curse of Yig," along with a healthy dash of anti-immigrant fervor:

> "But the real thing behind the way folks feel is simply race prejudice—and I don't say I'm blaming those that hold it. [. . .] a lot our New England ships used to have to do with queer ports in Africa, Asia, the South Seas, and everywhere else, and what queer kinds of people they sometimes brought back with 'em. You've probably heard about the Salem man that came home with a Chinese wife, and maybe you know there's still a bunch of Fiji Islanders somewhere around Cape Cod. Well, there must be something like that back of the Innsmouth people. (CC 272)

"The Shadow over Innsmouth" is at heart a racialist fantasy, and the early suggestions of miscegenation between New England folk and foreigners serves as a thin, misleading veneer of normal racism (Lovett-Graff also reads implications of incest in the story, given the remoteness and isolation of Innsmouth, and the insularity of the inhabitants), setting up expectations in readers that are later turned away. It is not long after hearing rumors of racial mixing that the unnamed narrator encounters the first individual who bears what he terms the "Innsmouth look," whose strange appearance causes him to question the idea:

> Just what foreign blood was in him I could not even guess. His oddities certainly did not look Asiatic, Polynesian, Levantine, or negroid, yet I could see why the people found him alien. I myself would have thought of biological degeneration rather than alienage. (CC 279)

As with the folk of Dunwich, the population of Innsmouth are described as degenerate—but unlike in "The Dunwich Horror," here Lovecraft presents an entire community tainted with the unnatural, with "dirty, simian-visaged children" and "almost every one had certain peculiarities of face and motions which I instinctively disliked" (CC 282). Here again, like the Martenses and Whateleys, we have one particular family more degenerate and despicable than the others—the Marshes, the center and cause for the alien blood in Innsmouth. What really sets the story apart is that the interbreeding is on such a wide scale—and purposefully done, as related by Innsmouth town drunk Zadok Allen, but more important to the story is the result:

> "When it come to matin' with them toad-lookin' fishes, the Kanakys kind o' balked, but finally they larnt something as put a new face on the matter. Seems that human folks has got a kind o' relation to sech water-beasts—that

everything alive come aout o' the water onct, an' only needs a little change to go back agin. Them things told the Kanakys that ef they mixed bloods there'd by children as ud look human at fust, but later turn more'n more like the things, till finally they'd take to the water an' jine the main lot o' things daown thar." (CC 297)

While not called out explicitly, the basic idea of humans and Deep Ones diverging from a common stock probably derives from Lovecraft's reading of Haeckel's studies in phylogenetics, particularly the human embryo's transition through several stages during development, including one with gills (cf. MF 748-49).

In Lovecraft's pre-1924 stories, the families could arguably be said to have brought their degeneration down on themselves—the first Jermyn married a white ape, the Martenses stuck to their own out of insularity, the de la Poers deliberately kept their internal cult, shutting out even other members of their family. Post-1924, many of the hybrid offspring are either unwillingly begotten, as in "The Curse of Yig" and "The Horror at Red Hook"—and in "The Dunwich Horror" it is unclear which party exactly initiated relations.

Only in "The Shadow over Innsmouth" is it clear not only that are the Deep Ones the primary instigators, but that they elicit the cooperation of the townsfolk. This is not the isolated case of a single birth, but a systematic effort to breed more hybrids, on a higher and more frightening scale. The original sin of Obed Marsh and the Innsmouth folk was not licentiousness—"I don't think he aimed at fust to do no mixin' nor raise no younguns to take to the water," as Zadok Allen put it—but the things from the sea had other ideas: "*they* wanted to mix like they done with the Kanakys, an' he fer one didn't feel baound to stop 'em" (CC 302-3). It was their urging that led Obed Marsh to take a "second wife *that nobody in the taown never see*" in a callback to the Ape Princess of "Arthur Jermyn," though with a frightful fertility more reminiscent of the Martenses, since she bears Obed three children, and Obed's fully human children interbred with them as well.

Of course, there is more to "The Shadow of Innsmouth" than a story of fish-men and a town of hybrids; it is a story of personal revelation and horror. The first time the unnamed narrator perceives an artifact from Innsmouth, it affects him strangely:

> Among these reliefs were fabulous monsters of abhorrent grotesqueness and malignity—half ichthyic and half batrachian in suggestion—which one could not dissociate from a certain haunting and uncomfortable sense of pseudo-memory, as if they called up some image from deep cells and tissues whose retentive functions are wholly primal and awesomely ancestral. (CC 277)

These pseudo-memories are revealed as racial remembrances of the kind used by Lovecraft in *The Dream-Quest of Unknown Kadath*, and by Machen in "Novel of the Black Seal." It is significant that Lovecraft stresses the biological nature of this race-memory, rather than a spiritual connection or reincarnation, as it reinforces the core idea of biological determinism—a truth that the narrator cannot escape, since it is an essential part of them. Lovecraft claimed to have felt something similar in his own life, an association with ancient Rome that "produce[s] in me a profound feeling of *stirred memories* and *quasi-identity*" and vivid dreams of himself living in Roman times. (SL 4.334)

The narrator's entire purpose before his detour to Innsmouth was to track down genealogical data—information that takes on new importance when it is discovered that he is, on his mother's side, the great-great-grandson of Obed Marsh and his unseen second wife. At first refusing to acknowledge this information, the narrator is beset by dark dreams of the sea, until in a dream he meets his grandmother and great-great-grandmother. "That morning the mirror definitely told me I had acquired *the Innsmouth look*" (CC 335). Confronted at last by the truth of his heritage, he resists committing suicide as Arthur Jermyn did, and as his own uncle did—and instead embraces the change as it comes.

Few of Lovecraft's characters come to such acceptance of their lot, and here is the awareness and transformation that Victoria Nelson looked for and never found—not of a refusal to address sex, but of the biological inevitability of heredity, the acceptance of self. Lovett-Graff draws parallels with Lovecraft's own genealogical researches, going so far as to suggest:

> What was a public allegory of immigrant sexuality and its threat becomes a private allegory (perhaps romance) of the family past and its promise. Following the path he had mapped out in his own mind on the degenerative nature of sexuality, Lovecraft finally comes face-to-face with his own degenerate origins (born of woman and a diseased father), for which the only surcease is to fantasize a return to the womb. Unable to rise above the reality of the body's sexuality, Lovecraft sinks comfortingly into the arms of Mother, letting the

promise of her protection mask the tragic condition of his biological being and origin. (Lovett-Graff 1997a)

Unlike Lovecraft's early fictional family trees, the Marsh line as depicted in this story is not simple or directly patriarchial—there are lines of descent from first wives and second wives with multiple children, mysterious blanks where the information on a great-grandmother or uncle peters out. Here, the narrator's maternal line is more important, since that is the one that leads back to Obed Marsh and his Deep One wife, and so we learn more of his grandmother and great-grandmother than his father or grandfather. Lovecraft himself was closer to his mother's side of the family, particularly after the death of his father, and his genealogical researches found more distinguished ancestors on the Phillips side than on that of the Lovecrafts. Though he liked to present himself as a pure-bred Anglo-Saxon, Lovecraft also discovered a few Celtic ancestors—a fact that Lovett-Graff made much of:

> The racial paranoia inspired by the hard hereditarianism of the eugenics movement could not leave an individual with so troubled a family history and so complicated a personal medical history unaffected. The strong resemblance between the narrator's genealogy and Lovecraft's, the same Lovecraft who feared the Celtic taint of a great-great-great-great-grandmother and her daughter and granddaughter, cannot be ignored. (Lovett-Graff 1997a)

The prominence of the matrilineal line makes the case of gender in "The Shadow over Innsmouth" a bit strange. The greater number of characters that actually appear in the story are male; most of the females—particularly the narrator's great-grandmother and great-great-grandmother—are not directly present, referenced only through dreams or genealogical notes. It is not until the narrator tracks down his great-grandmother that he sees a female with the Innsmouth look—a female relation he of course resembles. The de-emphasis and absence serve to accentuate the otherness of the matrilineal line. The exception is Anna Tilton, a neutral female presence who, like Mamie Bishop, serves as a source of data and little more.

The initial mistake of the narrator that the Innsmouth affliction is a kind of disease also suggests a reading of "The Shadow over Innsmouth" as a metaphor for sexually transmitted—and inheritable—diseases such as syphilis. This reading is tied in to the recurrent rumor that Lovecraft had congenital syphilis; but also crops up independent of such legendry, as in

Dale J. Nelson's comparison of Swiftian satire and horror:

> One recalls the blighted denizens of Lovecraft's Innsmouth, the batrachian "marks" transmitted from generation to generation, each victim experiencing the progressive emergence in his own features of inhuman ugliness. (Is it quite clear, by the way, that the visions of splendor which come to that story's narrator at the very end are to be taken as genuine, rather than as, in part at least, the effect of the Innsmouth blight upon his brain?) (Nelson 1990, 6)

Lovecraft's surviving notes on "The Shadow over Innsmouth" emphasize both his careful plotting of the Marsh family tree and a focus on the "hybrid generations," which include "halfbreeds," "quarters," and "eights," with regular generations marked every thirty years from 1847 to 1907. A small but tantalizing plot-fragment absent from the final draft mentions that once the Deep Ones had taken over and were set to breed more with the Innsmouth folk, "many women commit suicide or vanish" (Lovecraft 2006, 249-53).

"The Dreams in the Witch House" (1932)

An orthodox reading of "The Dreams in the Witch House" reveals little to no sexual material, implicit or explicit, and the primary interest of this tale in respect to the concerns of this essay is Lovecraft's treatment of a few female characters.

The chief antagonist of the story is Kaziah Mason, a female witch. Unlike many of Lovecraft's females, Kaziah is by nature of age or presentation essentially asexual—there is no note of her ever having been married, and she has no male interests in that line and no children. Also strangely asexual is Kaziah's particular tradition of witchcraft. Lovecraft draws from the Salem witch trials, as well as medieval folklore and superstition via Margaret Murray's *The Witch-Cult in Western Europe* (1921)—but Kaziah's actions are without the obvious sexual elements typical of such legendry: no supernumerary nipples, kissing the devil's backside, worship of Diana or some other mother goddess, etc. The lack of sexual context makes it difficult to say much about Kaziah Mason from a gender perspective; the best that can be said is that she is probably female because most of the accused witches in the Salem trials were female, and her most feminine attribute is the way her familiar Brown Jenkin suckles on her blood. We have no real idea of her motivations, goals, or desires, including why she preys on children or attempts an initiation of the protagonist, Walter Gilman, except to play to old stereotypes of the hag-figure and seducer of the innocent.

The minor female characters in the novel are even less fleshed out, the only notable one being Anastasia Wolejko—a mother whose child is stolen by Kaziah Mason. Unlike Lavinia Whateley in "The Dunwich Horror," Lovecraft does not make an issue of Wolejko's marital status or if the child is "legitimate," though the implication is that she is single and in a sexual relationship—"And her friend Pete Stowacki would not help because he wanted the child out of the way anyhow" (*DWH* 323). A *Monster of Voices* (2011) goes so far as to suggest Woljeko is a prostitute (Waugh 100).

Robert h. Waugh also suggests an unorthodox reading to the story as a series of erotic or wet dreams, and makes an effort to analyze the various dreams experienced by Walter Gilman in this somewhat metaphorical context. The reading focuses on Gilman's growing sense of excitement—which is understood as titillation as much as fear—that accompanies his strange journeys and encounters with Kaziah Mason, in whose bedroom he sleeps. The physical evidence of these dream encounters often confronts Gilman when he wakes—as after a wet dream the sleeper wakes to find the dried remains of ejaculation, so does Gilman awake to find physical evidence of his night-time excursions.

"The Thing on the Doorstep" (1933)

In the introduction to *More Annotated Lovecraft*, Peter Cannon writes:

> "The Thing on the Doorstep" is the only Lovecraft story with a strong or important female character—though of course the malign Ephraim Waite has usurped his daughter Asenath's consciousness. [...] Lovecraft avoids exploring the possibilities inherent in this gender-swapping situation [...] (9)

The truth is more complex. Asenath is the strongest and most important female character in the work that came out under Lovecraft's own name, but he had written several previous stories featuring strong women in leading roles, notably "The Curse of Yig" and "Medusa's Coil." Will Murray in "Lost Lovecraftian Pearls: The 'Tarbis' Collaboration" (1999) suggests that the very obscure Lovecraft/E. Hoffmann Price collaboration "Tarbis of the Lake" (1934), on which Lovecraft lent considerable advice, may also have been an influence, as it similarly involved a woman who could project her mind and spirit into a corpse—or vice versa. The story was written in the manner of "Through the Gates of the Silver Key" during Lovecraft's visit to Price in New Orleans in 1932, with each taking a turn at the manuscript; but this original work had to be significantly revised by Price before he could sell it to *Weird Tales* in 1934. Price reportedly also cannibalized "Tarbis" as a spicy for *Spicy Mystery Stories* in 1935.

While Lovecraft does not explore the more lascivious possibilities of gender-swapping (aside from a single suggestion), the entire crux of the story depends on Asenath/Ephraim's desire to change gender. It is more accurate to say that "The Thing on the Doorstep" is the only story in Lovecraft's fiction where gender becomes a major issue for discussion.

The courtship and marriage of Edward Derby and Aesnath Waite is one of the few romantic relationships in the Lovecraft Mythos. Edward Derby contains many autobiographical parallels with Lovecraft, which suggests the story as an allegory of his brief marriage to Sonia (Joshi 1996, 172). Likely literary influences on the story include Barry Pain's *An Exchange of Souls* (1911), about a scientist who exchanges personalities with his wife (*TD* 438), and Edgar Allan Poe's "Ligeia" (1838), whose title character and marriage appear to have strongly influenced the description of Aesnath and the courtship.

Asenath Waite is the daughter of Ephraim Waite of Innsmouth "by an unknown wife who always went veiled" (*TD* 344), and it becomes clear later in the story that Asenath is one of the Deep One–human hybrids from "The Shadow over Innsmouth." Lovecraft describes her as "dark, smallish, and very good-looking except for overprotuberant eyes"—the latter a reference to "The Shadow over Innsmouth," or again to Poe's Ligeia, whose large eyes are her key feature. Also like Ligeia, Asenath is an occultist of a far higher grade than her potential husband: she served to initiate them into greater mysteries and briefly returned from the dead by possessing a corpse. Another possible inspiration is the Urning or "woman trapped in a man's body" in Havelock Ellis's *Sexual Inversions*, if Lovecraft read that work.

Of course, the crux of the character is that while the body of Asenath is female, the consciousness that drives that body is male—that of Ephraim Waite, as Burleson points out in his article "Lovecraft and Gender":

> What do we make of this man-concealing womanly exterior, this woman in whom—the interiority here is clearly suggestive of the fact that Ephraim has "raped" his daughter in the most extreme way, usurping her very mental identity; he is illicitly inside her—in whom lurks a concealed male presence? (Burleson 1992, 23)

The confusion of gender explains certain odd behaviors, such as when Asenath "would frighten her schoolmates with leers and winks of an inexplicable kind, and would seem to extract an obscene and zestful irony from her present situation" at an all-girls school (*TD* 345). Ephraim had taken on his daughter's body to extend his existence, but once in that body became aware of certain esoteric limitations:

> Her crowning rage, however, was that she was not a man; since she believed a male brain had certain unique and far-reaching cosmic powers. Given a man's brain, she declared, she could not only equal but surpass her father in mastery of unknown forces. (*TD* 345)

Joshi is quick to note that this passage is not quite as openly misogynistic as it appears, and he quotes a 1934 letter to show that Lovecraft believed in a difference in kind of intelligence rather than degree (*TD* 441): "The feminine mind does not cover the same territory as the masculine, but is probably little if any inferior in total quality" (*SL* 5.64).

A similarly easy-to-mistake sentiment is voiced in the passage "She wanted to be a man—to be fully human—that was why she had got hold of him" (*TD* 351). It is to be remembered Asenath's physical body is only half-human, the mother by inference a Deep One—this causing Burleson to note: "[N]o feminist critic need see in this any remark to the effect that a woman's humanity is in question" (Burleson 1992, 23).

When the dual nature of the character is intuited by Edward Derby, his confusion over the true "gender" of his wife causes such confusion—"I'll kill her if she ever sends me there again. . . . I'll kill that entity . . . her, him, it . . . I'll kill it! I'll kill it with my own hands!"—that he is forced to declare Asenath/Ephraim without gender, a neuter "it" (*TD* 350). This issue of gender language is reinforced elsewhere in the story, as the narrative drives the reader to identify Ephraim/Asenath as something less than a human being—with the revelation of Asenath's Innsmouth blood—and finally to recognize "it" as an inhuman "thing," left lying on a doorstep.

Robert M. Price points out that Ephraim and Asenath are biblical names. Ephraim translates to "very fruitful" and Asenath to "belonging to the father." In Genesis 41:52 and 46:20, Asenath is the wife of Joseph and mother of Manasseh and Ephraim. In "The Thing on the Doorstep," the parent/child relationship is reversed. The connection was first noted by Price in "Two Biblical Curiosities in Lovecraft" (1988).

Edward Derby "remained single—more through shyness, inertia, and parental protectiveness than through inclination" (*TD* 343) until the age of thirty-eight, when he met Asenath Waite. Like Denis de Russy in "Medusa's Coil," Derby was immediately smitten:

> Edward met Asenath at a gathering of "intelligentsia" held in one of the students' rooms, and could talk of nothing else when he came to see me the next day. He had found her full of the interests and erudition which engrossed him most, and was in addition wildly taken with her appearance. [. . .] It seemed rather regrettable that Derby should become so upheaved about her; but I said nothing to discourage him, since infatuation thrives on opposition. [. . .] About this time Edward brought the girl to call on me, and I at once saw that his interest was by no means one-sided. She eyed him continually with an almost predatory air, and I perceived that their intimacy was beyond untangling. (*TD* 345-46)

A justice of the peace administers the wedding, and following the honeymoon the couple move into a house in Arkham. The relationship that follows is dominated by Asenath; Edward Derby sees less and less of his old friends and family, "for Asenath had concentrated in herself all his vital sense of family linkage" (*TD* 348)—an exacerbation of a typical period after marriage, this time fueled by extensive hints of their occult studies and the suggestion that Asenath is telepathically displacing Edward's consciousness with her own. The relationship apparently ends when Edward tells his friend that he had mustered the will to force Asenath off to New York—where he hoped "she'd go west and get a divorce" (*TD* 356)—although this turns out to be a lie.

Some critics read this story as an allegory for Lovecraft's marriage and divorce. In this regard the story has difficulties, but it remains a popular interpretation. Joshi summarizes it best:

> [. . .] if Derby's youth and young manhood are an amalgam of Lovecraft and some of his closest associates, his marriage to Asenath Waite brings certain aspects of Lovecraft's marriage to Sonia manifestly to mind. In the first place there is the fact that Sonia was clearly the more strong-willed member of the couple; it was certainly from her initiative that the marriage took place at all and that Lovecraft uprooted himself from Providence to come to live in New York. The objections of Derby's father to Asenath—and specifically to Derby's wish to marry her—may dimly echo the apparently unspoken objections of Lovecraft's aunts to his marriage to Sonia. (Joshi 2010, 864)

In terms of biographical details among the characters, himself, and his ex-wife, Lovecraft does not replicate the exact facts his relationship with his wife; for example, the age relationship between Sonia and Lovecraft is reversed in Edward and Asenath, with Edward being the older of the pair by fifteen years, while Lovecraft was in fact seven years younger than Sonia—although this may be a deliberate construction, as Lovecraft was at least once mistaken as the older of the couple, just as Asenath eventually was. Nor was it Lovecraft who pushed for an end to his relationship with Sonia, as Edward did with the possessive Asenath, but Sonia who asked Lovecraft for a divorce. However, other aspects of the fictional relationship do seem to echo some of Sonia and Lovecraft's marriage: the duration of the marriages is roughly the same, and like Derby, Lovecraft never learned to drive. Even allowing for such parallels, the best that can be said is that events in Lovecraft's life inspired parts of "The Thing on the Doorstep," and some of the emotional aspects of the story reflect his understanding of the marriage.

Even if the story is not a literal rewriting of his marriage in his own words, wrapped in his fictional mythology, knowledge of Lovecraft's marriage allows a deeper reading of the story. The literal reversal of gender suggests the reversal of typical gender-roles in his marriage. In her own testament Sonia claims to have been deferential in many matters, but it is a sad fact that Lovecraft's inability to secure work in New York made her the chief breadwinner for the couple—in an era when the husband typically provided for the wife. That Sonia was aware of his possible feelings of emasculation is made clear in her own account. From *The Private Life of H. P. Lovecraft*:

> I effaced myself entirely and deferred to him upon all matters and domestic problems regardless of what they were in order to remove or reduce if possible some of the complexes he might have had. Even to the spending of my own earned money I not only consulted him but tried to make him feel that he was the "Head of the House". (Davis 1992, 12)

Despite this assertion, Sonia was undoubtedly the dominant force in the relationship—the one who pushed for both their marriage and their divorce, and who always initiated sex. Whether Lovecraft consciously drew on his relationship or not, the reversal of cultural gender-roles in Lovecraft and Sonia's marriage may well have inspired the literal assumption of the position (and body) of the incapable Edward by the masterly and domineering Asenath.

The pairing of the dominant Asenath and the weak Derby is matched implicitly against the far more staid Upton and his barely visible wife. Kálmán

Matolcsy has written the most insightful interpretation of Upton's wife:

> Asenath's figure, her overflowing and diffuse body is counterbalanced in "Doorstep" by Daniel Upton's spouse, a constrained, somewhat restricted, genuine angel of the house, about whose purity no doubt is raised. [. . .] The fact that she does not see Asenath's decomposing body—Daniel's wife is always shunned, evanescent, and ethereal (she never appears in body throughout the story)—offers an instance of the gendered version of the Lovecraftian "cosmicist" thesis, that is, witnessing the horror equals knowing it, knowledge is always harmful, and both knowledge and harm are closely tied to gender. (Matolcsy 172)

Mrs. Upton is unseen in the story, and so can suffer no criticism of her appearance, heritage, or habits; she can be seen as an idealistic image of a wife rather than a real person. Upton's wife is the antithesis of Asenath Waite—and as a consequence, she has quite literally almost no place in the story at all; the female Upton is not just uninteresting, her characterization is barely worth mentioning except to give some tenuous example of the stereotypical image of a housewife. It is on consideration of the poor, nameless fate of Mrs. Upton that the reader comes to appreciate that, flawed, terrible, and domineering as Asenath may be in the story, at least she is in it—or is she, if the "real" Asenath was trapped in her father's body, again the female rendered mute and invisible off the page?

It is relatively easy to consider "The Thing on the Doorstep" an early example of transgender or transsexual speculative fiction—if not a particularly sympathetic one, given that the transformations and relationships are forced and possessive, the masculine warring to overcome or escape from the feminine. Yet the eternal interest of this tale lies in the questions that naturally arise from the gender-bending or body-switching implied in the sexuality and gender identities of Derby and "Asenath." Joshi asks: "If, as the story suggests, Lovecraft regarded the mind or personality (rather than the body) as the essence of an individual, is this marriage homosexual?" (Joshi 2010, 582), and a few more questions assert themselves. Asenath's body may be biologically female, but the mind or soul that drives it is male—and carries with it stereotypical male attitudes and behaviors. Does that make "Asenath" a prototypical transgender character? If "she" considers herself male, and had sex with the male Derby, does that make "her" homosexual or bisexual? What does Derby feel about the situation, particularly when he is literally emasculated, transposed into his wife's body for periods of time—and how much of what Asenath did in Derby's body would countenance sexual abuse? While never addressed, the possibility that Asenath-in-Derby's body had relations with Derby-in-Asenath's body is also a possibility. Finally, what to make of all these questions with regard to what we know of Lovecraft? Of his friends, his mother, his marriage? These are questions without definitive answers; Lovecraft is dead and his letters are silent as to particulars. What is left is speculation and interpretation—but as Cannon noted, such questions go unasked and unanswered in the story itself.

Probably it was a deliberate aesthetic choice. Lovecraft was surely versed in marriage rites and knew more of sexuality and homosexuals at that point than ever before in his life. To make no mention of it, but not provide some narrative escape mechanism for the marriage bed, would be perfectly in keeping with the idea that a gentleman simply does not discuss certain subjects. Possibly it was an omission of the mind: Lovecraft was so far removed from thinking about intercourse that he wrote the story without giving the gender-bending implications any consideration beyond the hideous facts behind the survival of the Ephraim intellect. The result is what it is: a threshold of speculation crossed by many later scholars, critics, readers, and authors.

"Supernatural Horror in Literature" (1927; revised 1933)

A significant scholarly assay of the literature in Lovecraft's own lifetime, "Supernatural Horror in Literature" remains an important document providing his views of his precursors and his philosophy of the weird. Various works cited and praised by Lovecraft have been noted as influences on his own fiction, particularly with regard to his entries on favored and influential authors such as Edgar Allan Poe, Arthur Machen, and Lord Dunsany, and through the inclusion of obscure works such as Robert W. Chambers's "The Harbor-Master" (1897), Irvin S. Cobb's "Fishhead" (1911), and Herbert Gorman's *The Place Called Dagon* (1927), all significant influences on "The Shadow over Innsmouth."

Lovecraft gives little mention in the essay to sexuality, but neither does he shy away from mention of demon lovers, incubi, succubi, and various marriages to supernatural entities that populate many of the stories. These elements of supernatural lust and romance represent a continuing theme that crops up perennially in weird fiction, that of the supernatural romance.

Concerning this theme, J. Vernon Shea remarks: "Howard was almost completely indifferent to the *feminine* figures of fantasy and mythology which have allured other writers: Circe, mermaids, lamias, nymphs, and vampires" (10). Shea's comment is fair, as Lovecraft deliberately eschewed many traditional monsters in his fiction, but it is not entirely accurate. Though Lovecraft does not pursue this particular theme in detail in his essay, he does make note of the repetition of certain concepts like the corpse-bride and statue-bride (Lovecraft 2000, 25–26). While marriage to a supernatural bride is not a major factor in Lovecraft's fiction, it does have its place—"Arthur Jermyn," "Medusa's Coil," "The Mound," "The Shadow over Innsmouth," and "The Thing on the Doorstep" all partake somewhat of the concept, and a kind of inversion can be seen in other tales—"The Dunwich Horror" where Yog-Sothoth stands in for the demonic bridegroom as given in Machen's "The White People"; "The Man of Stone," where instead of marrying a statue a man and wife become statues; "The Horror in the Burying-Ground," where a woman's fiancé is mistaken for a corpse, and such.

The lack of emphasis on sex or sensuality in the text, beyond what is necessary to give an accurate account of the stories in question, is not surprising given both Lovecraft's known preference against ribaldry for its own sake and his specific emphasis throughout the essay on promoting the idea of "cosmic" horror, which focuses not on the individual or the relation of two individuals, but on more impersonal and vast forces that dwarf the scope of human endeavor; throughout the essay he laments stories that must end happily, where virtue must prevail, or that become entangled in commonplace romance. As a consequence, much of the detail of interpersonal relations in the stories is left out.

Lovecraft gives equal mention to female authors of the weird, judging their works on merit and not by the sex of the writer. Given the importance of their contributions, it is notable that he does not make an effort to downplay their achievements, notably in the case of Mary Wollstonecraft Shelley, author of *Frankenstein; or, The Modern Prometheus* (1818), where he writes: "criticism has failed to prove that the best parts are due to Shelley rather than her" (Lovecraft 2000, 35). In fact, there are only two real criticisms with regard to gender in the entire essay. The first concerns the archetypes of the early Gothic novel: "the saintly, long-persecuted, and generally insipid heroine who undergoes the major terrors and serves as a point of view and focus for the reader's sympathies" (Lovecraft 2000, 28). Lovecraft's dislike of this particular trope in part explains his treatment of the female characters in his own stories and revisions. The second is his failure to recognize the importance of gender in some of the weird fiction he cites, notably Charlotte Perkins Gilman's "The Yellow Wall Paper" (1892), even though Lovecraft was aware Gilman was a feminist. However, it may be this is simply because Lovecraft was focusing on the story as a weird tale, or that the protagonist possibly might be seen as an extreme extension of the Gothic heroine type he disliked.

Collaborations

In addition to the works that appeared under his own name, Lovecraft made a small business out of revising and ghostwriting the works of other writers such as Zealia Brown-Reed Bishop, Adolphe de Castro, and Hazel Heald, as well as collaborations with writers such as E. Hoffmann Price and C. M. Eddy, Jr. For the most part, Lovecraft exercised a rather heavy hand as a revisionist or as a collaborator, often rewriting large sections of the story until the end result was arguably mostly his own work; as a ghostwriter he would often keep only a few elements of the original idea or outline and the rest would be pure Lovecraft. However, it is notable that his revisions are notably different from the work that appeared under his own name, often with more female characters and a greater tendency for romance as an element of the plot, and a few of these works are worth examining separately.

A special case worth mentioning is "Bothon" (1946). Nominally attributed to Henry S. Whitehead, there is some evidence that Lovecraft may have contributed to it, or else that August Derleth may have written it based on Lovecraft's synopsis (Joshi 1996, 196). The story is notable for containing a romantic element, as the eponymous hero Bothon leads an invasion of Atlantis to claim the hand of Ledda, the emperor's niece, but the Lovecraftian material is too scant for further comment.

"Poetry and the Gods" (with Anna Helen Crofts) (1920)

This early collaboration by Lovecraft features a central female character, Marcia. It is a brief, dreamlike tale of gods, romance, and poetry, vaguely Dunsanian in tone, and mostly unremarkable except as Lovecraft's earliest known work with a female collaborator. Joshi speaks accurately of it:

De Camp curiously remarks of this tale that "the prose has a feminine ring foreign to Lovecraft"—inspired, one suspects, by nothing more than the fact that a woman is the central character (this may indeed have been Miss Crofts' addition). The prose is, however, no more "feminine" than that of Lovecraft's other quasi-Dunsanian tales. (Price 1990, 4)

"Ashes" (with C. M. Eddy, Jr.) (1924)

The first revision by Lovecraft for Clifford Martin Eddy, Jr., this tale is almost, if not entirely, Eddy's work; Lovecraft notes only that he corrected it, and it is included here only for completeness (SL I.257). Joshi sums up "Ashes" succinctly: "It is a pointless and hackneyed tale with a nauseating romantic element which, by the standards of 1923, might almost have been termed pornographic" (Price 1990, 5). Joshi is probably referring to one particular passage:

> The feel of her soft, yielding body held close to my own was the last straw. I cast prudence to the winds and crushed her tightly to my breast. Kiss after kiss I pressed upon her full red lips, until her eyes opened and I saw the lovelight reflected in them. (HM 334)

"The Loved Dead" (with C. M. Eddy, Jr.) (1924)

Based on a draft by Eddy, revised by Lovecraft, "The Loved Dead" created a sensation when it appeared in *Weird Tales*: authorities in Indiana tried to have the issue banned for obscenity (Joshi and Schultz, 156). It is also the most explicit story Lovecraft ever contributed to in his lifetime with regard to love and sex—though at first it is the mere presence of the dead that elicits a sensual, though not explicitly carnal, response. It is not until midway through the story that the necrophile is discovered: "stretched out upon a cold slab deep in ghoulish slumber, my arms wrapped about the stark, stiff, naked body of a foetid corpse! He roused me from my salacious dreams" (HM 353).

Schultz in his article "On 'The Loved Dead'" also notes:

> When the narrator describes his love for the dead, Lovecraft uses alliteration to indicate the narrator's growing excitement. Lovecraft's poignant sense of what he called "expectancy" is transformed into a bizarre parody of sexual anticipation. (Price 1990, 59)

The general character of the necrophile is familiar to Lovecraft's readers, since the basic archetype appears in several of his stories: the unnamed, obsessive, and sensual seeker of the macabre was prominent in both "The Lurking Fear" and "The Hound" (1922). It is tempting to look for aspects of Lovecraft's own character and history reflected in that of the unnamed narrator, even elements of his own sexuality, and the bare bones are there—the sickly childhood, the death of grandfather and parents—but the details are wrong, and it is probably best not to read too much into the character.

The degree of Lovecraft's contribution to Eddy's tale is a matter of some debate. All agree that the original idea for the story and first draft were Eddy's. Joshi gives the opinion that Eddy and Lovecraft contributed about equally to the final story (*HM* xvii), and "Lovecraft probably added a few details to the plot [. . .] but revised or wrote much of the actual prose" (Price 1990, 6), which was standard for Lovecraft in his collaborations and may explain Frank Belknap Long's claim that "Lovecraft wrote 9/10 of C. M. Eddy's 'Loved Dead'" (Price 1990, 56). Muriel Eddy in *The Gentleman from Angell Street* (1961) insists that Lovecraft had simply "read the original manuscript and touched it up in places" (Eddy and Eddy 18). In the Summer 1948 *Arkham Sampler*, August Derleth quotes Eddy's version of events as follows:

> The yarn started out to be a little short study in psychology under the tentative title of *The Leaping Heart*, i.e., a heart that leaped from sheer joy whenever in the presence of the dead. [. . .] H. P. L. discussed it with me, and we decided that it might do for *Weird Tales*. One point on which we were agreed was that too many stories told by a hero now deceased leave the reader completely up in the air as to how the story could ever have seen the light of day. H. P. L. calmly informed me that my protagonist was suffering from a medically-recognized mental ailment, and that he couldn't be blamed for anything he did during the course of the story. He even named the malady—a long Latin term which I had never heard before. Once I had placed my protagonist in the graveyard, the story wrote itself. (Eddy 21)

Lovecraft himself wrote: "It may interest you to know that I revised the now-notorious 'Loved Dead' myself—practically re-writing the latter half. [. . .] I did not, though, devise the necrophilic portion" (*LRB* 61).

"The Last Test" (with Adolphe de Castro) (1927)

This revision contains the closest thing to a stereotypical romance among Lovecraft's stories—the put-off courtship of Georgina Clarendon and John Dalton. Unlike most of the revisions and ghostwritten tales, we have access to the original text by de Castro: a non-supernatural tale entitled "A Sacrifice to Science" (1893), published first in the *Californian Illustrated Magazine*. In comparing the two texts, it is clear that Lovecraft took the courtship entirely from de Castro's original; his main contribution to the relationship was changing the name of the female character from Alvira to Georgina.

"The Curse of Yig" (with Zealia Bishop) (1928)

Zealia Bishop was one of Lovecraft's ghostwriting clients, and "The Curse of Yig" was one of three stories he wrote under her name. In content, "The Curse of Yig" owes much to Machen. As with Mrs. Cradock in "Novel of the Black Seal," the pioneer woman Audrey Davis is found alone and insensible after the death of her husband—and like Mrs. Cradock, it is hinted that more occurred than was shown in the events of that night: "'*That* is what was born to her three-quarters of a year afterward. There were three more of them—two were even worse—but this is the only one that lived'" (CrC 194).

It is interesting to note that of Lovecraft's few pregnancies in his stories—all of which occur off the page—"The Curse of Yig" and "The Dunwich Horror" are the only two referred to at length, and both have the traditional full term of a normal human pregnancy: nine months. It is likely that Lovecraft simply did not think of or did not care to play with the idea of different rates of gestation, as some later authors did. Audrey Davis incurs the curse of Yig earlier in the story by killing a brood of newborn serpents "comprising as many as three or four"—the exact number of children she later bore as the fulfillment of the curse (CrC 180). The surviving child is a hybrid in the mode of Helen Vaughan of "The Great God Pan," though not one that could ever pass for human. All in all, "The Curse of Yig" is something of a thematic trial run for several elements of "The Dunwich Horror."

"The Curse of Yig" is also notable for its use of female characters, particularly Audrey Davis, who is prominent and proactive in the story, and the minor supporting character Grandma Compton, who would reappear in "The Mound." Davis is responsible for both accruing and fulfilling the eponymous curse of Yig. Her fate is arguably worse than that of many of Lovecraft's male protagonists—none of whom are even forced to bear unwanted offspring—but otherwise is in keeping with theirs: madness and death.

"The Mound" (with Zealia Bishop) (1929–30)

A lengthy novelette, "The Mound" is inarguably the most significant contribution to Lovecraft's growing pseudomythology of all his ghostwritten or revised tales. "The Mound" is a "lost world" or "hollow earth" story, and almost reads as a sort of inversion or parody of A. Merritt's *Conquest of the Moon Pool* (1919), since it removes all the lighter, romantic (and ultimately sappy) elements of the plot, and taking a lead from the decline of the Roman Empire, with its insularity, lost territories, and growing fear of barbarian invasion and obsession with bloody entertainments. Other likely influences are the novels of Edgar Rice Burroughs, particularly the subterranean, psychic Mahar race in *At the Earth's Core* (1914) and *Pellucidar* (1915).

In describing the ancient civilization of K'n-yan, Lovecraft is free to present a sort of idealized science-utopia—but one that has decayed so that the great pinnacles of achievement have been lost, the highly cultured race stagnant and dying, and the progressive efforts of eugenics degenerated into horrors. The highest accomplishments of the civilization are marvels of science, including advances in biology and eugenics: "The ruling type itself had become highly superior through selective breeding and social evolution [. . .] and thus, by raising the naturally intelligent to power, drained the masses of all their brains and stamina" (CrC 274).

While poor genetics, this understanding of eugenics and class would have produced a world that conformed fairly well with Lovecraft's idyll—a class-and-race-based society where the different tiers were naturally suited to their social status by their inborn attributes. In addition to this "master-race" were various specially bred slave races—again, partly human in their makeup. One of the most sickening was the quadruped *gyaa-yothn*:

> The flesh they ate was not that of intelligent people of the master-race, but merely that of a special slave-class which had for the most part ceased to be thoroughly human, and which indeed was the principal meat stock of K'n-yan. [. . .] That part of them was human, seemed quite clear [. . .] (CrC 281)

This is the second instance ("The Rats in the Walls" being the first) of a deliberate breeding program for human or human-like creatures in Lovecraft's fiction. Here again we see the degeneration of a human population by sex, only this time the process is artificially managed rather than occurring through natural inclination. In the society of K'n-yan humans are just another type of beast, no different from dumb animals—a somewhat satiric affirmation of what many evolutionists have claimed, with an end result reminiscent of Swift's *A Modest Proposal* (1729).

The religion of K'n-yan is based on the worship of many Lovecraftian entities considered deities. Notable among these are "Yig, the principle of life symbolized as the Father of all Serpents," first mentioned in "The Curse of Yig," and Shub-Niggurath, "the All-Mother and wife of the Not-to-Be-Named One," who was "a kind of sophisticated Astarte" (*CrC* 289), first mentioned in "The Last Test." This is one of the few instances when Lovecraftian entities are firmly cast as "gods" to be worshipped, and the fairly beneficent natures depicted here are somewhat anomalous, suggesting an unreliable narrator or a writer deliberately subverting his own typical devices.

Tellingly, in the society of K'n-yan "the civil and social distinction of the sexes had disappeared" (*CrC* 275). It has no marriage but is based around "the large affection-groups, including many noblewomen of the most extreme and art-enhanced beauty, which in latter-day K'n-yan took the place of family units." (*CrC* 290-91). It is possible that the "affection-groups" are a remnant of the philosophies of Lovecraft's friend James F. Morton and the "free love group" he once engaged in (Everts). It is difficult to say what effect Lovecraft's own marriage or views on marriage contributed here, but this sexual element becomes crucial:

> [. . .]a female of his affection-group who conceived for him a curious individual infatuation based on some hereditary memory of the days of monogamous wedlock in Tsath. Over this female—a noblewoman of moderate beauty and of at least average intelligence named T'la-yub—Zamacona acquired the most extraordinary influence [. . .] (*CrC* 296)

Unfortunately for T'la-yub, even before they set out on their escape attempt, her human companion has firmly decided he would never marry her, and her fellows in K'n-yan exact a terrible revenge on her for her betrayal. The double betrayal—by her lover and by her people—arguably makes T'la-yub the most sympathetic character in the story, though this is in part obscured by Zamacona's self-centered narrative and disagreeableness over her non-humanity.

"Medusa's Coil" (with Zealia Bishop) (1930)

Lovecraft's last ghostwritten tale for Zealia Bishop again features a major female character, the *femme fatale* Marceline Bedard. It is also inarguably one of his most singularly racist stories. From very early on, the tone is set with the suggestion of miscegenation: "Romantic young devil, too—full of high notions—you'd call 'em Victorian now—no trouble at all to make him let the nigger wenches alone" (MC 25). This remark is directed toward one of the main players in the tale, Denis de Russy. The de Russys are revealed to be an old Southern family of relatively high social standing and few branches; it is no surprise that by the end of the tale the line is extinct. While pursuing his studies in Paris during the decadent 1890s, Denis meets and marries Marceline Bedard, the priestess of a small cult among the students, who claims to be "the left-handed daughter of Marquis de Chameaux" (MC 27). In this context, "left-handed" is synonymous with "illegitimate." In appearance, she was beautiful:

> She did have an air of breeding, and I think to this day she must have had some strains of good blood in her. She was apparently not much over twenty; of medium size, fairly slim, and as graceful as a tigress in posture and motions. Her complexion was a deep olive—like old ivory—and her eyes were large and very dark. She had small, classically regular features—though not quite clean-cut enough to suit my taste—and the most singular head of jet black hair that I ever saw. (MC 28-29)

Denis, for his part, is infatuated with his beautiful young wife, with what his father describes as "puppy-love," though Marceline does not quite return the feeling. In this, Antoine appears to take on Lovecraft's own opinion of such sappy romanticism. The arrival of Frank Marsh, an old friend of Denis, adds the element of jealousy to the mix, and for the first time in a Lovecraft story we are faced with an actual romantic triangle: Marceline infatuated with Frank, Denis infatuated with Marceline, and Frank both Denis's friend and painting a nude portrait of his wife.

The whole thing comes to a bloody and supernatural end, with the final maddening revelation delivered by Frank's portrait, which like the eponymous *Picture of Dorian Gray* (1890) records the true soul and nature of Marceline Bedard—and something else: "for, though in deceitfully slight proportion, Marceline was a negress" (MC 68) This ending, combined with other elements in the story, is the most clear and emphatic statement concerning actual miscegenation (as opposed to implicit miscegenation, as in "Arthur Jermyn" or "The Shadow over Innsmouth") or simple negative portrayal of immigrants, Jews, blacks, etc. in the Lovecraft Mythos, and is the intended final horror from relatively early on, as revealed by Lovecraft's surviving notes (Lovecraft 2006, 243-44).

The best that can be said about the ending is that it may reveal in some way the depth of Lovecraft's own fears: by making it the terminal revelation, Lovecraft gives the slight ancestral fact the same weight as the secret of the Dunwich Horror. "Medusa's Coil" shows in literary form both how far Lovecraft had changed from his early days—a strong female character, interpersonal relationships real and imagined, and the use of implicit and desired promiscuity are all absent from his earliest fiction—and how he did not, because in many ways the final revelation is no different from that of "Arthur Jermyn." In both cases, the capstone of the terrible revelation is miscegenation—not on the part of the individual, but of some ancestor, yet enough to make the descendant a shocking and vile figure, at least to the other characters in story, and by extension is intended to invoke something of the same effect in the reader.

"The Man of Stone" (with Hazel Heald) (1932)

This revision is noted by some for its similarities to "The Mask" from Robert W. Chambers's *The King in Yellow* (1895): both stories feature an occult petrifying chemical, two men, a woman, and jealousy. Both stories result in the resolution of the love triangle by way of the chemical—but where Chambers leaves two characters alive and one dead, Lovecraft's ending has all three characters dead of murder or suicide at the end, reminiscent of his high school play *Alfredo* (Joshi and Schultz, 3). However the final survivor is the female character Rose, who turns the tables on her husband and kills him—but chooses suicide rather than be apart from her lover, in the vein of *Romeo and Juliet*. Her final entry in the journal that comprises most of the story is a very rare occurrence of Lovecraft writing from the perspective of a female. It is tempting to draw a parallel between this star-crossed romance and the supernatural tales of statue-brides with which Lovecraft was familiar, where the bride becomes a statue rather than the other way around.

"The Horror in the Burying-Ground" (with Hazel Heald) (1933/35)

A more macabre ghostwriting assignment, "The Horror in the Burying-Ground" is similarly the tale of two men and a woman, although the details of the relationship are much more cynical and more reminiscent of

"The Last Test": instead of two men vying for the affection of one woman, here we have a woman, Sophie Sprague, trapped between two evil men—her brother and a morbid suitor. Sophie gains ultimate advantage, or at least survival, over the two male characters, though she is literally haunted for her actions. While Sophie is an effective part of the story, the narrative rarely focuses on her; the reader is being told the story by an unnamed narrator, and so her actions are only noted as they appear to the nameless witness, with the reader left to piece together the true underlying events and motivations. The story is also understood in the context of the wider tradition of weird fiction as a sort of inversion to the old tale of the corpse-bride: in this case, the fiancée is plagued by the persistence of her corpse-groom.

Themes and Parallels

With regard to sex, love, and gender in the Lovecraft Mythos, there are themes and ideas that Lovecraft used repeatedly or developed over several stories. These themes are not explicitly sexual, and may not even have been intended, but have been recognized, utilized, and further developed by later writers in the Cthulhu Mythos, and I think it worthwhile to examine a few of them here.

Sexual Symbolism in Lovecraft

The absence of women and sex in the Lovecraft's Mythos has spurred attempts at both a post-mortem Freudian psychoanalysis of Lovecraft and a critical search for sexual symbolism in the Lovecraft Mythos: "In the face of such radical exclusion, certain critics have concluded that his entire body of work is in fact full of particularly smoldering sexual symbols" (Houellebecq 57–58). As Joel Pace wryly put it:

> If history and time could ever be rearranged so that Dr. Sigmund Freud could have paid a house call to the residence in which Howard Phillips Lovecraft spent his final years, the small house near the top of Providence's College Hill would not have had a room large enough to accommodate all the scholars who would wish to be flies on the wall. (104)

Lovecraft's opinion on the matter is voiced most clearly in "Beyond the Wall of Sleep" (1919) when he wrote of Freud's "puerile symbolism" (*TD* 11). The popularity and idiosyncrasy of this view is noted by Stephen

King in his introduction to Michel Houellebecq's *H. P. Lovecraft: Against the World, Against Life* (2005):

> It can be argued that such "great texts" as "The Dunwich Horror" and "At the Mountains of Madness" are about sex and little else, and that when Cthulhu makes one of its appearances in Lovecraft's tales, we are witnessing a gigantic, tentacle-equipped, killer vagina from beyond space and time. I'm not trying to make light of Lovecraft, only pointing out that if the Elder Gods are seen from a psychoanalytic standpoint, especially from the standpoint of psychoanalysis as it existed in Lovecraft's time, then we're in a Freudian three-ring circus. (13)

King's argument is essentially correct, and echoed by L. Sprague de Camp and others (de Camp 1975, 300). "Amateur Freudians" could well argue that the one-eyed, fifty-foot sea creature from "The Horror at Martin's Beach" (1922) in Lovecraft's revision with his future wife Sonia is a symbolic penis; that the "sticky whitish mass" that is all that remains of Wilbur Whateley in "The Dunwich Horror" is symbolic of the aftermath of ejaculation (*TD* 225), and that the fireplace of the Martense house in "The Lurking Fear" is a symbolic womb—the latter a minor point in Bennet Lovett-Graff's essay "Lovecraft: Reproduction and its Discontents: Degeneration and Detection in 'The Lurking Fear'" (1995). A good example of this sort of slightly lurid speculation can be found in J. Vernon Shea's "H. P. Lovecraft: The House and the Shadows" (1966):

> It would be very easy to explain that Lovecraft's unconscious dread of his mother made him create womb-symbols, horrible creatures from the deep dark sea (a fishy odor is vulgarly associated with the vagina). A psychoanalyst could also make much of the title figure of Howard's "The Outsider", saying that a recurrent dream of being hideously diseased or of falling apart with decay indicates a deep-seated fear of harming the love-partner. (11)

Similarly, St. Armand's *The Roots of Horror in the Fiction of H.P. Lovecraft* (1977) implicitly suggests that the monsters in Lovecraft's stories, at least those derived from his dreams, are the product of his normally inhibited sexual urges expressing themselves while he slept (92; cf. Joshi 1996, 259-60). Such an argument might at least give readers new cause to consider the gugs from *The Dream-Quest of Unknown Kadath* (1926-27), whose fang-filled mouth "opening vertically instead of horizontally" (*DWH* 188-89), resemble not incidentally the folkloric vagina dentata. The symbolic images given above are probably not intended to have any overt sexual symbolism—the remains of Wilbur Whateley, at least, are more likely homage to the dissolution of Helen Vaughan in "The Great God Pan" (whether her remains are in fact symbolic is another matter). Grant Morrison in *Lovecraft in Heaven* (1994) equates Lovecraft's nausea at the smell of seafood with his disgust for sex via the smell of Sonia or Susie's vagina— and he was not alone. J. Vernon Shea makes a note of it, as does Stephen Sennitt (Shea 11; Mitchell 2010, 202).

One of the most extensive contemporary evaluations of sex and symbolism in the Lovecraft Mythos is Gavin Callaghan's *H. P. Lovecraft's Dark Arcadia* (2013), a heroic effort to re-examine Lovecraft's fiction and its symbols with respect to Lovecraft criticism, the biographical details of his life, and various literary, historical, and psychological influences. While I do not agree with bulk of Callaghan's conclusions about Lovecraft or the symbolism in his work, *Dark Arcadia* is a significant work.

Whether or not any of this interpreted symbolism rings true is entirely subjective; to quote St. Armand: "On the subject of the sexual roots of Lovecraft's symbology, I shall let the reader draw his own conclusions" (92).

Weird Sex

Human interaction is not the focus of Lovecraft's fiction; his philosophy of writing as revealed in "Supernatural Horror in Literature" and his letters was to attempt the cosmic. The mundane details of human life, like sex, were entirely at odds with the atmosphere he strove to create. Yet sex was a part of the history of weird fiction, an element that Lovecraft had read and recognized in the form of succubi, incubi, lusty satyrs, and strange marriages to statues and undines from diverse tales. So there was a place for sex in Lovecraft's fiction, provided that the sex was an expression of the weird. As Caitlín R. Kiernan put it: "Lovecraft who only *seems* a prude until one realizes how preoccupied so many of his stories are with sex, very weird sex, indeed, no matter what dim view he took" (Kiernan 2012, 10).

Looking at Lovecraft's stories in this light, it is unsurprising to find that the majority of sex in the Lovecraft Mythos—really most of it aside from some stereotypical romance stuff in his revision-work, such as "Medusa's Coil"—is of an unnatural kind, typically with at least one deceased, inhuman, or partially inhuman partner. The sex itself is never featured on the page, of course, so there is no idea how strange the act itself might be, but the results of such weird couplings tend to speak for themselves. Wilbur Whateley and the Dunwich Horror, the hybrid fish-people of Innsmouth, the serpent-children of Audrey Davis, and the ape-like Arthur Jermyn all violate, to different degrees and in different ways, the human form and the normal procreation of man and woman, bodily representing "a malign and particular suspension or defeat of those fixed laws of Nature" (Lovecraft 2000, 23). Other authors have addressed this idea more openly and certainly in more explicit detail, but Lovecraft himself was operating in fairly established weird fiction territory and at least in the immediate footsteps of "The Great God Pan."

The Lure of the Forbidden

Sex thrives on the breaking of taboos, the shiver of excitement that comes with doing something you're not supposed to do; the more forbidden an act may be, the more obscene the material, the greater the thrill. It should come as no surprise that the arcane literature of the Lovecraft Mythos features many of the same basic traits as pornography in the United States of the 1920 and '30s—hidden from the public, suppressed or kept under lock and key by intelligent men, not talked about openly, prone to disgust the uninitiated, passed around in secret by groups of degenerates, amassed by loners in terrible libraries, yet a subject of abiding and almost frenzied interest. The worried anticipation of Lovecraft's protagonists and narrators, and his penchant for tantalizing and seductive hints rather than outright revelation or denial creates an intellectual burlesque that both reader and protagonist endure. Lovecraft's most decadent characters, such as the protagonists in "The Hound" and "The Lurking Fear," are obsessed with forbidden lore and ecstatic in their discoveries of it.

In setting up certain elements as forbidden and obscene, Lovecraft creates and then breaks new taboos with each story, evoking new sensual thrills. By making some of these elements common background material, he builds a framework of taboos that readers carry with them from story to story. The very mention of Shub-Niggurath or Innsmouth means nothing to a Mythos virgin, but invokes connections in the mind of an experienced reader of Mythos stories—readers themselves become something of a seeker of the forbidden, reveling in the latest details of the Mythos. The presiding passion of both reader and protagonist in the Mythos tale is thus *libido sciendi*—the desire to know, not just what happened, what happens next, or how the story ends, but what new revelations of the Mythos will be learned. John Taylor Gatto in his article "Whispering in the Dark: A Peek at Lovecraft's Dirty Story" (1978) describes the sensation as "a curiosity and taste for thrills that is downright prurient and pornographic" (109). The article is a revised excerpt from Gatto's Monarch Notes series entry *The Major Works of H. P. Lovecraft: A Critical Commentary* (1977). Of all the critical literature, Gatto may have the distinction of going the farthest in an effort to wring a sexual metaphor out of Lovecraft, which results in remarkable passages like the following:

> Those familiar with Lovecraft's tricks react immediately to the first characterization of the protagonist as an "enthusiastic amateur" for this is just the sort of well meaning young lady that old Grandpa Theobald loved to diddle with, a little complacent, a little cocksure, and raring to go after the forbidden fruit. (109)

Forbidden Knowledge, Personal Transformation

> In Lovecraftian horror the adept is faced with a new understanding of the order of the cosmos; in erotica, the rules are often social, requiring the adept to confront their preconceived notions of sexuality, gender and relationship dominance. When the two are combined, the effect is powerful. The subversion of social norms is magnified through the transformation of self on a literally cosmic scale. (Cuinn 312–13)

Once a character in the Lovecraft Mythos obtains or experiences the forbidden, what follows is typically a mental or physical transformation. It may shatter existing preconceptions, shaking the characters' faith in the world that they know, or it may lay bare some personal horror that they can no longer ignore. The concept dates back at least as early as Arthur Machen's "The Great God Pan" and was fully expressed in Machen's prelude in "The White People." The negative, transformative effects of forbidden knowledge is featured in many stories in the Lovecraft Mythos, though the exact details differ: Arthur Jermyn destroys himself, the unnamed narrators of "The Shadow over Innsmouth" and "The Outsider" embrace their change, Edward Derby of "The Thing on the Doorstep" becomes transferred into his wife's body (and eventually her corpse), and so on.

There are parallels that can be drawn between this process of realization and sexual education, which has both academic and natural aspects. Natural awareness of sexuality usually takes place around puberty when body and mind undergo their changes, while knowledge of the actual "facts of life" is transmitted via books, peers, older teachers, or actual sexual experience. The transmitted or discovered knowledge that comes with sexual education and experience is not mere dry facts—it involves and helps shape the developing sexuality; readers of a textbook on sex may discover things about themselves, just as characters in Lovecraft may realize a sudden monstrous insight from their occult studies.

In a way, the sexually explicit Cthulhu Mythos stories are a direct expression of this theme of knowledge and personal transformation. Sexual knowledge and experience over a period of time begets jadedness, where old and familiar pleasures do not have quite the same thrill, and new or more intense material may be required to obtain the same satisfaction. Thus where Lovecraft would spend the majority of the story hinting or suggesting at changes, later writers favor more direct stories and develop in detail what Lovecraft would have left discreet or implicit.

Miscegenation and Mis-generation

> [W]hy are the Outré Beings so eager to mate with humans? There are two possible answers. The first is that they are not; rather, it is the wizards and cultists that force them to do it against their will. Unfortunately this simply rephrases the original question to why the wizards or cultists are so eager to do it. (O'Brien, 11)

In "The Dunwich Horror," "The Curse of Yig," "The Shadow over Innsmouth," "Arthur Jermyn," and "The Horror at Red Hook" Lovecraft presents cases of miscegenation—alien entities procreating with the human race, spawning hybrid entities that mingle features of the two. In "Arthur Jermyn," "The Horror at Red Hook," and "The Shadow over Innsmouth" this process is a rather bald allegory in some cases for human miscegenation, the racist concept of "corruption" of European descent by "inferior races" (cf. Joshi 1996, 162-63). Less obviously, it is an allegory for the dilution of a culture by contact, the practices and social norms of the alien culture influencing and sometimes entirely replacing those of an existing one. Most later Cthulhu Mythos authors, however, are focused on a detail Lovecraft probably did not intend: apparently, all these Mythos entities are physically capably of having sex with humans, and at least some of them are willing or wish to do so. Sex is a motive and plot-driver that many humans understand, and once a Mythos entity is understood to be a sexual entity as well, it opens up new vistas of stories beyond those written by Lovecraft, and many authors have taken advantage of this fact.

If readers choose to observe the families in Lovecraft's fiction as extensions of the main narrator or character—as literal parts of their being—then the concealment of an ancestor is equivalent to hiding the biological evil already within the character, and the ultimate revelation of that ancestor reveals his own immutable taint and degeneration. Lovecraft's focus on physical determinism—that people are trapped, by circumstances they cannot control, in the biological mechanism of their bodies, inheritors of the sins of their parents and ancestors—is more prevalent in the Lovecraft Mythos than in much of the Cthulhu Mythos, because it is such a bleak worldview, where nothing the individual does in his lifetime can change the unassailable facts, and to marry or have children is only to share the horror with loved ones. When faced with the truth of their biological destiny, it is not enough for some of Lovecraft's characters to kill themselves, as in "Arthur Jermyn"; they also seek to kill their children as well, to cut off the diseased branch of the family entirely rather than propagate the affliction.

The Role of Women

Women are underrepresented in the Lovecraft Mythos. Most of the protagonist or narrator characters are male, as was customary for pulp fiction of the period, and like Lovecraft himself often evinced little apparent romantic interest of any kind. Bruce Lord's summary is exemplary of the general criticism of women in the Lovecraft Mythos:

> Narrators mention their wives in no real detail, and usually only in connection with their sons. In "The Rats In The Walls" and "The Shadow Out Of Time" Lovecraft introduces the theme of father-son relationships to no small degree, while essentially bypassing the husband-wife relationship. Lavinia Whateley may indeed be the least insignificant female character in Lovecraft's entire body of work; the only possible exception, Asenath Waite of "The Thing On The Doorstep," is a complex and not entirely female character [. . .]

However, a more accurate presentation is given in Ben P. Indick's "Lovecraft's Ladies" in *Essays Lovecraftian* (1976):

> [. . .] a hasty count of feminine names in a recent index of his stories and their characters produces at least several dozen. Quite obviously, de Camp's statement, as well as popular supposition is incorrect. True, none of his narrator-protagonists is feminine, and sexual discussion or even romantic warmth are

absent; however, he was hardly ignorant of women, and in his serious as well as in some of his lighterhearted works, women are important characters. (80)

Gina Wisker goes further, defining Lovecraft's females as liminal characters:

> Lovecraft's women dramatize and embody the concerns of the early twentieth century, the disgust and abjection of reproduction, fear of the weird more generally, and imperial concern of the invasion of the foreign and alien Other through miscegenation. [. . .] Many of Lovecraft's female figures are creatures constructed in a context of social and cultural exclusion, disgust, and fear of age, women whose social positions are marginal and strange. [. . .] The portrayal of women who are living vehicles through which monstrous aliens can be reproduced ("Innsmouth", "Dunwich") is a rich and unusual contribution to the variety and mix of monstrous women in genre fictions. (32–33)

All these approaches have their particular insights. Certainly, there are more female characters in Lovecraft than most fans and critics seem to recall, from maiden aunt Mercy Dexter and the widow Rhoby Harris of "The Shunned House" to Queen Nitokris in "Under the Pyramids" and Dame de Blois in "Psychopompos." Equally true, women are rarely major protagonists and antagonists in the tales (though with notable exceptions such as Marceline Bedard), and their supporting roles tend to be limited presences. The most exceptional and memorable of Lovecraft's female characters, like Asenath Waite, Lavinia Whateley, and Keziah Mason, are certainly liminal characters that act outside of traditional societal roles, and that in part is what makes them exceptional in these stories.

The majority of Lovecraft's most prominent female characters are present in his revisions and ghostwritten works, notably those for female clients. This may beg the question of how much the use of female characters was insisted upon by the clients, or taken for granted from their outlines/story ideas/drafts. It does seem likely, given several of the more conventional romantic plots in stories like "The Man of Stone" and "The Horror in the Burying-Ground," that these female clients had an influence on the fiction. Ultimately, however, Lovecraft essentially wrote the stories, or at least the bulk of them, and it is his treatment of the female characters that is of interest, not necessarily whether they were created by him. Even if Lovecraft did not originate some of the characters in his revisions, he still undoubtedly originated several important female characters in works under his own name—Kaziah Mason, Asenath Waite, and Lavinia Whateley especially.

Greater prominence in a story is not generally a factor for long literary life in the Lovecraft Mythos, and female characters receive the same dooms as their male counterparts—madness, death, and destruction. Marceline, Kaziah, Asenath, and T'la-yub are all violently killed in the course of their stories, and Audrey suffers rape and madness. Lavinia Whateley, once she fulfills her purpose in bearing the children of Yog-Sothoth, is treated callously by her son, forbidden to attend the rites, and eventually disappears entirely. T'la-yub is not even given the peace of death, but has her corpse mutilated and reanimated. It is indicative of Lovecraft's attitude toward women that most of his female characters are also married or seek monogamous relationships, sometimes with ulterior motives (Asenath, Marceline, T'la-yub). The exceptions are typically spinsters like Grandmother Compton, or those outside normal social convention or independent-minded like Lavinia Whateley. Marital status does not seem to be a deciding factor in the fate of a female character.

The Unseen Mothers

One of the earliest and most notable treatments of women in the Lovecraft Mythos is in "Arthur Jermyn," where the females of the Jermyn line are notable by their absence. Never described in any detail or even named on the page, these women are present in the genealogical narrative only as necessary to propagate the next generation, and then conveniently disappear from the family history. Lovecraft's tendency to focus on the male, name-bearing members of the line, particularly in "Arthur Jermyn," "The Lurking Fear," and "The Rats in the Walls," by consequence pushes the women off the page. Indeed, in "The Lurking Fear" all the Martense daughters go unnamed and unacknowledged on the page, their existence only implied by further generations. Indick gives a possible explanation for this postage-stamp portrayal of women:

> A number of these feminine names are merely parts of the genealogies which are so important in his fiction, befitting his antiquarian interest, and establishing a realistic depth in the families in which will so often appear a degenerate or alien strain. More often, the subsidiary female characters are humorless but busy home-makers, which is in itself hardly atypical of the life of the wife and mother of the 17th through 19th centuries. (80)

The females of a family line are essential—indeed, one of the inherent paradoxes of focusing on the male transmission is that while the identity of the father may be in question, the mother of a child is always known from birth. In "The Curse of Yig" and "The Dunwich Horror," the question is by default the paternity of the offspring, with the mothers being acknowledged as a matter of course. Understanding this, Lovecraft sometimes uses the "hidden mother" (or grandmother, great-grandmother, etc.) to deliberately obscure the issue of genealogy, as in "Arthur Jermyn," "The Shadow over Innsmouth," and "The Thing on the Doorstep."

The absence of females, their literal namelessness and facelessness, and particularly the sudden and inexplicable disappearance of Lavinia Whateley from the pages of "The Dunwich Horror," are sometimes taken as examples of Lovecraft's misogyny, "the muting and vanishing of women" (Lord). There is some fairness to this observation and reproach, because in reducing the unseen mothers down to the simple mechanical function of bearing children and limiting not only their narrative but biological input, Lovecraft essentially demeans women to a single role and diminishes their vital contribution in that part.

Indeed, in terms of their offspring, it is rare for Lovecraft's mother characters to contribute to the same degree as the father characters; one or the other is almost always dominant in the mix. For "Arthur Jermyn," it is the Ape Princess, with the wives of her son and grandchildren apparently contributing little to the line; in "The Lurking Fear" the distinctive mismatched eyes of Gerrit Martense carry down to the latest, most degenerate generation; Lavinia Whateley's greatest contribution to her twins is their grandfather's chin (although the unnamed twin also apparently carries her albinism, unlike Wilbur), etc. The closest true admixture of features is in "The Shadow over Innsmouth," where the unnamed narrator has the same eyes as his ancestor Obed Marsh—and also the latent Innsmouth look from Obed's Deep One wife.

Considering the autobiographical aspects in his work, there is always the question of how much of Lovecraft's own relationship with his mother is at work in his stories. For example, it is possible to draw parallels between Lovecraft and Wilbur Whateley in "The Dunwich Horror," as Stanley C. Sargent did in *The Taint of Lovecraft*, since both author and character shared a similar upbringing—an absent father, a prominent grandfather with his aging library, and a single mother. But how Sargent reconciles the "slatternly" Lavinia Whateley with the "touch-me-not" Susie Lovecraft, I am at a loss to explain.

Robert D. Marten in "The Pickman Models" (2004) delves into Lovecraft's family tree in an effort to find genealogical influences on his fiction, and unearths colonial ancestress Ann Marbury Hutchinson, whose colorful history includes accusations of witchcraft and a monstrous birth. As entertaining as literary necromancy with Lovecraft's family tree may be, there is a trap here: in trying to discern more of Lovecraft by reading into his characters and stories, readers risk seeing their own prejudices reflected in the material regardless of known facts. For example, comparisons may be drawn between Susie Lovecraft and Audrey Davis of "The Curse of Yig": both were single mothers (of sorts) and spent time in a sanitarium, but the details of the story have little actual relation to the life of Lovecraft's mother, and any comparison between the two is a strained and probably fruitless effort.

The Wise Woman

> The intrusion of Lovecraftian horror into our world [. . .] often inverts the patriarchy by empowering the female who has "crossed over" and embraced the new reality. For the empowered female, this is an act of joy, not horror, punctuated by orgasm, fertility, and the dominance of the female over the male. (Cuinn 320)

In certain Lovecraft Mythos stories, a female character is more intelligent, proactive, or versed in occult lore than the main male characters in the story. Most prominent are T'la-yub of "The Mound," Marceline Bedard and Old Sophonisba of "Medusa's Coil," Keziah Mason of "The Dreams in the Witch House," and Asenath Waite of "The Thing on the Doorstep." These females are usually presented as equal or near-equal to the male characters, often possessing considerable occult knowledge and skills that a male character lacks; they serve to initiate men in their studies or worship, and finally die and are resurrected in some fashion. They are more or less female counterparts to the stereotypically male wizards and warlocks of the Lovecraft Mythos such as Joseph Curwen (although Asenath is a slightly different case, as "she" was a female body possessed by a genderless mind). All these examples may be based on Poe's "Ligeia" to some extent; the parallel is strongest in "The Thing on the Doorstep" and "Medusa's Coil" and weakest in "The Dreams in the Witch House" and

"The Mound," simply because in the latter two stories the romantic relationships between the female characters and their male protagonists are either one-sided or non-existent.

It is not coincidental that these females share not only their occult experience, but also sexual experience; by marrying their pupils they initiate them not only into the mysteries of the supernatural but the mysteries of sex, or at least the marriage-bed, since T'la-yub, Marceline, and Asenath all seek monogamous unions for their own purposes. The purpose of the women in these unions appears uniformly to bind the men to them more intimately—whether in a religious, legal, or emotional sense (or a combination thereof) is unclear, but in every instance certainly to their own advantage, and at least in the case of Asenath and Marceline to the disadvantage of their husbands.

The Anti-Gothic Heroine

"[T]he saintly, long persecuted, and generally insipid heroine who undergoes the major terrors and serves as a point of view and focus for the reader's sympathies" (Lovecraft 2000, 28). Thus does Lovecraft describe a formulaic Gothic female, as first appeared in the character Isabella in Horace Walpole's *The Castle of Otranto* (1764). Lovecraft's prominent female characters are almost the inverse of this trope: they are rarely the point of view of the narrative, they are never saintly, and, rather than undergoing the major terrors, they are usually the cause or contributors thereof. While this may have been coincidental, Lovecraft may also have been making a conscious or unconscious attempt to break from a Gothic trope he disliked.

For example, of those prominent non-antagonist female characters, none can be described as "saintly," since all of them at one point or another commit acts of violence or evil, or by inaction allow a murder or death to take place. Audrey Davis in "The Curse of Yig" invokes the curse by killing the children of Yig and in a fit kills her husband; Rose in "The Man of Stone" is emotionally unfaithful to her (admittedly abusive and evil) husband and eventually poisons him in revenge or self-defense; Sophie Sprague in "The Horror in the Burying-Ground" stands silent while both her brother and suitor are buried alive; and Lavinia Whateley in "The Dunwich Horror" could be regarded as promiscuous and a willing participant in the rites on Sentinel Hill.

Rather than being the mere subjects or victims of horror, Lovecraft's major female characters are typically the catalysts for the terror in his stories. Audrey Davis evokes the curse of Yig on herself and her husband; Rose's attraction to another man spurs her warlock husband into making his chemical brew; the quest for Sophie Sprague's hand leads to two men being buried alive; Lavinia Whateley literally births the Dunwich Horror. Even as catalysts, Lovecraft's females tend to remain somewhat sympathetic characters, because of their long suffering. Rose is trapped in a bad marriage, Lavinia Whateley is socially ostracized and eventually forbidden her freedom, Sophie Sprague is trapped between an abusive brother and a creepy suitor. Unlike the passive victim-heroines of Gothic romance, Lovecraft's women tend to take some action to resolve their situation when opportunity allows, but also typically become trapped or suffer the consequences of their actions.

As a counterpoint to this view, Sara Williams has put forward the theory that it is Lovecraft's male protagonists who have taken on the aspect of the Gothic heroine, citing Walter Gilman of "The Dreams in the Witch House" as an example of such a character as subject to hysteria as any Gothic novel heroine. In this context, Keziah Mason and other predacious women could be seen as gender-flipped versions of the villainous Gothic antagonists who incite and play on hysteria in women (Williams 59).

Lovecraft's Slatterns

If there are no Gothic heroines in Lovecraft's fiction, and chastity and virginity are no shields against the creatures and forces of the Mythos, the matter of sexual promiscuity in his works is more ambiguous. The best examples come from the two lovers' triangles of a sort in Lovecraft's revisions "The Man of Stone" and "Medusa's Coil," where the attractions felt are never consummated. The "bad girl" Marceline Bedard attempts a physical affair and is rebuffed, while "good girl" Rose is sorely tempted by her growing love for another man than her husband; both stories end with the women in question dead. In other stories, the evidence for promiscuity is even slighter: T'la-Yub of "The Mound" is part of a polyamorous society but specifically develops a monogamous inclination, and Lavinia Whateley, though described as slatternly, is never attached to any particular male figure. The majority of Lovecraft's other females are in monogamous relationships, with extramarital sex only occurring as a result of rape, or evince no sexual interest at all, such as Kaziah Mason. Another possible example is Anastasia Wolejko, also of "The Dreams in the Witch House," who is intimated to be without a husband, thus presumably a widow with surviving child or a woman who had a child out of wedlock, and is "friends" with another man would prefer the child out of the way.

Of all these characters, none attempt to maintain affections with two separate male characters at the same time—Marceline Bedard and Rose both turn their attentions from their husbands, T'la-Yub abandons her affection-group for her conquistador, Anastasia Wolejko is not listed with any other "friends," and Lavinia Whateley shows no other interaction outside her family. If these characters might be considered "promiscuous" by Lovecraft's standards, it is unclear if they are singled out for unusual punishment in this regard; terrible things happen to many characters in the Lovecraft Mythos regardless of gender, and the deaths of Marceline Bedard and Rose are no more horrific than the rape and madness of Audrey Davis. Even in the cases of Bedard and Rose, the cause of their deaths was the occult forces pervading their lives as much as their attempts at or temptation to have an affair.

Rape in the Lovecraft Mythos

Rape as a crime against women carries special poignancy for many reasons, not least because of the possibility of pregnancy from unprotected sex. In the Lovecraft Mythos, where a woman can bear the hybrid offspring from a Mythos entity, this carries with it a special kind of horror, and for some, rape and impregnation are sexual fetishes, taboos that add thrill to a narrative. Given his lack of bedroom scenes, it is no surprise that Lovecraft says almost nothing of rape in his stories, but it does crop up at least twice.

In "The Curse of Yig," Audrey Davis kills a nest of four snakes and is forced to bear four snake-human hybrids in return. The second case is a few lines in "The Horror at Red Hook," where four women who were being held prisoner—and with ill-born children—are discovered after the police raid. In both cases, the act of rape (it is not much of a stretch to assume rape in either case) occurs off the page, and in both cases the results of that forced sexual activity are hybrid children. A more ambiguous case is the conception of the Whateley twins by Lavinia Whateley and Yog-Sothoth; there is simply not enough information to clarify if it was a case of cosmic rape or a willing participation, though Lavinia's willing participation in other rites may be an indication against rape.

Women in the Lovecraft Mythos are not suggested to have been raped except when the act results in a child as in "Novel of the Black Seal." With so few instances it is difficult to generalize, but it is possible that Lovecraft only chose to include the suggestion of rape in a story when a hybrid child is desired, as no form of consent would make sense within the framework of the story. Other Mythos entities, such as the Deep Ones in "The Shadow over Innsmouth," do not appear to commit rape—they desire willing human partners—although Lovecraft's notes for the story suggest he may have been willing to hint at rape earlier on.

Searching for Shub-Niggurath

If human females are in the minority in Lovecraft's fiction, female inhuman entities are exceptionally scarce. The Ape Princess, T'la-yub of K'n-yan, and the Deep One wives of Innsmouth are the only such creatures that are definitively female, and they are far closer to human than many of Lovecraft's iconic aliens. Yig and Yog-Sothoth, because they both "fathered" children by human women, are generally seen as masculine; likewise, Nyarlathotep assumes the form of a male human in Lovecraft's stories and poetry. Great Cthulhu, Rhan-Tegoth, etc. are generally indeterminate, insofar as they are not clearly depicted as having any human gender, but are sometimes referred to by gender-neutral masculine pronouns rather than "it" or "that." As a consequence, readers of the Lovecraft Mythos have generally recognized two "major" entities as probably female: Mother Hydra and Shub-Niggurath.

Mother Hydra is referenced in a single line from "The Shadow over Innsmouth": "'an' the children shud never die, but go back to the Mother Hydra an' Father Dagon what we all came from onct—Iä! Iä! Cthulhu fhtagn!'" (CC 304). The title "Mother" gives the most immediate and definitive identity to a female entity, and when paired with "Father" the context of the reference suggests that Hydra and Dagon are progenitors of their race, like Adam and Eve. Nothing more is directly spoken of Mother Hydra in the Lovecraft Mythos, and of Father Dagon there is scarcely more, save that the Esoteric Order of Dagon is presumably named for him and may or may not be related to the entity in Lovecraft's early short story "Dagon" (1917). The names themselves give little additional information: the hydra of Lerna is a classical Greek water-monster, and Dagon is a biblical deity of the Philistines sometimes associated with fish or fishing; both are far away from the alien syllables common of Lovecraft's exotic entities, and may be mere human titles or adapted names. Mother Hydra and Father Dagon never make an appearance in this story or any other, and even within the context of the story they have a mythical, quasi-biblical quality to them; but whether they are "real" within the fictional world of the Lovecraft Mythos is almost irrelevant, since their only purpose is to hint at a greater culture beyond the seedy, dilapidated, and inbred limits of Innsmouth.

Shub-Niggurath is another poorly defined entity, though used more often by Lovecraft. References to Shub-Niggurath are typically via the exclamation "Iä! Shub-Niggurath!" often accompanied by "The Black Goat of the Woods" or "The Goat with a Thousand Young." (Another reference to a "Black Goat" occurs in Lovecraft's revision to Duane W. Rimel's "The Tree on the Hill" [1934], but it is not clear if this is the same entity.) From this repeated phrase we can discern little, except that it seems a very common exclamation used by magicians and those familiar with the Mythos. The "Goat" referenced brings to mind the satyr-like figure of Pan or Satan, the "Woods" gives possible connotations of a nature deity or the primeval forests, while the "Thousand Young" suggests fertility, which again may be connected to the Pan figure, both in traditional myth and as developed by turn-of-the-century literature such as Arthur Machen's "The Great God Pan," and possibly "The Red Hand." Whatever the relation between Shub-Niggurath and the Goat, it is not until "The Mound" that Lovecraft provides some additional insight: "a shrine of Shub-Niggurath, the All-Mother and wife of the Not-to-be-Named One. This deity was a kind of sophisticated Astarte, and her worship struck the pious Catholic as supremely obnoxious" (CrC 289).

As with Mother Hydra, the usage of specific terminology ("wife" and "All-Mother") suggests that Shub-Niggurath is a female entity; the term "All-Mother" combined with a reference to Astarte suggests a deity of love or fertility. To a degree, this reading is made difficult by the uncharacteristic nature of the passage as compared with much of Lovecraft's other writing—a document by a Spanish conquistador chronicling an alien culture, as translated by an American centuries hence, and with several salient details that reverse earlier depictions of Mythos entities like Yig and Cthulhu. As a result, Shub-Niggurath and other "deities" are presented as benevolent, in almost a classical Greco-Roman sense, with their respective roles and human relations to one another, elements that appear very seldom elsewhere in Lovecraft's writing and may be a clue to readers that not everything is to be taken at its face value.

Similarly, the information on Shub-Niggurath from "Out of the Aeons" derives from a modern translation of a scroll predating known human civilizations about "T'yog, High-Priest of Shub-Niggurath and guardian of the copper temple of the Goat with a Thousand Young" who believed the "Mother Goddess" Shub-Niggurath was one of "the gods friendly to man" and that "with the power of Shub-Niggurath and her sons" he could oppose another god, Ghatanothoa. (MC 199). This confirms that Shub-Niggurath was seen as a female entity, worshipped by human beings in prehistory, that her worship was somehow connected to "the Goat with a Thousand Young," and that she was considered a "Mother Goddess" (similar to the Magna Mater of "The Rats in the Walls") who had "sons"—either actual progeny, or metaphorically by her worshippers. This sort of exposition and traditional sword-and-sorcery background is again very atypical of Lovecraft, and there may be a hint of an unreliable narrator here, as though the translator were imposing on the story a more traditional format; but despite this the feminine nature of Shub-Niggurath is very clear in both accounts.

In contrast, another title possibly affiliated with Shub-Niggurath is "Lord of the Woods" from "The Whisperer in Darkness" (1930), as the two are closely related in the text. The masculine title of "Lord" suggests an alternative possible interpretation for Shub-Niggurath, or possibly lends itself to Shub-Niggurath as a hermaphrodite, as Ramsey Campbell interprets in "The Moon-Lens" (1964).

Aside from these few fragments, Lovecraft made jocular mention of Shub-Niggurath (including the occasional "Iä! Shub-Niggurath!" interjection) in his letters. These are not properly part of the Lovecraft Mythos, but at least some later writers consulted and drew inspiration from them. In his 1933 family tree, for example, Lovecraft lists Shub-Niggurath as a child of Darkness, who joined with Yog-Sothoth to create Nug and Yeb, two entities that are featured in many of Lovecraft's revisions, and by descent from them were related to Cthulhu, Tsathoggua, Clark Ashton Smith, and Lovecraft himself (SL 4.183). A 1936 letter to Willis Conover gives the most complete description of Shub-Niggurath Lovecraft ever provided:

Yog-Sothoth's wife is the hellish cloud-like Shub-Niggurath, in whose honour nameless cults hold the rite of the Goat with a Thousand Young. By her he has two monstrous offspring—the evil twins Nug and Yeb. He has begotten hellish hybrids upon the females of various organic species throughout the universes of space-time (cf. "The Dunwich Horror") [. . .] (SL 5.303)

Efforts to reconcile this form of Shub-Niggurath with the goat-like visions evinced by "The Black Goat of the Woods" and the fecundity implied by "The Goat with a Thousand Young" have been made, most notably in Brian McNaughton's "Mud" (2000).

While it is impossible to say that Mother Hydra and Shub-Niggurath are the only major non-human female Mythos entities, they are probably the only two such that could be considered, by the weight of evidence, predominantly identifiable as female in the same way that Yog-Sothoth and Yig are predominantly identifiable as male. Given the scarcity of their descriptions, these two entities—particularly Shub-Niggurath, with her possible connection to fertility—have a greater prominence to readers of the Mythos than might be expected. Readers and writers interested in exploring sex and Lovecraft's Mythos have been naturally attracted to the resident female entities when addressing the subject of sex and the Cthulhu Mythos.

Asexual Aliens

The stories examined above are concerned about sex, love, and gender in the Lovecraft Mythos; the complement to this notion is the deliberate instances of asexual reproduction that Lovecraft wrote into the Mythos, through alien races like the plant-like Old Ones from *At the Mountains of Madness* (1931) and the body-hopping Great Race of Yith from "The Shadow out of Time" (1934-35), and more obscurely through the contamination of "The Colour out of Space" (1927), the sorcerous displacement by Joseph Curwen in *The Case of Charles Dexter Ward* (1927) and Ephraim Waite in "The Thing on the Doorstep," and somewhat more ambiguously through entities of indeterminate sexuality such as the shoggoths; and Cthulhu, whose octopoid spawn are mentioned in *At the Mountains of Madness*.

While I give "The Colour out of Space" as an example of asexual reproduction, Robert H. Waugh's "Lovecraft and Lawrence on the Hidden Gods" (2007) suggests a dualistic sexual symbolism:

[...]bisexual details find their place in "The Colour out of Space." The stone and its hollow globules are both male and female, testicles and womb. The lightning-bolt is a male fertility motif, but the iridescence of the Colour suggests Iris, the goddess of the rainbow. It lies in the water of the well, but it ascends to the constellation Cygnus, the swan into which Zeus transformed himself in order to seduce Leda. The Colour manifests itself as both male and female. (45)

Likewise, consider Richard Upton Pickman of "Pickman's Model" (1926) and *The Dream-Quest of Unknown Kadath*, who is hinted to be a changeling entity that spent part of his life as a human and part of his life as a ghoul. The concept of changelings, the substitution of a child of one race for another, was a popular motif in fairy tales. However, in weird fiction as early as Machen's "Novel of the Black Seal" the idea of the "fairy child" was more associated with rape and miscegenation rather than the discreet swapping of human infants. Lovecraft's contemporaries Clark Ashton Smith and Robert E. Howard reflected this in "The Nameless Offspring" (1932) and "The Children of the Night" (1931), respectively. However, the presiding scholarly view of Lovecraft's fiction, at least since George Wetzel's "The Cthulhu Mythos: A Study" (1955), is that Pickman was a changeling in the old sense, and as he grew older he reverted to type; the idea has since been popularized and promulgated by Donald R. Burleson, Robert M. Price, and others. Lovecraft's conception of ghouls has been highly influential on the works of later authors, most notably Brian McNaughton and W. H. Pugmire, the latter of whom has revisited the concept of the ghoul-changeling in "Born in Strange Shadow" (1996).

Lovecraft's deliberate use of asexual reproduction in his fiction stands in contrast to the often-present but implicit sexual reproduction discussed above; in these stories Lovecraft does not simply hide the sexual act, but removes it entirely, while retaining the reproductive impulse—the ability and desire to continue the species or the self in new forms—by a number of different methods derived from his readings in science (the Elder Things' spores, etc.) and science fiction (mind-transfer, etc.). Bruce Lord posits Lovecraft's repeated use of asexual reproduction as a direct outgrowth of his own views towards sexuality, biological determinism, and generational degeneration:

> Lovecraft's fiction is rife with examples of societies and individuals that propagate themselves using means other than sexual reproduction, and are thus able to circumvent the pitfalls of degeneration. Not as surprisingly, in the majority of these instances, asexual reproduction is cast by Lovecraft as a prefera-

ble and more 'advanced' or 'superior' means of propagating a species (by this point it should be clear that terms such as 'advanced' and 'degenerate' hold a great deal of currency in Lovecraft's descriptions of his creations when positioned against the seemingly inescapable path of degeneration that plagues humanity). In "At The Mountains Of Madness" and "The Shadow Out Of Time," Lovecraft continues his agenda of supplanting assumptions of humanocentricism by envisioning societies capable of operating without the detrimental effects of sexuality. Additionally, in "The Thing On The Doorstep," Lovecraft presents us with one of his most complex tales with regards to sex, gender, and attempts at circumventing the perils of reproduction via sexual means.

As a parallel thought, consider "Herbert West—Reanimator" (1921-22), a gruesome update and revisitation of the central element in Mary Shelley's *Frankenstein*. The creation of Frankenstein's Monster has been considered a masturbatory fantasy in some respects: the idea of man creating life without a woman. One possible reading of "Reanimator," and by extension Lovecraft's other cases of asexual reproduction, may be considered in a similar light.

Of course, even in Lovecraft's advanced alien societies, asexual reproduction is no guarantee of freedom from the perils of degeneration. The Old Ones from *At the Mountains of Madness*, for instance, become degraded over time:

> If anything, the later contours shewed decadence rather than higher evolution. The size of the pseudo-feet had decreased, and the whole morphology seemed coarsened and simplified. Moreover, the nerves and organs just examined held singular suggestions of retrogression from forms still more complex. Atrophied and vestigial parts were surprisingly prevalent. (*TD* 266)

Slightly more difficult cases for consideration are Lovecraft's asexual and ambiguously sexual Mythos entities, such as Cthulhu, Shub-Niggurath, ghouls, night-gaunts, etc. Many of these are not given any explicit gender or sexual identity in any of the tales, and their alien anatomy, when described, lacks details of genitals or secondary sexual characteristics like breasts. Most of the Mythos entities are sexless as far as the Lovecraft Mythos is concerned, save for those who establish some sexual ability by procreating with humanity (Yig, Yog-Sothoth, the Deep Ones, etc.) or in cases where the reproductive habits of the entire society (Elder Things, the Great Race, and the inhabitants of K'n-yan) are dealt with in some detail. The "default" gender for many of these entities in common use is, by general convention of the English language, given to be male (i.e., marked by the masculine pronouns him, his, he); Lovecraft is not averse to using the gender-neutral "they" or "it" as occasion warrants; but when describing Great Cthulhu, for example, the use of the masculine indeterminate is much more prevalent. Other Mythos authors are sometimes more keen to define the sex or sexlessness of the ambiguous entities in the Lovecraft Mythos, and driven by Lovecraft's use of the masculine tend to render Cthulhu and other entities as male rather than as female, neuter, or of some alien gender.

In stories with asexual alien races, Lovecraft did not avoid the concept of family or social organization, as noted by S. T. Joshi:

> It is a fact of no small interest that all three of Lovecraft's comparatively utopian societies have done away with sex in the normal human fashion. This is understandable in the cases of the Great Race and the Old Ones, since both these races are totally non-human in biology and could thus hardly propagate like humans. Both reproduce by spores; consequently there is little place for family life in the two civilizations. (Joshi 1989, 4-5)

The surveys of civilization for both the Great Race and the Old Ones, for example, both contain accounts of the alternative social structures:

> Being non-pairing and semi-vegetable in structure, the Old Ones had no biological basis for the family phase of mammal life; but seemed to organise large households on the principles of comfortable space-utility and—as we deduced from the pictured occupations and diversions of co-dwellers—congenial mental association. (TD 302)

> Family organisation was not overstressed, though ties among persons of common descent were recognised, and the young were generally reared by their parents. (DWH 363)

The two systems are interesting to contrast with Lovecraft's sole advanced alien civilization that utilized sexual reproduction—the populace of K'n-yan from "The Mound," with its old hereditary lines mostly forgotten and the populace divided into non-familial "affection groups." Nowhere in these societies is there room for romantic love as humans understand it, even absent the need or desire for sexual attraction; but the focus on mental congeniality and mutual affection strongly recalls Lovecraft's expressed opinions in "Lovecraft on Love" and supports Joshi's contention that "Lovecraft was essentially reflecting his own social views when writing such passages is obvious from the manifestly sympathetic tone in which the passages are written" (Joshi 1989, 5).

Joshi's interpretation also has to be measured against the rest of Lovecraft's fiction, where the family unit was paramount, and his own life, where he was conscientious of his surviving immediate family to a great degree, and through genealogical research traced connections back to more distant ancestors. It is a question for the reader as to whether the lack of family structure and freedom from sex (or at least, sexual mores) better demonstrates the evolution of these entities, or their alienage from humanity. These societies obviously do not reflect Lovecraft's upbringing— but then again, they may reflect something of his adult life, when his biological family narrowed and he found amicable and mutual non-sexual affection with a surrogate family—his many correspondents, particularly those whom he visited in their homes such as R. H. Barlow and Frank Belknap Long.

Homosexual Interpretation

The number of male characters in the Lovecraft Mythos, often close friends and acquaintances, who work closely together and are intimate in confessing details of their lives and family histories, as seen for example between the narrator and Edward Derby in "The Thing on the Doorstep" or Frank Marsh and Denis de Russy in "The Mound," may give the impression of an implicit homosexual subtext. This is a subjective interpretation and usually considered along the same lines as considering Lovecraft himself a closeted or latent homosexual, despite his negative views toward homosexuals as noted earlier; but it is considered here for completeness.

On the surface, the friendships between Lovecraft's male characters appear chaste and platonic, harkening to similar literary same-sex friendships and partnerships that Lovecraft was aware of and would have drawn from, notably Phillipps and Dyson, Arthur Machen's pseudo-detectives from *The Three Impostors*, "The Shining Pyramid" (1895), and "The Red Hand" (1895), and Sir Arthur Conan Doyle's Sherlock Holmes and Dr. Watson—and from Lovecraft's many own long and non-sexual friendships with men. That some of his friends were themselves homosexuals does not detract from this interpretation. Bruce Lord suggests that this may be an angle by which to interpret Lovecraft's fiction:

While I do not subscribe to the theory proposed (too reductively) by some that Lovecraft was a repressed homosexual, (I find viewing Lovecraft to be simply asexual more accurate) Lovecraft's apparent (and likely subconscious) tolerance for homosexuality presents some interesting possibilities.

Whether or not they have a conscious or subconscious homosexual context, the interpretation of some stories of the Lovecraft Mythos as allegorical to homosexual experience is valid and worthy of consideration, as Robert M. Price did in his article "Homosexual Panic in 'The Outsider.'" Consider a simple allegorical interpretation of "The Shadow over Innsmouth" as a journey of self-discovery for a closeted homosexual, exposed for the first time to a homosexual community fearful of persecution, asserting his heterosexuality by exposing them, and then discovering and finally embracing his own sexuality. Of course, a more negative reading of the same story may combine it with suggestions of sexually transmitted disease and degeneration. The inspiration for a homosexual interpretation of this sort was suggested by a footnote in Price's "Homosexual Panic" article.

Several stories in the Lovecraft Mythos can be similarly interpreted in this manner, such as "The Loved Dead" (replacing homosexuality with necrophilia). For completeness I should mention "The Trap" (1931), written by Henry S. Whitehead and revised by Lovecraft. An unorthodox reading of this tale may suggest a homoerotic subtext in the close relationship between a schoolboy and his male teacher, and the image and associated sensations given for penetrating to the other side of the mirror as a metaphor for anal sex. This reading may partially be due to rumors that Whitehead was a homosexual.

In later Mythos fiction, the close non-sexual friendship between male characters has become reinterpreted, sometimes by making one character female, as in Pugmire's "Some Distant Baying Sound" (2009) or the comic *The Chronicles of Dr. Herbert West* (2008), and other times by making one or both characters homosexual—explicitly so, in the case of Mythos-based erotica.

3. Sex and the Cthulhu Mythos

The Cthulhu Mythos extends beyond Lovecraft's fiction. It begins properly with Lovecraft's friends, co-creators, and collaborators such as Robert E. Howard, Clark Ashton Smith, August Derleth, and Robert Bloch, who shared their fictional deities, monsters, tomes, and locations among one another. Later authors would borrow from their Cthulhu Mythos stories when writing their own works or seek to create sequels, prequels, pastiches, and homages to continue the stories written by Lovecraft and his friends. The Cthulhu Mythos, beyond the control of any individual or single ethos, would in time expand far beyond the limits of Lovecraft's approach to sex, broaching into such territory as female protagonists, realistic sexual and romantic human relationships, erotic literature, and pornography.

Fritz Leiber described Lovecraft as a "transition-writer" who did service for horror and speculative fiction as other transition-writers "between the stories observing all sexual taboos and the stories observing none" (*LR* 478). While the prudish Lovecraft never threw out all sexual norms, he did write or have a hand in stories explicitly or implicitly discarding some of them—bestiality ("Facts concerning the Late Arthur Jermyn and His Family"), eugenics/selective breeding programs ("The Rats in the Walls," "The Mound"), incest ("The Lurking Fear"), interbreeding or miscegenation ("The Shadow over Innsmouth"), necrophilia ("The Loved Dead"), polyamory/polygamy ("The Mound"), and rape ("The Curse of Yig"). As restrained as his depictions may have been, they did provide the taboo-breaking starting points that allowed other authors to go beyond Lovecraft, to create new fiction and ideas.

The scope of the Cthulhu Mythos is so vast that only a representative fraction can be addressed here. In light of that, this chapter will be something of an inverse format to the preceding chapter: it begins with a summary and discussion of some of the novel themes that have developed in the Cthulhu Mythos, followed by a survey of the key works and authors for the development of the Mythos in terms of love, sex, and gender, both in terms of specific authors like Ramsey Campbell, Brian McNaughton, and Edward Lee and in terms of seminal anthologies such as *Eldritch Blue* (2004), *Horror Between the Sheets* (2005), and *Cthulhurotica* (2010) that express the continued development of this subset of Cthulhu Mythos literature.

New Developments

> No matter how a creator's journey into the world of Lovecraftian eroticism began, there are a myriad of reasons for entering it willingly: the attraction of the forbidden, the delightfully creepy atmosphere that lends itself well to rule breaking and sexual encounters, plausible deniability and the option to avoid personal responsibility, or just a need to face the ultimate challenge. (Cuinn 311)

Writers in the Cthulhu Mythos have not been constrained by Lovecraft's self-imposed limitations in describing sex, sexuality, gender, women, and relationships. However, early authors contemporary with Lovecraft were also not entirely free to develop their own approaches. Weird fiction venues were restricted, and there was a limit to how much sexuality was tolerable in *Weird Tales* under Farnsworth Wright, who would permit Mrs. Brundage's nudes on the covers but rejected tales like Clark Ashton Smith's "The Witchcraft of Ulua." Likewise, Arkham House under August Derleth exercised at least some editorial censorship over the Mythos works published there. Even so, Lovecraft's moral limitations or artistic sensibilities were not always shared by his contemporaries. The fiction of Robert E. Howard, Clark Ashton Smith, Robert Bloch, and other original contributors to the interconnected fiction that would become the Cthulhu Mythos is less restrained in many cases, depicting a much wider range of characters, characterization, and interaction than in the Lovecraft Mythos. Sexually explicit Cthulhu Mythos fiction came about somewhat later, with notable material appearing in the mid-1960s, a generation or so after Lovecraft's death.

The timing is probably not coincidental. Children who had first encountered the Mythos from *Weird Tales* and Arkham House in the 1940s and '50s would be reaching adolescence and adulthood in the 1960s and '70s. As with comic books, pop music, and other media, the Cthulhu Mythos would experience cycles of rediscovery and reinvention as writers and creators attempted to update, analyze, and in some cases sexualize their childhood.

3. Sex and The Cthulhu Mythos

Sex was an area with great potential for new Cthulhu Mythos authors specifically because Lovecraft and his contemporaries did not, or could not, write such stories in their own time. Whether or not there was an audience for such fiction, there were few if any publishers that would take them. *Weird Tales* remained the primary market for weird fiction until the 1950s, and aside from the nudes on the covers the contents were generally very tepid; the Spicy magazines simply did not extend to weird fiction at all—*Spicy Mystery Stories* declined Clark Ashton Smith's "Mother of Toads," and Smith was forced to expurgate the story to get it into *Weird Tales*. As a forbidden area that had seen practically no development, authors looking to create new and original Mythos fiction were free to develop material in this direction without fear of retreading old ground. The sexual implications Lovecraft included in the Lovecraft Mythos—the negative space left to the imagination by the impregnation of Lavinia Whateley in "The Dunwich Horror," for example—would later be revisited by many authors who chose to elaborate on the undeveloped or unspoken elements in the plot: How had the cosmic sex act occurred? What if Lavinia Whateley had triplets, instead of twins? What if Mamie Bishop had also consorted with Yog-Sothoth? What if old Wizard Whateley was possessed by or stood in for Yog-Sothoth, and impregnated his daughter incestuously? These questions and many more were asked and answered in later Cthulhu Mythos fiction, based on what Lovecraft wrote, but also on what Lovecraft deliberately did not write; not just the unanswered questions, but the unasked.

Michel Houellebecq once wrote concerning the addition of erotic elements to the Mythos:

> There are indeed those who have tried to introduce erotic elements into the framework of a primarily Lovecraftian tale. The results have been absolute failures. Colin Wilson's attempts in particular tend clearly toward catastrophe; there is a constant feeling that the titillating elements have been added merely to draw in a few additional readers. And in truth it cannot be otherwise. The combination is intrinsically impossible. (59)

This is probably the unvoiced opinion of many Lovecraft scholars, but I would argue against it. Sex and the Cthulhu Mythos is, as I hoped to show in the preceding chapter, not an "intrinsically impossible" combination, but a significant part of the Lovecraft Mythos, open to other writers to explore and develop. Certainly there is no inherent contradiction in the usage of sexual and erotic elements in horror or weird fiction; Bram Stoker's *Dracula* (1897) and the image of the sexually seductive vampire it helped spawn is probably the premier example to prove such a point. The question is whether there can be a story that is truly Lovecraftian that is also sexually aware or explicit—and I believe such stories exist, such as Ramsey Campbell's "Cold Print" (1969).

As the Cthulhu Mythos expanded and developed, certain common themes and ideas emerged and gained general prominence in the collective consciousness of readers and fans, and a subset of these is specifically applicable or customary to the more mature and adult Cthulhu Mythos tales. A brief examination of some of these themes is beneficial before addressing a survey of sex and the Mythos.

Family Trees of the Gods

The artificial mythology of the Lovecraft Mythos differs substantially from the classical and Christian mythologies with which Lovecraft was familiar. Lovecraft offers very few descriptions on how the separate beings and races relate to one another, and aside from "The Dunwich Horror," "The Curse of Yig," and *The Dream-Quest of Unknown Kadath* there are no instances of a named entity dallying with mortals in the manner of Zeus. In his lifetime Lovecraft never published an official genealogy of the Mythos entities he created or incorporated in his stories, but the spare outlines of some such relationships were in place. In his letters, Lovecraft did publish a few genealogies and relationships of the gods, always in a jesting manner, such as when he wrote:

> Yog-Sothoth's wife is the hellish cloud-like entity Shub-Niggurath, in whose honour nameless cults hold the rote of the Goat with a Thousand Young. By her he has two monstrous offspring—the evil twins Nug and Yeb. He has also begotten hellish hybrids upon the females of various organic species throughout the universes of space-time (cf *The Dunwich Horror*). (SL 5.303)

Lovecraft also gave a fanciful genealogy showing how both Clark Ashton Smith and himself were descended from Azathoth by means of Shub-Niggurath and Yog-Sothoth's twins Nug and Yeb—Lovecraft of course included both Cthulhu and Nyarlathotep in his ancestry, while for Smith he drew a line from Tsathoggua (SL 4.183).

Other authors writing in the Mythos seized upon familial relationships as a means of both expanding on existing entities and incorporating their own original creations into the sparse framework of the Lovecraft Mythos.

Following their own muses, authors like Clark Ashton Smith, August Derleth, Lin Carter, and Brian Lumley would draw up their own "Family Tree of the Gods" or in their stories create familial relationships explaining the origins or generations of Azathoth, Cthulhu, Tsathoggua, Yog-Sothoth, and their spawn. Of course, this meant that in at least some cases Mythos entities were cast as sexual entities, and even assigned genders and mates. The full effect of following different authors' individual takes on the genealogies of Mythos entities through their stories results in a massive, sometimes contradictory, and often slightly ridiculous chart not unlike those produced by mapping the divine genealogy of the Greco-Roman family trees or, for a more contemporary parallel, the literary mashup of Philip José Farmer's Wold Newton family from *Tarzan Alive* (1972) and *Doc Savage: His Apocalyptic Life* (1973). If we accept certain of these familial relations as fact—for example, Wilbur Whateley's direct descent from Yog-Sothoth makes him the several-times great-uncle of Tsathoggua—we can see how silly and confusing such genealogical efforts tend to be!

Lovecraft also chose not to provide extended family trees of the degenerate and miscegenated families that populated his fiction, and later authors also seized on this unrealized potential to hang their plots and characters. The Lovecraft Mythos generally concerns unbranching lines of lineal descent such as the Jermyns, or a single branch of a more sprawling family tree, such as the Whateleys in "The Dunwich Horror" and the Marsh family in "The Shadow over Innsmouth." Later writers would add their own scions of Lovecraft's tainted families, innumerable Whateley, Bishop, and Marsh cousins, uncles, and grandnephews, and nieces cropping up out of the literary woodwork. A few cases such as August Derleth's "The Shuttered Room" (1959) even combine the disparate families with intermarriages—possibly encouraged by Ephraim Waite's Innsmouth wife from "The Thing on the Doorstep." Less often, Lovecraft's insular, degenerate, and sometimes tainted or inbred clans would also serve as the basis and inspiration for similar families in the works of other authors. In many cases, the family trees are as much a matter of narrative practicality as a desire to impose order on the Mythos. By creating relationships between Mythos entities and characters, writers could more easily place their own creations with respect to the existing Mythos—building off of the work of Lovecraft, his peers, and their followers, adding on to existing work as Clark Ashton Smith, Frank Belknap Long, and Robert E. Howard had done.

Some of the greatest points of interest for many authors and fans are the individuals who represent intersections between the sprawling but mostly human family trees of the Whateley and Marsh families and the cosmic genealogies of Mythos entities. In the Cthulhu Mythos, Wilbur Whateley and his unnamed twin were not unique in their generation, but serve as a template for later writers in the Cthulhu Mythos to revisit and reuse in their own original stories, and as a baseline to explore other pairings duplicating the roles of Yog-Sothoth and Lavinia Whateley. The revelation of familial heritage key to Lovecraft Mythos tales like "The Rats in the Walls" and "The Shadow over Innsmouth" would recur often, with as much or more attention paid to the participants as to the offspring. In particular, there has been a tradition of Mythos stories featuring cosmic miscegenation starting at least with Machen's "The Great God Pan" (1890), Lovecraft's "The Dunwich Horror" (1928), and Clark Ashton Smith's "The Nameless Offspring" (1932).

Naming the Unnamable

Cthulhu Mythos fiction is transgressive by nature, ignoring or breaking the boundaries and conventions of literary genre, physical law, human culture, and sexual taboo. Violation has tremendous effect on readers, both to attract and repulse, but simple shock value loses power with repetition. To most contemporary readers Machen's "The Great God Pan" and Eddy and Lovecraft's "The Loved Dead" are not obscene, but tame and quaint, if not actually hokey. This is part of the reason so many pastiches of Lovecraft fail: formulaic fiction reduces its impact, just as repeated viewings of the same pornography tends to lessen arousal. Sexually explicit Cthulhu Mythos stories draw some of their attraction and interest from introducing new and more extreme taboo violations to a jaded audience: the very combination of sexually explicit material with Mythos horror represents an effort to stir interest by engaging the reader with a different approach.

In both pornography and literature, crude depiction for its own sake is almost meaningless and has very little lasting impact. Devoid of context, plot, and some skill with words, rote description of a sexually fetishized Cthulhu Mythos falls flat once the novelty of reading about yet another human raped by a Great Old One wears off. Fortunately, these kind of stories appear to be in the minority, but many of the same basic sexual ideas—sex with Mythos entities (often but not always nonconsensual), impregnation by Mythos entities, sexual fulfillment beyond normal human limits—recur often. For many authors the idea of combining sex and the Cthulhu Mythos still appears to be the crux and driving motivation behind a story, rather than a necessity of the plot and action in the story. In such Cthulhu Mythos media the result is often little better than Mythos-flavored pornography or erotic horror literature. Conversely, stories where sexual and Mythos material both serve the story and are appropriate to the plot are arguably some of the best, most mature work in the Cthulhu Mythos oeuvre.

If the general absence of sex in the Lovecraft Mythos left room for later authors to add on to the Mythos, much the same conceptual elbow-room exists with regard to women, gender, love, and human relationships as well, and the number of stories featuring female characters, romantic elements, etc. has risen along with those depicting sexual elements. The acceptance of sexually explicit material is not a prerequisite for a Cthulhu Mythos story addressing such themes. Lovecraft managed a gender-bending story in "The Thing on the Doorstep" without actually addressing the issue of whether Asenath and Edward ever had sex. But the very fact that he did not address it at all in the story has become one of the major factors of criticism for that story: because it was not talked about, sex became glaring in its absence to many readers as they worked through the potential implications. Such unspoken currents in a narrative are often beneficial, if done correctly, allowing readers to fill in the details from their own imagination—and if they are writers, that is exactly what they can do with their own Cthulhu Mythos stories.

The *Necronomicon* as Pornography

> A few volumes were illustrated pornographic works of a quite spectacular character, exploring depths of perversion I had never even imagined. Into the flames they went. (Price 2008, 6)

> Doris didn't like the *Necronomicon*, although she considered herself an emancipated and free-thinking young woman. There was something sinister, or to be downright honest about it *perverted* about that book—and not in a nice, exciting way, but in a sick and frightening way. All those strange illustrations, always with five-sided borders just like the Pentagon in Washington, but with those people inside doing those freaky sex acts with other creatures who weren't people at all. (Shea & Wilson 94)

Given the parallels between Mythos literature and pornography as forbidden, censored literature, it makes sense that at some point Mythos literature would be mixed in with the likewise forbidden erotic works, and in time literally become pornography—the occult content sexualized, the Lovecraftian contents made sexually explicit in text or illustration. In the earliest examples, the occult literature simply shared space on the bookshelf with other forbidden works—but forbidden for different reasons. As Peter Tupper noted:

> You couldn't just walk into a store and buy a copy of de Sade's *120 Days of Sodom* or Burton's *Arabian Nights* or *Kama Sutra*. You had to know a guy who knew a guy, and just to lay hands on such a book, to possess such rare sexual knowledge was an initiatory, transformative experience. Lovecraft's library of fictional, sanity-altering books comes from the same ideas. He was writing at the tail end of that historical period when knowledge could be kept hoarded by an elite of white, upper-middle class men, before mass literacy and cheap printing made that kind of control impossible. Nowadays, if the *Necronomicon* did exist, it would probably have been scanned and circulated all over the Internet. ("HP Lovecraft, erotica, and why they actually go together")

In Clark Ashton Smith's "The End of the Story" (1930), the hidden works of the monastery library include "the somewhat infamous *Histoire d'Amour*, by Bernard de Vaillantcoeur, which was destroyed immediately upon publication, and of which only one other copy is known to exist" (CF 1.23). Robert E. Howard's "The Children of the Night" (1931) depicts a similar library where *Nameless Cults* is shelved next to the Mandrake Press edition of Boccaccio (either *Amorous Fiammetta* [1929] or else *Ten Tales from the Decamaron* [1930]). Robert M. Price has pornographic works in the same pile to be burned with the *Book of Iod* and the *R'lyeh Text* in "Beneath the Tombstone" (1984), and in "A Thousand Young" (1989) the *Cultes des Goules* shares shelf space with the Marquis de Sade's *One Hundred and Twenty Days of Sodom* (1785). However, the connection and confusion between Mythos and pornographic literature is most clearly expressed in Ramsey Campbell's "Cold Print" (1969), where a seeker after certain rarified erotica unwittingly stumbles across the *Revelations of Glaaki* instead.

From being classed as forbidden works alongside pornography, Mythos tomes were sometimes also intermixed or infused with a sexual element—the Mythos volumes that contain love-spells or erotic illustrations as well or as part of their occult contents. This is first notable in Robert Bloch's "Philtre Tip" (1961), where a professor writing a dry academic text on an exciting topic, *Aphrodisia, A Study of Erotic Stimuli Through the Ages*, includes a recipe from von Junzt of *Nameless Cults* fame; another example in this development is when Ramsey Campbell introduces *Witchcraft in England* in "The Faces at Pine Dunes" (1980) with naked witches dancing on the cover, and in many of the pages. Of course, there is a degree of truth in these depictions: many real-world occult works did feature love magic of some sort, but the idea that a book of Mythos lore might contain prurient as well as cosmically horrific content is a middle ground leading to the depiction of Mythos books as principally pornographic in and of themselves.

Part of the appeal of Mythos tomes is their verisimilitude: the scholarly histories devoted to them, the academic debate over the etymologies of their titles, and the way the title suggests the often unseen contents. Sexualized Mythos works sometimes reflect the same penchant, for while the titles are often suggestive or explicit and often puns on established Mythos tomes or stories, the same appeal remains. For example, in *The Pornomicon* (2005) Logan makes an effort to provide an etymology for his fictitious volume: "Pornomicon . . . derived from the Greek Word 'Porne', meaning prostitute. But the word on the whole means nothing to me" (Logan 5). Caitlín R. Kiernan makes use of the same root when she recasts Lovecraft's Pnakotic Manuscripts as "the fabled *Pornographies of Pnakotus*," recalling when the term "pornography" originally referred to an academic treatise or history of prostitution (Kiernan 2007, 28).

The actual depiction of Mythos tomes as pornography, rather than sitting next to erotica on the bookshelf, is more common in erotic fiction and is particularly prevalent in adult comics and graphic novels that can actually include depictions of pages, scenes, and other material from the pornographic Mythos tome. For example, a page from the *Necronomicon* is included in *The Convent of Hell* (1997) by Barreiro and Noé, showing a passage of script above an image of phallus-headed tentacle, and *The Pornomicon* is based on a homoerotic variation of the *Necronomicon* with some passages and pages depicted.

In some cases, the *Necronomicon* or similar Mythos tome is not simply a prop in the story but a character in its own right, with its own purpose and power—and in this case too, a Mythos book may take on elements of pornography. For example, in Kiernan's "The Perils of Liberated Objects, or, The Voyeur's Seduction" (2009) the Mythos tome reflects the subconscious desires of its owner as erotic and horrific imagery.

Body Horror

There is an element of horror in the physical alteration of the human body, and a fascination that accompanies such changes. Humans undergo many such transformations, some rapid—the stiffening of the normally flaccid penis or the erection of the nipple during sexual arousal—and some relatively slow and gradual, such as the onset of puberty or the stages of pregnancy. These are explicitly sexual and natural examples, and body horror takes part of its attraction not only from the transgression of the human form but from the violation of sexual taboos, sometimes enhancing or subverting natural processes to arrive at distinctly unnatural and inhuman results. The result is not terribly dissimilar to the human marvels and oddities of yesteryear's carnivals, the "freaks" and sideshow performers whose strange anatomies thrilled crowds with the variety of the human form. If not handled with care, however, the plausibility of terrible growths and transformations does not quicken the pulse of the reader, but becomes a farcical exercise; the horror is lost as the sheer implausibility of the entity or events becomes comical.

Body horror is not solely about the actual transformation of the human form by mundane or supernatural means; it is also concerned with the psychological effects on the characters, how they react to the change that has taken place or that may still be taking place, and how their perception of themselves changes in response to the changes in their body. In popular horror, the transitions involved are usually based on some external force—the vampire's victim dies and rises from the grave as a vampire, the victim of a werewolf is scratched and on the full moon becomes a werewolf. These "contagious" monsters are mostly absent from the Lovecraft Mythos, where bodily horrors are almost always inherent (often inherited), irreversible, and insurmountable unless the victim chooses suicide (as Arthur Jermyn does, and the protagonist in "The Shadow over Innsmouth" almost does), or embraces their inhumanity (as Wilbur Whateley does, and the protagonist in "The Shadow over Innsmouth" ultimately does). The hardline biological determinism of Lovecraft is not present in the entire Cthulhu Mythos, but is a starting point that many authors make use of.

Lovecraft Mythos stories that deal with physical degeneration or transformation are accompanied with mental and perceptual changes, often with the character incompletely aware of the changes their body undergoes; in the Cthulhu Mythos these transformations are usually given greater attention, detail, and elaboration—sometimes to the point of fetishization, attaining a sexual element even if it does not involve any genitalia or secondary sexual characteristics. As the body of Cthulhu Mythos literature has developed, several common body horror themes have become widespread, most notably pregnancy.

Pregnancy

> The most common use of love & sex in Mythos stories is procreation, but as we have seen this is potentially more complex than simple sex. Even the rape of a human by an Outré Being is more involved than simply the physical violation. And the complexity increases when the story moves away from procreation to examine the impact of the Mythos on social and interpersonal interaction. (O'Brien 306)

The understanding of procreation as the purpose or consequence of sex has been with mankind throughout history, and while sex is never featured explicitly on the page in the Lovecraft Mythos, the sexual action in the stories is mainly concerned with procreation rather than recreation. We as readers will never know if Yog-Sothoth lusted after Lavinia Whateley (or vice versa) in any conventional sense or the method of their intercourse, but we see the result of their pairing in the offspring they produced. Of the pregnancies in Lovecraft we know almost nothing, save that at least in Lavinia Whateley's case it appeared to be exactly the traditional nine months. Writers after Lovecraft do not limit themselves in that regard, and so pregnancy becomes prominent and more common—sometimes the impregnation is the incident of rape by a Mythos entity as in "The Curse of Yig" or "Novel of the Black Seal," other times it is an intentional result of some act, as in "The Dunwich Horror" or "The Shadow over Innsmouth." Some Mythos "pregnancies" are completely unconventional, more akin to parasitism or violating known biology and genetics.

The horrors of gestation are terrible and traumatic to women, and many different aspects of impregnation, pregnancy, and birth have their own attendant sexual fetishes. There is the act of impregnation, almost always synonymous with sex, which is a violation of the (almost always female) person to the greatest degree; like sexual disease and damage to the genitalia, pregnancy is one of the life-altering and enduring personal physical possibilities of sex, particularly unwilling sex in the case of rape. As the fetus or fetuses (or eggs, pods, seeds, parasites, etc.) grow and the pregnancy progresses, the would-be mother or parent is forced to come to terms with all the symptoms of her pregnancy, the physical alterations of her body and behavior (pregnancy sickness, strange food cravings, spreading hips, growing belly, swelling and lactating breasts, darkening nipples, etc.)—and more, since with the gestation of a hybrid or alien entity, the difficulties of the pregnancy are often heightened or strange. Finally, there is the act of birth—not simply a danger to the potential parent, but the point in time where he or she must come face to face with the result of their labors. The birth itself is often as sexualized and violating an experience as the insemination, a climactic re-enactment of the sexual act as the new life comes forth from the womb or body.

Pregnancy in the Cthulhu Mythos is not always violent and sexualized, but the increased occurrence and description of impregnation and pregnancy is part of the increased awareness and admissibility of sex in Cthulhu Mythos literature as a whole. Impregnation is more often a motivation for characters and entities in the Mythos, a goal toward which they work for their own reasons—following a biological imperative to breed, in the example of the Deep Ones of "The Shadow over Innsmouth," or so that the hybrid spawn can serve them in some way that they cannot, as Wilbur Whateley was to have done in "The Dunwich Horror." As such, pregnancy is also a possible consequence for characters involved with the Mythos. Lovecraft ended many tales with a parting revelation of some terrible truth that the narrator had refrained from saying for the entire duration of the story; in the post-Lovecraft Cthulhu Mythos the parting revelation may as likely as not be that a certain character is pregnant—potentially with the spawn of a Mythos entity. A good example of such an ending can be found in Edward Lee's *The Innswich Horror* (2010) or M. L. Carter's "Prey of the Goat" (1994).

The Tentacle as a Sexual Symbol

Sexual symbolism in the Lovecraft Mythos has already been discussed briefly; later authors expanded on those symbols they perceived, developing them in their own stories. The proliferation of the tentacle as sexual symbol in Mythos stories and media has gone hand-in-hand with the proliferation of Mythos entities as both tentacled and sexual beings. The sexual objectification of the tentacle and tentacled entities largely predates the Lovecraft and Cthulhu Mythos; the main interest with regard to this essay is how the Mythos fits into the history and development of tentacles in a sexual manner. For the purposes of this section, "tentacle" includes vines, pseudopods, and any other prehensile appendage.

There are essentially two main categories of sexual use of the tentacle in general media: the tentacle as a prehensile tool to engage in bondage play, groping, and frottage; and the tentacle as a phallic symbol and often an actual genital organ used by an inhuman entity, either as an aspect of alien anatomy or when an actual penis cannot be depicted, used to penetrate a character in a sexual way or for a sexual purpose. A third, far less common usage involves the suckers present on cephalopod arms, which are sometimes used as a surrogate for oral play, to kiss and suckle at the flesh, and in some cases to cause characteristic wounds and scars. Suckers and the concurrent sucker-play appears to have become less common as the tentacles drifted away from their biological roots in literary and artistic depictions, and as the tentacles themselves typically became more stylized. In some cases suckers and their sexual function were replaced by an actual mouth or other orifice on the tentacle. Penetration typically follows the standard methods for phalluses: anal, oral, and vaginal. However, at least a few cases of Mythos fiction such as *The Dunwich Romance* (2011) and "Ink" by Bernie Mojzes (2011) include male and female urethral penetration by small tentacles. The best summary I've ever found of the literary utility of tentacle is sex in the chapter "Tits and Tentacles" from *The Erotic Anime Movie Guide* (1998):

> The visual grammar permitted by the tentacle is extremely useful to the pornographer. With no restriction on length, it permits penetration without blocking the view. It can also be used as a form of restraint, permitting multiple penetration, sexualised bondage and ease of access. Best of all for the tentacle as a pornographic device, while it may often look suspiciously like a penis, to the extent of possessing a foreskin or glans, or even ejaculating upon climax, it is not a sexual organ by definition. (McCarthy and Clements 58)

Consider this against China Miéville's argument in "M. R. James and the Quantum Vampire" (2008):

> A Weird tentacle does not 'mean' the Phallus [. . .] Which is why, despite the seeming isomorphism of interests and recent inevitable cross-fertilisation, *haute* Weird is radically opposed to the sub-genre of pornographic 'hentai' manga and anime known as 'tentacle rape'.

Miéville has a half a point: the idea of the tentacle as a literal phallic object for performing real or simulated coitus came after Lovecraft, and was primarily the invention of Toshio Maeda in the 1980s to skirt censorship in Japan. However, to say that the concept of tentacle-as-phallus was entirely absent from weird fiction is erroneous. Consider the toothy tentacle that literally takes the place of Wilbur Whateley's penis in "The Dunwich Horror."

The earliest examples of the erotic in tentacle art and literature emphasize the grasping/bondage play, while the penetrative aspect is a much later development. In current depictions, the first two different aspects are often combined, so that a single entity with multiple tentacles can hold/fondle a single subject and penetrate it, sometimes in more than one orifice at the same time.

In Japan, the tradition of sexualized tentacled entities is often traced back to the period of *Tako to ama* (1814; *Diver and Two Octopi*, popularly known as *The Dream of the Fisherman's Wife*, *The Image of Tamamori*, etc.), an infamous erotic woodcut executed by the famed Japanese artist Katsushika Hokusai (who was by coincidence a favorite of Lovecraft's, though Lovecraft is not known to have ever seen *Tako to ama*) and based on a work by his master, Katsukawa Shunshō; similar erotic depictions were made by other artists of the era, analogous to European popular erotic depictions of "Leda and the Swan" in depicting a mythical scene for prurient interests. For a more in-depth examination, see Danielle Talerico's "Interpreting Sexual Imagery in Japanese Prints: A Fresh Approach to Hokusai's Diver and Two Octopi" in *Impressions: The Journal of the Ukiyo-e Society of America* 23 (2001), and Ricard Bru's "Tentacles of Love and Death: From Hokusai to Picasso" in *Secret Images of Picasso and the Japanese Erotic Print* (2010).

Hokusai did not invent this erotic scene, but his image is the most popular, widely known, and influential such work. *Ukiyo-e* prints by Hokusai and other Japanese artists became immensely popular in Europe and inspired the influential *Japonisme* style. Among the many influenced by Japonisme and Japanese print artists such as Hokusai was Aubrey Beardsley, the famous illustrator of the *Yellow Book* magazine and the first edition of Arthur Machen's *The Great God Pan and The Inmost Light* (1894). For more, see Linda Gertner Zatlin's *Beardsley, Japonisme, and the Perversion of the Victorian Ideal* (1997). The enduring and widespread popularity of Hokusai's erotic woodcut is in part one of the reasons it is cited as an example for a tradition of tentacle erotica in Japanese art, though contemporary usage of tentacles differs greatly from Hokusai's era.

The introduction of *ukiyo-e* to Europe was coincidental with the introduction of popular novels prominently featuring giant octopuses, squids, and krakens by Victor Hugo's *Les Travailleurs de la mer* (*The Toilers of the Sea*, 1866) and Jules Verne's *Twenty Thousand Leagues under the Sea* (1870), a similarity of theme that was noted in a review of Hugo's novel (Bru 56-58). These stories drew upon and expanded the Western sea story tradition and the kraken legend as exemplified in Lord Tennyson's poem "The Kraken" (1830), which has been noted as a possible influence on or inspiration for "The Call of Cthulhu" and Cthulhu in particular, notably by Will Murray in "The Dunwich Chimera and Others" (1984), T. S. Miller in "From Bodily Fear to Cosmic Horror (and Back Again): The Tentacle Monster from Primordial Chaos to Hello Cthulhu" (2011), and G. W. Thomas in "Writing the Mythos: A Lesson in Squidgy History" (2011).

Around the end of the century emerged Western artworks that appeared inspired or at least influenced by Hokusai's pearl-diver and octopodes. Famous Decadent artist Félicien Rops's painting *La Pieuvre* ("The Octopus," c. 1880), for example, contains a woman being attacked and sexually penetrated by the tentacles of an octopus, and the latter theme is also portrayed in Fernand Khnopff's frontispiece for *Istar* (1888), a novel by occultist Joséphin Péladan. In "Tentacles of Love and Death: From Hokusai to Picasso" it is noted:

> In France at the end of the nineteenth century, the octopus could be both an erotic and a malevolent creature, and so manifested a dual symbolic existence fully in tune with *fin de siècle* aesthetic movements in art and literature. [. . .] The octopus also had both erotic and frightening connotations during the Edo period. A number of engravings show the beast as a source of terror, with giant anthropomorphic octopuses attacking people, such as those appearing in Hokusai's manga volumes which were so popular in Europe at the end of the 19th century. (Bru 62)

The image of the woman-and-octopus would reappear throughout the period in Decadent works, and with the continued circulation of Japanese prints would influence many later artists and writers. For example, the Belgian 1906 edition of H. G. Wells's *The War of the Worlds* (1898) was illustrated with *The Martian Claims a Victim* (1906) by Henri Alvin-Corrêa, which depicts a tentacled, octopodesque Martian clutching a nude female victim. Likewise the weird art of Clark Ashton Smith, which was much admired by H. P. Lovecraft and Samuel Loveman, reflects a conscious influence from the Japanese and those influenced by the Japanese prints, as revealed in a letter from Smith to Samuel Loveman dated 9 August 1915: "I care very little for the elaborate realism of Western art, anyway, and shall base my manner more on that of the Japanese . . . I confess that I care more for the drawings of Beardsley and Dore than for anything else in Occidental art" (Smith 1973, 4). Reproductions and descriptions of Smith's art in *The Fantastic Art of Clark Ashton Smith* (1973) and *Grotesques and Fantastiques* (1973) reveal the use of tentacles in depicting several of his aliens and Mythos entities, though not in any kind of erotic context.

Tentacles also appeared in the occasional monster or strange figure in early weird tales such as M. R. James's "The Treasure of Abbot Thomas" and "Count Magnus" in *Ghost-Stories of an Antiquary* (1904), and Arthur Machen's "Novel of the Black Seal" (1895). The literary depictions are mostly devoid of sexual content (a poetic exception is A. C. Hilton's "The Octopus" [1872], which in a comedic parody of Swinburne presents the deathly embrace and "kiss" of an octopus in terms of a lover), but in the context of the artistic atmosphere at the time they were produced may have had an underlying subtext of sex and horror. Other examples of Western artwork that combined tentacles with sexuality include Gustav Klimpt's *Jurisprudence* (1903) for his series of University of Vienna Ceiling paintings, and Pablo Picasso's *Erotic Drawing: Woman and Octopus* (1903).

At the very least Machen and James's tentacles represent pre-sexual steps in the development and use of tentacles in weird fiction, and served as inspiration for later authors like Lovecraft and Clark Ashton Smith. Indeed, "Novel of the Black Seal" may be the most immediate source for tentacles in Lovecraftian fiction, from this line: "Something pushed out from the body there on the floor, and stretched forth, a slimy, wavering tentacle, across the room, grasped the bust upon the cupboard, and laid it down on my desk" (Machen 2001, 173). The parodist Arthur A. Sykes recognized this aspect of Machen's fiction when he wrote "The Great Pan-Daemon" (1897): "He-she-it transfixed me with a lurid leer, with a cobra-glance of quenchless lubricity, and the octopus-tentacles of a noisesome lust-fury wound themselves round my very soul" (Locke 44).

The most important appearance of images featuring tentacles in a sexual context or as subtext in the West probably began with the lurid pulp covers. Octopodes appeared in sailor/ocean fiction, science fiction, and fantasy pulp magazines such as *Argosy* (1882–1978), *Amazing Stories* (1926–

2005), and *Weird Tales* (1923-54)—in fact, the cover for the inaugural issue is an example of this trope. The majority of pulp covers of course did not feature either shapely women or tentacles, but the individual elements— scantily clad, half-naked, or naked men or women and tentacles, feelers, pseudopods, etc.—were featured separately with some frequency, and in a few cases they came together to show women threatened by or enwrapped in tentacles or tentacled entities, either by natural cephalopods, the tentacle-like bodies of snakes and such or, more commonly in the fantasy and scientifiction pulps, the tentacles of bug-eyed aliens, monsters, and robots—possibly to emphasize their alien nature to humanity and the human form, possibly as a convenient source of bondage instead of rope.

Females in bondage (tied up, handcuffed, gagged, etc.) were a staple of pulp magazines and Golden Age comic books like *Sensation Comics* and *Wonder Woman* before World War II, and later the covers and contents of exploitative fiction novels. The sexual impact of such images and stories is beyond the scope of this essay, though interested readers might start with Jean Gregorak's "Horror Is What a Girl Would Feel: Narrative Erotics in Depression-Era Pulp Fiction" in *Delights, Desires, and Dilemmas: Essays on Women and the Media* (1998). Women enwrapped by a python, elephant proboscis, or alien tentacle might be considered a subset or extension of this sort of pulp art.

It is difficult to say exactly how and when the Cthulhu Mythos became associated with tentacles. Lovecraft, Clark Ashton Smith, Robert E. Howard et al. certainly employed them in their fiction, but they were employing an element already used by Wells, James, Machen, etc., and the use of tentacled entities is not exclusive to Mythos fiction during the period. A large part of the association is probably due to the fact that Lovecraft, as the primogenitor of the Mythos, had several of his most prominent inhuman entities sport tentacles, feelers, or similar appendages, including the unclothed Wilbur Whateley of "The Dunwich Horror"; Rhan-Tegoth of "The Horror in the Museum" (1932) with its "dense growth of dark, slender tentacles or sucking filaments" (MC 162); and of course, the "pulpy, tentacled head" of Cthulhu from "The Call of Cthulhu" who would go on to become the essential mascot of the Mythos, with his octopoid spawn mentioned briefly in *At the Mountains of Madness* (CC 141) and "The Shadow out of Time." Any and all of these uses by Lovecraft may have inspired the general trend of using tentacles in contemporary and later Mythos fiction, or associating the Mythos with tentacled monsters. After

Lovecraft's death, August Derleth for his part regularly used the image of tentacles and octopoid-headed entities in his Mythos fiction and probably contributed to making tentacles a regular and recurring element of Mythos entities makeup.

Tentacled beings continued to be developed outside of Mythos fiction at the same time and in the same venues, such as the octopus-god Khalk'ru in A. Merritt's serial novel *Dwellers in the Mirage* (1932), first published in the *Argosy*, and C. L. Moore's "Shambleau" (1933), which also first appeared in *Weird Tales*. If nothing else, "Shambleau" is the first instance I could find of a female tentacle monster: "'I only know that when I felt—when those tentacles closed around my legs—I didn't want to pull loose. I felt sensations that—that—oh, I'm foul and filthy to the very deepest part of me by that—*pleasure*—and yet—'" (Moore 2009, 45). I am cheating a little here, for while neither story is explicitly a Mythos tale, both Moore and Merritt were correspondents with Lovecraft and familiar with his work; the three collaborated with Robert E. Howard and Frank Belknap Long on the round-robin story "The Challenge from Beyond" (1935). *Dweller* is sometimes credited as Merritt's take on a Mythos story, though it was written before he met Lovecraft in 1934, because of the similarities between the octopus-god Khalk'ru and octopus-headed Cthulhu, as well as other elements.

Even in the pulps the tentacle was sometimes associated with sex, as seen in Robert E. Howard's "Xuthal of the Dusk" (1933):

> A dark tentacle-like member slid about her body, and she screamed at the touch of it on her naked flesh. It was neither warm nor cold, rough nor smooth; it was like nothing that had ever touched her before, and at its caress she knew such fear and shame as she had never dreamed of. All the obscenity and salacious infamy spawned in the muck of the abysmal pits of Life seemed to drown her in seas of cosmic filth. And in that instant she knew that whatever form of life this thing represented it was not a beast. (Howard 2002, 238)

Charles Hoffmann noted this instance in "Return to Xuthal" (2010):

> In depicting Natala being violated by Thog, he was a good half-century ahead of his time. Today there is an entire pornographic sub-genre of Japanese anime commonly referred to as "tits and tentacles." These adults-only animated characters portray the plight of young women, usually teenage schoolgirls, who are sexually abused by monsters very much like Thog. (106)

From the pulps, the image of the tentacled monster, alien, mutant, robot, etc. entered the American cultural image lexicon and was a minor but recurring theme in genre literature, such as Philip José Farmer's *Image of the Beast* (1968), comic books like Marvel Comics' *Conan the Barbarian* (1970-93), and horror films including Roger Corman's *The Dunwich Horror* (1970). Through translation and transmission of Mythos stories and American pop art, this implicitly sexual tentacle art and literature was introduced to Europe and Asia following World War II, where different censorship laws encouraged the growth of more explicitly sexual themes, and most importantly different sexual themes, than were common in American depictions of sexually suggestive tentacled entities. For example, tentacled monsters, aliens, and mutants continued to be featured in the pages of Wally Wood's E.C. Comics-esque portfolio *Weird Sex-Fantasy* (1977) and *Métal Hurlant* (1974-87), often with much more explicit sex and violence than was allowed in American and British comics of the same era because of regulation of the comic book industry in the US and UK on account of moral panics against crime and horror comics like those produced by E.C. Comics in the mid-50s. The bondage/frottage aspect of tentacle sex, at least from an artistic viewpoint, appears to have reached maturity in the 1980s with comics like Italian comics artist Paolo Serpieri's *Morbus Gravis* (1985), the first in a series of graphic novels featuring Druuna, an updated pulp magazine heroine often imperiled and grappled by tentacled monsters.

Nineteenth-century manga did feature penetrative sex with octopodes, but not penetrative tentacle sex: when an octopus would have coitus with a human woman, the artist would provide it with a penis. Jason Thompson in his article "The Long Tentacle of H. P. Lovecraft in Manga (NSFW)" traces the modern concept of penetrative tentacle sex to the anime adaptations of Toshio Maeda's *Urotsukidōji* and *Demon Beast Invasion* anime (manga 1986, anime 1990). In an interview, Toshio Maeda elaborated on his reasons for this depiction:

> At that time [pre-*Urotsuki Doji*], it was illegal to create a sensual scene in bed. I thought I should do something to avoid drawing such a normal sensual scene. So I just created a creature. [His tentacle] is not a [penis] as a pretext. I could say, as an excuse, this is not a [penis], this is just a part of the creature. You know, the creatures, they don't have a gender. A creature is a creature. So it is not obscene - not illegal. ("Manga Artist Interview Series [Part 1]")

The idea of penetrative tentacle sex in comic art was not unique to Japanese manga of the period, as illustrated by "Love in Arms" by Bob Lee and Brad W. Foster in *Fever Pitch* (1988), where a woman imagines penetrative sex with an octopus. However, the idea did not really catch on in the US until the 1980s and 1990s with magazines like *Heavy Metal* (1977–present) and anime such as *La Blue Girl* (1993).

Heavy Metal is an English translation of the French comic magazine *Métal Hurlant*, which included serializations of Serpieri's Druuna series, comic pastiches and adaptations of Lovecraft's stories, and more, while *La Blue Girl* is another adaptation of a Toshio Maeda manga featuring tentacle sex, brought to the United States to cater to an adult audience during the beginning of American popular interest in Japanese manga and anime. Few of the works given above have an explicit connection to the Cthulhu Mythos, but their debt from prior art and influence on subsequent art make them pivotal in understanding how tentacle sex developed and became affiliated with the Mythos.

With the awareness of the idea of penetrative sex with tentacles, the application of that idea to a genre famed for its tentacled monsters like the Cthulhu Mythos was probably inevitable. The two core concepts—the sexualization of the old pulp art and the use of tentacles as substitute penises for explicit sexual penetration—naturally converged based on their common elements (sex, tentacles) and became associated almost by proxy with a genre whose mascot was the octopus-headed Cthulhu. An example of the use of tentacles as long, prehensile sex organs in connection with the Cthulhu Mythos is a scene in Barreiro and Noé's *The Convent of Hell* (1997), and in a looser sense many of the sexual images in H. R. Giger's *Necronomicon* (1977) undoubtedly qualify.

Lovecraft and his contemporaries probably never intended the general sexualization of tentacles (with the possible exception of the depiction of the nude and dying Wilbur Whateley in "The Dunwich Horror," whose tentacle is so suggestively located in place of a penis and may have been an effort on Lovecraft's part to squeeze the scene past editor Farnsworth Wright), but built on their existing use in weird fiction. Their probable major inspiration is a scene in Arthur Machen's "Novel of the Black Seal," where the hybrid or changeling Jervase Cradock, under the influence of the Seal, releases a tentacle from his body. In that story, the tentacle is an example of primitive powers and abilities that have survived among the aboriginal, non-human race, abilities attributed to "lower order" animals such as snails and amoeba, alien to humanity. Lovecraft and his fellow writers utilized a very similar idea repeatedly in some of their work, depicting some of their Mythos entities as deliberately primeval, but magnified to an epic scale—hence Lovecraft's gigantic shapeless shoggoths from *At the Mountains of Madness* (1931) and Clark Ashton Smith's eponymous, protean creature in "Ubbo-Sathla" (1933), both of which are likely inspired by Ernst Haeckel's concept of a primordial *urschleim*. This original symbolism inherent in the tentacle was generally lost by imitators, leaving the tentacle as a calling-card of the Mythos "style" without the underlying substance. It is likely that over-identification of the Mythos with tentacle sex is simply an extension of the over-identification of the Mythos with tentacles in general.

For all that we can trace a general outline of the history and development of tentacle sex, there remains the major issue that the perception of the trope does not quite equal its realization. Only a very small fraction of Cthulhu Mythos material actually makes any use of tentacles for sexual purposes, and the majority of such stories and media are relatively recent. Put simply, tentacle sex is far less prevalent in the Cthulhu Mythos, even the subset of erotic Mythos fiction, than popular opinion holds—but it does exist.

From a literary perspective, the use of tentacles as a sexual symbol allows writers to give sexual function and identity to a Mythos entity without explicitly lumping it in with common human conceptions of gender—that is, while the entity becomes a sexual entity, it is still at least somewhat identifiably alien. However, the use of tentacles for penetrative sex draws on Western culture assumptions associated with penetrative sex—the penetrator (in this case, the tentacled monster) implicitly takes on a "masculine" role, and the person penetrated takes on a "feminine" role in the coitus. This relationship by default tends to give rise to the perception of Mythos entities with tentacles as male, whether or not they are otherwise depicted as having a recognizable gender. This perception is not always explicitly true, but is an example of a common heteronormative bias. Definitively female tentacled entities do exist in some works, as well as male victims, but both appear to be in the minority; where they do exist, the Mythos stories sometimes exhibit very strong parallels to homosexual, bisexual, and transsexual literature, with questions of sexual identity versus gender identity.

Likewise, the nonhuman aspect of a tentacle entity and the sexual nature of penetrative sex have given rise to the predisposition of the tentacle entity as rapist, so much so that in general context "tentacle sex" and "tentacle rape" are almost synonymous. Common depictions of tentacles in media may support this view, sometimes deliberately, by showing only the tentacles interacting with the human and obscuring or omitting the body of the tentacle-monster, and combining the early bondage/groping aspect of tentacle sex with the penetrative aspect. The effect given is that of a faceless perpetrator imposing sexual dominance on another—a clear enough analogy of a rapist. The rapist aspect also tends to reinforce the inherent characterization of the tentacle entity as male, not because females cannot be rapists, but because culturally males are both more strongly associated with the penetrative sex partner and rapists than women. Of course, simply because the tentacle entity is perceived as male—or hypermale, given the multiplicity of substitute phalluses and their size with relation to the normal human member—it may also elicit strong reactions of homophobia, homoeroticism, and fear or desire of sodomy.

Much of the details of tentacle sex rely on the inherent unreality of the act, permitting an exaggeration of sexual characteristics, actions, and consequences beyond what the real world would permit. With the obvious unreality comes a moral and emotional distancing in the reader, expanding the boundaries of what would commonly be acceptable—just as cartoon violence is both harsher and more harmless than vaudeville slapstick, since the characters involved can deform and destroy each other and yet suffer no real or permanent harm. Joel Powell Dahlquist and Lee Garth Vigilant encapsulate something of this view with regard to tentacle sex in Japanese manga:

> Tentacle sex/rape of nubile girl-women isn't doubling back on any reference in the real world. There is no real thing to simulate. It exists for its own purpose as an erotic phantasm of the strange and teratological. [. . .] Tentacle hentai offers the telegenetic signs of the most perverse and debased sexualities. It opens for fantastic examination a sexuality that transgresses all "simulated" moralities of the "real" world [. . .] A *"real" porn actress would never survive teratological tentacle sex—in all orifices.* [. . .] After all, manga sex and tentacle hentai are just cartoon fantasies where demons and aliens with tentacles are dominating—in the most vicious ways—other *cartoons.* They are not *real.* (Dahlquist and Vigilant 99-100)

Of course, the degree of "reality" in any given instance of tentacle sex is determined by the author of the work and can be tweaked both for the audience and the desired effect; tentacle sex is an expression of "a malign and particular suspension or defeat of those fixed laws of Nature" (Lovecraft 2000, 23) as set forth in Lovecraft's theory of weird fiction, which may be played for horror, arousal, gruesomeness, or comedy.

Alien Heats

In the Lovecraft Mythos, many Mythos entities typically have little to no sexual identity—in "The Call of Cthulhu," for example, Cthulhu is not stated to have a sexual preference, desire for sex, or even an established gender identity (though the default pronouns used are male)—with the exception being Yog-Sothoth in "The Dunwich Horror," the Deep Ones in "The Shadow over Innsmouth" and "The Thing on the Doorstep," Yig in "The Curse of Yig," etc. Writers in the Cthulhu Mythos would expand on these elements in later stories, adding dimensions of sexuality and gender to already extant Mythos entities that lacked them and creating new Mythos entities with sexual identities already in place as part of their character. The result that emerged is what Machen, Lovecraft, and other early writers of the weird hinted at but never explicit recounted: the Mythos entity as a sexual partner to human characters.

The defining trait shared by all the outré creatures in the Lovecraft Mythos is that they are alien to humankind, and it is this otherness that most facilitates their adaptation to sexual characterization. Alien entities bridge the gap between the literature of the fantastic and erotic fantasy, allowing a greater exploration of sexual possibilities beyond traditional conceptions and normal human and physical limitations. Fantastic, alien, and supernatural creatures are not restricted to Mythos fiction, and are part of a long tradition of sexual traffic between humans and fantastic races in folklore and myth, which has developed and been a part of the literary traditions that led to current fiction, as Lovecraft himself noted in various bride-tales referenced in "Supernatural Horror in Literature." The development of sexuality in Cthulhu Mythos fiction is thus a part of the development of sexuality in genre fiction as a whole; where non-Mythos science fiction and fantasy may focus more on orcs, elves, vampires, werewolves, centaurs, near-human aliens, and other novel or folklore-derived fictional species, the distinction of whether a particular sexualized monster is a Mythos entity or not is, barring clear indicators from the writer, a subjective and mostly meaningless one. Arguing that a particular interdimensional being from outside known time and space is a Mythos critter or "simply" an alien or demon is literary hair-splitting.

The sexualization of Mythos entities serves many different purposes for writers, some of which can be easily addressed here. The appeal of the sexual Mythos entity is in its transgressive nature—not just of cultural taboos against mating outside your tribe, caste, or society, but outside your species and in some cases beyond the limits imposed by biology and the laws of physics. The addition of the sexual element personalizes the horror of the impersonal cosmic entities written of by Lovecraft, adding sexual terror and titillation by opening the Mythos entity up to fantasies of rape, penetration, sexual dominance, and reproduction. Mythos entities lend themselves to these scenarios by the difficulties encountered by humans in trying to communicate with them, the traditionally antagonist nature of human-Mythos being interactions in the Lovecraft Mythos, and by their superhuman power. More, Mythos entities in their strange anatomies allow writers to express novel and unusual sensations, textures, smells, tastes, and emotions that are not traditionally associated with most forms of human sexual intercourse, feeding an appetite for sexual novelty, attempting to stimulate mental interest in the reader by appeal to things uncommon to their sexual experience, and in some cases playing directly to specific fetishes, some of which may not be physically realizable but must be played out or expressed through the printed page, illustration, animation, interactive video, or computer game, etc. For example, tentacle play as described above is not typically physically realizable to a great extent, and the art and fiction associated with the fetish typically exceeds the anatomical limitations of the human body.

For their own part, the ability and desire to interact sexually with humans is, in the context of the Mythos entities themselves, largely derived directly from the few instances of sexual interaction given in the Lovecraft Mythos. Of the known instances in Lovecraft's fiction—Yog-Sothoth, Yig, the Deep Ones, etc.—in every case the sexual act appears essentially for the purpose of reproduction and results in conception. In the case of Yig and Yog-Sothoth, this appears to be in fulfillment of a higher purpose: to fulfill the Curse of Yig and to father a child to open the gates for the Old Ones, respectively. For the Deep Ones, the purpose is unclear or unspoken; the narrator is simply told that "*they* wanted to mix like they done with the Kanakys" (CC 302), which may be part of a specific plan of breeding or a simple desire to slake inhuman lusts; and the ambiguity in this matter has led to development of the Deep Ones along both lines.

The drive and ability to copulate with human beings also humanizes Mythos entities. The sexual urge is one that human beings understand, and by applying it to Mythos entities it reduces the unknowable and alien aspect of Lovecraft's cosmic horrors to an entity, however strange or powerful, that needs to get laid. Just as human sex is recreational as well as intended for reproduction, the desires of Mythos entities graduate in some stories from practical impregnation in accordance with a specific purpose or fulfillment of alien biological imperative to a pleasurable pursuit. Rather than have sex solely to produce hybrid offspring, some Mythos entities have sex for fun.

While many Mythos stories necessitate rape on the part of the human to their alien sexual partner, sex and even rape are far from unique to human experience, as the animal kingdom will attest in astonishing variety. In the Lovecraft Mythos, the sexual interactions of Mythos entities and humans run the gamut from consensual to nonconsensual, with some cases being difficult to interpret. In practical terms, the tendency for Mythos entities to dominate humans sexually appears to be an outgrowth of the Lovecraftian idea that Mythos entities surpass humanity in all things. The image of an overpowering entity engenders, in at least some individuals, fantasies of sexual domination, violation, and subjugation. This sexual power dynamic is discussed further in Jennifer Broznek's essay "The Sexual Attraction of the Lovecraftian Universe" in *Cthulhurotica* (2010).

While there are stories of Mythos entities raping humans, there are also stories where the human is a submissive "willing victim," an active and consensual partner in the sex act, the active or dominant initiator of the sex act and so on. As sexually capable creatures, Mythos entities become capable of taking on any role reserved for sexual entities in human literature: lover, parent, slut, prostitute, blushing virgin, rapist, victim of rape, etc. This use of Mythos entities most typically lends itself to a mixture of the weird and blue comedy, romance, psychological horror, and other forms of art and discourse.

As a final note on this subject, there are exceptions—Mythos entities that can pass for human and are given a sexual identity in the context of the story primarily by being presented as normal human beings, with typical human sexual desires and purposes. The most prominent examples are Deep One hybrids that have yet to express their alienage, and the special case of Nyarlathotep, whose occasional form when dealing with humans is as a tall, dark-skinned human male. Because of their ability to blend in with human beings, these Mythos entities typically do not exhibit the full range of strange anatomies and motivations described above, and for the majority of the stories focusing on them the characters are described and defined in human terms—rather than being alien, they are presented as quirky or exotic, with only hints or a familiar name to clue the reader in that the character is not quite what they seem. This informs readers of the Mythos of the possible alien nature of the character; the other characters in the narrative lack this metatextual knowledge and react to the pass-as-human Mythos character normally, but the reader's response is heightened in expectation for when the entity's true nature is revealed.

Parody

Lovecraft and the Cthulhu Mythos have long attracted parody, often to comment on the peculiarities of Lovecraft and the fiction he wrote and inspired, often with a degree of love and affection. Some of these parodies specifically highlight the issues of sex and gender in the Mythos; Peter Cannon's "The Hound of the Partridgevilles" (1999) and Mark E. Roger's "The Book of the Dunwich Cow" from *The Adventures of Samurai Cat* (1984), for example, both highlight and make light of the inherent silliness that comes of cosmic miscegenation and human social and genealogical relationships with Mythos entities.

Pornographic parodies of Lovecraft's work or the Mythos are considerably rarer. In the few examples I've run across the traditional purposes of parody are diminished but not entirely lost—the works still include inherent criticism of the genre in the elements that the author chooses to use and exaggerate, but added to this is the desire to titillate in a specific medium, using the tropes of the source material. That is, the author writes for the specific purpose of featuring explicit sex between specific characters of Lovecraft or the Mythos, or to include that sex in a specific Mythos setting, using distinctive elements of the Mythos. Given that the Lovecraft Mythos is rather open to use, unlike other copyrighted works, the line between original adult contributions that use Lovecraft's characters and follow his stories a little too closely and pornographic parodies can be very fine indeed.

For example, *Herburt East: Re-fuckinator* (2012) is a commentary of the implied homosexual subtext that can be read into Lovecraft's works. It inverts the expectations of the reader by taking Lovecraft's original text, complete with setting and characters, and transforming it into a raunchy episodic homoerotic novel, and it highlights both its own nature and Lovecraft's florid language with punning twists. The reader can appreciate it both as an amusing "take that" and a hardcore pornographic work. By contrast, in the hardcore pornographic film parody *Re-Penetrator* (2005) the commentary is nearly nil—the entire point of the parody is to watch the characters of Dr. Herbert Breast and the buxom corpse he reanimates engage in coitus. Rather than attempt to reinterpret the text, the creators of *Re-Penetrator* act out a specific fantasy using a stripped-down version of Lovecraft's character and setting.

Lovecraft as a Sexual Character

Fictional versions of H. P. Lovecraft, characters based on Lovecraft, and explicit reference to Lovecraft as an author of Mythos tales and his fiction are present in a number of Cthulhu Mythos tales, and in some of these portrayals Lovecraft's sexuality is a key part of the character. These fictional Lovecrafts—and I include here those characters who are based on Lovecraft and references to him in a fictional context—rely on both biographical information about Lovecraft and the myth of Lovecraft developed from decades of anecdotes, rumor, and past characterization. In large part, Lovecraft's appearance as a sexual character bespeaks the continued interest in the sexual themes and dynamics in both his life and his work, both real and imagined.

In the majority of depictions, the fictional Lovecraft is asexual—or, at the very least, has no place in the story to display sexuality, and so does not. This is not out of line with what is known about Lovecraft; also in accordance with his known history, in those stories where the fictional Lovecraft is actively sexual or noticeably attracted in an amorous manner, the character is almost exclusively depicted as heterosexual. Despite some speculation on the flesh-and-blood Lovecraft's sexual orientation, the homosexual or bisexual Lovecraft character is largely absent, though W. H. Pugmire in *Letters from an Old Gent* (2012) presents sentiments where the post-mortem divide between Lovecraft and Samuel Loveman is presented in terms of a lover's tiff.

Except for a brief period in his life, Lovecraft was a bachelor, and nearly every instance of the fictional Lovecraft character is alone as well; parents dead and aunts, if mentioned, generally unseen. This is the impression that was probably received by Lovecraft's younger correspondents, such as Robert Bloch, August Derleth, and R. H. Barlow. The lack of female contact supports the general asexuality of the fictional Lovecraft and tends to emphasize the non-sexual emotional bond between the fictional Lovecraft and other male characters in the story. Where Lovecraft's wife does appear, the relationship is often romanticized, sexualized, or both. In the comic adaptation of *The Dream-Quest of Unknown Kadath* (1997-99) by Jason Bradley Thompson, a few poignant panels show a Sonia-analogue at an amateur convention with Randolph Carter; George Kuchar's black-and-white biographic comix *H. P. Lovecraft 1890-1937* (1975) shows a sexually aggressive Sonia in the marriage-bed; Edward Lee in *Trolley No. 1852* (2010) likewise has his fictional Lovecraft recall his ex-wife's rapacious sexual appetite, as does Grant Morrison's *Lovecraft in Heaven* (1994). Richard Lupoff's alternate history novel *Lovecraft's Book* (1985)/*Marblehead* (2006) focuses on when the marriage is at an end in all but name—yet they cling to that name. Sonia is living in New York, Lovecraft in Providence, but divorce has not yet reared its head, and Sonia for her part is willing to resume the relationship, physical and otherwise, but Lovecraft is standoffish. Lupoff puts great if subtle focus at times on the lack of physical interaction between the two, when Lovecraft could have kissed Sonia or gone to bed with her but steadfastly refused to resume such relations. The depiction favors Sonia suffering Lovecraft's indifference and willing to resume the marriage, with only Lovecraft himself (and perhaps his aunts) as an impediment to their continuation as a couple. Touches from Sonia's memoir are evident, but it is not listed in the bibliography.

Several fans have imagined what it would be like if Lovecraft wrote erotic or pornographic fiction featuring his Mythos. The earliest published examples I've found are magazines in amateur press association mailings like the Robert E. Howard United Press Association (REHUPA) mailings in the early 1980s, including references to such tales as "The Horror of Red Hooker," "The Shunned Mouth," "The Cunts of Ulthar," "Beyond the Walls of Sheep," and even complete pornographic parodies such as "At the Mammaries of Madness" and "The Man with a Thousand Members" in the amateur pornzine *Weird Tails*. Following in this vein is Peter Cannon's "Asceticism and Lust: The Greatest Lovecraft Revision" (1988), a light-hearted satire that takes the form of a brief article describing a hitherto undiscovered collaboration between Henry Miller, author of the erotic novels *Tropic of Cancer* (1934) and *Tropic of Capricorn* (1939), and Lovecraft entitled "The Tropic of Cthulhu." While written in jest, Cannon takes great care to support the story of the collaboration with considerable detail drawn from the lives, letters, and writings of both Lovecraft and Miller, making as plausible a case as possible for when and how the two gentlemen might really have conspired together on such a project and why. Lee's much more explicit *Trolley No. 1852* uses the framing story of Lovecraft writing erotica for a spicy magazine, the narrative of which contains a character based on Lovecraft himself, and which ends with Lovecraft's sexual encounter with his female editor.

Besides Lee's take, several other versions of the fictional Lovecraft are sexually active or romantically inclined. Peter Cannon's *The Lovecraft Chronicles* (2007), for example, postulates an alternate biography where Lovecraft did not die in 1937, but almost married again. Kenneth W. Faig, Jr. in *Tales of the Lovecraft Collectors* (1995) reveals that Lovecraft had a teenage affair with a local girl resulting in an illegitimate daughter, a point approximately echoed in S. T. Joshi's novel *The Assaults of Chaos* (2013), which shows Lovecraft losing his virginity with an Irish-American classmate in high school; Edward Lee's *The Innswich Horror* (2010) reveals Lovecraft's dalliance with an Innswich native leading to a bastard son; and the film *The Last Lovecraft: Relic of Cthulhu* (2009) centers around another imaginary descendent of Lovecraft.

As a complement to this occupation with Lovecraft's fictional descendents, there are also works that focus on Lovecraft's parentage and conception. Some of these, such as Peter H. Cannon's *Pulptime* (1984), conclude that Lovecraft was not the child of Winfield Scott Lovecraft: Cannon ascribes Lovecraft's birth to an affair with Sherlock Holmes! Most works, however, focus on Lovecraft's parents, particularly Winfield Scott Lovecraft's syphilis-driven hallucinations and the suggestion that Lovecraft may have inherited congenital syphilis from his parents. Perhaps the most evocative and explicit works along this line are Grant Morrison's *Lovecraft in Heaven* (1994) and Alan Moore's *Recognition* (2003).

Gender, Sexuality, and Mythos Writers

The men and women behind the Mythos are all sexual beings, and in many cases this aspect of their nature is reflected in their Mythos work and worthy of examination. That said, in this chapter I have not made an effort to single out writers based on their sex or gender alone. If any authors are discussed here, it is because I have felt that their work in the Mythos is important and worthy of examination, regardless of their gender or sexuality. Their sex, whatever it may be, is primarily of interest in shedding light on how and why they have written as they have done. To put this in some perspective, a brief examination of sex and gender in terms of Mythos writers may be beneficial.

A scientific study of gender and sexuality among published Mythos writers has not been done—and would be very difficult, given the relative obscurity of many, and the penchant for pseudonyms—but a very rough survey of names in Chaosium's Call of Cthulhu fiction line tends to support the idea that the vast majority of Mythos authors are male; though if names are anything to go by, the number of female Mythos writers has been steadily increasing over the last several decades, or at least are being published with greater frequency. This is not particularly revelatory given that the Cthulhu Mythos has its beginnings in weird and pulp fiction, which in the United States of the 1920s and '30s was dominated by male writers and editors.

The first female writers associated with the Mythos were Lovecraft's collaborators in the amateur press such as Anna Helen Crofts, Elizabeth Berkeley (pseudonym of Winifred Virginia Jackson), and Sonia Haft Greene, and female revision clients such as Zealia Reed Bishop and Hazel Heald. Lovecraft's contemporaries who contributed to the growing Mythos while he was alive and immediately after his death were almost exclusively male—the most notable female pulpster of the era associated with Lovecraft is his correspondent C. L. Moore, who collaborated with Lovecraft in "The Challenge from Beyond" (1935); her stories such as "Shambleau" may show some influence from the Mythos (and certainly influenced later authors), but she did not participate in the creation of books, entities, people, and places in the manner of Robert E. Howard or Clark Ashton Smith.

Whoever may be considered the "First Female Mythos Writer," women were underrepresented—basically unrepresented, in the case of Arkham House anthologies and collections—in Mythos fiction for several decades after Lovecraft's death. This began to change in the 1960s with the advent of writers like Joanna Russ, the continued spread of the Mythos to new generations, and the proliferation of Mythos publications under other publishers. One of the most encouraging developments of recent years is the appearance of female editors of Mythos fiction collections, such as Silvia Moreno-Garcia and Paula Stiles, editors of *Historical Lovecraft* (2011) and *Future Lovecraft* (2011), and Carrie Cuinn of *Cthulhurotica* (2010), along with female Mythos novelists such as Molly Tanzer, who wrote *A Pretty Little Mouth* (2013).

The early Mythos tales from Lovecraft and his contemporaries through approximately the death of August Derleth display a notable bias representative of their long dominance by male writers, most strongly a majority emphasis on male characters and protagonists. Pastiches, sequels, and continuations tend to continue or exacerbate these early Mythos writers' habit of downplaying or neglecting female characters. This early block of fiction can also be viewed to have a strongly heteronormative bent, largely in keeping with the prevalent sexual attitudes of the 1920s through 1960s—and despite the known sexual orientation of at least some of the Mythos writers for this period. Acceptance of homosexuality, bisexuality, and alternative sexual lifestyles has ebbed and flowed with the times, but for long periods in American history it was not socially acceptable, safe, or even legal to openly be non-heterosexual or write about non-heterosexuality, as tragically demonstrated by the suicide of R. H. Barlow in 1951.

Openly non-strictly-heterosexual Mythos writers of any gender are thus generally associated with the 1980s and later—not because they did not exist prior to that point, but presumably because social attitudes did not generally permit such openness in sexuality until then. By much the same token, open homosexual, bisexual, and transsexual characters in Mythos fiction were relatively rare until the advent of Mythos writers who were openly non-heterosexual themselves. The gender and sexuality of Mythos writers are not automatically expressed in their Mythos fiction—just because a writer might be a lesbian does not mean she is restricted solely to writing homosexual characters any more than a male heterosexual author is restricted to writing about heterosexual men and women.

The result of society's greater acceptance of different sexuality, coupled with the loosening restrictions to Mythos publishing following the death of August Derleth, was not exactly an "explosion" of female and non-heterosexual writers and characters in Mythos fiction. Rather, there was a gradually increasing openness toward authors and Mythos fiction of all stripes, which happened to include women, homosexuals, etc. This greater inclusion has given the Mythos readership such notable contemporary authors as Poppy Z. Brite, Stanley C. Sargent, Wilum H. Pugmire, and Caitlín R. Kiernan, among many more, and the Mythos as a whole is richer for their contributions.

Key Works and Authors

What follows is a survey of the work of the most important and notable authors in the Mythos oeuvre with respect to love, sex, and gender. It does not pretend to be a complete or exhaustive discussion of such materials, but rather focuses on those that have the most influence and literary merit, or which are otherwise notable. I include not simply writers of adult-oriented Mythos fiction but also editors of magazines and anthologies of such fiction, whose influence in the selection and presentation of works is such a critical and influential factor in the development and dissemination of sexually-mature Mythos tales. Editors, in their philosophy, skill, and taste, determine in a large part what stories are published and ultimately read, and the prominence of August Derleth and Robert M. Price here is an acknowledgment of their efforts and judgment in that respect as much as their writing.

For all that the Cthulhu Mythos is more widely known and recognized today than ever before, new and original Mythos literature has always been something of a niche market, and many of the works mentioned below are or were offered by small and specialty publishers—not just of purveyors of collections and novels specializing in the weird like Arkham House or Chaosium, but comic book publishers like Last Gasp and Avatar Press, and ebook publishers like Circlet Press. These small-press publishers are important in part because they are more willing than larger publishing houses to print daring works, specialize in certain strange and adult fare already, or are simply less picky about what they publish. The mention of works from small and unknown publishers is not an effort toward obscurism or intended to reflect sexually aware Mythos tales as a minority fringe on the outskirts of accepted fiction; these works are included for their significance toward the subject, not their individual impact. The inclusion of these works here is an active effort to avoid the academic conceit that certain media, because of their crude construction or mayfly existence, are beneath notice. Indeed, given that the Mythos was born in the pages of pulp magazines and amateur writing, it would be hypocritical to ignore these works simply because they exist in non-prose media—and, in some cases, have even been adapted from prose to comic book form.

There is no set canon among the Mythos, no rules that authors must follow to include Cthulhu or the *Necronomicon* in their fiction. Most authors and fans are in tacit agreement in referring to the Lovecraft Mythos as a common source, but even in this it must be remembered that in the earliest stories Lovecraft incorporated the creations of others just as much as they borrowed from him. For that matter, none of those authors in Lovecraft's circle of correspondents were forced to make their fiction agree with Lovecraft either, and the Mythos material in many of the original stories is little more than a connective tissue of shared background elements. Clark Ashton Smith and Robert E. Howard in particular did not, for the most part, set out to write "Mythos" fiction—they wrote their own fiction, which because they shared certain elements with Lovecraft, or that Lovecraft and those that followed him borrowed, became part of the Cthulhu Mythos. Later authors wrote more fiction that was about the Mythos itself, such as Derleth's *The Lurker at the Threshold* (1945) or Lin Carter's "The Winfield Inheritance" (1981). As a consequence, many stories are part of the Mythos only for a single mention of a Lovecraftian tome or entity, like Manly Wade Wellman's "The Letters of Cold Fire" (1944). There are also many works with no overt reference to the Mythos, but which nevertheless are indebted to Lovecraft—stories that borrow from the themes, concepts, and tropes of Lovecraft, but do not use any of the setting or background material, even the use of a single Mythos name; I refer to these here as Lovecraftian stories. Generally speaking, I have avoided mentioning Lovecraftian stories or those with minimal Mythos material unless they are significant or influential.

If there is a single unifying theme to tie these authors together with Lovecraft in regard to their approach to sex and the Cthulhu Mythos, it is that sex is presented as a transgressive act. Robert E. Howard includes lusty abominations that leer at scenes ripped from flagellation literature, Clark Ashton Smith indulges in cuckoldry and necrophilia, Ramsey Campbell drags us through the gutter-world of pornography and fears of sexual inadequacy, Brian McNaughton captivates readers with tales of possession and incest, W. H. Pugmire titillates them with the easy but undefinable sensuality of the creatures in Sesqua Valley. All in their own way these and other writers explore beyond the boundaries of "normal" sex, and through the lens of the Mythos proceed from mere decadence, carnality, kink, and the prosaic facts and fantasies of sex to take on the added illicit thrill of the impossible, the forbidden, and the unknown.

Some readers may come to the conclusion that the contemporary fiction of the Cthulhu Mythos is more sexualized than that of the past, and will find in the latter parts of this chapter that material fit for the Spicy pulps has given way to pure pornography. However, I would remind everyone that these authors are not representative of the Mythos or their generation; they are the extraordinary pioneers who pushed the boundaries of the possible with sex and the Mythos—and the farther we follow, so too the weirder and more transgressive things get. Still, just because the most extreme writers of today are doing hardcore Lovecraftian pornography does not mean that most Mythos authors of today are so sexually explicit in their writings.

Robert E. Howard

> "I don't know that they contain any more sex than is necessary in a delineation of the life of a lusty bygone era," Lovecraft said. "Good old Two-Gun didn't seem to me to overstress eroticism nearly as much as other cash-seeking pulpists—even if he did now and then feel in duty bound to play up to a Brundage cover-design." (Lovecraft and Conover 2002, 43)

Lovecraft's adumbration to his friend and correspondent Willis Conover is generous, but plays down or misses the more intimate details of sex in Robert E. Howard's fiction, the process that went into writing those stories, and Howard's own background and source material. A full examination of the sexual dynamics of racism, gender balance, and real and perceived sexual chauvinism in Howard's works is too long to go into here, so the following is somewhat compressed to present background specifically relevant to Howard's Mythos fiction.

With the exception of Lovecraft, Robert E. Howard has received the greatest attention of biographers and bibliographers of any of the *Weird Tales* writers, and the microscopes of several generations have been trained on every aspect of his short life, omitting nothing, even his knowledge and familiarity with sex. The full extent of Howard's sexual experiences and preferences is a matter of debate. In *Dark Valley Destiny* (1983) the de Camps painted Howard as sexually repressed, probably a virgin, and in an unhealthy (though not sexual) relationship with his mother and, by extension, all other women . . . not unlike L. Sprague de Camp's assessment of Lovecraft in *Lovecraft: A Biography* (1975). General consensus holds that there is little to no evidence of Howard having had sex, and that his close relationship with his mother made relations with other women difficult—the latter emphasized by Novalyne Price Ellis in *One Who Walked Alone* (1986), which consists mainly of her journal entries during the period of

3. Sex and The Cthulhu Mythos

her tempestuous on-again/off-again relationship with Howard. Novalyne relates that Howard kept his hands to himself, but sex raised particular points of conflict between the two at times, such as when he gave Novalyne *The Complete Works of Pierre Louÿs*, a volume of erotic literature, for Christmas (Ellis 1998, 133), and presumably again when Howard suggested she might write for the Spicy pulps (*REH* 3.418); whether this was due to inexperience with dealing with women—not knowing they might be offended by such material—or a desire to engage with Novalyne on a different level is never quite clear.

The Christmas episode does raise an interesting and somewhat underexplored biographical detail: the presence of a number of works of erotica in Howard's library, as noted by Steve Eng in the appendix to *The Dark Barbarian* (1984), particularly several works of sadomasochism such as "A *History of the Rod* [. . .] [Glenn Lord] suggests this book and other flagellation erotica in REH's library may reflect his unsuccessful try at writing for such pulp magazines as *Terror Tales* and *Thrilling Mysteries*" (Eng 189). The latter titles are examples of the "shudder pulps" or "weird menace" pulps, which featured sadistic tortures, both in the writing and especially on the covers; the latter led New York City mayor Fiorello LaGuardia to censor pulps with lurid covers, including *Weird Tales*. With regard to Lord's comment that Howard chose the books for research purposes, this may be somewhat accurate: *A History of the Rod* (1865), *Black Lust* (1931) (aside from the erotic and flagellation content, the novel is also a history of the siege of Khartoum and may have inspired or contributed to Howard's spicy story "Guns of Khartum" [1975]), and several other books listed in his library are old Victorian curiosa disguised as and little distinguishable from mundane histories or anthropological works of the period save for their subject matter. However, absence of interest in the subject would appear to be contraindicated by the presence of several scenes of flagellation in Howard's fiction, as noted by Charles Hoffman—though again, as Lovecraft noted, these scenes were also more likely to earn a cover illustration from *Weird Tales*, so it is possible he wrote them in with commercial interest.

Besides the flagellation erotica, two other titles of interest in Howard's library are *Untrodden Fields of Anthropology* (1898) and *Musk, Hashish and Blood* (1899). The latter is mentioned by title in Sax Rohmer's novel *Dope* (1919), and Howard was an avowed fan of Rohmer, though *Dope* was not in his library at the time of his death. It is possible that Howard saw the title drop in the story and inquired after the book, much as he asked

Lovecraft about the *Necronomicon*. (MF 37). *Untrodden Fields* is another Victorian anthropological work; its focus on the degeneracy of civilizations may have been a minor influence on or contribution to Howard's views on the subject. While the exact edition of either book that he possessed is unknown, both books were published by Falstaff Press—which advertised in the pulps, and by coincidence was one of two private publishers Lovecraft recommended to a seeker of curiosa (Lovecraft 2007a, 34).

Howard's interest with flagellation erotica would intersect with the Mythos in "The Black Stone" (1931), arguably his most significant Lovecraftian tale. In that story, the narrator is struck by a whim to visit the Black Stone and experiences a vision or dream of those long-gone pagan rites, which focuses on a pair of sacrifices—a naked young woman and a child—and on an ecstatic, nude dancer being whipped into a bloody frenzy by the priest:

> The lashing continued with unabated violence and intensity and she began to wriggle toward the monolith on her belly. The priest—or such I will call him—followed, lashing her unprotected body with all the power of his arm as she writhed along, leaving a heavy track of blood on the trampled earth. She reached the monolith, and gasping and panting, flung both arms about it and covered the cold stone with fierce hot kisses, as in frenzied and unholy adoration. (Howard 2001, 12)

This bald flagellation scene is an expansion and exploration of the ritual scenes in Lovecraft's "The Call of Cthulhu" and "The Horror at Red Hook," with greater attention given to the details of the orgiastic rites, and the monolith is given greater prominence as a phallic symbol—the more so when the woman collapses to embrace and kiss it. Howard would have known of the use of flagellation in pagan celebrations, such as in the worship of Cybele, from his reading of Plutarch, as well as from such books in his library as *A History of the Rod* (1886) and *Sex and Sex Worship* (1922). The dark-haired female is the centerpiece of both the action and the narrator's attention; presenting herself nude to the crowd, she willingly surrenders to the beating, which drives her to an ecstatic frenzy of motion and final supplication. This provides considerable contrast with the also naked, bound, and weakly resisting sacrificial victim offered to the toad-monster. While both women are nude, the dancer embraces her status and is invigorated by it, while the girl to be sacrificed has been rendered as powerless as a victim in a rape fantasy. While the sacrificial victim's final fate is unrevealed, Howard's prose suggests a carnal sacrifice, as the toad-monster is described in terms of lechery and lust—a major departure from Lovecraft's typically asexual entities.

Other applications of this flagellation material by Howard are most evident in his stories for *Spicy-Adventure Stories* (1934-36) magazine, printed under the pseudonym Sam Walser; the stories were censored by the editors before they saw print, and a few were rejected outright for violating the magazine's strict writing guides. The uncensored versions of these spicy stories were republished in *Spicy Adventures* (2010). Howard also tried his hand at confession stories, which are reprinted in *Lurid Confessions* 1 (1986); and weird menace stories, which are reprinted in *Shudder Stories* 1-2 (1984).

In 1935, Howard wrote to Lovecraft about how E. Hoffmann Price had gotten him into the spicy field:

> In my efforts to make new markets I've been "splashing the field" as Price calls it. One market I tried was *Spicy Adventure*, a sex magazine to which Ed is the star contributor. I sold the first yarn I tried, but doubt if I could make that market regularly, as it requires a deft, jaunty style foreign to my natural style. However, I'll probably try it again. Why don't you give it a whirl? You can use a pen name if you like; I did, and I think most of its contributors do. The maximum length is about 5000 words. That sort of yarn is easy to write, if not to sell. If they reject it, you've only wasted a day or so. They like good strong plots, but the sex element is a cinch; any man can write that part of it. Just write up one of your own sex adventures, altered to fit the plot. That's the way I did with the yarn I sold them. (MF 909)

Regrettably, Lovecraft's next letter is nonextant, so we don't know what his response to Howard's suggestion was, or even if he acknowledged it. The bit about Howard's own "sex adventures" is likely a good example of his supplying a tall tale, perhaps to hide his lack of sexual experience, or else as a joke. The story in question ("The Girl on the Hell Ship," published as "She-Devil"), as with every "spicy," featured no sex on the page by editorial fiat.

Price offered to revise some of Lovecraft's stories for the *Spicy* market, as he would go on to do for Clark Ashton Smith: "Maybe I could thus cash in on some of your rejections from WT! Though introducing bawdy touches concerning Cthulhu or the Elder Ones would tax my imagination" (Murray 1999, 52).

More explicit prose and verse not intended for publication found its way into Howard's letters to his friend Tevis Clyde Smith, reproduced in *The Collected Letters of Robert E. Howard* (2008). A few have also been reprinted in chapbook form: the plays *Song of Bastards* and *Bastards All!* and the memorable poem "Ancient English Ballade" ("Oh, come, friend Dick, go whoring with me!") in *Lewd Tales* (1987); other poems, along with a spicy and an untitled synopsis for another appeared in *Risqué Stories* 1-5 (1984-86). Howard's spicy stories and his other fiction never overlap in setting, though there are a few instances where he cannibalized or revisited an earlier plot, and he utilized several of the same or similar sexual themes in both his spicy and non-spicy work, so there are certainly parallels between the two. The image of a woman being whipped, for example, occurs in the spicy "Daughters of Feud" (written 1936), the Conan tale "Xuthal of the Dusk" (1933), and the Cthulhu Mythos story "The Black Stone" (1931), and bespeaks the way his interest in sadomasochism—whether to earn a Brundage cover or not—expressed itself in his writing.

Much of Howard's reading in sexual matters did not make it into his Mythos fiction. While the background of many a "lusty bygone era" in his weird fiction takes great inspiration from the Lovecraft Mythos, such as the strange cult of Kathulos in the serial novel *Skull-Face* (1931), the tentacled monster Thog of "Xuthal of the Dusk" (1933), and the god that is not dead but lies eternally beneath "The Cairn on the Headland" (1933), only a few his stories are explicitly Mythos tales. With regard to the Mythos proper, one of Howard's great contributions is a stunted precursor race to humanity with ties to lingering pagan religion and witch-cults—a synthesis of concepts from Arthur Machen in "Novel of the Black Seal," "The Shining Pyramid," "The Red Hand," and possibly "The White People" with Margaret Murray's *The Witch-Cult in Western Europe* and other works. The idea appears to have originated from both Howard's reading of Machen and his correspondence with Lovecraft (MF 26-27, 32-33). Jeffrey Shanks in "Theosophy and the Thurian Age: Robert E. Howard and the Works of William Scott-Elliot" (2011) suggests that the theosophical concept of "root races" likewise may have informed or inspired Howard.

Lovecraft never explicitly used Machen's race of troglodytes in his own fiction, although elements of it may remain in the degenerate, multiethnic cults of "The Call of Cthulhu" and "The Horror at Red Hook"; the fullest development of this theory by Lovecraft is the mini-essay "Some Backgrounds of Fairyland," originally from a letter to Wilfred B. Talman. Likewise, Lovecraft and Howard shared some degree of belief in physical, generational degeneration. Compare the Martense clan in "The Lurking Fear" and how Howard's pre-human race was also driven to a nocturnal existence—but where Lovecraft made the Martenses descend into apes, the Children of the Night become more reptilian, though not quite to the degree of the Serpent-People of Valusia in Howard's Kull tales.

These Little People or Children of the Night allowed Howard to give full expression to a kind of fantasy racism—a prejudice and genocidal urge that becomes embedded in many of Howard's characters and is often directed against their racial antagonists. Or taking a cue from Machen's Jervase Cradock in "Novel of the Black Seal," their mixed-raced descendents are often intimated to be the products of rape—such is the case in "The Children of the Night" (1931): "What foul shape stole into the Ketrick castle on some forgotten night, or rose out of the dusk to grip some woman of the line, straying in the hills?" (Howard 2001, 78), and again in "Worms of the Earth" (1932): "but they steal forth at night to grip women straying on the moors" (Howard 2001, 31). The latter story contains one of the most remarkable sexual characters in Howard's Mythos fiction: Atla, the witch-woman of Dagon-moor, whom Bran recognizes as half-human and half-other: "By the mottles on your skin, by the slanting of your eyes, by the taint in your veins" (Howard 2001, 30). In the story, Atla's price for her aid is a night in the king's bed:

> "I am half-human, at least! Have I not known sorrow and yearning and crying wistfulness, and the drear ache of loneliness? Give to me, king—give me your fierce kisses and your hurtful barbarian's embrace. Then in the long dreary years to come I shall not utterly eat out my heart in vain envy of the white-bosomed women of men; for I shall have a memory few of them can boast—the kisses of a king! One night of love, O king, and I will guide you to the gates of Hell!" (Howard 2001, 31-32)

Atla shares many similarities with Jervase Cradock—and, by extension, Wilbur Whateley. Her appearance is not entirely human and is generally loathsome to normal humanity, and her heritage gives her access to peculiar powers that are mostly only hinted, but include the ability to speak the hissing speech of the Little People, just as Jervase Cradock could sometimes lapse into the dark tongue of his progenitors and Wilbur Whateley was conversant in Aklo; she also serves as a link between the mundane and the supernatural, just as the others do. Beyond this, Atla's defining characteristics are that she is a woman while Jervase and Wilbur are male, though in their respective stories the latter are essentially asexual, while Atla possesses and acts on a very human desire for companionship—or, at the very least, a session of physical lovemaking.

Howard himself seemed surprised at the story's reception, as he noted in a letter to Tevis Clyde Smith: "The readers took well to my 'Worms of the Earth' story, much to my surprize. I didn't know how they'd like the copulation touch" (REH 2.485). This focus on rape and half-breeds suggests a certain fascination with miscegenation in Howard's fiction (both Mythos and non-Mythos), and recalls the attractive and sexually aggressive black women who appear in several of his stories, including the black queens in the weird Solomon Kane story "The Moon of Skulls" (1930) and the spicy "The Ship in Mutiny" (written 1936). It is a matter of some debate how much this emphasis on sexually attractive and aggressive black women—and, by a consequence, of mixed-race characters in his fiction—was influenced by Howard's experiences in real life, and a Southwestern culture that placed particular negative emphasis on half-breeds and mulattos. One particular episode in Ellis's memoir stands out—an account of an argument about white men who visit black prostitutes and beget mixed-race children, which left Howard sputtering (Ellis 96).

Male and female homoeroticism is often perceived in Howard's stories, though it would be a stretch to claim that any of his major characters are homosexual as he conceived and portrayed them. Interested readers may check out chapter 7 ("Is Conan Dating Clark Kent?") of Harry Harrison's *Great Balls of Fire! An Illustrated History of Sex in Science Fiction* (1977) for a look at perceived homoeroticism in Howard's works and adaptations.

The strong masculine portrayals of Howard's male characters—often abetted in reprints by hypermuscular, near-nude depictions in the accompanying artwork—are recognized as sexually appealing; the physical interaction of more than one such character, such as a violent conflict between two half-naked barbarians, or the tender groping trunk of Yag-Kosha from "The Tower of the Elephant" (1933), can be read as scenes of homoeroticism, though there is no indication that Howard ever considered them as such. He himself curiously characterized female-on-female violence in his stories as lesbianism (MF 909). This understanding or representation was not based on love, affection, or sexual attraction between two women, but the sexually charged conflict between two contrasting women—one blonde and one brunette, one white and one black, one of a "wholesome" race and one of a "degenerate" or "savage" race, etc.

Clark Ashton Smith

The aesthetic cross-fertilization between Lovecraft and Clark Ashton Smith could be traced as far back as *Home Brew* and their exchange of letters, but their respective imaginations did not really overlap until Smith began his brief but prolific spurt of story-writing for the pulps in the 1930s. Both authors took inspiration from Edgar Allan Poe, Arthur Machen, etc.; but Smith also received inspiration from George Sterling, French Romantic and Decadent literature, Baudelaire, and James Branch Cabell.

Smith wrote his stories before the idea of a "Cthulhu Mythos" was recognized by most readers of *Weird Tales* or conceived by August Derleth, and when taken with the fact that much of Smith's fiction is interrelated, sharing fantastic settings like Averoigne, Hyperborea, or Zothique, characters and entities like Eibon and Tsathoggua, and references to events from other or previous tales, it is difficult to distinguish what Smith stories may be considered part of the Cthulhu Mythos—and if such a distinction is really meaningful. Later authors like Lin Carter have muddied the waters further with a penchant for tying in Smith stories and creations that initially had nothing to do with the Mythos.

H. P. Lovecraft and Clark Ashton Smith had very different attitudes and experiences on sex, and their Mythos fiction reflects in part this difference. It is known that as a young man Smith fell passionately in love with a blonde woman who took ill and died, and afterwards he gave his deepest love to brunettes; he joked of affairs with married women in his letters, the true extent of which is unclear; and late in life he married Carol Jones Dorman, who survived him and wrote an uncompleted memoir titled *The Man Who Walks the Stars*, the manuscript of which resides at the John Hay Library (Smith 2003, 32n2; Behrends 5-6). The combination of love and death, as well as affairs and cuckoldry, are themes that would recur often in Smith's creative output, from the romance and sexuality prominent in his poetry, including the suggestive "Saturnian Cinema" (written 1954) and the erotic "The Temptation" (1924) collected in Section V of *The Last Oblivion* (2002); and the weird play *The Dead Will Cuckold You* (1951). In Smith's short fiction, of which his tales related to the Cthulhu Mythos are a part, Tim Powers gave the best epitome:

> Eroticism abounds, though, whether as dangerous as the various deadly ladies in "The Kiss of Zoraida" and "A Rendezvous in Averoigne," or as grotesque and ultimately funny as the "national mother" in "The Door to Saturn," but

it's a fatal eroticism, and to give in to it is generally to be obliterated—though often we can queasily sympathize with the brave and foolhardy souls who choose just that. Lamiae, succubi, sirens—for the duration of a story, at least, Smith can convince you that plain love between a human man and woman is the lowest possible reading on a meter that stretches very high, though nearly all of the calibrations are in the red-lit danger zone. (CF 1.vii)

Donald Sidney-Fryer likewise noted that "Generally overlooked is the fact that a great many of Smith's 'tales of horror' are just as much tales of love" (1988, 11), and that "Smith relentlessly emphasizes the carnal qualities of death and dying" (1988, 13). Both statements ring very true, and Smith's weird fiction often features love leading to murder, necromancy, and necrophilia, as well as pining for a dead loved one or a romance with the undead. For a greater examination, see Steve Behrends's "The Song of the Necromancer: 'Loss' in Clark Ashton Smith's Fiction" (1986). For a more general approach to sex and death in fantasy, see Ann Morris's "The Dialectic of Sex and Death in Fantasy" in *Erotic Universe: Sexuality and Fantastic Literature* (1986).

Not that Smith deliberately set out to write erotica most of the time—far from it, as he wrote to August Derleth in 1933:

> As to the so-called sexiness, it would not interest me to write a story dealing with anything so banal, hackneyed and limited as this type of theme is likely to be. Too many writers are doing it to death at the present time; and I have ended by revolting literarily against the whole business, and am prepared to maintain that a little Victorian reticence, combined with Puritan restraint, would harm nobody. (Smith 2003, 220)

Despite this sentiment, Smith's penchant for the morbid, gruesome, and sensual in scene and subject matter would often see his best work rejected multiple times or require revision before it would see print, and Smith did once attempt to "splash the spicies," possibly under the suggestion of Robert E. Howard or E. Hoffmann Price. Will Murray in "An Informal History of the Spicy Pulps" (1984) reveals:

> An interesting sidelight to Price's Spicy work was two stories Clark Ashton Smith gave him after Smith found them unsalable. In 1940, Price rewrote them for *Spicy Mystery*. The first, "House of the Monoceros," appeared in the February 1941 issue as "The Old Gods Eat," while the second story's fate is unknown. It was titled "Dawn of Discord." Naturally, they were greatly changed in the telling. (Murray 1984, 38)

Smith's versions of "House of the Monoceros" and "Dawn of Discord" have since been reprinted in *The Miscellaneous Writings of Clark Ashton Smith* (2011). However, in his own efforts to write for the spicies, CAS related his failure in a letter to R. H. Barlow: "'Mother of Toads' is a sort of carnal and erotic nightmare and I can't decide on its merits. Spicy Mystery Stories rejected it after holding the ms. for nearly two months" (Smith 2003, 301).

A certain female character type in Smith's works is indicative of his approach: independent, magically skilled or powerful in some way, and rarely married or interested in marriage, but attracted to men and interested in sexual relationships. The leading example from his Mythos stories is Moriamis in "The Holiness of Azédarac" (1933), who is perhaps based on the titular "The Demoiselle d'Ys" (1895) by Robert W. Chambers. It is interesting to compare this kind of character with some of Lovecraft's and Howard's, such as T'la-Yub of "The Mound," Marceline Bedard in "Medusa's Coil," and Atla of "Worms of the Earth." While Lovecraft's females seek marriage or long-term commitment, Howard's and Smith's characters seek only affection, and only Moriamis looks for honest affection. The result is in part a difference in the tone of the story—Lovecraft and Howard going for weird horror, Smith striving for weird black humor—as much as the difference in the authors' history with and approach to women.

Still, if Lovecraft and Smith had their differences, so too did they draw from the same well. Smith's "The Nameless Offspring" (1932) is a cousin to Lovecraft's "The Dunwich Horror," both inspired by Machen's "The Great God Pan," as Smith revealed to Lovecraft in a 1931 letter:

> "Pan," by the way, has suggested to me an idea so hellish that I am almost afraid to work it out in story-form. It involves a cataleptic woman who was placed alive in the family vaults. Days later, a scream was heard within the family vaults, the door was unlocked, and the woman was found sitting up in her *open* coffin, babbling deliriously of some terrible demoniac face whose vision had awakened her from her death-like sleep. Eight or nine months afterwards, she gives birth to a child and dies. The child is so monstrous that no one is permitted to see it. It is kept in a locked room [. . .] (Smith 2003, 145-46)[1]

---

1. In 1933, CAS related an anecdote that is similar in theme to this story to Lovecraft: "Here, by the way, is a recent portrait–sketch of our Lord Tsathoggua, which I made for you the other day. My Indian wood-cutter saw it (as I think I mentioned on a card) and said instantly: 'That's one of the Old Boys.' He then proceeded to narrate a tribal legend about a young squaw who was carried away by some prehuman entity

Lovecraft wrote back:

> That daemonic-spawn plot of yours is tremendously powerful—a genuine improvement, I think, on the idea of which Machen is so fond—*Great God Pan, Black Seal* &c. I once had the idea of having a daemon begotten through some hellish evocation, & having the birth attended by the death from shock, of both mother & physician—followed by the swift growth of the nameless thing which escapes unseen from the fateful birth-chamber. The thing was to be a terror of the night in the rural region concerned—a looker into windows & devourer of lone travelers. But I gave up the notion when I saw how Machen had used it before me. (SL 3.286)

It is a curious sort of comment for Lovecraft to have made, since in essence he already had done that by writing "The Dunwich Horror" in 1928, but it is revealing that what both Lovecraft and Smith seized on from these Machen stories and used as a common element in both tales was the "daemonic-spawn" element. As with Lovecraft, Smith focuses primarily on the resulting progeny, leaving the act itself—and the perpetrator—unseen; nevertheless, the sexual element was a concern in seeing the story published (CF 3.312).

The most lasting impact of Clark Ashton Smith on love and sex in the Cthulhu Mythos was the expansion of the idea of sexual congress between the Mythos entities, particularly the heritage of Tsathoggua and his various descendents, which finally culminated in "The Family Tree of the Gods." Inspired by a humorous genealogy Lovecraft had included in a 1933 letter (SL 4.183), Smith furnished the first actual "Family Tree of the Gods" in letters to R. H. Barlow in 1934[2] (Smith 2003, 257) and Robert A. ("Rah") Hoffman in 1943 (Smith 2003, 340). The chart and notes were revised and expanded by Smith, then published in the Summer 1944 issue of the *Acolyte* and reprinted in *Planets and Dimensions: Collected Essays of Clark Ashton Smith* (1973), and with additional supplements from Smith's letters

---

into a cavern. Nearly a year later, the squaw emerged to the light, bringing with her an infant that was half human and half something else" (Smith 2003, 228). Given the date, the anecdotal tale had no direct influence on "The Nameless Offspring" (1932), but is included here for completeness and as an item of interest.

2. There are some trivial differences between the letters to Barlow, published in full in *The Dark Eidolon: The Journal of Smith Studies* 2 (1989), and the published "Family Tree of the Gods"/"From the Parchments of Pnom," but these do not affect the substance of the text.

as "From the Parchments of Pnom" in *The Tsathoggua Cycle* (2005). Rah Hoffman gives a good account of its genesis:

> [...] he came across a draft of one page of a letter he had written to Barlow years before. Barlow, he explained, had written asking for the family tree of Smith's gods, or "Old Ones," as Smith called them. So CAS had gone pseudo-seriously into it, sketching the tree, writing an extensive account of the genealogy of the line, and even inventing some imaginative names to fill in the gaps. (Sidney-Fryer 1978, 193)

The family tree is almost exclusively concerned with Smith's corner of the Mythos, the descent of Tsathoggua's family as given partly in his tales "The Door to Saturn" (1932) and "The Testament of Athammaus" (1932), and written at least in part to reconcile Tsathoggua's biography with Lovecraft's ghostwritten story "The Mound" (1929-30). In the tracing of generations, Smith moves from asexual reproduction to sexual reproduction:

> Azathoth, the primal nuclear chaos, reproduced of course only by fission; but its progeny, entering various outer planets, often took on attributes of androgynism and bisexuality. The androgynes, curiously, required no coadjutancy in the production of offspring; but their children were commonly unisexual, male or female. Hzioulquoigmnzhah, uncle of Tsathoggua, and Ghizghuth, Tsathoggua's father, were the male progeny of Cxaxukluth, the androgynous spawn of Azathoth. Thus you will note a trend toward biological complexity. (Price 2005, 3)

Later authors did not explicitly follow Smith's formula, but this early family tree—and Lovecraft's—helped establish the idea of familial or sexual interconnections and interactions between the various Cthulhu Mythos entities, and provided the basis for various works by Lin Carter and others.

In addition to Tsathoggua and kin, Smith also invented a number of other alien entities with unusual sexualities—the Blemphroim of "The Door to Saturn" (1932), who had degenerated to a headless state (similar to Howard's Little People or Lovecraft's Martense clan) and were ruled by a national mother who killed and ate her husbands; and the Voormis, apparently a hybrid race: "much was said of the genesis of the Voormis, who were popularly believed to be the offspring of women and certain atrocious creatures that had come forth in primal days from a tenebrous cavern-world in the bowels of Voormithadreth" (CF 5.54-55). Ubbo-Sathla is another of Smith's additions to the Mythos, a terrestrial "formless, idiotic demiurge" (CF 3.225) counterpart of sorts to Lovecraft's celestial blind idiot god Azathoth. The two serve similar purposes in Smith's Mythos work—Ubbo-Sathla the progenitor and ultimate source of all earthly life, while Azathoth the same for the Mythos entities Tsathoggua, Cthulhu, etc., as revealed in "Family Tree of the Gods." In both cases, the ultimate sources reproduce asexually, although more in the manner of amoebas and other primitive life-forms than the more developed asexual aliens of Lovecraft's Mythos. Bearing a stark similarity is the protean Abhoth from "The Seven Geases," but with a key difference: where Ubbo-Sathla is mindless as well as formless, the protean Abhoth is sentient and conscious, able to recognize its diverse offspring, and, like the titan Cronus, has a penchant for consuming its own multifarious young.

Robert Bloch

The initial spate of Mythos tales by Robert Bloch were written from 1935 to 1937, during the period when the young writer was in correspondence with and encouraged by H. P. Lovecraft; after Lovecraft's death new Mythos fiction came only sporadically from Bloch's typewriter, with the bulk of his creative effort going to more original short fiction, novels, scripts, and screenplays. The development of female characters and sexuality in Bloch's Mythos tales mirrors in many ways his development as a professional writer: early Bloch tales feature few female characters and little sex, but as he developed and branched out into other forms of fiction he included both more frequently and with greater skill, though his depictions of female characters are sometimes compromised by lingering stereotypes of women as fickle, helpless, prone to distress, etc. Some of Bloch's most notable non-Mythos stories with strong sexual elements include "Yours Truly, Jack the Ripper" (1943), "The Skull of the Marquis de Sade" (1945), and "A Toy for Juliette" (1967). Bloch never splashed the spicies and in later years evinced a somewhat old-fashioned dislike for obscenities, gore, and sex in writing and film, but he did place stories with gentlemen's magazines such as *Playboy*, *Hustler*, and *Gallery*.

In the early tales, the main characters have no distinct sexual identity, and sex only enters the story to highlight some taboo aspect or legend. In "The Mannikin" (1936), for example, the libel of incest is applied to the Maglores to highlight their reputation of insularity, outsideness, and witchery—much as Lovecraft implied with the Whateleys in "The Dunwich Horror"; and when Bloch wishes to illustrate the decadence of a party in

New Orleans in "The Secret of Sebek" (1937), he outlines a crowd that includes "a desperately bright debutante, with the predatory slut-eyes of a common harlot" (Bloch 2009, 115).

"The Brood of Bubastis" (1936) is explicit in that bestiality is the method by which the priests of Bast created their hybrids, but the actual sexual action is Lovecraft-style, firmly off the page and in the distant past, reminiscent of "Arthur Jermyn" or "The Rats in the Walls." The breeding program, coupled with the British setting, cult, and underground chamber, suggests the influence of "The Rats in the Walls." Bloch's treatment of female characters and relationships in these early stories is generally slight to nonexistent, with the most remarkable piece being "Mother of Serpents." The central focus of that story is the conflict between mother and son. However, readers looking for a foreshadowing of the Bates family from *Psycho* (1959) decades later will be mostly disappointed; there is little to nothing of the complex psychological behavior that would mark Bloch's later work.

Bloch's Mythos stories from the late 1940s onward have greater development of character, including sexual identity and interaction where appropriate, and represent both a greater experience with and maturity in dealing with women, sex, and relationships. "The Unspeakable Betrothal" (1948) is a poignant depiction of real emotions and realizations that occur to many women, but the psychological transition here is realized with a supernatural transition that translates it from effective drama to horror, similar in some ways to the encroaching madness in Gilman's "The Yellow Wall Paper," as catalyzed by the Mythos. The comical, adult "Philtre Tip" (1961) is an extended pun, and "The Terror of Cut-Throat Cove" (1958) is an example of hardboiled Lovecraftian fiction, complete with a woman a man could get himself into trouble over.

The culmination of Bloch's Mythos material is the novel *Strange Eons* (1978), which in its mature handling of sexual matters and female characters is true to many of the concepts of the Lovecraft setting but updated to a contemporary setting, and in many ways prefigures several developments by later Mythos authors. Bloch deliberately plays with sex in *Strange Eons*, not simply recognizing and utilizing the sexual themes in Lovecraft's stories but deliberately invoking them to foreshadow the outcome of the novel, as well as incorporating Lovecraft criticism and biographical information directly in the text for verismilitude:

["M]iscegenation." Waverly nodded. "Lovecraft had a puritan attitude toward sex, and yet this theme threads through his stories. Even in the early tales, his morbid dislike of 'foreigners' hints at something evil in the mingling of bloodlines, something that would debase civilized attitudes and drag mankind down to pre-human level.

"Remember the degenerate underground race he describes in *The Lurking Fear* and *The Rats in the Walls*? In *Arthur Jermyn* he told of the offspring of ape and human, but I think he was really getting at something far worse. Then, in *Pickman's Model*, he openly spoke of ghouls—creatures who feast on the dead and presumably are born from a necrophilic union.

"But all this was only a prelude to the real horror—not the mating of superior with inferior, of man with animal, of the living with the dead, but something even more disturbing—the mating of man and monster.

"Consider Wilbur Whateley and his twin brother in *The Dunwich Horror*—children of Yog-Sothoth and a human mother. Think about the villagers in *The Shadow over Innsmouth*, worshipping the Kanaka gods of Polynesia with sexual rites which spawned a race of beings that lived on land until they developed the 'Innsmouth look'—fish-eyed, frog-faced mutations who finally wriggled back into the sea to join Great Cthulhu in the deep." Waverly gulped his brandy. "That's what Lovecraft was trying to tell us in his stories—there are monsters in our midst." (Bloch 1978, 29-30)

Here Bloch addresses the theme of miscegenation in the Lovecraft Mythos and provides a justification for it; the hybrid spawn are the outcome of a breeding program that outspans human history, to provide food for Cthulhu and the others. Anyone not familiar with the Mythos would miss most of the references Bloch uses, at least until some character on the page points them out, but Mythos fans can be expected to pick up on them and anticipate what Bloch has in store.

Reading *Strange Eons* at a higher level, with both an awareness of Lovecraft's stories and of the material on Lovecraft's life that had been published up to that point, it is clearly visible where Bloch was taking stabs or making use and reference to certain aspects of Lovecraft's personality and certain views and interpretations of his life, as well as his fiction. While recognizing and not exactly condoning Lovecraft's prejudice, Bloch nevertheless at least finds a use for it in the context of this novel.

Bloch's characterization of women in *Strange Eons* is undermined by the uses he puts to them in the story; while initially a sketch of intelligent, independent, and "liberated" women, their actions are almost entirely passive and reactive. Events happen to them or around them, but these women rarely instigate or take part in the events, and in the end are whisked off the page to be ravaged by the Old One and join Lovecraft's unseen mothers. Part of this is definitely Bloch playing to themes in the Lovecraft Mythos, deliberately invoking Lavinia Whateley and "The Dunwich Horror," but another part is probably the lingering attitudes of his day, or at least his instincts as a screenwriter. Bedroom scenes occur offpage, but the events are addressed with a Hollywood cut to the next morning, the dialogue and attitudes a bit too hardboiled and old-fashioned for the time when the book was written.

August Derleth

> I have often wondered why he put so little sex into his books. Before I met him, I assumed that this might be because he was a natural puritan, like Lovecraft; but my two days with him dispelled that notion. He could be sexually frank, even Rabelaisian, and the same quality appears in some of his letters to me. He may have felt that Wisconsin—and Sauk City in particular—might disapprove of a more open attitude to sex in the books; I don't know. If so, it was a pity, not because more sex would have given his books a wider sale, but because it was an aspect of his literary personality that he left unexplored. (Wilson 54)

As a tireless promoter of Lovecraft's work and publisher of Lovecraft's collected fiction, his *Selected Letters,* and various memoirs and biographical materials, August William Derleth was a significant force in how Lovecraft and the Mythos were received after Lovecraft's death. This includes much of the early impression of Lovecraft's sexuality: it was through Derleth that Winfield Townley Scott's original biographical article "His Own Most Fantastic Creation: Howard Phillips Lovecraft," Sonia Davis's edited memoir of her former husband, excerpts from Sonia and Lovecraft's letters to each other, and other materials saw print through Arkham House under Derleth's aegis. Derleth himself would sometimes weigh in on the subject of Lovecraft's sex life as well (Russell 114).

As an editor, co-founder of Arkham House, and anthologist, Derleth had the opportunity for a heavy hand in shaping the Cthulhu Mythos after Lovecraft died. While *Weird Tales* remained a primary outlet for new Mythos fiction, it was Derleth who selected and accepted stories for publication in a large number of anthologies, both at Arkham House and elsewhere. In this way, Derleth kept Lovecraft's fiction alive and in circulation and encouraged the early Mythos work of authors such as Ramsey Campbell, Brian Lumley, and Colin Wilson, while seeking to curtail the publication of other would-be Mythos writers. Derleth's editorial voice in selecting texts appears to have been generally permissive when it came to intimations of sexuality, as evidenced by Campbell's "Cold Print" appearing in *Tales of the Cthulhu Mythos* (1969), but it was evidently more stringent when it came down to vulgar language and overt sexuality, as revealed by Ramsey Campbell:

> One deletion he made, however, was anything that related to my "minor tendency to vulgarity," as he called it. He may even have felt slightly responsible for this, since he used to send me Henry Miller novels which were then banned in Britain, and later agreed to receive books from the Olympia Press in Paris on my behalf, since Olympia wouldn't mail to England, and send them on. You can see where he made one of the deletions, on page 199 of *Inhabitants*: "What's all this shit you're talking?" I had Leakey scream, but August took out the bad word without changing "talking" to "saying," and so the line reads oddly. I also, on page 201, had the robed man wearing "a necklace of small pink cylinders whose identity Leakey sickly suspected." But Derleth thought I meant the man and not the cylinders, and I didn't then have the courage to change the line back when I saw the page proofs. (Jaffery 72)

Campbell offered a slight expansion some years later:

> Another source of banned books was August Derleth, my friend and mentor and (in the days when Arkham House was pretty well his one-man operation) first professional publisher, who sent me Henry Miller's *Tropics* and Lawrence Durrell's *Black Book*. This led me to assume he wouldn't mind if I introduced a different kind of shock into my Lovecraft imitations, but he took the shit out of a line of dialogue. I still think it's what the character would have said, but I see that that may not be relevant to such a stylised form as Lovecraft pastiche. (Campbell 2002, 233)

Derleth's complete letter regarding "The Moon Lens," published in a subsequent, expanded edition of *The Inhabitant of the Lake* (2011), contains a fuller explanation:

> Secondly, you have a minor tendency toward vulgarity. "Shit" &c. may be in place in TROPIC OF CANCER, but it is out of place in a weird tale. The reader is not concentrating upon anything but the horror of your tale, and the intrusion of such language is unwarranted and distracting. It is certainly not a matter of prurience on my part, but only of the fitness of things. Whenever you use these offensive words (offensive in your context only, that is), any other word will do as well; they are not vital to your story, as they are vital to

Miller's, by contrast. In a Miller story "cunt" for woman is inevitable, and "woman" would be as out of place in his context as "shit" or "shitty" &c. are in yours. (Campbell 2011, 297)

These editorial decisions appear mirrored in Derleth's approach to his own fiction in that while he himself was no prude, and on occasion utilized sexual elements in his writing, he rarely did so in his weird fiction and never with vulgar language.

It is difficult to discuss Derleth's attitudes as a writer and editor without addressing something of his sexuality and attitudes toward sex. Derleth's sexuality had been the subject of gossip in certain circles for years before and after his death. For example, L. Sprague de Camp in his autobiography *Time & Chance* (1996) relates:

August's sexual proclivities have been the subject of gossip in science-fiction circles. Lin Carter once told me that, when he and his wife Noël made a brief visit to Derleth, August propositioned both during their stay. All I can personally testify to is that during Rusty's and my visit, August made no passes at either of us. (de Camp 1996, 242)

This is a fairly typical second-hand anecdote, but interestingly it refers to a very notable and recorded incident. Lin Carter and his wife only met Derleth once, thirteen days before the latter's death: the visit is described in *Lovecraft: A Look Behind the Cthulhu Mythos* (1972), and in some greater detail in "A Day in Derleth Country" (1971). Neither account mentions Derleth making a pass (or would really be expected to), unless it is alluded to during one small segment of the visit:

A third room was given over to Derleth's odd hobby of picking, drying and selling a succulent species of mushroom called morels. Augie remarked that during one stage of the drying process morels exuded an odor identical with that of male semen, which occasioned a few ribald jests. (Carter 1982)

These rumors influenced Derleth's reputation. Kay Price, Derleth's secretary, wrote:

As I grew older I listened closer to the gossip and rumors. They said Derleth was crude and obnoxious. He was a "home wrecker", "bisexual", "homosexual", and "drunk". [. . .] He laughed about his sexual reputation and said, "I wish I had time to do half of what the gossips accuse me of doing. I'd like to live up to my reputation, but unfortunately, I would have written two books instead of 150 if I did." (Price 1992, 58-59)

However, these rumors were not directly addressed until the publication of *Derleth: Hawk . . . and Dove* (1997) by Dorothy M. Litersky, one of Derleth's former students. Litersky's biography depicts Derleth as a closeted bisexual who engaged in multiple long-term relationships with both men and women, including some partners who were of high-school age at the beginning of the relationship. This depiction is based on Litersky's interviews with Derleth before he died, as well as her consultation of his papers and correspondence on deposit at the State Historical Society of Wisconsin and elsewhere. Derleth's published letters support some of Litersky's material and depiction of Derleth's character. For example, Litersky relates in one anecdote:

> Years later after Derleth's death Sara told her story to a class of young students and reporters of her walk in the woods with August. She was relaxing on a blanket when he proceeded to discard all his clothes except his socks and to dance under the trees. She said she was shocked and embarrassed and pretended to be asleep. (206)

While somewhat inexplicable to Sara (and Litersky), a letter from Derleth to Lovecraft suggests that nudism was a common practice for him, at least when the weather permitted: "I am brown as a berry, and have managed to rouse some indignation by being a one-man nudist colony on the hills only a third of a mile across the river from the village" (*ES* 632–33; cf. Moskowitz 82).

However, none of Derleth's printed letters include any reference to a homosexual relationship—nor would it be expected for Derleth to have stated such a thing to his correspondents. The best summary of his thoughts and feelings on the matter that Derleth ever expressed are in two letters to Lovecraft:

> I must confess, that though I am steeped in abnormal sex, having studied all kinds of perverts at first hand, the suspicion of necrophilia in A Rose for Emily never once entered my mind. [. . .] Here is a woman starved for something—what is it, love perhaps? Let us assume it is. But she knows nothing about it. Love to her means a possession, a having. What she had come to regard as hers seems to be too independent. She kills. Thus, she keeps, she possesses, she loves. Necrophilia may or may not enter into this relation; it's a minor point to me, since my own experience with people in this existence has led me to look on such things as part and parcel of life, though I am still conservative enough to be horrified by them, deeply. Yet I would be the first to jump to the defense of a necrophiliac, a homosexual, &c., largely because I know that so often these

poor creatures are incapable of helping themselves, have had their nerve systems tortured and twisted permanently from birth. (ES 406)

I can understand your detestation of sex irregularities in life as violations of harmony and I here fully agree with you. I had previously misunderstood you to mean protestation from a basis of morals, and on this basis I would have stood squarely opposed to you. I have known and still know many people who are sexually irregular, both homosexual men and women, and except for three cases out of perhaps 21, I have always found these people highly intellectual, fully aware of what they were doing, and in all cases quite helpless. Speaking perspectively and in the abstract, I could as easily conceive myself entering upon a monogamous homosexual relation as a heterosexual one—though perhaps practice would change that pointofview. To quibble about mere words, I should not say that perverts necessarily lived inartistically. (ES 543)

An unsourced quotation from Derleth proceeds along this line:

I have no inhibitions, had few all my life sexually, that if I wanted to masturbate, I did so without guilt; if I wished to make love to a member of my own sex, likewise; if I wished to make love to a woman, again, likewise, the only condition being that sexual pleasure must rise from love, or at least deep and genuine affection. (Litersky 211)

If these paragraphs do not answer any lingering questions regarding Derleth's sexuality, they at least elucidate some seeming contradictions in his actions and attitudes as a writer and editor. Derleth, whatever his personal feelings with regard to those he considered "perverts," acknowledged an intellectual interest in "abnormal sex," an acceptance of those who practiced what he considered abnormal sex, and a strong disagreement with "protestation from a basis of morals." While not willing to engage—or admit to engaging—in what he considered sexual perversion, Derleth did not consider such acts actually immoral, and by extension did not feel that literature discussing sex openly was immoral either, which explains why he sent books sometimes deemed obscene to a young Ramsey Campbell, and in his Mythos fiction did not always shy away from the risqué either.

As a writer of Cthulhu Mythos fiction, Derleth was fairly prolific—forty short stories counting "collaborations" and the short novel *The Lurker at the Threshold* (1945)—but this is only a small fraction of the total material he produced in his lifetime, with more than a hundred books to his credit before he died, including fiction, nonfiction, anthologies, and books of poetry, along with innumerable reviews, articles, essays, introductions, uncollected poetry, letters published and unpublished, etc.

Derleth was both a codifier who sought to emphasize and to establish more clearly certain aspects and relationships that Lovecraft had used in their own writing, and the primary pasticheur of the early Cthulhu Mythos. As such, the sexual elements in his work seem to reflect less his life and experiences than expansions and exaggerations of existing themes in Lovecraft's work. In several instances, Derleth's interpretation of Lovecraft's Mythos veers off from the standard reading of a Lovecraft text, and this gives a certain perspective to his viewpoint. In *The Lurker at the Threshold*, for example, he incorporates a passage from Lovecraft in the text:

> But in respect of Generall Infamy, no Report more terrible hath come to Notice, than of what Goodwife *Doten*, Relict of *John Doten* of *Duxbury* in the Old Colonies, brought out of the woods near Candlemas of 1787. She affirm'd, and her good neighbours likewise, that it had been borne to her, and took oath that she did not know by what manner it had come upon her, for it was neither Beast nor Man but like to a monstrous Bat with human face. It made no sound but look'd at all and sundry with baleful eyes. There were those who swore that it bore a frightful resemblance to the Face of one long dead, one *Richard Bellingham* or *Bollinhan* who is affirm'd to have vanished utterly after consort with Daemons in the country of New Dunnich. The horrible Beast-Man was examined by the Court of Azzizes and the which then burnt by Order of the High-Sherif on the 5th of June in the year 1788. (Derleth 2003, 23)

This passage is adapted from a fragment of Lovecraft's:

> But in respect of generall Infamy, no Report more terrible hath come to Notice, than of what Goodwife *Doten*, Relict of *John Doten* of *Doxbury* in the Old Colonie, brought out of the Woods near Candlemass of 1683. She affirmed, and her good neighbours likewise, that it had been borne that which was neither Beast nor Man, but like to a monstrous Bat with human Face. The which was burnt by Order of the High-Sheriff on the 5th of June in the Year 1684. (Lovecraft 2006, 256)

The passage reads similarly to that in Lovecraft's "The Unnamable," with its half-man half-beast, and to other references to unnatural births that were common in the legendry. Robert M. Price in his article "Legacy of the Lurker" notes that the unnatural Candlemas birth echoes the date Wilbur Whateley and his twin were born in "The Dunwich Horror." However, Derleth in adapting this fragment takes a different tack, at least initially: "[Richard Billington] had taken himself and his evil practices off into the deeper woods near Duxbury and there perpetuated himself in a secondary line which had ultimately spawned the horror" (Derleth 2003,

24). Nothing more is made of this dangling plot point, but it is an interesting point of departure and indicative of Derleth's later course: where Lovecraft's family lines tend to be dwindling, lonely affairs, Derleth's tend to be sprawling, tangled trees.

Derleth expanded on the expression of Lovecraft's notorious families by adding several new cousins, uncles, and other relations to the Whateley, Bishop, Marsh, Frye, and Corey clans, and more besides. Intermarriages between disparate Mythos families led to monstrous unions, most notably the combination of the Whateley and Marsh bloodlines in "The Shuttered Room." Simple genetics do not, as a rule, appear to govern these Lovecraftian clans, however: in the typical Derleth Mythos story or pastiche, the heir to a particular lineage is more likely to inherit the family house or property, and upon moving in either allow for the deceased's return or become possessed by the spirit of their ancestor, as occurs in "The Return of Hastur," "The Whippoorwills in the Hills" (1948), "The Horror from the Middle Span" (1967), *The Lurker at the Threshold*, and others.

Derleth's veering from the biological determinism that is such a hallmark of the Lovecraft Mythos is indicative of his general failure to capture or mimic the philosophy of Lovecraft's fiction; in the Derleth Mythos not all children of Innsmouth suffer the change, nor is the process of becoming a Deep One a simple matter of genetic inheritance. In at least two notable cases, Derleth abandons Lovecraft's Innsmouth for stories more in line with older weird works. "The Fisherman of Falcon Point" (1959) is much closer to a fairytale or legend cloaked in the dressing of the Lovecraft Mythos than a typical Mythos story, recalling tales of undines, mermaids, and water-brides, while "Innsmouth Clay" (1971) is a variation on the Pygmalion story, albeit including a few literal wet dreams:

> A really extraordinary experience in the night. Perhaps the most vivid dream I've ever had, certainly the most erotic. I can hardly even now think of it without being aroused. I dreamed that a woman, *naked*, slipped into my bed after I had gone to sleep, and remained there all night. I dreamed that the night was spent at love—or perhaps I ought to call it lust. Nothing like it since Paris! And as real as those many nights in the Quarter! Too real, perhaps, for I woke exhausted. And I had undoubtedly spent a restless night, for the bed was much torn up. (Derleth 2008, 254–55)

> Woke this morning convinced that I had not slept alone last night. Impressions on pillow, in bed. Room and bed very *damp*, as if someone wet had got into bed beside me. I know intuitively it was a woman. (Derleth 2008, 260)

In other fiction, Derleth did not so much abandon Lovecraft's ideas entirely as simply expand on them differently. "The Dark Brotherhood" (1966) is essentially a continuation of the asexual reproduction of the Great Race of Yith from Lovecraft's "The Shadow out of Time," only featuring a fictional Lovecraft analogue, an even more imaginary girlfriend, Rose Dexter, and aliens that choose to walk on earth as duplicates of E. A. Poe. At one point, Rose is captured:

> [. . .] in the one that lit the room with its violently pulsating and agitated violet radiation lay Rose Dexter, fully clothed, and certainly under hypnosis—and on top of her lay, greatly elongated and with its tentacles flailing madly, the rugose cone-like figure I had last seen shrunken on the likeness of Poe. And in the connected case adjacent to it—I can hardly bear to set it down even now—lay, identical in every detail, *a perfect duplicate of Rose!* (Derleth 2008, 226)

This scene has elicited a degree of relevant critical interest:

> Derleth, steeped in the works of his master and devoted to extending his fame, has here performed a greater service than he know or intended. It is all here: the blocked repetition of 'violent', the insistence on 'fully clothed', the carefully placed 'certainly' which absolves the woman of all participation, the 'elongated' and 'cone-like' alien, the hesitation about the possibility of setting down the account, and the shock and amazement that such a thing as reproduction should be. Much the same constellation of factors can be derived from an examination of the letters, and from such facts as are available about Lovecraft's brief and curious married life. (Punter 43-44)

Punter's interpretation demonstrates how Derleth's "posthumous collaborations" were received as extensions of Lovecraft's own work, and how Lovecraft's work in turn was viewed with respect to his legend and reputation for prudishness. In *The Literature of Terror* (first edition 1980, second edition 1996), Punter devotes a section to H. P. Lovecraft. Owing perhaps to the date of publication, when only de Camp's biography of Lovecraft was readily available, Punter's reliance on Derleth's posthumous collaborations and opinions of the Mythos, and his own undisguised distaste for Lovecraft's fiction and fan following, his brief overview contains several misconceptions and errors, and harps on Lovecraft's aversion to women and sex. This is deplorable not simply because Punter is incorrect about Lovecraft and Derleth, but because subsequent works such as Joseph Andriano's *Our Ladies of Darkness: Feminine Daemonology in Male Gothic Fiction* (1993), Clive Bloom's *Cult Fiction: Popular Reading and Pulp Theory* (1996), and Allan Lloyd-Smith's *American Gothic Fiction: An Introduction* (2004) have relied on Punter as a source and perpetuated his errors. While I do not wish to demonize Punter for his mistake, it is his poor example and its consequences that in part inspired this work.

Male characters do predominate in Derleth's Mythos fiction, with pairs of good male friends or relatives often coming together in close contact and adversity, such as in "Beyond the Threshold" (1941). As noted previously, there is abundant literary precedent for this sort of partnership without reading an implicit homosexual subtext into the work, but it becomes especially noticeable in *The Trail of Cthulhu* (1962), where by the final story Dr. Laban Shrewsbury has accumulated a group of five devoted men to his cause. Readers who perceive an implicit homosexual relationship would be forgiven for thinking that Shrewsbury is starting a harem! Female relations in the patrilineal family lines are, if anything, even more lacking and invisible than in the Lovecraft Mythos, being almost entirely absent in many stories, with the key ancestor in "The Return of Hastur" (1939), "The Sandwin Compact" (1940), "Beyond the Threshold," *The Lurker at the Threshold*, "The Horror from the Middle Span," and others always an uncle, great-uncle, grandfather, or great-great-grandfather, and so on.

This predominance of male characters seems to owe more to Derleth pastiching Lovecraft than to any natural instinct, and beginning in the late 1950s Derleth began to introduce more female characters, relationships between male and female characters, and sexual elements. Possibly with the demise of *Weird Tales* and his Mythos stories going straight to Arkham House anthologies, Derleth no longer had to contend with other editors of his work and took the opportunity for greater expression in this vein. This period of writing may also have been influenced by his divorce in 1959. Whatever the case, Derleth began delving into hitherto unknown territory with stories like "The Shadow in the Attic" (1964):

> I thrust forth a hand and encountered, unmistakably, a woman's naked breast! And at the same moment I was aware of her hot, fervid breath—and then, instantaneously, she was gone, the bed lightened, I felt, rather than heard, her movement toward the door of the bedroom. [. . .] I am ashamed to admit that I thought at first it had been Rhoda—which was only evidence of the mental confusion the incident had brought me to, for Rhoda was incapable of such an act; had she wished to spend the night in my bed, she would have said as much—she had done so before this. Further, the breast I had touched was not Rhoda's; her breasts were firm, beautifully rounded—and the

breast of the woman who lay next to me on my bed was flaccid, large nippled, and old. And the effect of it, unlike Rhoda's, was one of shuddering horror. (Derleth 2008, 187)

Pre-marital sex, a warlock's succubus that literally climbs into bed with the main character, a consideration of different aesthetics of the naked breast in the hand—such a story would probably have been too spicy for *Weird Tales*. That said, while Derleth did create some strong, confident, educated, and effective characters, such as Ada Marsh of "The Seal of R'lyeh" (1957) and Rhoda Prentiss of "The Shadow in the Attic," most of Derleth's female Mythos characters were explicitly introduced in the story for purposes of establishing a relationship with a male character or characters. Human women like Ada Marsh, Rhoda Prentiss, and Rose Dexter are all girlfriends, fiancées, or romantic interests; the succubus-cum-familiars of "The Shadow in the Attic" and "The Horror from the Middle Span" attach themselves to both the protagonists and their sorcerous uncles; the Innsmouth "mermaid" in "The Fisherman of Falcon Point" and the Deep One Galatea in "Innsmouth Clay" are supernatural brides whose sole purpose appears to be to transform the male protagonists into their proper mates.

Ramsey Campbell

One of the major new authors discovered by Arkham House, Ramsey Campbell began his career writing Lovecraft pastiches and then went on to find his own voice, breaking many of the unspoken taboos personal or professional that Mythos writers of the previous generation had abided by. In part, this was made possible by the early encouragement of August Derleth, and in part by the freedom of a small, specialty press like Arkham House from the pressures of mainstream publishing to conform to normative standards.

Campbell's early efforts, particularly the collection *The Inhabitant of the Lake and Less Welcome Tenants* (1964), are pastiches of Lovecraft's style and incorporate some of his material, but are refreshing in that they largely chronicle new horrors rather than rehashing Lovecraft's old ones, and inhabit a fictional English region of Campbell's own invention rather than the stereotypical Lovecraft country. The publishing of this volume was a hallmark of Mythos literature, the first volume of purely Mythos stories not attributed to Lovecraft or Derleth. Campbell continued to develop as a writer and ventured from Lovecraft pastiche set in the 1920s and '30s to more original material set in his own day. The strength of this approach can be seen in Campbell's "Cold Print," published in *Tales of the Cthulhu Mythos*, which broke many barriers regarding the use of sex in the Mythos and was astonishingly novel compared to the rest of the volume. T. E. D. Klein in "Ramsey Campbell: An Appreciation" (1977) summed it up best:

> The tale went on to include such untraditional elements as sexual frustration, loneliness, and outright horniness; pornography of the kind known euphemistically as "discipline"; hints of homosexuality and pedophilia; allusions to Burroughs, Robbe-Grillet, Hubert Selby, Jr., and B-movies [. . .] to say nothing of the such un-Lovecraftian details as bus fumes, slush, snot, and dogshit; all capped by one of the most breathtakingly gruesome endings I have ever read. (20)

August Derleth as the young Campbell's editor, publisher, and friend or mentor-figure was a major influence; while generally permissive toward content as an editor, Derleth was not always inclined to accept "vulgarity"; and as Campbell's first publisher, a rejection from Derleth would be devastating. As Campbell told it: "His feelings about what he regarded as the inappropriateness of vulgarity or sexual detail to horror fiction troubled me when I began work on *Demons by Daylight*, particularly since I then regarded Arkham as my only market" (Jaffery 104).

Of the stories in *Inhabitants* only "The Moon-Lens" contains any significant vulgarity or sexual detail, and of course that is the story that Derleth chose to censor somewhat—even then, Derleth deleted a minor expletive ("shit") but left in other language that might be questionable to prudes ("phallic" and "vagina"). Curiously, Derleth didn't mention the "necklace of small pink cylinders" at all, suggesting he either missed it entirely or was amenable to intimation without vulgar language and detail, which may also explain why Derleth accepted "Cold Print" for *Tales of the Cthulhu Mythos*. Whether the real or perceived constraints of Derleth's editorial voice greatly influenced the writing and rewriting of Ramsey Campbell's much-delayed next collection, the author has not said—but certainly Derleth's passing freed Campbell from any possible need to accommodate his mentor's editorial tastes.

In *Demons by Daylight* (1973), Campbell still utilized the same geography established for his Mythos stories in *Inhabitants* and continued to use supernatural elements, with certain places, entities, and objects acting as catalysts for the conflict within individuals, between individuals and their families, against uncaring societies, and between dream and reality. In

Demons Campbell broached dark and difficult topics in an intelligent, and if need be explicit manner, including sex:

> One of the chief reasons why *Demons by Daylight* was such a revelation in horror literature was the frankness with which Campbell addressed issues of sexuality and gender in his tales [. . .] Campbell's treatment of sex, while being as far as possible from the cheaply exploitative, confronts complex interpersonal issues with which we, as individuals and as a society, are still grappling. (Joshi 2001, 47–48)

The sexual focus in *Demons*, and in most of the rest of Campbell's fiction from this point on, is based less on infernal pregnancies and supernatural lovers and more on how human characters understand sex, as they try to figure out what they want, from who, and how to get it, with all the anxiety and frustration people normally encounter along the way. The supernatural element sometimes catalyzes these desires, as in "The Old Horns," and sometimes leaves them to deal with the consequences, as with the implied rape of "Made in Goatswood." Campbell would continue to develop the sexual identities of his characters, and sometimes even expanded to more sexually explicit writing, contributing stories exploring and combining sexuality, gender, and horror to anthologies like *The Devil's Kisses* (1976), edited by "Linda Lovecraft" (a pseudonym of Michel Parry). Campbell's erotic horror stories were later collected as *Scared Stiff: Tales of Sex and Death* (1986).

After *Demons* Campbell continued to add to the Mythos only sporadically, such as "The Faces at Pine Dunes" in *New Tales of the Cthulhu Mythos* (1980) (which he also edited), and the satiric pastiche "The Horror under Warrendown" for the Chaosium anthology *Made in Goatswood* (1995), a collection of stories by other authors based on Campbell's early Lovecraft pastiches. The possible culmination of his work, marrying the maturity of his fiction with some of the concepts in his earliest pastiches, is the novel *The Darkest Part of the Woods* (2002), but Campbell continues to put out the occasional Mythos work, such as *The Last Revelation of Gla'aki* (2013), a novella.

The early tales of *The Inhabitant of the Lake* contain the sexual story elements most obviously derived from Lovecraft and company. Supernatural parentage is reflected in Lionel Phipps of "The Horror from the Bridge," who is the product of a sorcerer and his corpse-bride, an idea that Campbell would revisit at greater length in *The Darkest Part of the Woods*. "The

3. Sex and The Cthulhu Mythos

Moon-Lens" is on the surface a clear pastiche of "The Shadow over Innsmouth"—the strange, isolated town with the repellant population and hints of terrible rites, the stranger who stumbles across this and barely escapes, only to discover he is one of them now—but interwoven is an effort at systemization and relation, tying together disparate references to Shub-Niggurath, connecting them to one of Lovecraft's few stories set in England ("The Rats in the Walls"), Machen's "The Great God Pan," the goat of the Sabbat and other occult symbols. The story is a hallmark for the Mythos in its use of explicit sexual imagery, highlighting the interpretation of Shub-Niggurath/the Black Goat as a fertility entity. The priest is girded, literally, with symbols of masculine fertility, and his speech to Leakey contains connotations of sex, sacrifice, and rebirth—a cyclical approach to reproduction that would become more pronounced in some of Campbell's later work. Leakey is taken into the cavern—literally the womb of the earth—and finds himself reborn in a new form as he leaves it. Some tales have an underlying sexual imagery which Campbell himself would only notice and comment on later:

> "The Inhabitant of the Lake". You think I'm exaggerating, or "reading in"? I would have thought so too, until I reread the story and fell over the buried sexual theme. Consider: the story deals with a creature covered with spines that come erect to enable it to inject fluid into the bodies of its victims. It is finally put out of action by one of the characters, who lops off one of its spines (on which, in a disturbingly unmotivated act, he has impaled himself); the story juxtaposes this image with the castration of a zombie. Now if I read all that in someone else's story I would feel pretty safe in discussing the sexual symbolism. (Campbell 2002, 357)

Starting with "Cold Print" (1969), Campbell moved to more mature fare. This is a story not about the kinds of pornography depicted as much as it is about the parallels between the uses made of "forbidden" literature of the Mythos and the censorship, stigma, and passion surrounding extreme pornography. It is a grown-up Mythos story in the sense that it uses an adult subject to reveal an established idea in a new light, highlighting the allure of the taboo by invoking another taboo. The same procedure of hinting and evocative titles that authors use to populate their Mythos stories with fantastic, eldritch tomes is used here to make readers shudder at books that hint of sadomasochism, homosexuality, and pederasty—without ever writing a scene containing any of those elements, or indeed any explicit sex act at all.

The distinction of "Cold Print" is the depiction of Sam Strutt as a fully realized character with sexual identity and desires. Strutt is a lonely pervert who imagines no one understands him and regrets that there is no one to share his interests. From his literary tastes we get the impression of a man interested in domination and sadomasochism (spanking, caning, etc.), focusing on his younger and weaker charges. His interests are not wholly pederastic or homosexual, but they drive him and thus the story. It is not a matter of obtaining adult books for a dry desire to complete a collection; Strutt needs the books—and the companionship of a confederate—to get him through the remainder of the holiday, and that is what drives him back to the shop, and in turn what drives the story. Dominant toward others, Strutt is submissive to and controlled by his own desire. It is this hunger or lust that compromises him, when the bookseller questions his motivations for reading the book—does Strutt visualize himself as the dominant party or the submissive? In reality, many dominant individuals have a submissive side as well, and so it appears to be the case with Strutt. In questioning Strutt's position, the bookseller undermines it and effortlessly assumes a dominant role—and as Strutt's position worsens, the bookseller grows more dominant, both physically and mentally, until Strutt becomes his victim. Campbell cites this as an example of "the theme of the fear of (and suppressed desire for) homosexual rape"(Campbell 2002, 357). In an interesting parallel, Vivian Ralickas in "Art, Cosmic Horror, and the Fetishizing Gaze in the Fiction of H. P. Lovecraft" (2008) suggests that a similar reading can be made of Lovecraft's "The Picture in the House" (1920), where an old man forces a disquieting volume on the younger intruder and forces him to read it, describing the scenario in similar tones of homosexual domination and rape.

Campbell's experience obtaining and reading forbidden books, such as the ones August Derleth helped him procure from Olympia Press, echoes the tensity of Strutt's search for Ultimate Press publications, provides at least some of the background in the real-world titles thrown out, and lends authentic flavor to the fictional book titles. Campbell's Catholic upbringing may have influenced the way the story plays on the subtle, adult fear that sins of the flesh might lead to sins of the spirit, reminiscent of Arthur Machen's discourse on sanctity and sin in "The White People": extraordinary venality could imperil the immortal soul.

"The Faces at Pine Dunes" (1980) is another story where the focus on a character and his sexuality is critical to the story. Michael is not just a young man living with his parents—he is a young man aware of and concerned with his sexuality and that of his parents, and the woman he meets at the bar; and he exhibits anxiety over his parents' perceived lack of sexuality, and relief when the woman seems to stir his body's interest. It is essentially a coming of age story set in the Cthulhu Mythos, but depicting a part of maturation that previous authors had ignored or failed to conceive. The pattern of descent that Campbell lays out, with each generation becoming more like the true image of the supernatural ancestor, is the long generational development of Arthur Jermyn or the Deep One hybrids as applied to Wilbur Whateley—the image of the pregnant woman in the stone circle recalls Lavinia Whateley's trips to Sentinel Hill in particular. Again, there is the suggestion of autobiographical elements in this story. The lack of sexual activity between Michael's parents reflects Campbell's own upbringing; their marriage broke down soon after he was conceived, so that by "1950, his parents no longer slept together, one reason being that his father made threats against her after sex" (Crawford 3).

Aside from these serious efforts at horror, Campbell has played with the boundaries of Mythos as genre literature somewhat. "Among the pictures are these:" (1981) is experimental fiction, a description of drawings from old notebooks that Campbell had made as a fourteen-year-old, influenced by Lovecraft and *Weird Tales* covers, unsurprisingly filled with sexual imagery (Campbell 1993, 360). "The Horror under Warrendown" (1995) is a satiric pastiche of a younger Campbell's Lovecraftian pastiches, written for the anthology *Made in Goatswood*, and it is from this viewpoint that the story is best understood.

After a long hiatus from the Mythos, Campbell returned with the superb novel *The Darkest Part of the Woods* (2002), a subtle work where a great deal becomes clear only on subsequent readings, when certain passages can be filtered for half-truths and certain scenes understood in a larger context, but the whole of the novel is an update, revisitation, and marriage of certain themes from Lovecraft's *The Case of Charles Dexter Ward* and "The Dunwich Horror" (and somewhat by extension Machen's "The Great God Pan" and "The White People"), Campbell's own fiction, and possibly elements of Derleth's *The Lurker at the Threshold*. Nathaniel Selcouth's sorceries are a combination of Joseph Curwen, Richard Billington, and Wizard Whateley's—the creation of a hybrid child, and when that fails, an effort to be born again in the image of a descendent. To this Campbell has added elements of necrophilia, rape (via magical coercion), and incest.

The real apprehension and tension that builds in *The Darkest Part of the Woods* is how the characters react to Sylvia's pregnancy as it progresses, and the mysteries surrounding the child's father. Even after we discover that Sam is the biological father, the tension does not let up as we see how the knowledge of his accidental incest, and the necessity of keeping it a secret, eat at him—and long before it is confirmed by Selcouth's journal, the reader will wonder at Sylvia's strange treatment of her unborn child and ask if it is Nathaniel Selcouth's reincarnation. The catalyst for the entire stage of events is Goodman—an ambiguous entity, like the Great God Pan, who set the events in motion by luring Selcouth to the woods, and later by inspiring the conception of Sylvia by Lennox and Margo. Sylvia for her part contains aspects of both Helen Vaughan and Lavinia Whateley, with her calm pride and mystery, though she does not survive to see the result of her efforts.

The Darkest Part of the Woods is exceptional among Mythos novels, and even among Campbell's own Mythos fiction, for its strong use of female characters—most notably Heather, Silvia, and Margo Price, as well as several friends, coworkers, townswomen, and other incidental female characters. Each of these women is fairly prominent in the book, particularly Heather and Silvia, and their characters are developed with meticulous attention. They are also, to a large extent, independent of men: Heather is divorced, Silvia has no husband or boyfriend, and Margo's husband is under psychiatric care; as a result, they are all forced to live more or less on their own. One possible peculiarity is that they all generally lack an active sex life. Heather is not seeing anyone, Margo hasn't had sex with Lennox since Sylvia was conceived, and Sylvia only has sex with Sam the one time. Even the males aren't getting any action; aside from Sam's accidental incest he is not confident around women his own age and isn't dating, Lennox is in a hospital and appears to lack a sex drive, and even Selcouth found breeding a chore. Campbell, consciously or not, is channeling something of Lovecraft here, where all the sex in the story leads directly to procreation and, innocent or not, is directed with terrible purpose.

Campbell's Mythos stories featuring sex are not pornographic and by many standards not even erotic, as the focus of the writing is not titillation or explicit depiction of sexual acts. Rather, Campbell uses the depiction of sexual curiosity, frustration, confusion, inexperience, desire, and intimation of paraphilia to provide sometimes conflicting motivations and insight into characters and their actions. Campbell's characters are for the most part sexual entities and are concerned about love, friendship, intimacy, gender roles, dominance, and satisfaction—whether or not they would express it in that language. Some of his stories address current and ongoing sexual conflicts in real life—for example, the more open sexuality of the current age against the sexual mores imposed by society and religion—and in some stories Campbell broaches taboo sexual subjects to lend a shudder to his stories, just as Lovecraft and Eddy did in "The Loved Dead." Of course, in other stories Campbell does much more than suggest and hint; an orgy (a literal orgy, not one of Lovecraft's off-the-page ceremonies) in "Dolls" includes a whipping with nettles on bare buttocks, though far less bloody than in Robert E. Howard's "The Black Stone"; "Merry May" (1986) features pedophilia as an essential element of the plot. These are subjects that are rarely spoken of in public, or at least casual conversation, and the stories gain power from a combination of frank discussion and sly intimation as they transgress.

While not a universal attribute to his fiction, Campbell has strongly featured children in some of his fiction, focusing both on their actions and their perspective, including how they handle sex. This comes into particular focus at times when such young adult characters are undergoing or have come through puberty and are trying to come to terms with their burgeoning sexuality. The latter is evident in at least two of his Mythos stories, "The Faces at Pine Dunes" and *The Darkest Part of the Woods*, and is also a strong element in several of the *Demons by Daylight* stories set in Campbell's Severn Valley. For a general overview of this theme in Campbell's fiction, see "The Child as Victim and Villain" in Joshi's *Ramsey Campbell and Modern Horror Fiction* (2001).

Many of Ramsey Campbell's tales that lack explicit Mythos references are still set in his fictional Severn Valley and contain evocative characterizations of sexuality and gender roles, such as the "The Second Staircase" (1973), which delves into aspects of gender-reversal and gender-identity that Lovecraft did not touch on in "The Thing on the Doorstep," the Machenesque combination of religious feeling and sexual urge in "The Old Horns" and "Made in Goatswood" (1973), and the sexually open relationships of the Brichester witch-coven in "Dolls" (1976).

Richard A. Lupoff

After the death of August Derleth, editorship of Arkham House passed briefly to Donald Wandrei, and then to James Turner. Under Turner's direction and in accordance with his tastes, Arkham House expanded its focus from dark fantasy and the weird to science fiction, and brought fresh perspectives on the Mythos from new authors like Richard A. Lupoff, whom Turner introduced to the Arkham House audience through *Lovecraft's Book* (1985) and the revised Golden Anniversary edition of *Tales of the Cthulhu Mythos* (1990), though the Mythos forms only a small part of Lupoff's prolific and varied corpus.

Lupoff's Mythos fiction is divided between pastiche and original work, and he appears to have approached both primarily as a writer of science fiction. His original works, including "The Discovery of the Ghooric Zone" (1977), "Lights! Camera! Shub-Niggurath!" (1996), and "Nothing Personal" (2010), are science fiction stories of the far future that utilize elements of the Mythos, while several of his pastiches including "Documents in the Case of Elizabeth Akeley" (1982) and "The Doom That Came to Dunwich" (1996) focus and expand on the science fiction elements in Lovecraft's own writing while updating the material to a contemporary setting.

The sexual and gender content of Lupoff's earlier Mythos fiction was hot stuff by Mythos standards: few if any stories to that point had ever broached anything quite as explicit in the Mythos as Lupoff had done in "The Discovery of the Ghooric Zone" or "The Devil's Hop Yard" (1978). Published a decade after Harlan Ellison's *Dangerous Visions* (1967), these works were relatively tame by the standards of New Wave science fiction, but show something of their influence in the mechanical, non-titillating detail regarding displays of sexuality, and the casual openness about and acceptance of sex by the characters.

Peter H. Cannon

Among Mythos readers, Peter H. Cannon is as well known as a Lovecraft scholar as a pasticheur, a learned editor of important books like *Lovecraft Remembered* (1998), and a prolific and insightful essayist who has contributed much to Lovecraft and Mythos criticism. One of his most notable works in this regard is *Long Memories: Recollections of Frank Belknap Long* (1997), a memoir of Lovecraft's long-lived and oft-neglected friend, correspondent, and fictioneer. As a result of Peter Cannon's relationship with the Longs during their twilight years, Long constitutes a significant influence on Cannon's Mythos-related writing—not so much any stylistic inspiration from "The Space-Eaters" (1928) or "The Hounds of Tindalos" (1929), but personal inspiration from the events and conversations of their long acquaintance. *Long Memories* paints a painfully poignant account of Frank and Lyda's waning days, and it illuminates how clearly Cannon portrayed them—and himself—as characters in his Mythos fiction.

Cannon's Mythos tales are typically pastiche by form, but parody by content—but they parody less the tropes and excesses of Lovecraftian fiction than the people and events behind them, most notably the life and history of H. P. Lovecraft, Frank Belknap Long, and their friends and family. While Cannon's fiction is always accessible to readers unfamiliar with the events so as to make a "straight read" possible, they are all specifically constructed to invoke, echo, or parody actual events and characteristics of Lovecraft, Long, or Mythos fandom and development in general. Cannon's single best work is *The Lovecraft Chronicles* (2004), a novel imagining what might have happened if Lovecraft had lived longer and received greater literary acclaim and success during his lifetime.

For the most part in Peter Cannon's fiction, sex and relationships are played for comedic value and are not central to the plot. This is most notable in his "Azathoth" series, which are run-on continuations of Lovecraft's "The Thing on the Doorstep" as the spirit of consciousness of Ephraim/Asenath Waite continues to transfer in and around the Waite/Derby bloodline. These stories deliberately call attention to details in Lovecraft's work, for example when the aged headmistress of the all-girls school Ephraim-as-Asenath attended reminisces about her young charge, with emphasis on the sexual implications of the situation. Cannon's female characters tend to be much more present and vocal than in Lovecraft's fiction, if slightly sensationalized in characterization for purposes of comedy and parody. This is particularly noticeable in the case of Ida Carstairs, the fictional counterpart to Frank Belknap Long's wife Lyda, though Robert M. Price avers Cannon's caricature is "only half as maniacal" (Price 2010, 95).

The basis of much of Cannon's parody is the patent or understood absurdity of the situation, the juxtaposition of established Mythos elements or ideas in different combinations or contexts from Lovecraft and most of the writers who followed him in the Mythos. Sometimes this is a matter of setting and narrative style, as in "The Sound and the Fungi" (2011), when Cannon pastiches Faulkner's *The Sound and the Fury* (1945), or Cannon's Lovecraft/Wodehouse pastiches in "Scream for Jeeves"

(1990) and its sequels. Elsewhere, Cannon has a penchant for odd Mythos miscegenations: where Lovecraft only included a few examples, Cannon liberally mixes things up in ways many Mythos fans would not expect, such as human/Mi-Go and human/Hound of Tindalos hybrids, simply because most Mythos writers followed Lovecraft's lead on such things.

Given the generally minor but pervasive nature of Cannon's use of sexual elements in his stories, I have chosen not to address the bulk of them in depth, and readers may take "It Was the Day of the Deep One" (1997) and "The Hound of the Partridgevilles" (1999) as examples of the kind of thing found in many of Cannon's other Mythos pastiches. Cannon's fiction about Lovecraft himself, particularly *Pulptime* (1984) and *The Lovecraft Chronicles* (2004), reflects more on Lovecraft's relationships, real or imagined, and is generally less sexually suggestive but more sexually aware, drawing in depth from Lovecraft's letters, writings, and memoirs.

Pulptime is a crossover between H. P. Lovecraft, Frank Belknap Long, and Sherlock Holmes, set during the Kalem Club period in New York City; the adventure ends with the revelation that Lovecraft is actually Holmes's son, the result of an American fling that Watson had carefully failed to record. Cannon was not the only one experimenting with Lovecraft as a fictional character at the time, as he relates: "I sent *Pulptime* to Jim Turner, editor of Arkham House, who in rejecting it confided they already had a novel with Lovecraft as a major character under contract" (Cannon 1997, 17). The latter would be *Lovecraft's Book* (1985) by Richard Lupoff.

Brian McNaughton

> He stood in my doorway like an avatar of ruin and knowledge, smiling a rueful smile. The combination of sex and death—attraction, embarrassment, pity, and fear, but especially attraction—was just too much for me. To this day I regret not inviting him in. (Pollitt 102)

In his author's note to *The Haunter at the Threshold* (2010), Edward Lee writes:

> I've dedicated this book to the late, great award-winning novelist Brian McNaughton. Though I never met Brian, I corresponded with him actively in the early '80s (he claimed I was his first "fan" letter not related to his porn books). His horror novels *Satan's Love Child*, *Satan's Mistress*, and *Satan's Seductress* were of a paramount influence. (By the way, those weren't his titles, they were the publisher's! The publisher was Carlyle Communications.) Though

some will easily object, I contend that never has Lovecraft's ground-breaking Mythos been so entertainingly redefined in contemporary terms than in those three wonderful books. (Lee 2010, 7)

"The Secret Master of Horror" embraced transgression and black humor, and his Mythos-related works are characterized by both strong sexuality and originality. McNaughton's treatment of adolescent sexuality, homosexuality, paraphilia, rape, etc. are comparable to Ramsey Campbell's in the scope of material covered, but the two differ in the manner of presentation, with McNaughton typically presenting sexuality and other transgressive matters in greater frequency and detail, but also typically for fun as much as for horror. This form of writing appears fairly natural to McNaughton, an expression of his style and attitude.

McNaughton began his career in the fanzines of the 1950s while in high school; he attended Harvard but did not take a degree, and for a decade worked as a newspaperman at the *Newark Evening News* until the paper folded, and he turned to other work, including a decade as night manager of a motel. In 1971 he began writing adult fiction with *In Flagrant Delight* (1971) by Olympia Press. Under his own name and pseudonyms he would go on to write at least twenty erotic novels and a couple dozen short stories published between 1971 and 1983. The vast majority of these works have no reference to the Mythos, nor does McNaughton's thriller *Buster Callahan* (1978; also released as *The Poacher*).

McNaughton continued writing erotic novels and short stories while working at other jobs. His breakthrough came in the late-1970s, when he convinced longtime publisher Carlyle Communications to print a series of non-erotic horror novels. Although stuck with editorially mandated titles by Carlyle, the novels *Satan's Love Child* (1977), *Satan's Mistress* (1978) and its sequel *Satan's Seductress* (1980), and *Satan's Surrogate* (1982) proved successful enough to help relaunch McNaughton as a writer of dark fantasy and horror fiction. Aside from the middle two books, the *Satan* novels are not part of the same series as the titles would indicate, and the share little with one another besides a common writer and certain common themes. However, the success of these novels signaled McNaughton's transition (or return) to weird and horror fiction, including contributions to *Weirdbook* (1968-97) and *Lore* (1995-98), and culminated in such masterpieces as *The Throne of Bones* (1997).

A large part of McNaughton's horror and dark fantasy work was inspired by the fiction of H. P. Lovecraft, Clark Ashton Smith, Robert E. Howard, and other Mythos authors; his Mythos fiction includes both those tales with Mythos elements, such as "The Doom That Came to Innsmouth" (1999), and those that generally lack direct Mythos elements but make reference to Lovecraft in the context of the Mythos such as "To My Dear Friend, Hommy-Beg" (1994), and "Ghoulmaster" (1996), which combines McNaughton's approach to ghouls from *The Throne of Bones* with Lovecraft's references to ghouls. McNaughton also mixes Lovecraft's fiction and references to Lovecraft's work as fiction together, as in "Beyond the Wall of Time" (1996), where Lovecraft appears as a fictional version of himself, and the novels *Downward to Darkness* and *Worse Things Waiting*. The bulk of McNaughton's work was original, such as the outstanding but non-Mythos tale "Meryphillia," an episode from his award-winning collection *The Throne of Bones* originally published in the anthology *Lovecraft's Legacy* (1990). McNaughton makes few references to other Mythos writers in his fiction, save for some disparaging comments about Derleth and a utilization of Colin Wilson's introduction to the Hay *Necronomicon* (1977).

In later life, Wildside Press issued corrected editions of McNaughton's earlier novels, restoring the author's original titles and updating the details. For example, the following passage from *Satan's Mistress* was removed in the later edition:

> I used to camp out at the newsstand when the monthly issue of *Weird Tales* was due, and I had to tear off the inappropriately lurid covers before I could smuggle the magazine past the surveillance of my parents. (McNaughton 1980, 172)

This is essentially the old legend of H. P. Lovecraft vs. the lurid covers revisited, as first related by Winfield Townley Scott; though internal evidence in the novel suggests that McNaughton probably picked it up from L. Sprague de Camp's *Lovecraft: A Biography*. Other internal evidence suggests that it may have been removed after McNaughton read S. T. Joshi's *H. P. Lovecraft: A Life* (1996) (cf. *Satan's Mistress* 173 and *Downward to Darkness* 100, where McNaughton replaces de Camp as a Lovecraft authority with Joshi). Of McNaughton's other horror novels, *Gemini Rising* (2000; first published as *Satan's Love Child*) lacks any specific reference to the Mythos, despite a very Lovecraftian plot, and *The House Across the Way* (2002;

first published as *Satan's Surrogate*), though very good, has only minor references in a few place names and the like.

Characteristic of McNaughton's approach to Mythos fiction is that every character in these novels of any significance has a sexual identity and has thoughts and actions regarding sex and potential partners; past, present, and speculative future sexual actions; and general thoughts on sex are regularly and consistently addressed throughout the books. Further, McNaughton's characters are aware of themselves as sexual entities, and from the perspective of an omniscient narrator the reader becomes aware of the characters' sexuality and understanding of the sexuality of other characters from their own perspective. The resulting effect sometimes gives the impression that everyone is thinking about sex nearly all the time. This is more than likely a holdover from McNaughton's pornographic works, but it also gives an unguarded, intimate look at the thoughts, feelings, and actions that characters would rarely share in a line of dialogue, such as parents silently evaluating their child's sexual orientation in light of behavior and perceived relationships with others.

The titillation of transgression is an expected part of the prose in the *Satan* novels and provides background and motivation for the characters, but these are not pornographic books in line with McNaughton's earlier, much more explicit adult novels. Much the same could be said of McNaughton's use of violence in these novels, providing the requisite gore but never being obsessed with the subject for its own sake. When the Mythos and sex do converge in McNaughton's novels, the result is always a particularly disturbing transgression: human motives and expressions often taken to inhuman extremes or combinations. Implicit in a number of these transgressive scenes are the popular theories of Sigmund Freud; McNaughton makes use of the image of the Oedipus complex and other outré sexual drives without deliberately calling them out to the reader. For example, *Downward to Darkness* reads something like a novel-length effort along the lines of Ramsey Campbell's "The Faces at Pine Dunes," given the early focus on adolescent sexuality and the later one on the sorcerous or spiritual inheritance of the family line, but probably derives more from *The Case of Charles Dexter Ward* and "The Thing on the Doorstep," both of which center on the reincarnation of a sorcerer via his descendents, and perhaps the implicit incest between Wizard and Lavinia Whateley in "The Dunwich Horror." The family dynamics at play in the Laughlin household are particularly notable, and reminiscent of the realistic family relationship of McNaughton's earlier novel *Gemini Rising/Satan's Love Child*. Both Frank and Rose entertain the idea of sexual liaisons outside their marriage, but never attempt to realize these fantasies until pushed by the magic and madness of the Halloween party.

Another theme of McNaughton's novels is characters that are self-aware—of their limitations, and of the Mythos as fiction. The latter is an idea first floated by August Derleth, who would insert copies of *Weird Tales* and the Arkham House collections of Lovecraft side-by-side with Mythos occult literature in his early short fiction, and was expanded by Robert Bloch in *Strange Eons*, in whose footsteps McNaughton follows by introducing characters like Martin Paige who knows of and appreciates Lovecraft's fiction *as fiction*, and because of that is not generally prepared to accept the Mythos as reality, even if he can recognize elements of it that he comes across. McNaughton's characters are often acutely aware of their own hangups and how their lives reflect culture at large; in *Worse Things Waiting* Toni acts as the altar in a Black Mass and notes the stale unoriginality of the ceremony, and Martin acknowledges how cheap his "real" writing is, which is often uncredited and unrewarded compared to the more profitable pornographic stories: "[H]e was also a writer of pornography, the ultimate science-fiction, where a single fact of physiology no more complex than the corking of a bottle is extrapolated into a whole new cosmos of sensation" (McNaughton 2000, 23).

Brian McNaughton also wrote a number of pornographic "romance" novels under the pen names Sheena Clayton[3] and Mark Bloodstone as well as his own, mainly for Carlyle Communications under imprints like Beeline, Tigress, and Pandora. The exact number and titles of his books I have been unable to determine, but the ones written as Sheena Clayton include *Love and Desire* (1982), *The Aura of Seduction* (1982), *Tide of Desire* (1982), *Danielle Book Two* (1983), *There Lies Love* (1983), and *Perfect Love* (1983)—all of which to greater or lesser extent contain references to the Mythos. For example, Edward Pickman Derby appears briefly as a member of a "Rats in the Walls"-esque Magna Mater cult in *Love and Desire*; Ramsey Campbell's Lovecraftian fictional grimoire *Astral Rape* from his novel *The Parasite* (1980) is prominent in *Danielle Book Two*; and the cult in *Perfect*

---

3. "Sheena Clayton was the illegitimate daughter of Sheena, Queen of the Jungle, and John Clayton, Lord Greystroke. I channeled her in several novels, of which TIDE OF DESIRE may have been the best" (McNaughton, 30 September 2000).

Love was founded by a Rev. H. P. Whateley from Arkham, Massachusetts. The remaining two books are essentially minor Mythos novels, though distributed and marketed in such a way as completely to miss that audience, or else more copies would no doubt have survived and be available.

Tide of Desire (1982) follows Antonia, a Deep One hybrid who discovers her heritage on Squampottis Island in Maine, among a schismatic sect that broke away from Innsmouth—the Reformed Order of Dagon. The balding, splay-footed appearance of the Deep One hybrids and the presentation of elements of the Deep One religion, especially "passing over," appear to prefigure McNaughton's later short story "The Doom That Came to Innsmouth" (1999). The novel comes to an abrupt, jarringly disconcerting "happy ending" very atypical for McNaughton's novels, as the novel was bowdlerized badly by the editors (Rodgers), and for years the original ending was thought lost. However, shortly before his death McNaughton found the original ending and was revising *Tide of Desire* for eventual publication at Wildside Press, under the title *Riptide*. This takes into account the statements of McNaughton (McNaughton, 30 September 2000) and Alan Rodgers, McNaughton's editor at Wildside (Rodgers), as well as a listing of a book named *Riptide* in a list of McNaughton's works at the front of *Guilty Until Proven Guilty* (2003).

Aura of Seduction (1982) shares some very similar plot elements to *Satan's Mistress* (1978) and *Satan's Seductress* (1980), as it concerns an occasionally incestuous mind-switching warlock and his daughter, Wilfrid and Nancy Corwin, and a continuation in some respects of *The Case of Charles Dexter Ward*. In the novel, down-on-her-luck stripper Jessica Swift agrees to become Wilfrid Corwin's personal assistant and becomes quite enamored with her simple-minded but well-hung charge—only to discover that Corwin and his daughter are part of a society of occultists that achieves immortality through serially swapping minds with others. The book contains many throw-away references to Dunwich, The Black Goat of the Woods, the Great God Pan, Nyarlathotep, etc.

In all cases with the Sheena Clayton novels, the narrator and primary protagonist is female, and the story contains numerous, frequent, and detailed sex scenes. The Mythos elements are background material, but often the main idea tied to them (a cult or occult group, astral projection, mind transference, etc.) is significant to the plot, both framing the sex acts and spurring the novel along to the next erotic moment, or to set up an unusual supernatural adult act. McNaughton also takes the word-count and the medium to address topics of sexuality, love, and censorship openly. This is most apparent in *Perfect Love*, where the eponymous Christian sect has an extremely vocal and low regard for women, which the protagonist discovers and attempts to revolt against. Likewise, homosexuality is more prominent, mostly lesbianism, and the female protagonist is usually at least somewhat sexually interested in women.

In 1971, Olympia Press's affiliate Ophelia Press published the science fiction adult novel *The Erotic Spectacles* by "Genghis Cohen," set near Miskatonic University in Arkham, Mass., but otherwise with no reference to Lovecraft or the Mythos. There are similarities in the construction and style of *The Erotic Spectacles* and *In Flagrant Delight*, and I believe "Genghis Cohen" may be another pseudonym for McNaughton.

Many of Brian McNaughton's published short stories remain uncollected, notably his adult fiction in gentlemen's magazines such as *Beaver*, *Hustler*, *High Society*, and *Chic* from the late 1970s to early 1990s, mostly written under his pseudonyms. Of the examples I have managed to track down, most are unremarkable straight pornographic material, sometimes with a supernatural or science fiction horror element. Exceptions are the eight "Wicked Walter" stories published in *Beaver* from 1981 to 1983.[4] The stories center on an Arkham police officer (later detective) and Miskatonic University graduate named Walter Finn, a hereditary witch who used his powers to solve other magical crimes. The "Wicked Walter" stories contain minor Mythos elements, but typically only as set dressing for typical (if fantastic) sexual encounters.

Of his later horror and dark fantasy stories, many contain notable sexual themes or references that were part and parcel of McNaughton's crude and black humor—stories like "The Dunwich Lodger" (1996), "Herbert West—Reincarnated" (1999), "The Doom That Came to Innsmouth" (1999), and "Mud" (2000), which so shock and transgress against the normally staid limits of Mythos sequels and pastiches, and were so inspirational to other writers like Edward Lee.

McNaughton has more female characters and protagonists in his nov-

---

4. "Wicked Walter" (July 1981), "The Panty Demon" (October 1981), "They Don't Write Them Like They Used To" (November 1981), "Glamour Puss" (February 1982), "The Enchanted Dildo" (July 1982), "The Great Cat-House Raid" (January 1983), "How Are They Hanging?" (February 1983), "I'll See You In My Dreams" (May 1983), and "Her Night to Howl" (unpublished).

els than in his short fiction, with complex relationships and motivations (some of which they are not consciously aware of), but villains tend to be male, and many female characters fall into certain hackneyed stereotypes, like the "brazen teenage slut" Shana Jennings of *Downward to Darkness*. McNaughton has a few openly homosexual supporting characters, but this has to be weighed against the casual use of homosexual pejoratives in his fiction, which is fairly typical of contemporary American society when it was written. Most of the characters take the "dykes" and "faggots" in stride, and McNaughton tends to make the character most guilty of uttering those terms the most concerned with homosexuality in general—which adds impact to the scene in *Downward to Darkness* where Frank is driven to accidentally sodomize another man.

Robert M. Price

> What on earth could be, you ask, more counterintuitive than a collection of tales about love & sex united by their focus on the mythology of H. P. Lovecraft? Actually, a very great deal. The link between Lovecraft's horrors and the mystery and (sometimes) terror of romance and sexuality are implicit and occasionally even explicit in Lovecraft's fiction. (O'Brien xii)

The expansion of sexuality in contemporary Cthulhu Mythos stories and its recognition in literary journals are in no small part due to the critical eye and tastes of editor, anthologist, critic, and writer Robert M. Price. Price notably served as editor of magazines like *Crypt of Cthulhu* (1981-2001) and *Cthulhu Codex* (1985-2000), and was long-running series editor of Chaosium's Call of Cthulhu Fiction line. Like August Derleth and Farnsworth Wright before him, Price was in a position to decide which stories would be printed or reprinted in the anthologies and magazines under his control, thereby being influential in introducing both new and old Mythos stories to the public, and commenting on them. In this regard, Price proved willing not only to acknowledge sexual material in old Mythos stories, but to print new stories with sexual themes and elements, as amply demonstrated in the *Shub-Niggurath Cycle* (1994), and articles that explored sexual interpretations or elements in Lovecraft's work, such as "Lovecraft and the Male Gender Role" (1982) in *Crypt of Cthulhu* No. 8.

Price's scholarly contributions in regard to Lovecraft, the Mythos, gender, and sex include such important milestones as "Homosexual Panic in 'The Outsider'" (1982), "Did Lovecraft Have Syphilis?" (1988), and

"Lovecraft and 'Ligeia'" (1992), as well as his editorial commentary and introductions in various anthologies. "The Thing in the Underwear," which Price wrote to introduce the collection *Eldritch Blue: Love & Sex in the Cthulhu Mythos* (2004), summarizes his attitude with regard to Lovecraft and sex:

> I say Lovecraft was fundamentally alienated from sexuality. It seems to me that he felt such sweaty, greasy wrestlings were appropriate only to the revels of Mulatto half-castes and Polynesian sailors in the Louisiana bayou, or among corrupted New Englanders committing miscegenation with horrific alien beings. [. . .] So Lovecraft viewed sex along with the Pterodactyl and the Trilobite as destined victims of evolution and superannuated, albeit not quite vanished from the earth. This means that for him, human romance and sexuality were essentially atavistic, and their encroachments in his tales a case of the return of the Chaos of the past, threatening to wipe away reason altogether if fools dare yield to perverse temptation and open the gates to their tidal wave. (O'Brien xii–xiii)

Price further explains that Lovecraft's fiction was not asexual, nor is sexual horror an inappropriate element for new fiction in the Cthulhu Mythos, a point Price expanded on in an interview with Sarah L. Covert:

> Sex is implicit in the Mythos even if we look no further than the ever-present theme of miscegenation with monstrous aliens. Romance would fit if one can manage to make someone's getting lost in the depths and terrors of the Old Ones into something to be taken seriously as tragedy. Otherwise it becomes burlesque. ("Robert M. Price Interview")

The best expression of Price's view with regard to sex and the Cthulhu Mythos is found in his own Mythos fiction. Price's fiction stems from his appreciation for the gradual accretion of the Mythos by writers like August Derleth, Lin Carter, Ramsey Campbell, and Brian Lumley, as they borrowed and built off of Lovecraft, Clark Ashton Smith, Robert E. Howard, and one another, and many of Price's stories are superior pastiches and continuations of Mythos fiction. When working in this mode, his expansions on the work of other authors tends to follow their own use of sexuality.

For example, when building directly on Lovecraft and Derleth's fiction Price tends to expand on the theme of miscegenation, such as turning the de la Poer line of Lovecraft's "The Rats in the Walls" into a separate race conceived by cosmic miscegenation in "Exham Priory" (1990), and following through on Mrs. Bishop's cryptic hints in the first two-thirds of August

Derleth's *The Lurker at the Threshold* to present her Narragansett ancestors and many of the folk of Dunwich as descendents of Tsathoggua in "The Round Tower" (1990). Likewise, in utilizing Ramsey Campbell's fictional English setting in stories like "Behold, I Stand at the Door and Knock" (1994) and the Peter H. Cannon collaboration "The Curate of Temphill" (1994), Price focuses on rape and (discreetly) paraphilia more than in other stories, and with intimations of homosexuality and pedophilia in some parts as well, echoing Campbell's "Cold Print." "The Green Decay" (1997) and "The Incubus of Atlantis" (1997) share the sensual adultery and cuckolding common of Clark Ashton Smith's fiction.

When writing in solely his own voice, Price's use of sexuality tends to build off both his love of pulp fiction and his scholarly expertise in religion. For example, "I Wore the Brassiere of Doom" by "Sally Theobald" for *Lurid Confessions* (1986) is based on the novel combination of Lovecraftian horror and the pulp-confession style, and was so convincing that one French bibliographer mistook it for authentic Lovecraft ("Robert M. Price Interview," 2010). The story was translated under the title "Le Soutien-gorge Ensorcelé" ("The Enchanted Bra") in *La Nurserie de l'épouvante* (1987), where the story was mistakenly presented as a Lovecraft original.

"Wilbur Whateley Waiting" (1987) perfectly captures the ennui and nostalgia of a pulp aficionado in a late 1980s swimming with commercial-minded *Necronomicon* hoaxes; and with a brief mention of "planetary sex magic," Price ties the conception of Wilbur Whateley in "The Dunwich Horror" with Aleister Crowley's infamous promotion of sexual magic and his novel *Moonchild* (1917). "A Thousand Young" (1989) is Price's most explicitly sexual story, but also one that relies on his other fields of study. Like Price, the narrator is versed in religion, philosophy, and psychology, erudite in confronting and transgressing sexual mores—and yet it is the quest of a scholar and an epicurean, who looks to an antiquarian index on old pornography for spiritual enlightenment and titillation rather than empty contentment of glossy nude magazines and videotapes of the era. This is the quintessential quest for Mythos knowledge or experience viewed through a carnal lens, and like the protagonists in "The Hound" the narrator eventually gets far more than he bargained for. Price walks a fine line throughout the story between too much and too little detail, consciously echoing his own comment that "to tease the reader's imagination would provide more shuddersome pictures, or at least shadows, than any explicit description he might provide" (Price 1994, 81). In this way Price's use of elements of religion and religious practice is particularly notable and fairly novel with regard to the Mythos.

This is not to say that Price was the first or only modern Mythos writer to use and discuss religion and sex in any degree—Ramsey Campbell discussed these issues in "The Enchanted Fruit" and "Made in Goatswood" in *Demons by Daylight* (1973)—but Price's approach and use of religion with regard to sex is a reflection of his greater knowledge and fluency in this area. Whereas Campbell may make manifest the lingering guilt from an upbringing of Catholic sexual mores in some of his stories and characters, Price is more apt to introduce the theological traditions and practices behind or underlying those same mores, to make reference to and comparison with the legends of other religions or to apocryphal biblical texts. A good example of the latter is Price's references to the Secret Gospel of Mark in "The Curate of Temphill," which intimates a possibly homosexual and pedophilic depiction of Jesus Christ.

Homosexuals exist in Price's Mythos fiction, although uncommon and always present to serve a specific story function, and at times Price has made a distinction between homosexuality and homosexual sex—that is, the actions that individuals take are sometimes different from their sexual preference, so that a normally heterosexual male will engage in homosexual sex for a given purpose; this does not appear to be a reflection of any of Price's personal beliefs, but again seems derivative of his religious and occult studies—in particular, the dispute over homosexual relations as a part of ritual magick. Lesbians by contrast are almost excluded from Price's Mythos fiction. Details of homosexual practice are absent, though Price did make reference to the high rates of HIV infection among homosexual men in "Feery's Original Notes" (1997):

> Many of our group are homosexuals, and in most cases not so much from natural inclination as by, how should I put it . . . by spiritual vocation. There is a kind of Tantric discipline that requires ritual coupling by way of macrocosmic-microcosmic emulation, mirroring certain planetary and astral conjunctions in the heavens, and this coupling must be devoid of the least particle of natural desire . . . I fear I risk offending you. But suffice it to say that our various ritual preparations did not in the end serve to fortify us against certain risks of a mundane nature. In short, Mr. Black at length confirmed that he had contracted the HIV virus, and then full-fledged AIDS. Thus far, I myself have tested negative. (Price 2008, 296-97)

Price, like Ramsey Campbell, uses homosexuality to mark a boundary of the "normal," which their respective protagonists transgress in their quests for ecstasy. Indeed, in comparing "Cold Print" and "A Thousand Young" we see that the protagonists are both lone seekers, wrapped up in themselves and their worlds, generally uncaring of others and anything beyond their own driving needs—but both desiring some outside contact to share their interests. One may prefer pornography and the other prostitutes, but both lack real human attachments in the form of friendship or romantic love, and their terrible error is in finding what they think they want and not being ready for it. The religio-sexual quests of both protagonists have distinct, though perhaps not directly intended, parallels with the ecstatic spirituality described in the works of Arthur Machen, most notably in "The White People"—these two men both may have "sounded the very depths of sin," but in comparison to the stark reality of the Mythos their wickedness is indeed "second-rate, unimportant" (Machen 2003, 62).

When engaged in pastiche, Price's gender depiction tends to follow his sources, contributing to a predominance of men in his Mythos tales. However, Price also sometimes utilizes the opportunity of a continuation or prequel episode to expand on female characters neglected in previous Mythos fiction; examples of this can be seen in stories such as "The Round Tower" (1990) and "Young Goodwife Doten" (1995), based on Derleth's *The Lurker at the Threshold*; and Price's collaboration with W. H. Pugmire in "The Tree-House" (1996), which features an aged version of Lavinia Whateley who had escaped "The Dunwich Horror."

It is almost incidental to note that Price is one of the few authors to feature incidents of tentacle sex in written Cthulhu Mythos fiction, with the "pseudopodic phalluses, teats, and vulvas it sent forth!" in "A Thousand Young" (Price 2008, 103) and "Behold, I Stand at the Door and Knock" (1994). These scenes mark Price's delving into the more gore-laden, super-sexualized, and surrealistic sexual violence of the sort that characterize slasher films, splatterpunk stories, and especially the more lurid moments of tentacle-sex from Japanese anime; the most notable Mythos story Price wrote in this oeuvre is "A Mate for the Mutilator" (2004), which appeared in the *Eldritch Blue* anthology.

W. H. Pugmire

> Since I do not believe that Lovecraft was gay, my letter in #56 suggests no such thing. The point of my letter was to suggest that Lovecraft had little interest in personal relations with women. Someone wrote of Lovecraft as being a "latent heterosexual," and this sums up my own views. The dark distrust of sexuality hinted in Lovecraft's fiction fascinates me, but his personal sex life is not something I care to know anything about. (Pugmire 1990, 45)

During the 1970s and '80s, the largest development of the Mythos and Lovecraftian fiction outside of Arkham House occurred in small-press magazines—cheaply printed paper pamphlets, mostly written by and for amateur fandom. Amateur press associations such as the Esoteric Order of Dagon (EOD) would compile magazines for mass-mailings, allowing wider dissemination of new poems, short fiction, and articles about Lovecraft and the Mythos to be disseminated outside of the editorial control of any one publisher. Many Mythos writers would be featured prominently in magazines, including Brian McNaughton, Robert M. Price, Stanley C. Sargent, and Wilum Hopfrog Pugmire—a transvestite punk writer, editor, and poet, the self-styled Queen of Eldritch Horror, whose magazine credits include *Midnight Fantasies* (1973-74), *Old Bones* (1976), *Queer Madness* (1981), *Visions from Khroyd'hon* (1985), *Revelations from Yuggoth* (1987-89), and *Tales of Lovecraftian Horror* (1987-99).

A hallmark of Pugmire's writing is the marriage of sensual language and atmosphere from the works of Edgar Allan Poe, H. P. Lovecraft, Clark Ashton Smith, and Oscar Wilde with an unsubtle but also unforced sexuality. While rarely sexually explicit, intimate and titillating contact between characters is common in Pugmire's stories, and the intimacy conveyed by kiss and caress, touch and taste is a fundamental part of his interaction between characters, not the least because it highlights their vulnerability or predacious nature. Implicit in intimate contact is the lowering of guards and the potential for violence, a promise that Pugmire sometimes bloodily fulfills. In his introduction to Pugmire's *Some Unknown Gulf of Night* (2011), J. D. Worthington best captures the apparent contradiction of sensual Lovecraftian fiction:

> [...] for Pugmire's work [...] is heavily sensual, potent with a latent or at times manifest sexuality (as well as an awareness of the disturbing links between sex and death) which may seem alien to its Lovecraftian origins in the mind of many. We should recall, however, Lovecraft's own evolving views on

such matters, and his praise of not only the French Decadents, but the work of such later, often sexually explicit, writers [...] While there is little doubt Lovecraft would not care for the focus on sexuality, there is good reason to suppose he would recognize it as artistically valid. In this, too, Pugmire shows both his difference from and insight into the views and work of his mentor. (Pugmire 2011, 10-11)

What is really exceptional about Pugmire's Lovecraftian fiction is that sexual or pre-sexual contact often occurs irrespective of the gender of the participants. Sexual attraction in Pugmire's work is not gender-blind, but neither does it hew strictly to easy delineations of whether a character is heterosexual, homosexual, bisexual, or asexual. Rather, a character's sexual attraction and response depend on the context of the scene and the events of the moment, so that characters that are primarily heterosexual can experience an instance of homosexual attraction, and vice versa. Thus many of Pugmire's characters do not exhibit a "fixed" sexuality, and can potentially receive or deliver a kiss or caress from anyone, even if they are primarily attracted to men or women. Pugmire never displays sexuality as unnatural in his works, nor does he attempt to display a conversion or seduction from heterosexuality to homosexuality or the reverse. It would be wrong to suggest from this behavior that Pugmire's characters are entirely bisexual or displaying the convenient sexuality of the moment; it is more accurate to say that the characters generally refrain from defining themselves gay or straight.

In part, this willingness to address non-heteronormative sexuality may be a reflection of Pugmire's own sexuality and tastes, such as his fascination with the life and writings of Oscar Wilde. In the afterwords to his stories in *Sesqua Valley and Other Haunts* (2008), he reveals how many characters and situations in his fiction were based on people and incidents from his personal and social life; men he had dated or been in love with, whether they had been lovers or not. However, it also functions as an expression of his settings, particularly in the Sesqua Valley where it highlights the alienness of the children of shadow in their abstraction from such concerns and human morality in general, the occasionally bestial instinctiveness they are prey to, and the heightened aesthetic atmosphere of the community and its residents. This can be most clearly seen in a few of the recurring characters: Adam Webster is a Decadent poet in a modern era, not exactly effete but open to encounters with men or women with little preference shown for either; Simon Gregory Williams, the Beast of

Sesqua Valley, is by comparison mostly asexual, his presiding physical lusts subsumed in his quest for magical knowledge.

While sexuality in Pugmire's work is fluid and not necessarily dark, in the majority of the romantic or sexual relationships in his tales at least one member is self-destructive and sometimes dies or is lost, such as in "Born of Strange Shadow," "The Imp of Aether," and "The Woven Offspring" (1998), among others. This violence is sometimes made apparent in one of Pugmire's recurring images of sex and violence: the bloody kiss, which also appears in stories such as "The Child of Dark Mania," "The Boy with the Bloodstained Mouth" (1989), and "The Fungal Stain" (2006).

Women are well represented in Pugmire's fiction, though rarely as recurring characters or in dominant roles. Again, this is in large part due to the nature of Pugmire's Lovecraftian tales, particularly those set in the Sesqua Valley, since all the children of shadow to date appear as male—and in Sesquan tales, humans of either gender tend to fail against the children of shadow. Even if they rarely dominate the setting, Pugmire's female characters are never simple sex objects and rarely unseen mothers, but usually as fully developed as any of the male characters.

Pugmire generally eschews many of the standard clichés of Mythos fiction, including those regarding sex and gender. Long family genealogies never come into play, capping out at three generations, with neither maternal nor paternal ancestors dominating, and typically without a supernatural aspect to the familial lines. Shub-Niggurath, the miscegenation of the Deep Ones, and the mind-and-gender swapping of "The Thing on the Doorstep"—three of the most popular subjects for Mythos authors in addressing sex in the Mythos—never show up in Pugmire's work in those contexts. Lavinia Whateley and her children by Yog-Sothoth only appear in a single tale, "The Tree House" (1995), which Pugmire wrote in collaboration with Robert M. Price, based on sonnet XXVI of Lovecraft's *Fungi from Yuggoth*.

It is not that Pugmire completely avoids these concepts—a hybrid entity birthed by a human woman and a Mythos entity occurs in "The Child of Dark Mania" (1997), for instance—but he chooses not to use those specific examples—the hybrids of Innsmouth, fertility cults centered around Shub-Niggurath, etc.—that have been used excessively by other Mythos writers. Instead, Pugmire tends to add a degree of sensuality and sexuality to other aspects of the Mythos. Nyarlathotep is the catalyst of a bond between brothers in "The Bloom of Sacrifice" (1995); "Born in Strange

Shadow" (1996) suggests an Oedipal relationship between foster-mother and her ghoul-changeling son; "The Imp of Aether" (1997) combines Derleth's fire elemental with transgenderism; and "Some Distant, Baying Sound" (2009) fantastically re-imagines "The Hound" by presenting the nameless narrator of that tale as a woman . . . among other things.

This appears to be a deliberate response and aesthetic point to go against the mediocre material that was perpetuated in magazines, the overuse of the most obvious Mythos aspects without any thought to the deeper philosophy and ideas behind them. Robert M. Price neatly encapsulated the problem:

> Prolonged exposure to fanzines [. . .] one soon concludes that the small readership for whom they are written has a great deal in common with the seedy protagonist of Campbell's "Cold Print." The Mythos has become like pornography, and it matters not whether there is any plot or chacterization to speak of, any more than it does in a cheap porn paperback or skin-flick. Just as long as the proper anatomy is all there, only in this case it is tentacles rather than testicles, beasts instead of breasts. (Price 1996, xiii–xiv)

Price also noticed W. H. Pugmire's response to this practice: Pugmire's magazine *Tales of Lovecraftian Horror* considered no overtly Mythos fiction. He expanded on this philosophy in his recurrent column "Lustcraft" in the same journal, emphasizing that the focus on atmosphere, language, and theme in Lovecraft's works was more important than name-dropping Mythos entities and texts while hitting the notes in hackneyed plots—and Pugmire practiced what he preached:

> My work cannot honestly be called "Lovecraftian" because I focus exclusively on supernaturalism; but Lovecraft's influence has kissed everything I've written. Sometimes that kiss is long and deep and blatant; but in the works I consider my best, the lips are lightly applied, though the passion runs deep. (Pugmire 1999, 3)

As with Lovecraft's contemporaries, when Pugmire utilizes Mythos elements it is primarily as background material and inspiration, preferring to develop his own characters and settings, primarily in the Sesqua Valley but also parts of Lovecraft's Arkham and Kingsport, so that a great deal of Pugmire's fictional output could be considered connected with the Mythos; all of it may fairly be called Lovecraftian, and much of it is sensual.

Caitlín R. Kiernan

> Herein lies weird sex. Very weird sex. Should your idea of "kinky" happen to begin and end with fleece-lined handcuffs and spankings, be warned—you may experience confusion, nausea, disorientation, annoyance, impatience, and, perhaps, narcolepsy while reading this book. Then again, you might be surprised. Either way, you've been warned, so no whining, please and thank you. (Kiernan 2005, 5)

The fiction of "H. P. Lovecraft's spiritual granddaughter" evinces both the continued aesthetic influences of Lovecraft and her own life experience as a paleontologist, musician, transsexual, and lesbian. Kiernan's fiction does not always contain explicit Mythos terminology, but much of it reflects the stamp of Lovecraft on Kiernan's own interests. Accordingly, it is unsurprising to find that many of Kiernan's Mythos and Lovecraftian stories feature strong female characters, including several prominent depictions of lesbians in stories such as "Paedomorphosis" (1998), "Derma Sutra (1891)" (2008), and "Fish Bride (1970)" (2009), and even a transsexual of sorts in "Pages Found among the Effects of Miss Edith M. Tiller" (2005). These women are not caricatures, and their relationships vary from modern-day descendents of J. Sheridan Le Fanu's "Carmilla" (1872) to realistic depictions of lesbians as flawed human beings. One of her best such relationships is depicted in "At the Gate of Deeper Slumber" (2009), where the unnamed narrator and Suzanne are not the perfect lesbian couple: they have disagreements, fights, and flaws. They quibble and worry over gender roles and each other's space. Suzanne refers to the narrator as a "butch dyke" in reference to the persona she projects, but the narrative itself reveals the uncertainty and discomfort—perhaps even jealousy—that accompany the invasion of her home by the Shining Trapezohedron. The narrator cannot give full force to her worries for fear of alienating her partner, and it is the fear of losing Suzanne that is the consuming dread of the piece, more than anything else. Kiernan has revisited this theme of love, loss, and the Shining Trapezohedron in her later piece "Ex Libris" (2012).

However, of greatest interest for the purposes of this work is the subset of Kiernan's fiction that consists of Mythos "weird erotica," a facet of her writing that she had not openly pursued until Subterranean Press approached her with the idea of doing a small volume of erotica; after receiving favorable responses from an online poll, she decided to write it (Kiernan 2005, 113). Of this erotic impulse, she noted:

> [. . .] my novels and short stories have usually avoided overtly erotic elements, because I feel they only serve to detract from more important aspects of the story. [. . .] However, there has often been a certain erotic undertone in my writing, one that's obvious *if* you know what you're looking for. There have been times when I've denied that this was so, for one misguided reason for another, but it's there [. . .] Of course, it rarely ever involves two people having anything as simple or orthodox as sex. (Kiernan 2005, 114-15)

With regard to her first efforts, Kiernan was somewhat disappointed:

> They were all essentially straightforward sexual encounters with the Other. And sure, sometimes the Other alters and organically subverts the narrators so fundamentally that they themselves become another facet of that Otherness (a recurrent theme of devouring, I suppose). [. . .] Where are the vignettes dealing with autoeroticism? Where's the hot Other-on-Other action? (Kiernan 2005, 115-16)

Sonya Taaffe in her afterward to *Confessions of a Five-Chambered Heart* wrote:

> The *other*. There must be lines drawn somwhere, or the act of crossing them is without meaning. A recurring motif [. . .] is the sexual meeting with something the narrator can neither categorize nor entirely understand, which is both damning and correct. (Kiernan 2012, 320)

Eventually her weird erotica output would include the *Sirenia Digest* (2005-present), *Frog Toes and Tentacles* (2005), *Tales from the Woeful Platypus* (2007), *The Black Alphabet* (2007), *The Crimson Alphabet* (2011), *Confessions of a Five-Chambered Heart* (2012), and *The Yellow Book* (2012), which contains "The Yellow Alphabet" that completes her Alphabetos Triptych. By the time the last two saw print, Kiernan had become more confident in her philosophy and efforts:

> I've been doing this for years stacked upon years now, haven't I? It may be I have cultivated an infamy, spawned an ill reputation, which I'd call an occupational hazard. For those who embrace the frisson, that fleeting or prolonged shudder. For those who show their darkest dreams and experiences to others (not to be mistaken with the *Other*), thereby opening themselves to accusations of corruption. But this is what fantasy does. Fantasy corrupts reality, as does dream. You can leave out all shameless mention of genitals, the satyrs, of mermaids, of frog toes and tentacles, and fine, fine, fine, but this, I conclude, does not change a thing.

> Death and sex, these are among the cornerstones of reality.
> Pain and pleasure.
> Fear of the unknown.
> Love of the Unknown, commingled with *eros* and *philia*. Desire without boundaries, no safe words, and I hardly care if this sort of thing *is not for everybody*. I steadfastly agree it's for more than are willing to admit. But, the rest of you, take my hand, and let's swim out past where our feet can touch the bottom. (Kiernan 2012, 12)

The distinction between Kiernan's weird erotica vignettes and other weird fiction and erotica is that she approaches the subject along the same philosophical lines as Lovecraft approached weird fiction, and deliberately so. Kiernan explores the links between "fear of the unknown" and "love of the unknown"; the strangeness and mystery that attracts and the fine line between the physiological response for being aroused and being scared. While human and Mythos entity copulation is an old idea that goes back to Lovecraft, he always left the details of the mating dance, seduction, courtship, and final consummation off the written page—and these are the areas that Kiernan explores in her weird erotica, focusing on the feelings and emotional attraction between these characters as much as the physical realities, the strange textures of alien flesh and appendages.

What sets Kiernan's weird erotica apart from other writers that combine sex and the Mythos is her skill and style in the telling. There is explicit sex in her stories, but that sex is depicted as part of and stemming from the plot, not the sole point of the piece and never a recitation of the mechanics of sex. Kiernan employs crudity and poetic license with precision; both are tools to be used to entice, titillate, or shock the reader, to set the tone and pulse for the scene, and emphasize and illustrate the action without delving into mechanical dreariness or purple prose. As Sonya Taaffe accurately observes:

> Some of the most striking images in this collection are of sexual congress, fundamentally presented *as* a transgressive act—stepping beyond the boundaries, an appropriately polymorphous definition as it applies to anything from simple kink to the transfiguring or annihilating communion of which the human sexual act is posited as a pale, striving reflection [. . .] (Kiernan 2012, 317)

Beyond being informed by the Lovecraftian view of weird fiction, Kiernan also uses elements from the Cthulhu Mythos in her work, showing a preference for Lovecraft's original stories. There is a peculiarity in her work that while Kiernan (like Pugmire) tends to avoid the most sexual-

3. Sex and The Cthulhu Mythos

ized elements of Lovecraft's tales, such as cosmic miscegenation and Shub-Niggurath, she does tend to incorporate some of the later, popular ideas of sex and the Mythos—which most notably manifest themselves in a tendency for tentacle sex, such as in "Pages Found among the Effects of Miss Edith M. Tiller." In general, Kiernan's Mythos fiction seldom offers any expansion on the collective cosmology; instead, she writes tales where the Mythos is the catalyst, allowing the wayward and curious lover to transform and self-destruct.

Aside from the prominence of women and alternative sexuality in her fiction, another theme in Kiernan's work is a convergence of pornography and Mythos occult literature. She has played around with the idea of a Mythos tome whose contents include sex magic, such as the dryly academic but detailed ritual for preparing virgin women to be offered to Ghatanothoa for sacrifice from *Unaussprechlichen Kulten* in *The Black Alphabet (A Primer)*, and conflated Mythos literature with pornography as "the fabled Pornographies of Pnakotus," recalling when the term "pornography" originally referred to an academic treatise or history of prostitution. In "Derma Sutra (1891)" a fanatical hunter of demons and monsters awakens from an opiate-induced sleep to find the words of *De Vermis Mysteriis* and the *Cthäat Aquadingen* inked onto her skin, even to the folds of her labia, which begins her quick seduction and corruption. Kiernan's most explicit and intriguing work along this line is "The Peril of Liberated Objects, or the Voyeur's Seduction" (2009), where an ancient red tome liberated from the Temple of the Elder Ones in the Dreamlands shares scenes of eroticism and horror with its chosen owner, who experiences the scene as both violator and victim—a voyeuristic impulse familiar to Mythos fans, who are themselves looking to experience an escape from life in the awful, novel, and sexual; as with Campbell's "Cold Print," this story holds up a mirror to the reader of weird erotica.

Another exceptional work in this regard is "Pickman's Other Model (1929)" (2010), Kiernan's best pastiche of Lovecraft, and a brilliantly original sequel, where an erstwhile colleague of Richard Upton Pickman traces back the model of a series of nude sketches to Pickman's crude early pornographic film called *The Necrophile* or *The Hound's Daughter*, and then to the model herself. It is also a carefully controlled story, where the descriptions of sexual material are sufficient and necessary for the plot, but no more. We can see this in part because Kiernan has touched on elements included in this story in other pieces, most notably "pas-en-arrière"

(2006) a weird erotica tale of another woman with the same anatomical anomaly. There is a graduated climax of material that echoes Lovecraft's technique of using more and more powerful adjectives as the story goes on—at first, artistic nudes, as any painter might have drawn as studies, but were lacking in Lovecraft's original portrait of Pickman as an artist. This novelty progresses to movies, then pornographic films, and finally returns to the revelatory truth in the original nudes.

Edward Lee

> Though a portion of H. P. Lovecraft enthusiasts are sure to curse me into the deepest pits of the Shoggoths for daring to 1) append one of the greatest horror stories every written, and 2) for doing so in such an indelicate, microscopically sexual, and scatological manner, I suspect that a good many readers may indeed enjoy this bit of work. (Lee 2011, 7)

Perversity, degradation, exploitation, brutality, blasphemy, excess, disgust, crudity, and explicitness are all elements of the literature of transgression; familiar tools for Mythos writers from Lovecraft and his contemporaries to authors of the present day. Yet there are few writers in the Mythos or otherwise who truly embrace transgression in their writing for a passage or a scene or a story, and only a select few who create large bodies of work unrelentingly filled with shocking, sensational content that combines gory violence, elaborate and graphic sexuality, and exploitation in daring, original, and admittedly sometimes schlocky narratives that venture from the disturbing to the absurd or the awesome. To paraphrase Roger Ebert, I may disapprove of a book for going too far, and yet have a sneaky regard for a book that goes much, much farther than merely too far.

The fiction of extremes has variously been deemed pornography, splatterpunk, hardcore horror, and bizarro fiction, but these are rough labels for a varied and eclectic range of writings—fiction that doesn't leave the gruesome or sexually explicit bits off the page, but rather revels in describing the forbidden in every raw, visceral, microscopic, and scatological detail. In Lee's own words:

> I find that whenever I'm reading something, part of me wonders what the work would be like if it were more explicit. Sometimes, of course, the prospect doesn't kindle me at all because there's no way the more explicit detail would be integral to the story; the result would be boring and cumbersome. Much of the time, however, the prospect is thrilling. If I'm reading Lovecraft or M. R.

James, for instance, I'll think, "Wow, wouldn't it be cool if stories like this were to-the-max hardcore?" ("Jordan Krall interviews Edward Lee")

Edward Lee calls his Mythos fiction in this vein "Hardcore Lovecraft," and as with many writers he eschews the wider Cthulhu Mythos and uses the Lovecraft Mythos as a jumping-off point and continual source of reference. Aside from Lovecraft, Lee takes inspiration from the early horror novels of Brian McNaughton as well as exploitation and horror cinema ("Jordan Krall interviews Edward Lee," 2011). Lee's "Hardcore Lovecraft" oeuvre includes the titles *Trolley No. 1852* (2009), *The Haunter of the Threshold* (2009), *Going Monstering* (2010), *The Innswich Horror* (2010), and *The Dunwich Romance* (2011). On the periphery are works like "The Scarlet Succubus" (1999) by Edward Lee and John Pelan, a Clark Ashton Smith–inspired short story set in Zothique; Lee's early novel *Coven* (1991), which references Lovecraft's life and Mythos; and the novel *Pages Torn from a Travel Journal* (2011), which treats Lovecraft as a character without directly naming him and ties in peripherally with Lee's infamous *Header* series. Lovecraftian influences are also evident in some of Lee's other works, notably the chapbooks *You Are My Everything* (2009) and *Family Tradition* (2002; with John Pelan).

While shocking by the standards of the mostly sexless Mythos, there is little to nothing in Ed Lee's various Hardcore Lovecraft works that is much more outrageous than in the Marquis de Sade's oeuvre—and even Lee has his limits. Male homosexuality tends to be mostly absent, and even female homosexuality is generally limited in extent; pedophilia is seldom addressed and never described on the page; and anything involving the Holocaust is right out ("Jordan Krall interviews Edward Lee"). Whatever readers may think of the quality of Lee's fiction or his approach, it is really no more than the most extreme example of the ongoing trend of greater sexual explicitness in works derived from Lovecraft, and it is from that perspective it should be understood and appreciated.

Lee's chosen style emphasizes hardcore, frequent, and escalating scenes of violence, pornography, and scatological acts, often with strong reliance on paraphilia, including coprophilia (feces), maiesiophilia (pregnancy), mucophilia (mucus), teratophilia (deformed or monstrous persons), masochism, rape fantasy, bestiality, and urolagnia (urine-drinking) among others, and in varied combination with a heavy emphasis on degrading and humiliating acts. Edward Lee's most infamous creation in this mode is the eponymous "header." Readers who want to know "What's a header?" are advised to search out any of Lee's relevant books—including *Pages Torn from a Travel Journal*—or the film *Header* (2006) based on Lee's original novel. You have been warned. Enjoy.

It should be emphasized that both in content and approach Lee's material is so over-the-top as to cross the line into fantasy and even absurdity, and Lee's plotlines combine the exploitative material with a wicked flourish of sardonic black humor and twisted cleverness that helps to keep the prose from becoming tired or too revolting—though there are points, especially in *The Haunter of the Threshold*, where the prose starts to drag and the plot stutters or gets lost in the requisite scenes of excess.

Much of Lee's material borrows from and elaborates on the Lovecraft Mythos, but with his own microscopic focus. For example, *The Innswich Horror* does not regurgitate the plot and sexual elements of "The Shadow over Innsmouth"; instead, Lee uses them as the basis for his own reimagining of events. The crossbreeding that was the purpose of the Deep Ones' visit to Innsmouth has been replaced with a massive human breeding project, using mutilated men as sires and unwilling women as mothers, with the objective of defeating the human race. The mutilation of the men and the forced nature of the breeding feeds the degradation and monstrous elements Lee usually plays with in his work. Part of what makes the novel a success is that Lee works these paraphilias seamlessly into the setting as necessary evidence of the plot for the reader to uncover. That said, some elements of Lee's Hardcore Lovecraft stories owe more to later developments in the Mythos. For example, in *Trolley No. 1852* the need to harvest the suffering of humanity as psychic sustenance recalls Colin Wilson's *The Mind Parasites* (1967), and the purpose of collecting human sperm to breed the servitor thoggs is reminiscent of later elaborations of Lovecraft's theme of cosmic miscegenation.

The regular appearance of pregnant women and the focus on the bodily changes of pregnancy—particularly swollen breasts and bellies—make blatant the element of maeisiophilia in Lee's fiction, but the uses Lee makes of pregnancy in his Hardcore Lovecraftian fiction are not always what one would expect. On the surface, there is the pregnant woman as an erotic figure, prominent in *Pages Torn from a Travel Journal*, *The Innswich Horror*, and *The Haunter at the Threshold*. However, despite the copious sex that occurs, the risk of becoming pregnant is rarely a major concern for most characters, either because of prophylactics, alien anatomy, or because the issue simply never comes up. When becoming pregnant does occur in the course of Lee's novels, it is always as a significant plot point—in *The Dunwich Romance*, it is part of the somewhat dark fairytale ending to find out that Sary Sladder is pregnant by Wilbur Whateley, and in the end of *The Innswich Horror* the same tactic is used with a bit more ambiguity with regard to the father.

Among his cast of degenerates, Lee makes special use of rural, backwoods folk as crude, ignorant, perverted, and uncivilized carriers of depraved sex and violence. Lee's inspiration for these characters probably stems from many sources, especially the films *Deliverance* (1972) and *Texas Chainsaw Massacre* (1974), but his depictions of the "Creekers" and their dialect also recall the ignorant, inbred folk of Dunwich and similar groups from the Lovecraft Mythos, and especially the more modern, sexually perverted white trash from Brian McNaughton's "The Dunwich Lodger" (1996). Again, Lee acts within the established traditions, but carries the caricature of immoral rusticity to new depths.

Overall, Lee's Mythos fiction is fairly gender-balanced; the major characters and narrators tend to be female as often as they are male. In terms of being subject to sexual humiliation, exploitation, and degradation, both male and female characters are likely to be subject to such efforts, with female characters tending to receive somewhat more attention and wordcount—though this may be because Lee generally avoids homosexuality in his Hardcore Lovecraft books, which tends to narrow the range of male punishments down to consuming something disgusting, verbal castigation, and physical violence without sexual penetration. Female prostitutes or former prostitutes in Lee's Mythos stories are generally painted in a more sympathetic light than other characters, often stressing their financial need and their status as social pariahs, while nymphomaniacs like Hazel Green in *The Haunter on the Threshold* are generally depicted as conflicted and often with limited control of their desires.

This empathy for mistreated women is in part reflected by generally positive or upbeat endings for the lead female characters in Lee's novels, but is nowhere more appropriate or well done than in *The Dunwich Romance*, where Sary Sladder, a deformed and poverty-stricken Dunwich whore whose life is a series of violent sexual episodes punctuated by verbal and physical degradation, begins what is at once a typical and outlandish kind of courtship. The half-human sorcerer Wilbur Whateley comports himself like a gangly teenager ashamed of his own body and courteous to a fault around Sary, but likely to engage in bloody and disgusting revenge on her behalf against the sadists and perverts who make up the townsfolk of Dunwich.

The Dunwich Romance works because it is exactly what it claims to be: an ornamentation on "The Dunwich Horror" that is also sexually explicit and with plot and prose worthy of a contemporary paperback romance novel, only with depravity turned up to the vicinity of the Marquis de Sade. When confronted with Sary Sladder, the reader is presented with Lee's vision of a character who could realistically fall in love with the half-human giant—herself degraded and deformed, cast out from normal society, yet perversely sexually attractive—and what Wilbur Whateley could be to fall in love with her. Wilbur in *The Dunwich Romance* is not exactly a sympathetic character, but compared to the perverse, detestable, and crude folk of Dunwich and their myriad violent ways and degrading treatment of Sary, Wilbur at least qualifies as an antihero. Their budding and ultimately doomed romance may be predictable, but it is carried out without missing a step.

The Mythos entities in Lee's Hardcore Lovecraft fiction are sexual entities and are served by cultists that are sexually perverse by most human standards; the protagonists are generally no less sexually active or excitable, but are almost uniformly not altogether malevolent—at least at the beginning. As with many Mythos works, the character development for most of Lee's protagonists involves a strong degree of corruption, but where typical Lovecraftian protagonists might be unhinged or subverted by the knowledge they gain, Lee's characters are forced to question (and, often, consciously act against and undermine) their moral framework. A typical Hardcore Lovecraft story will feature a transition or sexual awakening from the outer edge of the normal spectrum of human sexual activity into new frontiers, breaking a variety of "normal" human sexual taboos before graduating to sex with Mythos entities in various degrees.

In several of his Hardcore Lovecraft works, Lee uses the non-human anatomies of Mythos entities to explore the differing sensuality and capabilities of human-Mythos sexual interaction, but rarely for more than a scene. However, *The Dunwich Romance* lays out in microscopic detail a reproductive system and physique worthy of any serious science fiction work, with further elaborations revealed during sex scenes between Sary and Wilbur as they experiment. Whether Wilbur's continued lack of confidence in his ability to keep a woman sexually satisfied with mere thirty-minute rolling orgasms is an accurate depiction of teenaged inexperience or due to the author's desire to explore more elaborate tentacle-sex scenarios remains an open question.

Lee's Hardcore Lovecraft stories display an awareness and appreciation for Lovecraft's fiction and life, apparent through references, in-jokes, and allusions to Lovecraft's friends and family, the facts of his life, and many of his works. This is particularly noticeable in *Trolley No. 1852* and *Pages Torn from a Travel Journal*, where Lee presents Lovecraft as a sexual character. These depictions retain Lovecraft's known gentlemanly sexual reticence, but combine them with prodigious, if generally unused (until the events of the novel) sexual endowments. While readers unfamiliar with Lovecraft scholarship may grasp the joke, the real success of the characterization is more apparent to an audience that is familiar with some of the details of Lovecraft's life, and in this way the author shows his work in painting a loving caricature of Lovecraft, even as he takes liberties with Lovecraft's life to fit the needs of the story. Certainly, the idea of Lovecraft as a pornographer or a sexual dynamo would not be nearly as funny if Lovecraft hadn't a reputation for being so sexually reticent in his personal life.

Alan Moore

[. . .] actually put back some of the objectionable elements that Lovecraft himself censored, or that people since Lovecraft, who have been writing pastiches, have decided to leave out. Like the racism, the anti-Semitism, the sexism, the sexual phobias that are kind of apparent in all of Lovecraft's slimy, phallic or vaginal monsters.

This is a horror of the physical with Lovecraft—so I wanted to put that stuff back in. And also, where Lovecraft being sexually squeamish, would only talk of 'certain nameless rituals.' Or he'd use some euphemism: 'blasphemous rites.' It was pretty obvious, given that a lot of his stories detailed the inhuman offspring of these 'blasphemous rituals' that sex was probably involved somewhere along the line. But that never used to feature in Lovecraft's stories, except as a kind of suggested undercurrent.

So I thought, let's put all of the unpleasant racial stuff back in, let's put sex back in. Let's come up with some genuinely 'nameless rituals' - let's give them a name. So those were the precepts that it started out from, and I decided to follow wherever the story lead. It is one of the most unpleasant stories I have ever written. It certainly wasn't intended as my farewell to comics, but that is perhaps how it has ended up.

It is one of the blackest, most misanthropic pieces that I've ever done. I was in a very, very bad mood. [. . .] I wanted to be unflinching. I thought, if I'm writing a horror story, let's make it horrible. Let's make it the kind of stuff that you don't see in horror stories. Because William Christiansen had, perhaps unwisely, said: 'Look, you know you can go as far as you want.' I just got him to repeat that, and said: 'So... what, I can show erections? Penetration?' He said: 'Sure!' I don't know if he thought I was going to do it or not but . . . yeah, I did. It's a way that I haven't written about sex before. It's very ugly. [. . .] It reads very well: it's dark as hell. But it's kind of compelling. So I went back and read through the scripts for the following three issues, and I thought, 'Have I gone too far?' Looking back, yes, maybe I have gone too far—but it's still a good story. ("Alan Moore: Unearthed and Uncut")

Around 1994 David Mitchell of Oneiros Books approached Alan Moore to contribute a story for *The Starry Wisdom: A Tribute to H. P. Lovecraft* (1995). Moore's initial idea was for a novel called *Yuggoth Cultures*, which would consist of a series of short pieces, prose-poems, and vignettes— "cuttings, spores if you like"—from Lovecraft's poem-cycle *Fungi from Yuggoth*. Unfortunately, before Moore could complete more than six or seven pieces more than half of the only copies were lost in a cab in London, and the novel was abandoned. One substantial story, "The Courtyard," appeared in the *Starry Wisdom* anthology, and two other pieces, "Zaman's Hill" and "Recognition," were published in *Dust: A Creation Books Sampler* (1995) and later included in the revised 2003 edition of *The Starry Wisdom* (Moore 2007, 105-6).

"Zaman's Hill" and "Recognition" were adapted for comics by Antony Johnson with black-and-white art by Juan Jose Ryp and Jacen Burrows in the three-issue miniseries *Alan Moore's Yuggoth Cultures* (2003), and with various essays and extras was packaged as *Alan Moore's Yuggoth Cultures and Other Growths* (2007). Johnson and Burrows also adapted "The Courtyard" as a separate two-issue limited series: *Alan Moore's The Courtyard* (2003), which proved popular enough to be later be collected as a stand-alone slim trade paperback, and the accessory *Alan Moore's The Courtyard Companion* (2004); both *Courtyard* and *Companion* were issued together as a deluxe hardcover in 2004, and a color edition of *The Courtyard* was released in 2009.

Aldo Sax of "The Courtyard" is a caricature of a Lovecraftian protagonist: an intelligent white male, effectively asexual, somewhat condescending to others, traits that are manifested in racism and a slight disparagement of homosexuals. Like Lovecraft in New York, Sax is thrust into a milieu of others not like himself, which arouses disgust and disparagement in him, though never vocally. The teenage crowd is explicitly sexual; Johnny Carcosa's offerings even more so. What the reader gets is not the Mythos regurgitated once again, but an insightful re-imagining of the basic concepts—a nastier narrator describing a grittier world, with the reader left to decide, at the end, how much of the story Sax related was the Aklo talking.

Antony Johnson's comic script of "The Courtyard" retains the subdued sexual aspects of the story, keeping enough of Moore's distinctive language, which is terrifically effective when combined with Burrows's wonderfully restrained but detailed artwork (he shows us the cock-ring from Innsmouth with its tiny quills, a glimpse of *Pickman's Necrotica* of a human puppet molested by a shadowy, masked figure), and keeping the tone low and realistic to emphasize the transition to a fantastic set of double-page spreads when Sax receives the Aklo later on. Little is lost in the transition from prose story to comic strip, Burrows's detailed backgrounds filling in for many of Moore's word-pictures, sneaking in artistic references to the Mythos to complement Moore's literary ones, some of which are incredibly subtle (as Sax comes down from the Aklo and leaves Johnny Carcosa's apartment, the narrative shifts in perspective are represented as almost concealed scenes-within-scenes, reflected in windows and picture-frames, even as a couple ruts standing up and fully clothed against a tenement wall).

In 2010, facing a tax debt, Moore took up Avatar Press editor-in-chief William Christensen's offer to work with them again and wrote a sequel to "The Courtyard," with art again provided by Jacen Burrows. Released as a hornbook and four-issue miniseries entitled *Neonomicon* (2010), the series was later collected with a color edition of *The Courtyard* (2011) ("Alan Moore: Unearthed and Uncut"). As with its predecessor, *Neonomicon* would intimately combine sexuality with its reinterpretation of the Mythos, at once going back to the source material and re-imagining it with more contemporary sensibilities.

In *Neonomicon* Moore subverts, examines, and extrapolates from the sex tropes he observed in the Lovecraft Mythos, and the literature about Lovecraft and the Mythos that has built up around it. An important part of this narrative examination and subversion involves unveiling the horrors and secret knowledge that Lovecraft had only hinted at, keeping true to many of Lovecraft's concepts but with near-exploitative depictions designed to shock, tease, and repel. So there is the aggressive connection of Mythos material as pornography in the back of the "Whispers in Darkness" shop; the orgy of the cultists is not a pagan revel, but group sex designed to raise and capture orgone radiation; and the "cosmic rape" of conception and miscegenation with a Deep One is not hidden off the page, but presented as a brutal rape.

Special Agent Brears is the central character in *Neonomicon*, and it is her personality and experiences that drive the story, her past studies of Lovecraft in college and her struggle with sexual addiction that influence her decisions and set up the events in the story. Brears is a partial inversion of the stereotypical Lovecraftian protagonist as exemplified by Aldo Sax—female, not racist (judging by her partnership with a black man), and sexually promiscuous. However, Merrill Brears is neither a virginal, perfect Mary as in "The Great God Pan" or a slatternly, deformed Lavinia as in "The Dunwich Horror," because those are caricatures of women. Instead, Moore paints a more realistic portrait of a woman who is both open about her sexuality and ashamed by it, willing to strip down in front of her faithfully married partner or a group of cultists, but who calls herself a slut and a dirty whore when faced with Johnny Carcosa. As she put it to Lamper: "Look, who I fucked, it wasn't to do with liking them, okay? Usually, it was about hating me." Yet even during her confinement and sexual abuse, she retains a competent, intelligent, forceful, and resourceful character—without a gun pointed at her head, she is not squeamish about dealing with the Deep One.

The culmination of Brears's exposure to the Mythos is her pregnancy, whose Christ-parallels with Johnny Carcosa's annunciation place her as an heir to "The Great God Pan" and "The Dunwich Horror," and Moore approaches this with extremely elegant subtlety in Brears's final interview. Sax is, as I stated, a caricature of the Lovecraftian protagonist, and thus something of a cartoon of Lovecraft himself as Moore sees him—racist, intelligent, asexual—facing what is effectively his opposite, the Lavinia or Mary character, the mother of Cthulhu in all but name. With all the bullets fired and monsters dead, it becomes clear that final conversation is more or less the point of the preceding issues—that everything the reader has read and experienced so far has been leading up to an actual revelation, as with many of Moore's works, and Moore delivers with a recasting of Lovecraft's conceptions in a new format, ending with the revelation that R'lyeh is within her. As part of this realization, Brears comes to terms with herself and her sexuality.

With its graphic nudity, language, and depiction and suggestion of sexual acts; where the female lead character gets repeatedly raped and impregnated, some readers might conclude that *Neonomicon* is a mature work, and perhaps an exploitative one. However, the use of nudity and sex is an integral element in Moore's plot, not so much to shock readers, although it does do that, but to explore the themes of hidden and implicit sexuality in the Lovecraft Mythos; not to hide acts of rape off the page but to show them as the nasty, brutal realities they would be if they were real; and to examine the consequences on normal people—Lamper, dead; Aldo Sax, insane; and Brears, like the nameless protagonist of "The Shadow over Innsmouth," transformed and enlightened, accepting of her new role:

> I keep forgetting what this is and thinking I should get baby things. Jackets, a crib, a book of names . . . A book of new names, y'know? Not dead ones. [. . .] The strange aeons start from between my thighs and for all this other bullshit . . . it's the end. (Moore, Johnston, and Burrows)

Colin Wilson in "The Return of the Lloigor" (1969) gave one translation or epithet of "Necronomicon" as "book of dead names," which has passed into popular use. While faulty, modifying this back-formation with "Neo-" (new) gives the phrase "book of new names"—"Neonomicon."

Alan Moore's approach to the Mythos brings much the same ideology that characterizes his other work: it is provocative, original, and sexually aware, but also displays a strong awareness, examination, reflection, and sometimes subversion of the source material he draws on. Readers interested in exploring this area further should consult the collection of essays *Sexual Ideology in the Works of Alan Moore* (2012) and Moore's own historiography of eroticism, *25,000 Years of Erotic Freedom* (2009).

Moore's Mythos fiction contains a multitude of references to the Lovecraft Mythos and Lovecraft's life, but takes that material as a starting point and examines and extrapolates from there: where Lovecraft's imagery would hint or suggest, Moore delves into the gritty reality. The comic adaptations facilitate this verisimilitude by providing a plethora of visual details that subtly underscore the textual narrative. A brilliant example is Jacen Burrows's half-page panel showing the adults-only section in the rear of the Whispers in Darkness shop in *Neonomicon*, whose details include an inflatable sex doll with a gaping alien starfish-hole for a face, multipronged alien dildos and strap-ons,[5] and DVD boxes with titles like "C'TH'ORGY" and "The Dunwich Whorer."

---

5. Most of which, it must be said, outshines what is available in reality. However, it appears Burrows may have used Whipspider Rubberworks' "The Tentacle" sex toy as a visual reference for one.

Moore's Mythos fiction presents his perspective and understanding of the Lovecraft Mythos as interconnected with and reflecting the character of Lovecraft himself, and to a lesser extent Lovecraft's literary influences. The prose-poem "Zaman's Hill," for example, includes imagery that references Arthur Machen and Winfield Lovecraft's illness: "These are Machen-hills [. . .] whose calcinous rivulets spread like a tectonic syphilis birthing slow, massive hallucinations" (Mitchell 185). In *Neonomicon* there is a page where the visual panels of Agent Brears being raped by a Deep One are offset by a rather bland narration on Lovecraft's sexuality, bringing out all the old chestnuts—dressed as a little girl, dominated by a mentally ill mother and aunts, the failed marriage, etc.—both as a counterpoint to the brutal sexuality on-page, and to effectively transition to the next scene.

Moore has not shied away from sexual themes in his other works, but it is difficult to compare and contrast that material with his Mythos fiction, except in broad outlines. It may be significant, for example, that both "Recognition" and *Neonomicon* deal with instances of female rape, a subject that Moore has dealt with in *Watchmen*, *V for Vendetta*, and other works. However, the specifics suggest that this might be less a continuation of a theme than coincidence: in "Recognition" Moore refers to a specific incident regarding Winfield Scott Lovecraft's syphilis-induced hallucinations, and in *Neonomicon* he is deliberately invoking the references to rape in the Lovecraft Mythos. If there is a comparison to be made, it is that in all cases Moore does not glance over the brutality of sexual assault.

Cthulhu Sex Magazine (1998–2007)

> *Cthulhu Sex*: 1) A magazine intended for connoisseurs of horror and erotica. 2) Sexual intercourse with Cthulhu. 3) The malleable sexual organs of Cthulhu. 4) Cultishly inspired group pseudopodiphilia. (Morel 1)

The opening epigraph of *Cthulhu Sex* magazine changed slightly from issue to issue, but for the length of its twenty-eight issues editor Michael A. Morel brought its readership short fiction, poetry, and artwork of erotic horror. Despite the name, most of these works did not use or reference the Cthulhu Mythos, and the magazine's sole best-of anthology, *Horror Between the Sheets* (2005), only contains one explicit Mythos reference, "Cthulhu Sex (ahem!)–A Poem" (1998) by Katherine Morel. The key to *Cthulhu Sex* was the title, the combination of the eponymous avatar of the

Cthulhu Mythos and the promise of erotica deliberately invoked visions in readers and writers alike of depraved, perverted horrors and a willingness to publish them.

In this way *Cthulhu Sex* included darker, weirder, and more sexually explicit fiction and art than what most major publications were printing at the time, and provided a commercial and creative outlet for stories like Dan Clore's experimental "Why I Want to Fuck Cthulhu" (1998), Jean Ann Donnel's brief and hilarious "Shoggoth Makes Three" (2003), and Paul M. Collrin's "Dreams of Flesh and Stone" (2006), among many others, as well as a several adult-themed Mythos poems and dark and candid erotic artwork. Overall, the tone of the magazine was one of sensual horror rather than horrific erotica, emphasizing the elements of blood, sex, and tentacles.

Cthulhu Sex magazine was not alone in offering Mythos stories and art with sexual content, but it was the first commercial magazine to advertise itself openly as seeking and willing to publish such content, and to bank its marketing on the idea that readers would find the promised combination of sex and the Mythos provocative. While it is difficult to judge the wider impact of *Cthulhu Sex*, the magazine proved there might be a ready market of readers interested in Lovecraftian erotica, and who were willing to pay for it. *Cthulhu Sex* also had art and poetry included in the 2009 exhibit *Meanwhile ... at 594 Broadway* at the Museum of Comic and Cartoon Art in New York City. It is probably not just coincidence Lindsfarne Press, which published *Eldrich Blue* in 2004, advertised their books for sale in the pages of *Cthulhu Sex* magazine.

Eldritch Blue: Love & Sex in the Cthulhu Mythos (2004)

> The stories in this work deal frankly with sex and sexual situations, and the interior artwork depicts full frontal female nudity. They are meant for mature readers. Parental discretion is advised. (O'Brien xi)

The first anthology dedicated expressly to love and sex in the Cthulhu Mythos, *Eldritch Blue* consciously aped the style of the popular Chaosium Call of Cthulhu Fiction anthologies. Editor Kevin L. O'Brien distinguished *Eldritch Blue* from books like *The Shub-Niggurath Cycle* (1994), whose stories included sexually suggestive entries like Robert M. Price's "A

Thousand Young," because he was looking for a unifying conceptual theme rather than than a single Mythos element:

> I wasn't looking for love stories that simply had a Mythos twist; nor was I looking for stories that simply had sexual content in them. I wanted to see stories that tied the love and/or sex back into the Mythos in some fashion; stories that explored the interaction between the Mythos elements and the romantic/sexual elements. (O'Brien viii)

With this guiding vision, O'Brien focused not so much on the development of sex and love in the Mythos as on Cthulhu Mythos stories that were also stories about love and sex. Similar to the editors of the Chaosium anthologies, O'Brien shares his own thoughts on each story, interpreting them according to his own vision of the Mythos. This vision is spelled out most explicitly in his afterword "Love (and Sex), Mythos Style," which posits that Mythos entities are basically antagonistic to human life and use love and sex as a means to control and subvert humanity and to generate intermediaries to interact with humans. O'Brien's reading of the stories ties back into some of the themes of the Lovecraft Mythos, most notably biological determinism, but is only one interpretation of what is really a diverse collection of fiction.

Most of the stories in *Eldritch Blue* do not deviate from the established sexual themes of the Mythos, focusing on alien miscegenation between humans and Mythos entities, impregnation, half-breed spawn, etc. with slight variations and different combinations of various Mythos elements, settings, and characters. The innovation in these stories, when it is present, is the focus on the human impact of sex and the Mythos, treading new ground by showcasing unusual aspects of human sexuality as mail-order brides, couples dealing with infertility, sadomasochistic alien insects, virgins, strippers, and prostitutes, etc. The majority of the fiction avoids explicit sexual language and description of sex acts; there are fewer Mythos stories of erotic horror than Lovecraftian horror stories whose plot requires love or relationships to be involved in some fashion. With such a broad approach, it is somewhat surprising that the authors of *Eldritch Blue* evince a very limited view of carnality: all the relationships in the anthology are strictly heterosexual, with no exploration of other sexual affinities, paraphilia, or attendant aspects like pornography, etc.

Eldritch Blue is a milestone for Mythos fiction dealing with love and sex because it was the first, but as an anthology it is not entirely successful.

Love, sex, and the Cthulhu Mythos might be a novel theme for an anthology, but is still very broad, and these stories do not have the connective narrative between the pieces typical of the Chaosium *Cycles*. Editor O'Brien makes an effort to provide this connection with his commentary and analysis, but his interpretations are often somewhat forced, because while some of the stories are more or less typical Mythos pastiches with sex implied ("The Tale of Toad Loop," "The Spawn of the Y'Lagh") or parodies ("Beast of Love") that fall into a familiar Mythos form and pattern, others are more akin to Lovecraft-flavored erotic horror ("The Violet Princess," "The Surrogate"), and O'Brien stretches to encompass them in his vision of the Mythos. For example, O'Brien declined to use Ramsey Campbell's "Cold Print" for the anthology because "it didn't fit the theme of this anthology" (113), choosing instead to reprint "The Faces at Pine Dunes;" and the sole Lovecraft story in *Eldritch Blue* is not "The Dunwich Horror" or "The Shadow over Innsmouth," as one might have guessed, but "The Thing on the Doorstep." These editorial decisions reinforce the idea that ultimately *Eldritch Blue* was not intended to be a collection of Mythos stories about things that bump uglies in the night, but given the contents it is easy to conclude that there are many approaches to love and sex in the Cthulhu Mythos, and *Eldritch Blue* provides a fair cross-sampling of them.

Cthulhurotica (2010)

> I'll admit that when I first put out the call for submissions, *Cthulhurotica* seemed to most people like it would be a collection of literary tentacle porn. I got stories that introduced a lovely setting but spent the next two thousand words having sex all over it. I got writers who wanted to take a gory horror story they'd written for something else, slap "Innsmouth" over the town's "Welcome to . . ." sign, and call it Lovecraftian. I got potential readers telling me they couldn't imagine "Lovecraft" and "Erotica" in the same sentence, and never (ever!) wanted to see my book in print. (Cuinn 5)

The second major anthology to take sex and the Cthulhu Mythos as its theme, *Cthulhurotica* is a collection of new Lovecraftian fiction. In format the contents are more eclectic (art, poetry, short fiction, and essays) and editor Carrie Cuinn does not attempt to place the material within any particular narrative or scholarly framework, letting the pieces stand and speak for themselves. The most significant drives of the anthology are the lack of sex and positive female characters in the works of Lovecraft:

Whether it was a symptom of the time he lived in, or a personal choice, Lovecraft rarely included positive female characters in his stories. Asenath Waite, from "The Thing on the Doorstep" was actually an evil old man wearing a girl's body like a suit, and his other major female character, Lavinia Whateley from "The Dunwich Horror" was merely a servant of a greater evil. Lovecraft usually limited his women to a mention that the main character had a wife, one who faded from the story a sentence or two later. To be fair, Lovecraft didn't just limit female sexuality—none of his characters are romantic or sexual either. He simply left it out. We don't want to only expand the role of the female in the mythos, we also want to include a spectrum of gender and sexuality models, to better reflect today's society. ("WNW talks with Carrie Cuinn, the woman behind the Cthulhurotica anthology")

Cuinn's view of Lovecraft's female characters is blithe, but her assessment is mostly valid. Characters like Lavinia serve as an archetype that many subsequent female characters in the Mythos are based on, for good and ill, and many pasticheurs who aped Lovecraft carried on or exacerbated the gender imbalance in his work. The female characters in *Cthulhurotica* are not always strong or forceful, but the anthology does contain more prominent, proactive female characters, both supporting and as protagonists, than in most Cthulhu Mythos collections, and from the perspective alone could be seen as successful to Cuinn's purpose. As well, *Cthulhurotica* has a greater number of homosexual or bisexual characters than the norm for Mythos fiction. These factors coincide with a very low level of sexual violence, particularly violence against women. There is very little rape or forced sexual encounters, and none of it described explicitly or with derogatory language.

Despite the title, *Cthulhurotica* is neither a volume of Mythos tales nor erotica, though most use the Mythos in some fashion and all use sex to some degree. As with most contemporary Mythos fiction, the stories draw on or take inspiration from the Lovecraft Mythos almost exclusively. While the principal focus remains on sex between Mythos entities and humans, the purpose of that sex is generally focused on pleasure instead of (or in addition to) procreation. Many of the stories borrow more strongly from the ideas and tropes of Mythos sex that have percolated into the popular consciousness than from any specific image or passage in the Lovecraft or Cthulhu Mythos, such as Mythos entities subsisting on sexual energy ("Riemannian Dreams") and tentacle sex ("Descent of the Wayward Sister" and "Daddy's Girl"). The latter may in part be due to Cuinn's somewhat blithe assumption that tentacle sex goes hand-in-hand with the Mythos. On the other hand, the freedom from slavish devotion to the Mythos has given readers such outstanding weird sex stories as "The C-Word," "Flash Frame," and "Infernal Attractors" that can stand on their own, but whose hidden meanings reveal themselves when considered against the backdrop of the Cthulhu Mythos.

Whispers in Darkness: Lovecraftian Erotica (2011)

> I wanted *Whispers in Darkness* to exist because I needed to see how sex would play out in Lovecraft's dark and alienated world. Would the knowledge we are nothing drive people to antisocial manipulation? Or would the certainty that the universe simply does not care about us push us together and cause us to care even more about each other? The answer, it seems, is yes. (Blackmore)

Editor Jen Blackmore's anthology of Lovecraftian fiction is the first to be comprised primarily of horror erotica, though there is less of horror and more of erotica. The stories in this e-book contain explicit descriptions of sexual intercourse, and those sexual activities are generally characterized as fun or enjoyable activities for both participants, but shy away from being schlocky or exploitative; these are not poorly plotted, poorly written fuck stories where sex is the sole point. The explicit sex is part of the narrative, a natural outgrowth of the plot or the crux of it, but at the same time they are Lovecraftian works—not pastiches or parodies for the most part, but homages and derivative works that use and pay tribute to the Mythos. As with many contemporary stories of the Mythos, the contents of *Whispers in Darkness* reflect the modern conception of sex in the Mythos as much as they do embellishments on the entities, locations, and elements of the Lovecraft Mythos; a majority of the stories, for example, feature scenes of tentacle sex in one form or another.

The appeal and success of *Whispers in Darkness* is that it is not just Mythos-themed erotica; instead, the contents are extremely literate and engaging Lovecraftian stories that are also erotic and uncensored. The writing is of consistently high quality and style, and unabashedly explicit. There are no guilty feelings in this anthology, no abhorrence that isn't pinked with strange attraction, no sexual element hinted at but left shyly off the page, but also no lust that isn't mixed with other, deeper emotional attachments between the parties. The stories are for the most part fun as well as arousing, not always humorous but always interesting, and the authors are free to include other themes than just eroticism—the desire to know, censorship, and the value of pornography form a theme in "Koenigsberg's Model," for example. This speaks to the nature of the anthology itself as a valid literary and artistic expression.

Other Authors and Works of Note

> "By the way, I met up with Herrmann Mülder recently," I said—"you know, the guy who wrote the *Ghorl Nigral?* Says he's writing a sequel. It will deal with the love-life of Yog-Sothoth." (Lovecraft and Conover 2002, 185)

In the course of this chapter I have omitted any number of writers who have contributed to sex and the Cthulhu Mythos. There are simply too many authors of Mythos stories to cover them all adequately, and not all of their contributions have had significant impact on the Mythos readership. In many cases, these tales simply continue sexual themes and ideas begun by Lovecraft and his contemporaries without expanding or exploring them: for example, cosmic miscegenation resulting in hybrid offspring is ingrained in the Mythos, as are tentacled beasties of every description. This does not mean such writings cannot be influential. From Lovecraft and Heald's "Out of the Aeons" (1933) arose the bones of Lin Carter's Xothic Cycle of stories, focusing on the children of Cthulhu, to which Brian Lumley later added a daughter Cthylla in *The Transition of Titus Crow* (1975), and the theme was revisted by Tina L. Jens in "His Darkling Daughter's Womb" (1997) . . . and so on and so forth in like manner has the Mythos grown, building on previous works.

If I have neglected Lin Carter and Brian Lumley in this essay, it is not because their work is insignificant, but only because their use of love, sex, and gender in their Mythos fiction is less influential than that of their contemporaries like Ramsey Campbell. Lumley in particular transitioned from Lovecraft pastiches to science fantasy novels and novellas set in the the various worlds and Dreamlands of the Mythos, and his love and gender elements tend to proceed along the lines of planetary romances as set by Edgar Rice Burroughs (with perhaps a touch of Robert E. Howard), with strange queens, princesses, and demigoddesses vying for the protagonist's affections. Only in *Khai of Ancient Khem* (1980; later reprinted simply as *Khai of Khem*) does Lumley significantly deal with rape and sexual perversion. Many writers with less Mythos or Lovecraftian word-count than Lumley to their credit have produced works more concentrated on sexuality and the Mythos—far too many to list here, but a few at least are worth mentioning, to give readers an idea of the scope and variety of the material available.

C. Hall Thompson's early Lovecraftian novella "Spawn of the Green Abyss" (1946) is a weird love story between a human suitor and a woman pledged to a sea-god. Stanley C. Sargent's brilliant "The Black Brat of Dunwich" (1997) has two researchers tracing the steps of "The Dunwich Horror" and encountering an old man who recasts the account with Wilbur Whateley as a hero and Armitage as a villain, suggests Wilbur is a product of incestuous union between Lavinia and old Wizard Whateley (who served as a stand-in for Yog-Sothoth), and even intimates a budding homosexual relationship. Poppy Z. Brite's oft-anthologized and reprinted Lovecraftian story "His Mouth Shall Taste of Wormwood" (1990) reads something like an even more decadent, oversexed version of "The Hound" but set in a modern New Orleans. Nancy A. Collins's "The Thing from Lover's Lane" (1996) is the acclaimed tale of teenage horniness gone wrong when a cheerleader is raped and impregnated by Shub-Niggurath and her boyfriend catches the blame for it. Micheal Shea's "Fat Face" (1987) deals with a prostitute whose customer is much more than he seems. *Cthulhu Sex* alumnus Mark McLaughlin is one of the best writers to mix sex, Mythos, and comedy to outrageous and hilarious effect, recently collected in *Best Little Witch-House in Arkham* (2013). All are examples of Mythos and sex together at their best.

Most new Mythos writers begin with or return to the Lovecraft Mythos, building off of Lovecraft's stories and fiction, but some few choose instead to pastiche or take inspiration from other writers and address sex and the Mythos through that lens. Clark Ashton Smith is most notable for receiving some of the more adult-oriented pastiches such as "The Mastophilia of Amlimla" and "The Vulvifora of Vuutsavek" in *Tales of Sex and Sorcery* (2009) by Simon Whitechapel (as Charlotte Alchemilla Smythe), and "The Scarlet Succubus" in *The Last Continent: New Tales of Zothique* (1999) by Edward Lee and John Pelan. *The Scarlet Succubus* is the title of a short novel of Zothique that Smith had planned but apparently never wrote, which would "exploit the imaginative and mystic possibilities of sex—an angle that seems rather neglected in this day of raw and mundane realism" (Smith 1989, 272).

Other authors have broken new ground, writing fiction that is not primarily Lovecraftian or Mythos but definitely uses elements of it. An examplar is Nick Mamatas, whose Beat novel *Move Under Ground* (2004), in the style of (and starring) Jack Kerouac, is set in a Lovecraftian world where reality is breaking down. Likewise, Mamatas's *The Damned Highway: Fear and Loathing in Arkham* (2011), written with Brian Keene, places gonzo journalist Hunter S. Thompson on a trip to Lovecraft Country. Both relive the sex tropes of the 1960s through a Cthulhuvian lens, drugs and warped reality colliding with the distinctive personal philosophies and styles of the historical characters, so that readers are treated to visions of secret orgies where Nixon is buggered by a tentacle, or Jack Kerouac is almost drawn down into the embrace of tree-like shoggoths shape-shifted into titillating Beat chicks, or a particularly rapacious Allen Ginsberg is unhinged by the proximity of Cthulhu.

By contrast, some Mythos works simply have not had a significant impact, either critically or with the readership of the Mythos. *Nightmare's Disciple* (1999) by Joseph S. Pulver, Sr. follows a serial killer whose firm belief in the Mythos motivates him to perform a variety of sex-charged murders and mutilations, with the detectives picking up the pieces behind him following his journey of discovery. *The Colour out of Darkness* (2006) by John Pelan similarly combines sexual sadism with the Mythos, as cultists addicted to the liquid green essence of a Mythos entity revel in acts of violence and sexuality while police detectives seek to stop them. This lack of impact is not because of or in spite of their sexual content, but only because the stories themselves failed to make an impression on the Mythos readership at large. Increasingly, sex is so accepted in contemporary fiction that what would have been remarkable to see in an Arkham House anthology before Derleth died passes in Lovecraftian anthologies today with little or no comment. Forty years ago Ian Watson's "The Walker in the Cemetery" (2010), which includes a spawn of Cthulhu explicitly double-penetrating a character's vagina and anus with its tentacles, would never have passed unmolested into a Cthulhu Mythos anthology.

In this chapter I have purposefully neglected until now a few authors who began writing stories using elements from the Cthulhu Mythos in their work, but outside the general stream of the Mythos publishing narrative. By the latter I refer to writers after Lovecraft who did not begin their Mythos writing at Arkham House, or *Weird Tales*, or any of the various Lovecraft magazines, and generally do not show the influence or awareness of wider Mythos fiction in their fiction. These byblows and odd cousins include famed regionalist Fred Chappell, whose novel *Dagon* (1968) combines a kind of Lovecraftian influence and snippets with the Southern Gothic style. In a tale almost entirely devoid of outright supernatural elements a preacher moves into the old family plantation and begins a downward spiral of degeneration and sexual degradation at the hands of a local teenage seductress who may be a priestess of Dagon. Likewise, mainstream horror writer Graham Masterton has used the figure of Misquamacus from *The Lurker at the Threshold* (1945), Yog-Sothoth, and various other Lovecraftian characters and conventions in many of his novels and short stories, most notably *The Manitou* (1975) and its sequels, *Revenge of the Manitou* (1976), *Burial* (1992), "Spirit Jump" (1996), *Manitou Blood* (2005), and *Blind Panic* (2009); and the novel *Prey* (1992). In the Manitou series, Misquamacus seeks to be reborn into the new century, to gain his revenge on Europeans who destroyed his people. Masterton, who has written dozens of sex instruction books in addition to his many novels and short stories, typically features a healthy dose of sex in his novels as well.

One of the strangest developments is a very small subset of paranormal romance fiction that incorporates elements of the Cthulhu Mythos. Most prominent in this regard is Margaret L. Carter, particularly her novella *Tentacles of Love* (2007), a light-hearted erotic romp where a woman marrying into an eccentric Massachusetts family with characters borrowed from all across Lovecraft's fiction (including the groom's twin brother, a conglomeration of iridescent globes and tentacles/basement-dwelling nerd named Wilbur obsessed with Japanese tentacle anime) discovers that her husband has tentacles too—but she still loves him. As M. L. Carter, she also contributed "The Prey of the Goat" (1994) to *The Shub-Niggurath Cycle*. This more serious horror tale has a preacher's wife receive a strange amulet of Shub-Niggurath as a bequest, which causes her to become possessed—and eventually pregnant with an inhuman child. However, these explicit references to the Mythos are relatively rare, as shown in Carter's other two Lovecraftian romance novels, *From the Dark Places* (2003) and *Windwalker's Mate* (2008); both are slightly more serious works that both deal with sexually available single mothers and their supernaturally conceived, psychic young children. Similarly, Robyn Wolfe's brief novelette *Arkham Dreams* (2011) does not, despite the title, contain much in the way of Mythos references.

In mentioning these few titles, I hope to impress upon readers that there is more to sex and the Cthulhu Mythos than those works I have examined in this chapter, and that the sexual trends that began or are represented in that fiction continue to be developed, sometimes in strange directions and unexpected genres. The works I have mentioned I consider some the most notable for their content, or of those outside those authors and anthologies I had hitherto contained myself to. Readers may be assured that many more stories containing sex and the Cthulhu Mythos are out there.

Sex and Mythos Poetry

A number of the early contributors to the Mythos, particularly Lovecraft, Clark Ashton Smith, Robert E. Howard, and August Derleth, were poets whose subject matter sometimes mixed the weird and fantastic with sex and eroticism. Still, it was rare that any elements of the Mythos would directly appear in their work, the most notable example being Lovecraft's sonnet-cycle *Fungi from Yuggoth* (1929-30), which was published piecemeal in *Weird Tales* and other magazines. None of these early works directly combine sex and the Mythos, but the poetic output of these seminal Mythos authors established a precedent for poetry that inspired others.

So in parallel to the prose Mythos there arose a poetic tradition of sorts united in Mythos theme, imagery, and literary allusion; notable poets who have tried their hand in this vein include Lin Carter, Darrell Schweitzer, Robert M. Price, Stanley C. Sargent, Ann K. Schwader, W. H. Pugmire, and Nick Mamatas among many others. Some of this Mythos poetry deals with sex as subject matter or includes erotic imagery. It is best to understand Mythos poetry as a collateral and complementary effort when undertaken by Mythos authors—sometimes in imitation of Lovecraft, Smith, and Howard, such as Lin Carter's *Dreams from R'lyeh* (1975) and Ann K. Schwader's *In the Yaddith Time* (2007), which were inspired by Lovecraft's *Fungi*. The latter is particularly interesting for both its female narrator/heroine and its inspiration from Richard Lupoff's "The Discovery of the Ghooric Zone."

Minor verse was also an excuse (if any was needed) for Mythos writers to make light of their own fiction and its tropes; for instance when Robert M. Price parodies Carter's *Dreams* with his "Mildew from Shaggai" in *Crypt of Cthulhu* No. 61 (1988). It is most often the satirical material where the poets take themselves and their subject matter less seriously that topics on sex, love, and gender would find expression and publication in magazines like *Crypt of Cthulhu* and *Cthulhu Codex*. Mythos poetry with outright erotic themes and imagery remains rare, probably due to the very limited venues for publishing such material, such as the sadly defunct *Cthulhu Sex* magazine. Some Mythos poetry with adult themes is still published in anthologies and collections, such as Pugmire's metafictional "Songs of the Sesqua Valley" in *Sesqua Valley and Other Haunts* (2012).

Mythos poetry often demands that the reader have an understanding of Lovecraft and the Mythos to fully appreciate the substance, if not the language and construction, of the poems. Examples include Nick Mamatas's *Cthulhu Senryu* (2010) and David Jalajel's *Cthulhu on Lesbos* (2011). Eroticism is not a focus of either work, but in places the poets' approach and construction clearly shows an awareness of sexuality and taboo. Jalajel's Sapphic stanzas, for instance, are culled from Lovecraft, and whenever these selections include the word "queer" Jalajel includes it but also strikes it out—invoking Lovecraft's older, innocent use of the word and its modern connotation as a pejorative against homosexuals at a stroke.

Lovecraftian poetry, like Lovecraftian fiction, takes inspiration from and makes use of ideas and imagery from the Mythos without including explicit references to the Mythos. I good recent example is "Subcutaneous Hentai Blues" ("fever dreams of impossible couplings . . .") from skawt chonzz's collection *R'lyeh Sutra* (2011).

Mythos Ebook Erotica

Erotic literature has historically been transient, disposable literature. While present in some form in every literate society, with rare exceptions popular erotica tends to be quickly forgotten and poorly preserved. So it is that the history of Mythos erotica before the advent of the Internet is sketchy and incomplete; many of Brian McNaughton's novels and short stories in adult magazines remain unidentified and uncollected, and who knows what else has never found its way into wider publication or republication?

The advent of e-publishing has allowed the wider development and dissemination of erotic literature than at any previous period in human history; and this has resulted in a flowering of available pornographic material and erotica via the Internet, and the proliferation of specialized erotica aimed at specific fetishes and audiences. Mythos-related adult works are only a relatively small part of the total, and include both commercial ebooks and noncommercial fanfiction. To gain an understanding of how the Mythos is used and depicted in such works, I will briefly survey a number of commercial erotic ebooks that strongly feature the Mythos or label themselves as Lovecraftian. Some of works under consideration are clearly derived from the Mythos, even if they make no direct use of it. For example, *The Tentacles of the Elder Gods* (2012), a series by Lindsey Purl, involves a tentacled elder god named "Kum-Shaggurath" and characters such as Professor Whateley and Professor Olmstead. Grace Vilmont's *Uhluhtc's Sacrifice* (2013) simply reverses Cthulhu's name, but this is the only allusion to Lovecraft's creations and work.

There is no work so mean or devoid of merit, either in its subject matter or its execution, that it cannot reveal something to the discerning reader; so it is with Mythos ebook erotica. While many of the following works are inconsequential or poorly written, I believe that for all their technical or literary flaws they demonstrate many popular depictions and understandings of sex and the Mythos. At the very least these pieces reveal a literary undercurrent that is mainly missed or dismissed by academia. These are unfiltered, uncensored Mythos stories, and they have found an audience.

Three trends seem to mark the outpouring of Mythos-themed ebook erotica: penetrative tentacle sex, male homosexuality, and pregnancy or impregnation. While not present in every story, these themes tend to be very common and are often combined, so that a homosexual erotic narrative may contain scenes of penetrative tentacle sex, or penetrative tentacle sex may lead to impregnation. Tentacle sex, pregnancy, and the Cthulhu Mythos have been discussed at some length previously, but in many cases here the immediate influence of Japanese adult anime and manga is very obvious. Stories like "I Was Impregnated by Cthulhu!" by Penny P. Zahn, "Booty Call of Cthulhu" by Roxie Ferouge, "Cthulhu's Caresses—Lovecraftian Erotica" by Amy Morrel, "I Fucked Cthulhu" by Deliah Fawkes, "Tentacles in Suburbia" and "Summer of Tentacles" by Polera North, and "The Shakti" by B. Tolliver are all examples of these kinds of stories, featuring tentacle sex and/or pregnancy and the Mythos in various combinations and settings.

The emergence of a homosexual Mythos erotica subgenre is not, as it might appear at first, very unusual even given the relative lack of openly homosexual characters in the Mythos; traditionally the bulk of Mythos readership is male, some fraction of which must be homosexual, and the absence of such characters and scenarios provides an obvious vacuum for erotica authors to fill. Similar subgenres can be seen in other male character-dominated genre literature such as westerns and comic book superheroes.

Bisexual and lesbian-oriented Mythos erotica is less prevalent, but not absent. The stories vary from Johnny Murdoc's "The Horror in Dunwich Hall," with its bare gloss of Mythos references and tentacle sex to Lula Lisbon (writing as D. P. Lustcraft), and her parodic homoerotic rewrite of Lovecraft's "Herbert West—Reanimator" as "Herburt East: Refuckinator." Two notable authors in this subgenre are David Holly and Charlotte Mistry, who both write homoerotic fanfiction but for very different audiences.

Charlotte Mistry's trilogy of homoerotic tentacle sex stories "Dark Descendents," "Tentacles of Ink," and "Cult Sacrifice" are advertised as Lovecraftian erotica and contain no overt reference to the Mythos. Instead, the stories take something of their darkly fantastic atmosphere, setting, and inspiration from the Lovecraft Mythos. They are representative of a small class of similar stories that are inspired by the Mythos and borrow elements and tropes from it but are not directly connected with the Cthulhu Mythos, as they contain no mention of Mythos entities, books, or places by name. More pointedly, the stories all focus on homosexual encounters between two men and seem more aimed at a female audience.

David Holly borrows more from the Mythos for his homoerotic stories "The Fire Dance of Yog-Sothoth" and "In Deep Dendo," both of which are collected in *The Devil's Demand* (2013). Both stories feature an emphasis on helpless nominally straight or bisexual characters becoming corrupted into homosexuality by exposure to the Mythos, anal and oral penetrative sex with cartoonishly well-endowed multiple partners and tentacles, and the narrators coming through the experience intact by accepting the homosexual pleasures they've come to know. The Mythos references are frequent, at times rather sloppy and heavy-handed, but no more so than in the majority of heterosexual Mythos-based ebook erotica.

Where other stories are based on general Mythos tropes or are derived more or less directly from the Lovecraft Mythos, the "Blackstone Erotica" series of e-novellas by Justine Geoffrey and put out by Martian Migraine Press—including "Red Monolith Frenzy," "Green Fever Dreams," "Summonings: Anicka and Kamil," "Summonings: Yvette's Interview," and the forthcoming "Yellow Sign Bound"—are based on the wider Cthulhu Mythos. "Red Monolith Frenzy" is a sequel of sorts to Robert E. Howard's "The Black Stone," where the eponymous Justine Geoffrey goes to the degenerate and perverted town of Stregocavair, inhabited by an inbred race of oversexed mutants, where she awakens the god of the Black Stone with a sexually charged word of power and becomes the Priestess of the Black

Stone. In "Green Fever Dreams" Justine's sex-magic-fueled adventures continue in London, where she becomes embroiled with a dominatrix cultist who plots to summon Dagon via a sex rite with a Deep One beneath the Spa N'th-lei. "Summonings: Anicka and Kamil" is a prequel to the events of "Red Monolith Frenzy," where High Priestess Anicka uses her brother Kamil in an incestuous ritual to summon Daolath, while "Summonings: Yvette's Interview" is a prequel to "Green Fever Dreams" featuring an occult BDSM adventure with characters from Spa N'th-lei.

"The Black Stone" is a natural starting point for Mythos erotica, though Justine G. does not follow Howard's original rather extreme sadomasochistic bent and so makes more use of the setting and imagery than much else. Besides moving beyond Lovecraft into the wider Mythos, the author demonstrates a considerable degree of erudition about the Mythos in general, borrowing from the work of Mythos scholar Will Murray, Alan Moore's *Neonomicon*, and Ramsey Campbell among others. Like Edward Lee, Justine G.'s approach pushes the limits of explicit sexuality that uses the Mythos, and currently represents the most creative and ambitious Mythos ebook erotica.[6]

---

[6] Justine G.'s erotica series has been collected and published by Martian Migraine Press as *Priestess* (2013), and the same press has recently produced the anthology *Conqueror Womb: Lusty Tales of Shub-Niggurath* (2014).

4. Beyond Cthulhurotica

The Cthulhu Mythos has spread beyond the standard boundaries of literature, so that Lovecraft's influence and references to Mythos entities and tomes can be found in all manner of media, some of which involve love, sex, and gender in the Mythos. This chapter gives brief coverage to these relations in other media, which as I hope to show are intimately bound up with Mythos prose fiction, being both inspired by them and influences on later Mythos works.

The section "Sex and the Lovecraftian Occult" looks at a subset of Mythos literature or scholarship that is generally so segregated from literary critiques, fact-based biographies, and prose fiction that I thought it best to address it separately. The section deals with occult interpretations of Lovecraft and the Cthulhu Mythos, particularly an examination of how the writer-magicians address sex in their works, with an emphasis on the sexual magicks they detail and profess. Like Mythos-based erotica, the Lovecraftian Occult is not always held in high regard by literary figures in the Mythos, but it has had an observable influence on Cthulhu Mythos literature and deserves examination.

"Sex and the Mythos in Art" examines the influence of sex on visual artwork inspired by or based on the Mythos, including a discussion of certain popular forms that tend to reappear in different contexts. While this is a briefer section, I feel it provides reasonable background to understand the more visual media in the subsequent sections.

"Sex and the Mythos in Comics" surveys the Mythos in sequential art. Comic books and graphic novels are no less literature than prose short stories and novellas (and I have mentioned a few of them previously, including the work of Alan Moore in the last chapter), but the addition of artwork renders them a unique medium with its own history and tropes generally separate from those of prose fiction. This section ends with a brief look at Sex and the Mythos in Anime and Manga, examining some of the characteristic elements of sex in these Japanese media.

"Sex and Mythos Cinema" concerns the use of sex and nudity in Mythos film and television. Particular attention is given to the emergence of explicit Mythos pornographic films, which have generally been neglected in the literature to date.

"The Mythos and Rule 34" is an overview of the sexualization of the Mythos on the Internet, looking especially at fanart, fanfiction, and webcomics. Given the scale of the available content on the Internet, which is constantly growing and changing, this survey is not in any way exhaustive and must be mostly restricted to general comments. However, wherever possible I will reference resources and examples that illustrate or support the assertions and observations made in this section.

Sex and the Lovecraftian Occult

> A common theme in many of the ceremonies we have collected is the explicit combination of sexual acts and Lovecraftian deities. (Gonce and Harms 122)

The popularity of Lovecraft, the *Necronomicon*, and the attendant mythology of the Cthulhu Mythos has inspired and informed a parallel tradition of occult literature, a significant fraction of which deals with sex magic and sexual symbolism. "Occult literature" in this section includes grimoires such as the Simon *Necronomicon* (1977), works of theory such as Kenneth Grant's *The Magical Revival* (1972), and magical fiction. While all these types of works incorporate Lovecraftian elements to some degree, they are best examined and understood within the context of occult theory and history, and so are distinct from the Mythos fiction addressed previously.

In reviewing this permutation of Mythos-derived or -inspired work, many of the same observations with regard to the Cthulhu Mythos apply, such as primary emphasis on the Lovecraft Mythos and Lovecraft himself, and the common misinterpretation of Lovecraft's life, philosophy, and ideas based in part on the posthumous collaborations written by August Derleth and the flawed biography by L. Sprague de Camp. However, while occultists may use the Lovecraft Mythos and Lovecraft scholarship as source material, they derive almost nothing from non-Lovecraft Mythos fiction, and there is relatively little cross-pollination between this Mythos fiction and Lovecraftian occult literature. So it is best to consider these works as a parallel tradition, with occultists like Kenneth Grant drawing on the works of Aleister Crowley, Arthur Machen, Lovecraft, and Derleth among others, and Phil Hine, Stephen Sennitt, et al. in turn drawing in part on Grant for their works.

The Cthulhu Mythos has not borrowed excessively from Lovecraftian occult literature, despite the fact that authentic occult traditions have periodically been incorporated or mentioned in Cthulhu Mythos fiction. For example, Robert M. Price incorporates references to Aleister Crowley's tradition of ritual sex magic in "Wilbur Whateley Waiting" (1987), "Feery's Original Notes" (2008), and arguably "A Mate for the Mutilator" (2004); likewise, Alan Moore makes use of Wilhelm Reich's orgone theory in *Neonomicon* (2010). However, references to the Lovecraftian occult do exist in Mythos fiction, for example when Moore (himself a practicing magician with at least a passing familiarity with the Lovecraftian occult) makes mention of the Typhonian Trilogies in *Neonomicon*.

Lovecraftian occult literature has been highly influential in some of the iconography of the Mythos, best evidenced by the ubiquity of the "Necronomicon Gate" symbol from the cover of the Simon *Necronomicon* designed by Khem Caigan. Likewise, the claims of Lovecraft made in Lovecraftian occult and pseudo-occult work are sometimes persistent and influential, such as the repeated reference to Lovecraft's connection to Egyptian Freemasonry from Colin Wilson's hoax introduction of the Hay *Necronomicon* (1978), or claims that Lovecraft was an unconscious adept who wrote the truth as fiction, or otherwise was possessed of some special occult knowledge that informed his stories.

To help understand the metaphysics and historical context of the works discussed here, this section will begin with a bit of background material. Lovecraftian magical literature is primarily influenced by a handful of writers; I've chosen to address a selection of them separately, with notes on certain derivative or related works and groups. Due to the difficulty and cost of sourcing some of the original works in question, parts of this account will be based on secondary sources.

Background

Magia sexualis in Lovecraftian occult literature draws on a number of sources, but the most important is Aleister Crowley. As an occultist Crowley was a syncretist as well as a synthetist. He drew on Western esoteric traditions, most notably the ceremonial magic and initatory structure of the Hermetic Order of the Golden Dawn and Freemasonry, and Eastern esoteric traditions, particularly yoga and some elements of Tantra, and combined them to produce an original, composite system that he continued to evolve and refine throughout his life, adding new rituals of his own devising. A key component of Crowley's system was the advocation of a new ethic: "Do what thou wilt shall be the whole of the Law." This freedom of license was directly counter to the Victorian prudence of Crowley's upbringing and was a companion to similar sentiments on the importance of sexuality as evinced by contemporaries like Havelock Ellis and Sigmund Freud, who believed that sex was a central component of human existence and psyche.

This philosophical freedom to satisfy sexual impulse began to take a more overtly magical turn around 1910, when Crowley was introduced to the practices of the Ordo Templi Orientalis (O.T.O). Crowley was initiated to the highest degrees and revised the higher degrees of the order, which already included autosexual (VIII°) and heterosexual (IX°) sex rites, by introducing anal or homosexual rites into the XI°. Crowley composed and practiced a diverse array of sexual magic:

> [M]entally meditating on his penis—masturbating—while thinking of gods and angels; consecrating talismans with combinations of semen, vaginal juices and menstrual blood; prolonging and intensifying sex through visualization [...] beseeching gods for information, money and material possessions during sex. (Urban 122)

The theory behind the rites was that in sex lay the supreme magical power, the creative power that could conceive life, and that if the magician had sufficiently meditated on the appropriate sigil, image, or desired goal, and in the appropriate method, this power could then be directed away from the creation of a physical child to magical purposes. As Crowley wrote in *Liber CDXV–The Paris Working* and his novel *Moonchild* (1917), even the conception of a magical child was possible. In describing the sex magic rituals and the theory behind them in his various publications such as *Liber CDXIV–De Arte Magica*, Crowley not only used alchemical symbolism and other aspects of Western occultism, but made reference to, adapted, and incorporated certain terms, principles, and practices of Indian tantra into his own system.

In addition to the sex act itself and sexual symbolism, Crowley wrote and made use of some related practices. In *De Arte Magica* Crowley wrote of

"Eroto-comatose Lucidity," a practice of prolonged sexual activity designed to produce exhaustion and an altered state of consciousness where the subject can commune with God. The male and female secretions of sex acts were held to have a certain power to anoint and empower sigils and talismans, and also to be consumed during the "Mass of the Phoenix" from *The Book of Lies* (1913). The ingestion of sexual secretions continued to be a minor theme in some Lovecraftian occult workings, as can be seen in a variation of the Mass of the Phoenix in Ripel's *The Magick of Atlantis: Sauthenerom* (1985) and the inclusion of "consecrated sexual fluids" in the entheogenic elixir of the Miskatonic Alchemical Expedition (Gonce and Harms 117). For more on the latter, see Hine's articles "Some Brief Notes Regarding the On-going Work of Our Miskatonic Alchemical Expedition" (http://philhine.org.uk/writings/ktul_maexp.html) and "Cthulhuoid Copulations" (http://philhine.org.uk/writings/ktul_copul.html).

Crowley's system of sex magic is primarily androcentric; women are considered assistants, sometimes ignorant of their place in the symbolism of magical ritual. In some usages this was a form of magical role-play, where an earthly woman would take on the spiritual office of Babalon, the Scarlet Woman, Mother of Abominations, as counterpart to Chaos, the masculine creative principle in Crowley's Thelema, but in general Crowley's sexual rights are designed for the active use and benefit of men.

After Crowley, the most significant occultist drawn on by Lovecraftian magicians is Austin Osman Spare, an artist and former member of Crowley's magical society A∴A∴. Spare developed his own simplified magical system based around transgressing the artificial limits set by conventional religion and morality. A primary method of Spare's system (called by Kenneth Grant "Zos Kia Cultus") was the construction of a mystical sigil, an ideogram representative of the magician's desire, which would then be charged and brought to reality by entering an altered state of consciousness. Often enough this altered state was achieved by extreme exhaustion through sexual excess, similar in method, if not precisely theory, to some of Crowley's sex magic, notably the "eroto-comatose lucidity" and the process of visualization and use of symbols in the VIII° and IX° O.T.O. degrees, but with fewer trappings and less ceremony.

In Spare's system, the goal and key to magical success is liberation from self, abandonment to the unconscious mind achieved through embracing sensuality. For example, he described a ritual saturnalia or sabbat:

[T]here is a secret meeting place and an elaborate ceremony which is an extensive hypnotic to overwhelm all psychological resistances; thus, the sense of smell, hearing and sight are seduced by incense, mantric incantation and ritual, while taste and touch are made more sensitive by the stimuli of wine and oral sexual acts. After total sexual satiation by every conceivable means, an affectivity becomes an exteriorized hallucination of the pre-determined wish which is magical in its reality. (Grant 1972, 197)

Spare's conception of the sabbat owes something to the burgeoning development and spread of Gardnerian Wicca and related modern witchcraft movements in the 1950s and '60s, fueled in no small part by the witch-cult hypothesis of Margaret Murray and Sir James George Frazer's *The Golden Bough* (1890), which had likewise found its influence in the fiction of Lovecraft and Machen.

Kenneth Grant

British occultist Kenneth Grant achieved notability in magical circles as one of the heirs of Aleister Crowley and Austin Osman Spare, and through Grant's efforts many of Spare's writings were eventually published, as well as Crowley's magical diaries and autohagiography (with Crowley's literary executor John Symonds). Through his own writings, and as the founder and head of the New Isis/Nu Isis Lodge (1954–62) and the Typhonian Ordo Templi Orientis (1955–2011; now the Typhonian Order), Grant practiced and elaborated on the spiritual philosophy of Thelema and the systems of ceremonial sex magic developed by Crowley, Spare, and others.

Grant's writings have been controversial, not least because he chose to incorporate elements from works of fiction into his magical system, most prominently from the Lovecraft Mythos. Grant had postulated that Lovecraft's fiction represented an unconscious occult understanding since at least 1970 in an article for *Man, Myth and Magic* entitled "Dreaming out of Space." These views were codified in Grant's first major occult publication *The Magical Revival*, essentially an historical exegesis of Crowley's magical system of Thelema from prehistory through eminent post-Crowley magicians including Jack Parsons, Dion Fortune, and Austin Osman Spare. In that book Grant noted apparent correspondences between Crowley's *Liber AL vel Legis* ("The Book of the Law") and Lovecraft's *Al Azif* or *Necronomicon*, as well as similarities between aspects of occult theory and the fiction of Arthur Machen, Lord Dunsany, Sax Rohmer, and others. It was part

4. Beyond Cthulhurotica

of Grant's thesis that Lovecraft had unconsciously captured real occult knowledge in his Mythos fiction, despite Lovecraft's avowed materialism and statements in his letters that the *Necronomicon* et al. were fictional works.

This incorporation of Lovecraft's material as "occult truth" (rather than literal historical truth, though Grant muddles the two in his books) represents one of Grant's major innovations to magical practice. Traditionally occultists had sought authority in the supposed antiquity of their tradition or source text (such as The Hermetic Order of the Golden Dawn or Gardner's New Forest Coven), magical instruction received from supernatural entities (such as Crowley's *Liber AL vel Legis*), or original techniques or permutations on existing methods (such as Austin Osman Spare). Grant's borrowings from and references to Lovecraft and Machen in his occult writings, and his insistence on the magical truth of their fictional concepts, opened up new avenues for occultists. Chaos magicians in particular would embrace the idea that as long as someone believes in a concept, even a provably false one, it does hold power for them.

Grant further refined his magical system in a series of books collectively known as the Typhonian Triologies—*The Magical Revival, Aleister Crowley and the Hidden God* (1973), *Cults of the Shadow* (1975), *Nightside of Eden* (1977), *Outside the Circles of Time* (1980), *Hecate's Fountain* (1992), *Outer Gateways* (1994), *Beyond the Mauve Zone* (1996), and *The Ninth Arch* (2002)—as well as various supplementary publications. The Typhonian Trilogies are works of theory instead of discrete formulae or rituals, and represent Grant's interpretation, exploration, and expansions of the magical systems of Crowley and Spare. They feature an increasingly confused admixture of occult concepts, borrowing liberally from tantra, parapsychology, fantasy and weird fiction, anthropology, ufology, and books "received" from interplanar entities or spirits.

In the course of these nine books, Grant manages to draw connections or correlations between the weird fiction of Lovecraft (including the posthumous collaborations of Derleth), Arthur Machen, and a vast array of occult topics, entities, and conceptions, so that a significant chunk of his corpus could be inferred to utilize, refer, or connect to material derived from the Mythos in some fashion—and thus much of Grant's magic system can be seen to use the Mythos as well. For example, a large portion of Grant's writing revolves around exploration of an occult cosmology based on the *qliphothic* tree of death, an inversion or mirror negative of the kabbalah *sephirothic* tree of life, inhabited by entities that Grant equated with Lovecraft's Mythos entities. Using Crowley's sexual rituals as a basis, Grant believed that one could journey to this realm or "Mauve Zone" in astral form, and the magician could communicate with various entities there. Likewise, Grant expanded upon Crowley's magical use of sexual fluids by equating it to the Sanskrit term *kala*, a concept based on the Sanskrit word for "time," but with the additional meaning of "lunar fluids" that are "situated in the organism of the human female" (Grant 1992, 253). Grant then applied his concept of *kala* to the Mythos: "The emissaries of the Old Ones seek nourishment of a kind that is available on earth only *via* the lunar *kalas* of the nubile human female" (Grant 1992, 30).

The androcentrism of Crowley and Spare's magical systems is still very much present in Grant, with a focus on phallic and masculine symbolism, but slightly balanced by an emphasis on women as active participants contributing to the rituals and with their own creative power, though in his accounts of rituals women still seem generally to be objectified, so that they may officiate a ceremony but are often the subject of the ceremony as well. The best examples of this are Grant's accounts of psychic or spiritual sexual congress with Mythos entities, particularly the infamous "Rite of Ku" supposedly performed at his New Isis Lodge:

> At the climax of the ritual Lî shed her robe and, like a white shadow, incredibly reptilian, slithered over the rim of the tank. As her form clove the waters eight phallic feelers reached up and seized her. They engaged her in a multiple *maithuna*[1] in which each tentacle participated in turn. Lî's hair, black as night, formed a slowly waving arabesque, each vivid tendril etched against the mauve-zone with Dalinian precision. The eightfold orgasm that finally convulsed her was registered by the votaries around the throne. Violent paroxysms displaced the black hoods, revealing shining heads and the protuberant eyes of the batrachian minions of Cthulhu. (Grant 1992, 18–19)

In another such rite with a female celebrant in an elaborate set-piece of Leng with a mechanical shantak-bird led to a similar sticky end:

> Then, a seething mass of white slugs and maggots fused into serpentine ropes which crawled over the snow and converged upon the altar, using the body of the priestess as a ladder. They left traces of their ascent glittering upon her legs, her throat and her face, yet left unstained the immaculate black grown, for they vanished beneath it and reappeared *via* the declivity between her

---

1. Sankrit, "coupling;" "the genitals in sexual congress" (Grant 1992, 256).

4. Beyond Cthulhurotica   251

breasts. On reaching the summit of the altar they formed an undulant mass of tentacles [. . .] (Grant 1992, 54)

There are only two sexual matters derived from Crowley that Grant does not address in depth in these books with regard to the Mythos: homosexual sex magic and supernatural conception. Of the two, homosexuality is the more disapproved by Grant, and his mentions of it in *Aleister Crowley and the Hidden God*, *Nightside of Eden*, and elsewhere are primarily designed to refute Crowley's homosexual rites as misinterpretations and explain why the magical symbolism is incorrect and even harmful. Nowhere does Grant provide or suggest homosexual magic in direct relation to the Mythos.

Supernatural conception is one of those matters where Grant failed to draw what to other readers might seem direct and obvious parallels. Despite the emphasis placed on the production of a magical child by Crowley and others, Grant never really acknowledges the similarities between Lovecraft's "The Dunwich Horror" and Crowley's *Moonchild* except for a very brief mention in *Aleister Crowley and the Hidden God*:

> In *Moonchild* the incarnation was effected in and through the normal sexual formula, and although the full impact of the moonchild's advent is not described, the reader is left with the impression that, whatever it may have been, it was some sort of a monster in human form endowed with superhuman powers. But no entity incarnating via the usual channels of sex, no physical intrusion of another dimension into the ambience of humanity could possibly exercise power in any but a terrestrial sense. This is because the "power" has been earthed or enfleshed. [. . .] I refer to Howard P. Lovecraft whose occult experiences, disguised as fiction, vividly adumbrate the awful possibility at which Crowley but vaguely hints in *Moonchild*. (Grant 1975, 34–35)

Elsewhere in his writings Grant never seems to make plain the connection between the "magical miscegenation" of entities and humans in the remote past which he claims resulted in the hybrid, animal-headed gods of ancient Egypt and the similar cosmic miscegenation in the Cthulhu Mythos. The closest he comes in this regard are passages such as the following: "Speaking of extraterrestrials inevitably evokes, if not the Great Old Ones themselves, then Their emissaries or minions. They sometimes mask themselves, like Machen's Jervase Cradock, in deficient human forms" (Grant 1992, 6).

Grant was not the only occultist working Lovecraftian elements into their writings at the time; Anton LaVey famously incorporated two such rites by Michael Aquino in *The Satanic Rituals* (1972). However, Grant was the most influential of those early occultists in the development of subsequent Mythos occult literature, and the most focused on sexual magic. Grant picked up on these developments in some of his publications, referencing the Simon and Hay *Necronomicons*, the Esoteric Order of Dagon (an occultist group), and the eccentric American occultist Michael Bertiaux in several of his works. Colin Wilson reciprocated Grant's interest by dedicating a substantial chunk of his introduction to *The R'lyeh Text* (1995), the sequel to the Hay *Necronomicon*, to Grant's focus on the "morbid" sexual subtext that Wilson also perceived in Lovecraft's work.

Aside from Grant's influence on the Lovecraftian occult, his works are also referenced in Mythos fiction, most notably Alan Moore's *Neonomicon* and possibly inspirational for the characterization in "Feery's Original Notes" (1997) by Robert M. Price.

Michael Bertiaux

A part of Kenneth Grant's *Cults of the Shadow* (1975) and later works concerns the magical practices of Michael Bertiaux, the author of a voluminous and eclectic multi-year magical correspondence course, partially collected as the massive *Voudon-Gnostic Workbook* (1988); he is also the leader of several groups of occultists. Grant and Bertiaux shared an interest in sexual magic as well as Lovecraftian magic, and corresponded at some length (Gonce and Harms 113-15). As I lack access to Bertiaux's published materials, the description of his magical system is derived almost entirely from notes by Grant and Gonce.

Bertiaux's system is based primarily on Haitian Voodoo, but incorporating material from a variety of magical systems and ideas including Crowley's Thelema and Wilhelm Reich's orgone radiation. The resulting system is segregated, with certain courses of magical instruction restricted by sex or other qualifications, and with a strong emphasis on the interplay of masculine and feminine forces, energies, or radiation. The Lovecraftian inclusions to his complex system appear relatively minor, and in practice Bertiaux's Lovecraftian sex magic rituals appear to be based predominantly on the participants taking on roles and engaging in sexual magical acts using symbolism and material derived from the Lovecraft Mythos as background.

According to Grant, Bertiaux had a "Lovecraftian coven" that performed sexual rites at two locations. One group was "structured upon the basic law of sexual polarity":

> This magical current is concentrated in Shub-Niggurath which—in Bertiaux's Coven—represents masculine energy in its blind and bestial form; the 'thousand young' being the *shaktis* or female vehicles of its manifestation. Bertiaux, as High Priest, enacts the rite of Lycanthropy by closing the circle, window, or cave through which the Great Old Ones gain ingress. That is to say, he impregnates the priestess with the seed of the sea-beast, thus co-creating with her the *teratoma* who manifests the atavisms latent in the deep. (Grant 1975, 187)

The second group, inspired by Rick's Lake in Derleth's "The Dweller in Darkness" (1944), reportedly visited a remote lake in Wisconsin to attempt evoking Deep Ones: "The participants at this stage actually immerse themselves in the ice-cold water where a transference of sex-magical energy occurs between priests and priestesses while in that element" (Grant 1975, 189).

While no writers have taken up Bertiaux's brand of Lovecraftian sex magic to my knowledge, it bears mentioning if only to show that such practices were not unique to Grant or his immediate influence (which is probably why Grant reported them), and Grant continued to refer to Bertiaux's magical practices in subsequent books. Thus, Bertiaux's Lovecraftian magic has had at least some impact through Grant.

Simon

The 1977 Schlangekraft edition of the *Necronomicon* by "Simon" was one of the earliest and remains one of the most influential occult works in the Lovecraftian tradition, fostered in no small part by the ready availability of the book and its accessory volumes, the *Necronomicon Spellbook* (1981), *The Gates of the Necronomicon* (2006), and *Dead Names: The Dark History of the Necronomicon* (2006), being made continually available in mass-market paperback. "Simon" is a pseudonym; the original *Necronomicon* at least is a collaborative effort, but subsequent works are probably by occultist Peter Levenda (Gonce and Harms 39-41).

Where Kenneth Grant had mapped Lovecraft's Mythos to Crowley's system, Simon takes another step further and attempts to map both to his personal version of Sumerian mythology. As a result, Simon's KUTULU and co. does not bear much likeness to either Lovecraft or Crowley, but it has the benefit of being much more approachable to the lay reader, and unlike Grant the material in the Simon *Necronomicon* is more liturgical than theoretical, with instructions, invocations, signs and seals, and other practical technical material for practitioners.

Simon acknowledges the link between sex and magic in his introduction to the *Necronomicon*, mentioning but not detailing the tantric sex magic of Crowley's O.T.O., the pseudohistorical witch-cult, and the sabbat orgies linked with witchcraft since medieval times, and goes on to say much more about the latter in *The Gates of the Necronomicon*. However, the Simon *Necronomicon* itself is not a book where the sexual act itself is part of the rituals; though at one point Simon does state that "the Priests of Old were naked in their rites" (Simon 1980, 100). Rather, sex, love, and gender form part of the attributes of various deities and spirits, most notably Inanna. Later works in the series suggests actual practical rituals to achieve effects of immediate benefit—summoning the spirit Zisi to heal a lover's quarrel, for example.

Occult writers who further developed the system of magic described in the Simon *Necronomicon*, such as Warlock Asylum (Messiah-el Bay) and Joshua Free, have also devoted more attention to sex and the place of the Simon text in the occult tradition. In *The Atlantean Necronomicon* (2010), for example, Warlock Asylum interprets the Simon *Necronomicon* as referring to the tantric sex rites of ancient Sumer, referencing Kenneth Grant's Typhonian Trilogies and anthropological works to explore some of the themes of fertility, menstruation, androgyny, etc. related to Inanna/Ishnagarrib/Shub-Niggurath and similar entities. Simon's melding of the Mythos to more traditional mythology, with all the strange generations and couplings inherent therein, also appears to have inspired later works, such as Frank G. Ripel's *The Magick of Atlantis: Sauthenerom, the Source of the Necronomicon* (1985).

In 2013, Peter Levenda released *The Dark Lord: H. P. Lovecraft, Kenneth Grant, and the Typhonian Tradition in Magic*. This is an exegesis of Grant's Typhonian trilogies, at the same time attempting to tie it more closely to the Simon *Necronomicon* and Lovecraft's Mythos. The result is more cogent and concise than Grant ever managed, though it adds little in the way of new material aside from a list of the *kalas*.

Phil Hine

> Let's face it, Sexuality is *weird*. Magic is *weird*. So when you start in on Sexual Magic, you're in for a double helping. (Hine 2008, 161)

A noted writer on chaos magic theory and an associate of the Esoteric Order of Dagon, Phil Hine's most significant contributions to Mythos occult literature are the chapbook *The Pseudonomicon* (1994) and the chapter "Liber Nasty" in his book *Prime Chaos* (1993). Hine's approach decries the crass mass-market commercialism of the Simon *Necronomicon* as well as the deliberate ambiguity and complexity of Grant, drawing on both without taking either too dogmatically or seriously. Hine emphasizes the personal and practical manipulation of the Mythos symbol system for magical purposes.

Hine has written a number of brief articles and essays on sex and magic, emphasizing that "sexual magic is about exploring and utilizing one's own awareness and experience of sexuality in order to bring about change, in accordance with will" (Hine 2008, 159). Hine effectively distills some of the core concepts of psychosexual magic espoused by Crowley, Spare, and Grant, such as the use of sexual tension or release to enter different states of consciousness or to fuel a working, but discards most of their ceremonial and theoretical trappings and preconceptions of gender and sexuality, most notably Grant's homophobic reinterpretation of Crowley's system of sex magic.

With regard to the Lovecraftian occult however, Hine is relatively concise:

> One of the commonest forms of sexual gnosis which can be applied to Mythos magic is the facilitation of altered states of consciousness brought on by sexual arousal, which can be used as a springboard for exploration of astral or dream zones. The use of sexual gnosis to charge obsessive fetishes is also an obvious application, as is the breakdown of taboos and revulsion's by exploring sexual gnosis outside of one's immediate references. (Hine 2009, 32)

This is in its way no different from the concept of transgressive sexuality behind Crowley's rites, though more plainly stated—the deliberate sundering of sexual taboos providing a mental or spiritual liberation. An example of the use of "revulsion" is given in Hine's ritual psychodrama "The Ghoul's Feast," designed to provide a symbolic transfiguration from human to ghoul following the lines of Richard Upton Pickman. Among the suggested activities is "engaging in copulation with another celebrant who has the appearance of a corpse" (Hine 2009, 42).

Taking inspiration from Lovecraft's "orgies" (such as in Louisiana swamp cult of "The Call of Cthulhu") and Spare's concept of the sabbat, Hine also offers some specific thoughts on "Frenzied Rites"—namely, the difficulty for participants to "abandon sexual taboos and self-restraint" (Hine 2009, 31), to lose themselves in true revelry and thus achieve an altered state of consciousness. Once the celebrants have lost themselves, broken free from the societal and personal limitations on their actions, they would be more open to magical possibilities as well.

The work of Hine has been influential on magician-writers such as Grant Morrisson and Stephen Sennitt, and has resulted in surprisingly original works of fiction such as the anthology *The Starry Wisdom* (1994). Sennitt in particular has written occult chapbooks of his own involving the Cthulhu Mythos, collected as *The Infernal Texts: Nox and Liber Koth*, and "Sex-Invocation of the Great Old Ones (23 Nails)" in *The Starry Wisdom*.

Donald Tyson

Straddling the boundary between literary and occult fiction are the writings of Donald Tyson's Necronomicon Series: *Necronomicon: The Wanderings of Alhazred* (2004), *Alhazred: Author of the Necronomicon* (2006), *Grimoire of the Necronomicon* (2008), *The 13 Gates of the Necronomicon: A Workbook of Magic* (2012), and the *Necronomicon Tarot* (2012). Tyson provides greater emphasis on the Lovecraft Mythos than many previous efforts, resulting in a system that is much more closely tied to Cthulhu Mythos literature than to the occult systems of Grant, Simon, Hine, et al.

Tyson presents his magical system in a simplified manner, organized for the aid of the reader, and with discrete rituals. In substance, this system is predominantly based on planetary magic, with some additional borrowings and influences, in particular the "gatewalking" rituals of the Simon *Necronomicon* and the tradition that has sprung up around that practice.

Shub-Niggurath is the primary focus of most of the sexual magic in Tyson's work, represented as a goat-like hermaphrodite, chaotic deity of perpetual fertility and sexual attraction. As with Simon, Tyson associates Shub-Niggurath with a conventional love/fertility entity, in this case the astrological Venus—but also emphasizes Shub-Niggurath as a deity of perverted fecundity, a mother of monsters. The devotees of Shub-Niggurath seek states of altered consciousness through sex and sensuality; Tyson gives details of one such rite, which appears to be a bowdlerized variation on Crowley's "eroto-comotose lucidity":

> On the day prior to the attempt to open the Gate of the East upon the path to the black throne, the follower of this way should rely on the aid of a partner to sustain his arousal without interruption continuously. This can be done with the aid of caresses, embraces, erotic art, sensual music, incense,

sensual baths, and oils for the skin. If necessary, the aspirant may sustain his own arousal, but this is more difficult as it divides concentration. Always the image of Shub-Niggurath should be held in the imagination, but in a form of the goddess that is attractive and seductive to the aspirant for her favor. Female disciples will choose to conceive her in her masculine aspect, unless they favor the love of women. (Tyson 2008, 148)

While this sustained arousal is being maintained on the day prior to the ritual of opening the gate, the follower of this path must not sleep. Fatigue of the senses is necessary to open the Gate of the East. Arousal should be maintained to a condition of discomfort that is almost painful. If Shub-Niggurath has heard and heeded the prayers of the aspirant, the goddess will help to sustain arousal, sometimes to a degree that seems almost superhuman (Tyson 2008, 148).

While Tyson does make allowances for female (and lesbian) devotees, the bulk of his language in this section and throughout the *Necronomicon* series is still generally androcentric and heteronormative. While Tyson does not denounce male homosexuality anywhere as Grant did, neither does he ever account for it.

Tyson is also notable for having written a full occult-flavored biography of Lovecraft to accompany his other works, *The Dream World of H. P. Lovecraft* (2010). While he mostly sticks to the facts, he is probably the first to ascribe to Lovecraft magical talents based on repressed sexual energy:

> It is the common practice in Eastern esoteric schools, such as that of Chinese tao, Tibetan bon, and Hindu tantra, to deliberately use suppressed sexual energy to provoke the awakening of magical or paranormal abilities, among them the gifts of astral vision and astral travel. In Lovecraft's case, this awakening may have occurred spontaneously, without him ever realizing what was going on, but it was no less potent for having been unsought. (Tyson 2010, 84)

In ascribing these talents to Lovecraft, Tyson does little more than repeat the same assertions as Kenneth Grant that Lovecraft unknowingly perceived occult truths and wrote them as fiction.

Tyson's strong adherence to Lovecraft's writing and scholarship, relatively simple and clearly organized occult techniques, and acknowledgment of the fictive origin of the *Necronomicon* and Lovecraft's fiction as fictions are the primary characteristics of his Lovecraftian occult literature. While he borrows principles, ideas, and even terminology from Grant, Simon, et al., and candidly discusses sex in the Lovecraft Mythos and Lovecraft's life, for the most part his occult works are mostly sanitized—no drugs, sodomy, ingestion of sexual fluids, etc. In this way, Tyson's *Necronomicon* series does not ignore sex or sex magic, but neither does it really explore or emphasize the transgressive nature of sex as Grant, Hine, et al. had done. This could merely be marketing, to make the books more acceptable to a large heteronormative audience, or simply Tyson's personal preference as a ceremonial magician.

Asenath Mason

Necronomicon Gnosis–A Practical Introduction (2007) is a condensed exegesis of Tyson's *Necronomicon* series, the Hay and Simon *Necronomicons*, Grant's Typhonian Trilogies, Hine's *Pseudonomicon*, et al. by Polish occultist Asenath Mason. Where most Lovecraftian occultists restrict themselves to working with Lovecraft's fiction (including Derleth's "posthumous" additions), Mason also incorporates later material from such Mythos writes as Ramsey Campbell and Brian Lumley. Much of the text is concerned with collating aspects of the various Lovecraftian occult systems and distilling them into a relatively coherent and accessible format, and punctuated by original pathworkings and rituals. In giving a list of magical techniques in the Lovecraftian tradition, for example, Mason gives the following description of sex magic:

> The Cthulhu Mythos include also many sexual elements. One of them are "sacred marriages" or sexual congress occurring between an Old God and a human partner. Such a situation is described in Lovecraft's story *The Dunwich Horror* [. . .] Sexual gnosis is a specific way of invocation, when the power of an invoked deity manifests through sexual impulses and is thus absorbed into the body and mind of a magician. This way the alien nature of Great Old Ones is more easily absorbed into consciousness. This is also one of the ways to achieve a trance state: at the moment of orgasm the mind is focused on a single experience and all other states of consciousness are left behind. An example of a magical working when sexual congress occurs between a male magician and the other force is union with Shub-Niggurath, a quasi-female deity of strongly sexual nature. Another practice by a male and a female magicians, one invoking e.g. Yog-Sothoth the other one–Shub-Niggurath. Then the congress occurs between the male and the female magician and the invoked powers are transferred to each other and united. Another sexual technique which can be applied to Necronomicon practice is the popular tantric tradition of achieving the state of ecstatic trance through awakening and raising the power of the Fire Snake. The serpentine deities in the Cthulhu Mythos, especially Yig, correspond to the tantric concept of Kundalini [. . .] (Mason 22-23)

4. Beyond Cthulhurotica   259

This is nothing particularly novel in terms of content, but it does represent the first concerted effort to unify and categorize the various sex magics developed in Lovecraftian occult literature so far under the same rubric. In the same section, Mason also briefly discusses creating servitors. This process appears to derive mainly from Kenneth Grant's discussion of homunculi and sigil magic taken from Spare:

> The procedure of their creation by a skillful magician does not differ from the popular modern techniques of chaos magic. And thus, first we have to specify a task or function they are supposed to perform, then create a sigil, give the Shoggoth a name, and finally activate the servitor by ritual means. The method of activation is through sexual energy (according to Kenneth Grant, the word "Shoggoth" is relating to Chaldean "shaggathai"—"fornication"). The whole operation of creating the servitor lasts 40 days, during which a magician feeds the Shoggoth with his sexual fluids mixed with his own blood. (Mason 23-24)

In the chapter "Sex, Blood, Chaos and Death—Presentation of Shub-Niggurath" (written with Adam Kosciuk), Mason alloys the disparate and presentations of Shub-Niggurath and the Goat with a Thousand Young from sources in Lovecraftian occult literature and Cthulhu Mythos fiction. The resulting history and examination of worship examines how Lovecraftian occultists correlated Shub-Niggurath with female deities and entities, and deities of fertility, love, and/or sex. The chapter ends with "The Black Communion," a rite of sexual sorcery between a male and female participant. The two enact ritualized coitus as priest and priestess of Shub-Niggurath. The female participant seeks identification with and possession by Shub-Niggurath, becoming her material avatar, and the male seeks spiritual communion with Shub-Niggurath through congress with the priestess.

The other chapter dealing strongly with sex magic is "The Serpent God Yig and the Power of Ecstasy." As with Shub-Niggurath, Mason places Yig as the original behind various snake deities, devils, and entities of myth and religion. Yig's sexual aspect derives in part from his depiction in "The Curse of Yig" and Tyson's use of Yig in his novel *Necronomicon: The Wanderings of Alhazred* (2004), but the primary magical mechanism of Yig is entering an ecstatic trance state fueled by the tantric concept of kundalini as expressed by Grant and Crowley—a metaphysical, libidinal serpent power that is coiled in the pelvis, and when awakened this phallic snake-power can induce the desired ecstatic state:

The priestess, inflamed to the point of orgasm, is "penetrated" by the deity, which in this practice is identified with Yig, when the serpent power rises up her spine and activates the chakras, the energy zones. At the moment of orgasm, the energy is moved to the centre of the Will, the Ajna chakra. The third eye opens and the vision of other planes and dimensions is achieved. [. . .] In the Tantric tradition, sexual fluids secreted during the orgasm are regarded as magically potent liquids. (Mason 156)

Mason provides a ritual along these lines to end the chapter "The Serpentine Ecstasy." In form it is a directed visualization exercise, descended from Crowley or Spare's attempts to achieve a magical effect by visualizing while masturbating. The goal of the exercise is to achieve a state of extreme arousal, to be aware of the kundalini power and direct it to rise, so as to energize the crown chakra and achieve possession by Yig proceeding through the visualization. While this does not specifically involve masturbation, it is heavily implied.

While Asenath Mason's *Necronomicon Gnosis* has not had as great an impact on the Lovecraftian occult as the work of Grant, Simon, Tyson, or Hine, it is representative of the substantial amount of material that those interested in the Lovecraftian occult and sex magic have to work with and the kinds of material they do produce, and thus represents the shape of future developments. Where Kenneth Grant wrote somewhat obscure books for a select audience, chock full of sex and relatively complex magical theory, Simon wrote an almost sexless *Necronomicon* with enduring mass-market salability. Tyson took a middle ground, more salacious than Simon but considerably tamer than Grant, and from the number of titles in his *Necronomicon* series has achieved at least modest commercial success—and despite the variety of its sources, it is from Tyson that Mason's book derives much of its style and paradigm. *Necronomicon Gnosis* is very much in line with the heteronormative baseline of the *Necromonicon* series, with scant if any mention of homosexuality and relatively conservative in the kinds of sexual material it addresses—no discussion of anal or oral *magia sexualis*, for example, and a far cry from the varied sexual material in Grant's Typhonian Trilogies.

Sex and the Mythos in Art

The earliest Mythos artwork consisted of illustrations for the fiction of Lovecraft and his contemporaries in the pulp magazines. With the lack of explicit sexual images within the text, the artists often had to stretch a bit to add in a bit of sexual detail to the accompanying images, such as Clark Ashton Smith's drawings of vegetation suggestive of genitalia for Lovecraft's "The Lurking Fear" in *Home Brew* (1922), and a few buxom naked worshippers and Deep Ones to accompany the publication of "The Call of Cthulhu" and "The Shadow over Innsmouth" in *Weird Tales* (1928 and 1942, respectively). Artists such as Virgil Finlay would occasionally add a bare-breasted female or nude, as for the dust jacket of *The Outsider and Others* (1939), but for the most part the Mythos artwork based directly on the stories of the Mythos, and the dust jackets and paperback covers of collections, remained within normal standards for genre fiction of the era. Nudity became more common beginning with the 1980s, as shown in the Tim White covers for *Tales of the Cthulhu Mythos* (1987) and *The Trail of Cthulhu* (1987), and continued on through the interior illustrations of *Necronomicon Gnosis* (2007) by Asenath Mason, Oliver Wetter's cover for *Cthulhurotica* (2010) and several of its interior illustrations, and so on. More explicit works were scarce in published Mythos-related works, though some graced the art galleries in *Cthulhu Sex* magazine.

The majority of Mythos commercial art—cover and interior illustrations for Mythos anthologies, novels, magazines, etc.—does not have openly sexual content, and most of that which does exist consists of bare female breasts. Mythos entities themselves tend to be depicted as genderless, with humanoids like Deep Ones or Cthulhu often shown naked but with crotches hidden or curiously blank; a notable exception is the Mythos art of Michael Bukowski (http://yog-blogsoth.blogspot.com), which does not shy away from depicting genitalia on depictions of Lovecraftian entities. Female Mythos entities by contrast often display naked breasts—as can be seen, for example, in Mike Dubisch's *Black Velvet Cthulhu* (2010) or Kirsten Brown's *Brides of Tindalos* (2010) illustration for *Cthulhurotica*. Explicit depiction of the vulva or vagina is much rarer, and illustrations of any form of sex in a Mythos context are generally restricted to pornography.

Sexual symbolism in Mythos art appears to follow much the same line as in Mythos fiction. The tentacle as a substitute phallus is probably the most commonly noted motif, and not always intentionally invoked. Robert M. Price once recalled, on an illustration for Brian Lumley's "The Statement of One John Gibson" for *Crypt of Cthulhu* No. 19 (1982):

Lin Carter took one look at my crude illustration of the dream metioned above, and cried, "Roberto! What's *this*?", because what I meant as Gibson grasping the dream-tentacle in horror looked for all the world like he was sitting up in bed grabbing his huge phallus, masturbating! (Lumley and Wiater 55)

Most depictions of tentacles in the Mythos probably are not meant to invoke the penis, but only as visual shorthand for the weird. For example, the figure for Wetter's cover of *Cthulhurotica* is a naked human female whose upper head resolves into flailing tentacles; this has nothing of the iconic imagery of tentacles threatening penetration or bondage, but everything to do with representing erotica (the naked female) and Cthulhu (tentacles), and this is all that is necessary to communicate the essential aspects of the anthology. A very similar approach was taken for the cover of *Whispers in Darkness: Lovecraftian Erotica*, juxtaposing a handful of tentacles against a naked female torso.

While as a whole Mythos art inspires highly original works based on the alien entities of the Cthulhu Mythos, some artwork also makes use of staple set-pieces of fantasy and horror. For example, the poster to the film *The Dunwich Horror* (1970) shows a supine woman being menaced by a monstrous head whose medusa-locks sprout monster-headed tentacles—the woman so positioned as to emphasize her cleavage, with her lower torso out of sight. This is really no more than an update to the classic Margaret Brundage covers for *Weird Tales* or a thousand other illustrations in magazines and novels of a woman on the verge of molestation.

In a Cthulhu Mythos context, such illustrations typically infer that the female (or more rarely male), who is often tied or bound to a stone or altar, is intended as an offering for some entity. This is not a unique image, or even original to the Mythos, but it is part of the visual language of Mythos art and literature. Just as readers know that a tentacle wending from the corner of a cover implies Cthulhu or its ilk, so too might a tentacle menacing a naked woman suggest the alien lusts for human women from "The Shadow over Innsmouth" or "The Dunwich Horror." Where most Mythos artwork plays these visual tropes relatively straightforwardly, with the female sex object cast as a powerless victim, in some Mythos art the roles are reversed, with the woman accepting or even seeking or dominating the union. Men may also take the role of sex object in such scenes, but this is generally rare and most prevalent in homosexual pornographic Mythos art such as in *The Pornomicon* (2005).

Outside of Mythos books, magazines, and other publications are visual works that reference or draw inspiration from the Mythos, a subset of which are sexually explicit and even pornographic. The connection between any given artwork to the Mythos may be relatively tenuous. The Swiss artist Hans Rudi Giger's collections *Necronomicon* (1977) and *Necronomicon II* (1985), for example, take some inspiration from Lovecraft's writings and are frequently sexually graphic, but despite the name they draw nothing directly from the imagery of the Mythos.

Where some artists may strive to achieve appreciation, awe, horror, shock, or titillation with their Mythos work, it is exceptional for a Mythos artist to attempt humor—and more exceptional still to combine it with a reference to sex or eroticism. Yet when this is done well, it is amusing and fascinating; the worm of horror and grotesquerie turns to become ridiculous, ghastly humorous, or even cute. The master of this form is undeniably Gahan Wilson, whose cartoons for *Playboy* and other publications are replete with monsters with a little cosmic miscegenation on their minds.

Sculpture remains an uncommon expression of Mythos art, though various small busts and statues have achieved a steady popularity over the years, though rarely sexualized. For example, artist and sculptor Jim Broers has produced a bare-breasted figure of *Shub-Niggurath* as a sort of female satyr figure; a work entitled *Rapture of Cthulhu* featuring three bare-breasted women prostrating themselves against a monolith topped with Cthulhu; and an original female character, *The Queen in Yellow*, based on Robert W. Chambers's *The King in Yellow*. Eolith Designs in the United Kingdom has also marketed a bare-breasted, female satyr statuette of Shub-Niggurath. In general, bare female breasts are usually the limit of sexual content for a Mythos sculpture.

By far the most explicit visual images of sexuality in the Mythos have occurred in the context of comics, film, and graphics published through the Internet, and the remainder of this chapter discusses these media.

Sex and the Mythos in Comics

Comic books, comic magazines, and graphic novels are the direct descendants of the pulps, and as such may be considered an extension of Cthulhu Mythos literature and a major medium for Cthulhu Mythos art, combining the difficulties and advantages of both. Along with adaptations of prose Mythos stories and poetry, Mythos comics include original works that showcase tremendous imagination and some of the best Mythos writing and art in any medium, and may be considered a major element in the proliferation of the Cthulhu Mythos in popular culture.

Comics are sequential art, where both words and illustrations combine to form a part of the narrative. Whereas Lovecraftian fiction tends toward evocative prose to achieve its effect with the reader, in comics and graphic novels the bulk of the details are often provided by the artwork—and so by its nature comic books have become the major medium for Cthulhu Mythos artwork, some of which contain nudity and others of which are erotic or pornographic. Nudity and eroticism in Mythos comic art are generally in accordance with the usual standards of the creator and publisher at the time. This is a laborious way of saying that the comic books featuring the Mythos are in general no more prurient than comic books without the Mythos, or than prose Mythos fiction of the same period. For example, when Richard Corben chose to adapt Lovecraft's "The Lamp" (2008) from *Fungi from Yuggoth*, the female character was particularly curvaceous, with large breasts and prominent nipples—not because of any particularly notable prurient interest, but because that is how Corben draws women in general.

The writing in Mythos comics goes beyond the words on the page, but encompasses the plotting, characterization, pacing, and narrative style. Mythos comics can be generally broken down into adaptations of prose Mythos stories (mostly but not exclusively Lovecraft's fiction), original works using the Mythos, and a vast number of works merely making scattered mention of Mythos elements like Cthulhu or the *Necronomicon*, or which, as with prose Mythos fiction, contains Lovecraftian ideas and elements but no direct mention of, reference to, or use of the Mythos. Depictions of sex and gender are in keeping with contemporary non-Mythos stories, and in general have become more inclusive of female characters and female character roles beyond love interests over time—and indeed, the use of visual media means that even the "unseen mothers" of Lovecraftian fiction often receive some depiction. Lovecraftian sexual themes addressed in the previous chapter are present here, particularly in adaptations, sequels, etc.; but from the 1960s onward, as knowledge of the Cthulhu Mythos grew in popular culture, elements like cosmic miscegenation became more common.

Sexual depiction in American comics was long subject to severe self-censorship under the Comics Code Authority (1954-2011), which

4. Beyond Cthulhurotica 265

among other things restricted the depiction of and reference to traditional horror tropes, violence, gore, sex, drugs, homosexuality, and the occult. While there are several unofficial adaptations of and references to the Lovecraft Mythos in pre-Code horror comics such as *The Vault of Horror* (1950-55), *Weird Fantasy* (1950-53), *Weird Science* (1950-53), and *Weird Terror* (1952-54), these had little or no sexual content. For more than a decade after the Code was implemented, however, there were almost no Mythos comics at all.

Eventually from the underground press there emerged underground comix and comic magazines such as *Heavy Metal* (1977-present) that rejected the harsh restrictions of the CCA. While Lovecraftian names and comics appeared sporadically in DC and Marvel Comics up to this point, it was in these new media that novel Mythos comic stories with more sexually mature images and themes appeared for the first time.

One of the earliest storylines featuring new adult material for the Mythos was "The Shoggoths" by Al Hewetson and Zesar Lopez in *Nightmare* comic magazine from Skywald. The incomplete series borrows little from Lovecraft aside from a few names and concepts, but the art is highlighted by the first nude human figures, and features miscegenation as a central (if mostly unspoken) theme in the development of humanity and its antithesis, the violent, hairy, ape-like Shoggoths.

Jaxon (Jack Jackson) was the first of the underground cartoonists of the 1960s and co-founder of Last Gasp Press, with a penchant for horror comics in the pre-Code E.C. Comics vein. His first foray at Mythos comics was an adaptation of "The Rats in the Walls" in *Skull* 4 (1972). Jaxon's second Lovecraftian effort was "Tales of the Leather Nun's Grandmother" in *Tales from the Leather Nun* (1972), a satirical and scatological collection of explicit sex, humor, and depravity from creators Jaxon, David Sheridan, Robert Crumb, Spain, Pat Ryan, and Roger Brand.

"Tales" is the first pornographic comics work involving the Mythos, with a great deal of the humor coming from the satirical takedown of the normally dead-serious Cthulhu Mythos, including dread Cthulhu accidentally receiving a facial. Artistically and politically the story is almost of a piece with the special Lovecraftian issues of *Skull*, also from Last Gasp. Jaxon's depiction of Cthulhu in the story is even borrowed from Simon Deitch's illustration on the inside front cover of *Skull* 4, which is notable for having a handful of tentacles (complete with suckers) in place of genitalia. "Tales" reflects the rise of pornographic works in underground comix, a crude, trippy story in direct contrast to the bland stories and artwork that characterized mainstream comics under the Comics Code Authority.

Underground comix inspired the development of independent comics with broader artistic sensibilities and higher production values, a middle ground between comix and mainstream comics—and here too, the Mythos found a niche. Mike Vosburg's character Linda Lovecraft debuted in *Star*Reach* 3 (1975) in "High Priestess of Sexual Sorcery" as a voluptuous sorceress dwelling in the temple of Cthulhu, based in equal parts on Lovecraft and Linda Lovelace (Arndt 70). Unhappy with the plotting, Vosburg retired the character after a few episodes and moved on to drawing comics for major comic publishers; he worked in Hollywood doing the cover sequences for the *Tales from the Crypt* television show. Vosburg would not resurrect the concept for twenty years.

The light-hearted and slightly ribald Linda Lovecraft stories set up scenes with the female Lovecraft in dishabille, lingerie, or nude, but was never openly pornographic:

> Mixing adult film references and H. P. Lovecraft was new at the time. I don't think anybody had tried that before. For me, it was a pretty interesting approach to horror. Lots of [mostly] implied sex but none of the grossness that often marred the underground comix. (Arndt 71)

At their best, the femme Lovecraft comics are like a lighter, PG-13 version of Howard Chaykin's *Black Kiss* (1988), mixing a noirish style of art and writing with elements of supernatural horror; at its worst they're a bit camp with plentiful cheesecake. The nudity and sexual situations are never explicit or pornographic, but more daring than *Savage Sword of Conan* or the Warren horror magazines that were being published at the time. In many ways Linda Lovecraft is another side of the underground comix coin from "Tales of the Leather Nun's Grandmother"—still transgressive for its day, but with cleaner art (in terms of both line and explicitness) and higher standards of storytelling. While central to many tales, Linda was rarely the protagonist per se, and there was little character development.

In response to this successful challenge by underground comix and mainstream comics venturing into uncensored comic magazines, the Code was generally relaxed and Lovecraftian concepts such as tentacular horrors and cosmic miscegenation began to be disseminated into comics through comic book series like *Conan the Barbarian* (1970-93) and *Savage Sword of Conan* (1972-95).

By the 1990s Mythos concepts, references, and their related sexual themes had become pervasive in comics and popular culture, to the point that they were featured prominently even in the occasional adult comic such as *Dagger of Blood* (1997), *Ramba* (1992–94), *Girl Meets Tentacles* (2010), and especially the erotic graphic novel *The Convent of Hell* (1997). Written by Ricardo Barreiro and illustrated by Ignacio Noé, *The Convent of Hell* is a nunsploitation erotic graphic novel notable for featuring elements of the Cthulhu Mythos and lavishly painted hardcore sex scenes, both of which were highly unusual at the time of its creation. Originally run as a serial and printed in Spanish and German, it was later translated into English with a slight abridgement.[2]

The Convent of Hell displays an unusual blend of influences. The scene where the portal is opened and the phallus-headed tentacles come out to molest the nun is a very unusual example of explicit penetrative tentacle sex in Western comics, very likely an example of the influence of Japanese manga. Sexual exploitation of nuns is characteristic of pornography in many Catholic-dominated countries, especially in Europe and South America, as reflected in film, novels, etc. Another possible influence is the films of Italian filmmaker Lucio Fulci, whose films *City of the Living Dead* (1980), *The House by the Cemetery* (1981), and *The Beyond* (1983) form a loose trilogy based around the idea of supernatural doors of doom, and which contain references to the Cthulhu Mythos. Arguably, there is a thematic conflation between Shub-Niggurath ("The Black Goat"), satyr, and the popular Christian image of the Devil, but it is not clear if this is what Barreiro had in mind or a happy coincidence.

However, if *The Convent of Hell* mishmashes Christian and Cthulhu Mythos to blasphemous effect, it is at least in reasonably good company with other European comics of the same era. In *Ramba 6* (1992), the oversexed Italian hitwoman faces a witch who invokes "Chtulu" to summon "Azatoth," a hairy, bat-faced, massively phallused demon. Other examples, some of which are translations of American comics, may be seen in *The Cosmical Horror of H. P. Lovecraft: A Pictorial Anthology* (1991). However, Barreiro's use of the Mythos is not dependent on what he had seen in horror movies or read in other comics; the references to the history of the *Necronomicon* show he had also at least read Lovecraft; and if you were try-

---

2. A three-page section where a child-like cherub is subject to oral sex, then crucified and killed, was removed, probably out of concern for American child pornography laws.

ing to open an extradimensional portal in the Mythos, Yog-Sothoth would be the natural selection, so the choice of names for invocation is not inappropriate, just strange when combined with popular Christian imagery.

Throughout the 1990s and 2000s, adaptations of Lovecraft and Cthulhu Mythos stories increased in number and sophistication, and original Mythos-based comics began to emerge from independent publishers like Adventure Comics, Caliber Comics, Cross Plains Comics, Millenium Comics, and Mock Man Press—publishers not generally subject to the still-lingering Comics Code Authority and willing to add a few risqué elements.

Mike Vosburg, for example, resurrected his *Star*Reach* creation as Lorelei "Lori" Lovecraft with "My Favorite Redhead" (1997), which is a reworking in part of "Nymphonecromania" (1977, *Star*Reach* 10), the last Linda Lovecraft story. Drawing on Vosburg's experiences in Hollywood, Lori Lovecraft is a B-movie actress a little too old for the sex roles but with a talent for sorcery. She starred in a series of one-shot comics, later collected in a pair of trade paperbacks and re-released as digital comics. Lori Lovecraft is a rare example of a female protagonist who is not chaste, sexless, a slut, or a rape victim, but a woman aware of and comfortable with her sexuality; after twenty years the femme Lovecraft was no longer particularly edgy, but compared to Linda, Lori actually gets considerable character development over the course of her series. Both Lovecrafts are uncommon examples of a female character in the center of the Mythos, empowered by their sexuality, and are representative of a much rarer positive sexuality that gets scarce play in the Mythos in any media.

The Cthulhu Mythos has long been incorporated as part of the tabletop role-playing industry, most notoriously in TSR's *Deities and Demigods* (1980) and Chaosium's *Call of Cthulhu* (1981) role-playing game. The popularity of *Call of Cthulhu* would spur considerable interest in the Mythos, as well as Chaosium's much-lauded *Call of Cthulhu* fiction line of anthologies and collections of both original and long out-of-print Mythos fiction. Fans inspired by *Call of Cthulhu* set out to create their own original material for the game and contributed to the body of Mythos art and fiction. One such group of fans formed Pagan Publishing in 1990, which began by producing the fanzine *The Unspeakable Oath* and later branched into RPG supplements and the popular *Call of Cthulhu* setting *Delta Green* (1997).

One of the popular and preeminent illustrators for Pagan Publishing was Blair Reynolds, a provocative and transgressive artist who also did work for Traveller and Blue Planet before quitting the gaming industry and forming his own publishing venture, Room 308. In 1996 he released the first issue of *Black Sands*, the first in what was planned to be a three-issue graphic novel. Unfortunately, Reynolds fell ill, and the remaining two issues have not yet been produced. *Black Sands* remains, however, an impressive accomplishment: a sexually explicit Cthulhu Mythos graphic novel with a mature plot.

Black Sands stands out as a momentous might-have-been. The writing is sparse in style but with a very controlled pacing that works well against the gorgeous, varied, aggressively transgressive black-and-white artwork. Unabashedly erotic and sexually explicit, *Black Sands* is a story where the sexual content is inextricably bound into the Cthulhu Mythos and the horror of the story, completely devoid of any of the humor or romance that tends to lighten such works. It is a rare Mythos work that manages to combine the starkness of the Mythos with sexuality without compromising on either, combining the fall into sexual depravity with the indoctrination into the worship of Nyarlathotep, reminiscent of Arthur Machen's concept of sanctity and sin from "The White People." As an incomplete work from an obscure press, *Black Sands* has not been hugely influential, but remains a stand-out example of what can be accomplished by combining sex and the Mythos in comics. All is not yet done with *Black Sands*, however. In 2013 Brian Reynolds finally released a novel, *Black Sands: Catalogue of the Ten Thousand Churches*, the first part of which is a reworking of "Betrothal," the first part of the *Black Sands* graphic novel.

In the last decade or so, as Lovecraft and the Mythos have gained further traction and have proven their commercial appeal to comic-buying audiences, we have seen the emergence of an increasing number of high-quality Mythos adaptations and original works by prominent comic creators such as Alan Moore, Mike Mignola, Michael Alan Nelson, John Coulthart, Richard Corben, Chuck BB, Roy Thomas, and Steve Niles. Their primarily independent publishers include Avatar Press, BOOM! Studios, Carnal Comics, Creation Oneiros, Dark Horse Press, and Moonstone, who are generally more daring in their offerings than major publishers Marvel and DC Comics. Most notable was the emergence of Alan Moore's contributions: *The Courtyard* (2003), *Alan Moore's Yuggoth Cultures and Other Growths* (2003), and *Neonomicon* (2010–11), with a new series, *Providence*, announced.

Erotic comics featuring elements from or inspired in part by the Cthulhu Mythos have not abated since they were first depicted in underground comix, but they have begun to develop a wider audience. Male homosexuality is uncommon in comic books, even in pornographic comics where it is often restricted to specialty series, and is practically unknown in Cthulhu Mythos comics, with the main exceptions being John Blackburn's bisexual series *Coley* (1989) and *Dagger of Blood* (1997), which feature a pair of lusty antagonists descended from Lovecraft's entities, and Logan's *The Pornomicon* (2005). Logan Kowalski is a French writer/artist of male homosexual pornographic comics, and his distinct style features rough-looking, bulky, bearish characters with exaggerated musculature and sexual characteristics. *The Pornomicon*, a one-shot comic, was initially released in French and German, and in 2006 was translated into English by Patrick Fillion and Fraz; Logan has also released "Pornomicon Legacy," a series of illustrations in the same vein. In the small field of homoerotic comics, *The Pornomicon* is the most prominent and notable to use the Cthulhu Mythos.

The Pornomicon is most exceptional in its use of homoerotic penetrative tentacle sex in the context of the Mythos—not unique, as there are other examples of tentacles penetrating orifices in Mythos prose literature, and certainly many manga that feature homoerotic tentacle sex, but the combination is unusual in Western comics and the most prominent sexual theme of the issue. It is debatable how much *The Pornomicon* may have been influenced from *The Convent of Hell*, as both feature distinct phallus-headed tentacles and begin in a religious institution whose chaste exterior conceals lusty behaviors, but the same argument could as easily apply to many Japanese manga, so must remain an open question.

It is evident that a considerable part of the desire to use the Cthulhu Mythos in *The Pornomicon* was the common association the Mythos has with tentacles, but beyond this Logan has gone to some pains to suggest an occult mythology and cosmology lurking behind the body horror aspects and homoerotic sex. The eponymous *Pornomicon* carries all the general attributes and serves the purpose of a copy of the *Necronomicon* in these pages, and is part and parcel of that cosmology. As with *Black Sands*, the esoteric knowledge of the Mythos becomes equated with carnal knowledge, but of an infinitely more extreme and taboo manner than what the characters are familiar with. This in turn provides excuse and explanation for the more extreme examples of Logan's artwork, taking the already unrealistically large and elastic genitalia and exploding them to positively cartoonish size under the influence of "Yog-Sototh" and Cthulhu.

Sex and the Mythos in Japanese Manga and Anime

Japanese manga and anime have had a particular impact on Western associations of sex and the Cthulhu Mythos. I have already discussed in a previous chapter how Japanese artists helped begin the tradition of tentacles in Western weird fiction, and that later Japanese manga introduced and popularized penetrative tentacle sex to avoid local censorship guidelines. In part this was possible because of the long period of self-censorship in English-language comics, which likewise had an influence on English-language animated films—it is no surprise that the rise of non-Code adult-oriented material in underground comix and comic magazines led to the production of ambitious, adult-oriented animation such as the works of Ralph Bakshi and *Heavy Metal* (1981). Japanese comics and animated works were censored by the state, but with fewer restrictions that led to the development of a number of sophisticated, adult-oriented works. When such manga were finally translated into English, they found a ready audience in the United States.

Lovecraft and other Mythos authors had been sporadically translated into Japanese since the 1940s; even Brian McNaughton's adult Mythos novel *Tide of Desire* (1981) was translated by the Nihon Male Order company, but the Mythos itself first reached mass popular attention with the introduction of the *Call of Cthulhu* role-playing game in 1986, which spurred the creation of licensed products, manga, and fiction. These Mythos-influenced products in turn were translated and shipped back to the Americas and Europe, finding a market both among general consumers intrigued with their style, art, and writing, and by those seeking pornographic materials—such as the titles Fantagraphics Books publishes under the Eros Comix imprint. The tropes of Japanese manga and anime became well-known in parts of Western popular culture, and the adult manga and anime series in particular helped shape the popular image and conflation between sex, the Cthulhu Mythos, and tentacle erotica. For example, *Girl Meets Tentacles* (2010) is in large part a Western parody of popular tropes from Japanese tentacle-eroticism hentai ("hentai" may be loosely translated as "pornographic work"), but also includes references to the Cthulhu Mythos by including the *Necronomicon* and other Mythos names. Readers should not take the mention of pornographic materials as exemplifying

Japanese Mythos works, any more than any of the American pornographic books, comics, and films covered here are typical of American Cthulhu Mythos media. Imports and translations from Japan tend to focus on some of the more pornographic and exceptional works.

Aside from their association with tentacle sex, manga and anime contain uncountable examples of references to and uses of the Cthulhu Mythos, and many of these stories contain romantic or sexual elements—far too many to list here, much less attempt to cover. In large part the sexual material in Japanese anime, manga, and derivative productions (video games, live-action films, etc.) is included or discluded primarily based on the intended audience. In the 2003 adult-oriented video game *Demonbane*, for example, the *Al Azif* is personified as a young woman who chooses detective Kuro Daijuji to protect her from cultists, and they later engage in a sexual relationship; the sex was excised in the 2004 anime adaptation *Kishini Hôkô Demonbane*, which was intended for a more general audience.

A notable example of a multimedia franchise in this regard is the Japanese series *Haiyore! Nyaruko-san*,[3] which began as a series of light novels by writer Aisora Manta and artist Koin, and has since expanded into a series of anime and manga adaptations. The basic premise of the series is that Mythos entities such as Nyarlathotep, Cthugha, and Hastur are in fact extraterrestrials, manifesting themselves on earth in the form of cute young girls (*moekko*). This is somewhat in contrast to a related genre of "monster girls," where monsters, demons, etc. are depicted in the form and sometimes with the personalities of prepubescent to adolescent girls. A Mythos-esque example of the latter is *Atlach-Nacha* (1997), an *eroge* visual novel (erotic interactive fiction computer game); the spider-like main character is a young woman loosely based on Clark Ashton Smith's creature of the same name.

Nyaruko from the planet Nyarlathotep arrives on earth to protect a human high school student named Yasaka Mahiro from another alien who wants to kidnap him for nefarious purposes. Nyaruko is attracted to Mahiro and wishes to pursue him, so she moves in with Mahiro and his mother and begins attending his high school. Meanwhile, Nyaruko's pres-

---

3. Japanese is a phonetic language, which means that translations of exotic or "unpronounceable" Mythos names are inadvertently given a very literal pronunciation. "Nyaruko" is a derivative of Nyarlathotep, which in this series is a planet occupied by a race known as the Nyarlathotepans.

ence has attracted her friends—Kūko (Cthugha), a fiery lesbian in love with Nyaruko; and Hasuta (Hastur), a male alien who is also attracted to Mahiro. These aliens move into Mahiro's house and squabble, compete for Mahiro/Nyaruko's affections, and protect the planet from the schemes of the other Outer Gods.

In general form, the anime series (neither the original light novels nor manga have yet been translated into English, but the anime is available with English subtitles) is that of a typical "love polygon" where a group of characters are entangled in overlapping romantic interests, set against the contrast of the invasive aliens and their various plots and Mahiro's ordinary life; many of the jokes are based on the Cthulhu Mythos, in particular the Japanese version of the *Call of Cthulhu* role-playing game. While the dialogue is sometimes suggestive and does contain openly homosexual characters, as a whole the series is not sexually explicit and the sexual references are generally only used as mildly risqué jokes: for example, in some of the short flash episodes notorious pervert Atlach-Nacha speaks openly about certain sexual acts in a way that causes the other characters to blush, but exactly what she said is bleeped out, so that the viewers only know through context that it was something naughty.

Sex and the Mythos Cinema

> All we need now is a series of Lovecraftian porn videos with titles like *Pickman's Nude Model, Wet Dreams in the Witch House, The Call Girls of Cthulhu,* or *Debbie Does Dunwich.* (Gonce and Harms 236-37)

For over five decades, film and television has captured and expanded upon the titillation, perversity, and romance of the Cthulhu Mythos, producing some of the most influential visuals and cinematic moments in all Mythos-based media, spawning sequels and inspiring works in art, comics, games, and literature. It is because of the influence of these films in shaping the popular image and conceptions of sex and the Mythos that Cthulhu Mythos cinema needs to be examined—and likewise, the Mythos has had a sizable impact on the cinematic scene beyond the sheer number of films and television programs based on the Mythos. Series such as *Necronomicon: The Journal of Horror and Erotic Cinema* (1996–2007), edited by Andy Black, a continuation of his *Necronomicon* (1993-95) film magazine, are the most apparent examples of this trend, which, as with

Cthulhu Sex magazine, uses a Mythos term as a byword for ultimate transgression or dark knowledge—in this case transgressive cinema. Film provides a unique medium to illustrate some of the unique visuals and sexual themes noted in the Mythos, but the reputation of the source material has often made the realization on film disappointing to many fans and critics.

There are several reasons why sex and the Cthulhu Mythos go together on film. The first is simply the capitalization on sexual themes in the Lovecraft Mythos; cosmic miscegenation between human and Mythos entities, for example, is most prominent and forms a key part of the plot and action of films like *The Dunwich Horror* (1970), *The Unnameable* (1988), *The Unnameable II: The Statement of Randolph Carter* (1993), *H. P. Lovecraft's Necronomicon* (1993), *Dagon* (2001), and *Cthulhu* (2007), among many others. Secondly, as Robert E. Howard and E. Hoffmann Price discovered with the Spicy publications, sex sells and can improve the commercial viability of the end product; and may be an end unto itself in a Mythos film. Thus the gratuitous female nudity in films like *The Dunwich Horror* (1970) and *Beyond the Dunwich Horror* (2008). Finally, the freedom to combine sex and the Mythos allows the creators to experiment with tropes and produce new and original works, such as the infamous head-giving-head scene in *Re-Animator* (1985) and the use of a homosexual protagonist in *Cthulhu* (2007). All three influences can be seen at work almost from the earliest Mythos movies.

The first films in the Cthulhu oeuvre were adaptations (however loose) of the Lovecraft Mythos, beginning with *The Haunted Palace* (1963), an adaptation of *The Case of Charles Dexter Ward*, and *Die, Monster, Die!* (1965), an adaptation of "The Colour out of Space." Given the period and the intended audience, these films did not feature nudity or sexual material directly, though they addressed Lovecraftian themes of cosmic miscegenation. Uncredited adaptations were also present fairly early on, particularly in foreign markets, such as *La Marca del Muerto* (1960) and *Curse of the Crimson Altar* (1968), which are loosely based on *The Case of Charles Dexter Ward* and "The Dreams in the Witch House," respectively. However, these kinds of films did have their impact on wider media. *Curse of the Crimson Altar*, for example, with its bizarre dream sequences involving semi-nude women, was made into an Italian photonovel in the *Racconti dell'Aldilà 2* (1975).

The first film adaptation of a Lovecraft story to go by the same name as the story, *The Dunwich Horror* is a collaboration between Lovecraftian filmmakers Daniel Haller (*Die, Monster, Die!*) and Roger Corman (*The Haunted Palace*), and remains one of the defining early entries in Cthulhu cinema. Following the same approach as Corman's series of Edgar Allan Poe adaptations, *The Dunwich Horror* expands on the original story, much to the chagrin of Lovecraftian purists: "Haller and Corman thus explicitly exhume the buried sexuality in Lovecraft's story. Corman's influence probably started the trend of sexualizing film treatments of Lovecraft's tales" (Gonce and Harms 236).

The Dunwich Horror is seminal in Mythos films for the creators' overt emphasis on the sexual elements of Lovecraft's story, most notably the element of cosmic miscegenation in the Whateley twins' conception, though in general the canned press for the film such as the posters and *The Dunwich Horror Press Book* (1970) heavily overhypes the lurid attributes of the film. Of their original additions, the most notable divergence from the story is the "romance" between Wilbur and Nancy—a very one-sided affair, given that Wilbur relies on hypnosis and drugged tea as much as his natural charm, rendering Sandra Dee's character little more than a limpid-eyed prop for the bulk of the film; her infamous but brief "nude" scene consists of a bared nipple provided by a body double.

An obvious artistic and commercial influence for this relationship was the film *Rosemary's Baby* (1968), which similarly featured a cult seeking to impregnate a young woman; but here the story is a generational one, with Sandra Dee's character literally taking the place of Lavinia, legs spread on a cross-shaped altar (movie photos show a scene not included in the final film, where the pregnant Lavinia is laid out on the X-shaped altar stone). Another scene of particular note is when Wilbur's unnamed, betentacled twin strips and (presumably) rapes or kills Elizabeth. This is perhaps the earliest suggestion of tentacle eroticism in Cthulhu cinema, though certainly not the last.

The sexual content in Cthulhu cinema peaked relatively early. The intimations of cosmic miscegenation in *The Haunted Palace* were made the centerpiece of *The Dunwich Horror*, complete with brief nudity, and this shortly gave way to the explicit hardcore sex acts in *Teenage Twins* (1976). The first pornographic film to feature any reference to the Mythos, *Teenage Twins* was the work of adult film director Carter Stevens and writer "Al Hazard"—the pseudonym for writer and pulp fan Richard Jaccoma, who is also remembered for his adult Sax Rohmer parody/pastiche novel *Yellow Peril: The Adventures of Sir John Weymouth-Smythe* (1978). Between several sex scenes, the plot develops: Gerald has obtained the *Necronomicon*, which he describes as the book of magic whose spells really work, translated into Sanskrit some 400 years ago by Abdul al-Hazred, bound in human flesh, and which Gerald believes is fueling some of their perverse desires.

The novelty of *Teenage Twins* is that Lovecraft and the Mythos were in a pornographic film, and not as parody but as a straightforward element of the plot. The source material for the description of the *Necronomicon* appears to come mainly from the works in Wilbur Whateley's library in "The Dunwich Horror," although the translations from the *Necronomicon* also include the invocation "ka nama kaa lajerama" from Robert E. Howard's "The Shadow Kingdom" (1929).

The spell of eternal life/potency is original to the film and, combined with the pentagram and "virgin sacrifice," seem in line with typical late-1960s images of black magic. Slightly more intriguing is the passing idea that the *Necronomicon* itself may have a corrupting influence just by its presence, an idea not really revisited until later in the Mythos oeuvre. However, for the most part this film seems to be an historical curiosity more than anything else, with no apparent impact on later works.

A substantial part of commercial Cthulhu cinema from the mid-1980s through the early 2000s can be traced back to the influence and individuals associated with *H. P. Lovecraft's Re-Animator* (1985). Gory, transgressive, and filled with black humor, director Stuart Gordon, producer Brian Yuzna, actor Jeffrey Combs, and screenwriter Dennis Paoli would go on to be a part of Mythos films including *From Beyond* (1986), *Bride of Re-Animator* (1990), *Necronomicon* (1993), *The Lurking Fear* (1994), *Castle Freak* (1995), *Dagon* (2001), *Beyond Re-Animator* (2003), *H. P. Lovecraft's Dreams in the Witch House* (2005), and *The Evil Clergyman* (2012), and so leave an indelible mark on sex and Cthulhu cinema.

H. P. Lovecraft's Re-Animator is an expansion and adaptation of "Herbert West—Reanimator" (1921–22), with the part of the unnamed narrator taken up by Dan Cain (Bruce Abbott), with West (Jeffrey Combs) a medical student transferred to Miskatonic University who leases Dan's basement. The female love interest is Cain's fiancée Megan Halsey (Barbara Crampton), the daughter of the dean. An exercise in transgression often recalled for its outstanding acting and physical effects, *Re-Animator* is, in terms of raw sexual material, most remarkable for the "head giving head" scene, where a disembodied head moves to perform cunnilingus. As the novelization put it:

Poised above Megan's crotch, the head looked up at her and smiled. "Yes . . . my love! *Yes!*"

With a twisted smile, he watched her quiver helplessly beneath him, then opened his mouth wide and disappeared between her legs. (Rovin 182)

Its importance to sexuality in Cthulhu cinema lies less in that scene, however, or in the amount of nudity it contains than in the impact it has had on both film and other media, which is far beyond that of any other film adaptation of Lovecraft. The *Re-Animator* franchise has included a novelization, additional films, comic books, short films, and a Broadway musical among other things, but the imagery of the film has had an influence far beyond these immediate productions. The really substantial influence of *Re-Animator* lies in how completely it has become the image of Lovecraft's story and character, particularly the image of the glowing green reagent, which has appeared essentially unaltered in such media as Edward Lee's *The Innswich Horror* (2010) and the pornographic film parody *Re-Penetrator* (2006). A similar softcore effort, *Actiongirls: Soldiers of the Dead 1* (2007), uses the green reanimating fluid but without any Mythos or Lovecraftian context.

Re-Animator is not a straight adaptation of Lovecraft's serial, and as the series progressed it continued to move beyond Lovecraft's material. *Bride of Re-Animator* (1990) essentially incorporates the remaining material from Lovecraft's serial and, recognizing the roots of Lovecraft's story in *Frankenstein*, is likewise a gore-filled revisitation of *Bride of Frankenstein* (1935), resulting in a weird love triangle as a disturbed Dan Cain is forced to choose between his living girlfriend and the piecemeal bride he and West have stitched together and reanimated.

The franchise moved beyond adaptation of Lovecraft's material and pastiche with *Beyond Re-Animator* (2003), which features less nudity than previous installments but focuses more on the sexual psychology and demeanor of the characters, particularly the latent incestual feelings of Phillips for his dead sister (Migliore and Strysik 315-16) and the dominating behavior of Phillips's love interest Laura (Elsa Pataky) under the influence of the warden. Visually the film continues to transgress, ending with a hilarious shadow-play of a rat fighting a severed, reanimated penis over the credits. Director Brian Yuzna elaborated on the origin of this scene:

[. . .] the owner of the company said, "Hey, you can reanimate a penis!" I locked onto that. "No, no, no—the boss said he wants a reanimated penis."

And I felt like we needed, once again, an outrageous sexual gag, like the head giving head. Dennis Paoli told me in these movies the danger to a woman is rape and the danger to a man is castration. Everything is on that level. (Migliore and Strysik 317)

The sophomore effort from the makers of *Re-Animator* was *From Beyond* (1986), which came armed with a bigger budget and a less satiric bent, but also much less raw material for a script. Lovecraft's "From Beyond" (1920) is only seven pages long, and the plot of the story is essentially exhausted in the pre-title sequence of the film. The film proper then is not an adaptation, but an expansion of the material playing on the same themes and characters; as *Lurker in the Lobby* puts it: "albeit with heavy emphasis on some very un-Lovecraftian multidimensional lust" (Migliore and Strysik 60).

From Beyond is more lurid than *Re-Animator* in terms of storyline and setting, even though it has far less nudity, because of the strong emphasis on sensuality, the inclusion of BDSM elements, and the symbolic imagery peppered throughout the movie. As Stuart Gordon put it in the director's commentary to the DVD: "How many phallic images could we put in this movie?" Rather than an exercise in exploitation, however, *From Beyond* remains a smart movie, with the emphasis on sexual sensuality in the film a logical progression from the increased sensual acuity in the original story. After *Re-Animator*, *From Beyond* is arguably the most influential of the Lovecraftian films in terms of influence and imagery; it may have inspired Cody Goodfellow's "Infernal Attractors" in *Cthulhurotica*. As an example of the pop culture sensibilities of Lovecraftian cinema at the time, Barbara Crampton did a photospread for *Playboy*'s December 1986 issue which contained several references to *From Beyond*. One photo had her re-don her lab coat and glasses to pose next to a resonator-style prop, while another had her back in the leatherwear (sans stockings) that she wore in Pretorius's sex dungeon.

The late 1980s and 1990s saw a spate of Mythos cinema, both adaptations such as *The Unnameable* (1988), *The Unnameable II: The Statement of Randolph Carter* (1993), and *H. P. Lovecraft's Necronomicon* (1993) as well as original works based on or incorporating elements of the Mythos such as *Evil Dead II* (1987), its sequel, *Army of Darkness* (1992), and made-for-cable films like *Cast a Deadly Spell* (1991). In most of these the sexual elements are unremarkable; there are simply too many films with female characters, love interest subplots, female frontal nudity, or simulated sex to cover them all. As the cost to shoot and distribute films decreased in the 2000s the number

4. Beyond Cthulhurotica 279

of Mythos films increased, as noted in the Films by Year index of *Lurker in the Lobby: A Guide to the Cinema of H. P. Lovecraft* (2006). Pornographic Mythos cinema returned in 2001[4] with *Mystery of the Necronomicon*.

As with Japanese Mythos prose and manga, relatively few of these films and anime are translated and made available for the English-speaking market (or mentioned in English-language reference works), but, as with English-language Cthulhu cinema, they appear to run the full gamut from the eldritch romance *Innsmouth wo Ōu Kage* (1992) to the hardcore erotic horror of *ExorSister* (1994). In this context, then, *Mystery of the Necronomicon* is significant both as an example of Japanese Mythos cinema that has been translated and made available to English audiences and as an unusual format: a four-episode hentai anime.

Mystery of the Necronomicon combines aspects of film noir, horror, and pornography, all tied together by a plot that conjoins two of Lovecraft's creations: Herbert West and the *Necronomicon*. The sex in this film is pure titillation; women throw themselves at Satoshi with fervor and frequency beyond belief, and some form of sex or nudity punctuates every chapter. Some unusual cultural and gender conventions in this film are apparent. For example, the penis is rarely depicted, and never in penetration, even though a scene involving a pair of lesbians using a double-ended dildo is apparently acceptable. Sexual violence against women is in general particularly prominent in this film, with several depictions of rape or forced sex, and one particularly gruesomely ironic scene where the women who had earlier used a double dildo are found murdered by being spitted together along a metal pipe.

In this respect, *Mystery of the Necronomicon* is no different from any other Mythos film that contains a bit of gratuitous sexual content, except in format (anime) and in the frequency, variety, and explicitness of the sexual material depicted, which in this case borders on that found in hardcore pornography. It is because of this explicit content as much as its status as an animated work that *Mystery* is an outlier in Cthulhu cinema, effectively bridging the gap between Mythos films with a bit of sex and outright Mythos porn. For example, unlike strictly pornographic works, *Mystery* has not been ignored in reference works and has a brief write-up in *Lurker in the*

---

4. More or less. 2000 saw the release of Max Hardcore's *Harder Than Hard*, which was scored to an album by heavy metal band 8MM Overdose; the final track and video is entitled "Necronomicon."

Lobby, whereas *Teenage Twins* does not. However, also unlike most Mythos works, *Mystery* more directly addresses (and depicts) topics such as lesbianism and rape, which are usually only alluded to in other Mythos films.

The first pornographic film parody of Lovecraft's work, or more accurately of the *Re-Animator* film adaptation, was *Re-Penetrator*. Pornographic parody is a long-established tradition in art and literature, and after twenty years *Re-Animator* (1985) was the subject of the first Mythos porn spoof. Released as a standalone DVD, an abbreviated version of the short film containing mostly the dialogue and plot scenes from *Re-Penetrator* was included as the penultimate chapter in *LovecraCked! The Movie* (2006), a low-budget horror-comedy film anthology based on Lovecraft and the Mythos.

While more than a little schlocky in conception and execution, with deliberately cheesy dialogue and props, *Re-Penetrator* did manage to capture at least some small echo of the transgressiveness of the original film, and the blood-spattered Joanna Angel won a 2006 AVN award for "Most Outrageous Sex Scene" in the film. Beyond being a pornographic parody, *Re-Penetrator* continues the *Re-Animator* tradition of pushing Lovecraft-derived material in new and bold directions (the "Bloody Sanchez" is a horror beyond even Gordon and Yuzna). The film was successful enough to spawn a series of pornographic spoofs of horror films, including Evil Head (2012), a parody of the Evil Dead film series including the Necronomicon ex Mortis.

One of the strangest films in the pornographic substream of Cthulhu cinema is *Beyond Tickling* (2007) by The Laughing Gas Zone, a black-and-white tickle-fetish short film based loosely on "From Beyond." The main novelty of *Beyond Tickling* is its focus on a paraphilia, and not one commonly associated with erotic Mythos works such as teratophilia or maiesiophilia. As neither an adaptation nor a parody, *Beyond Tickling* is also illustrative of the minimal characteristic elements that filmmakers felt necessary to invoke the Mythos in the audience: the entities from beyond, and the revelation that ends with madness. The importance of these elements is such that they are included even though they are not featured in Lovecraft's original story, but represent a common understanding of the Mythos by a general audience.

While many Mythos films include some element of sex or reference to the sexual themes in Lovecraft's work, few really approach the limits of what Lovecraft addressed, much less go beyond them. One of the most notable and controversial recent Mythos films in this regard is *Cthulhu* (2007):

"Innsmouth", though, more than anything reminded me of the experience of gay and lesbian friends, who after leaving home under duress in their teens, had to go back in their 30s when a parent was sick or a sibling needed help. Lovecraft said "Innsmouth" was about the horror of heredity. I think that particular horror is, if I'm not going out on too far a limb here, a part of some of the issues in certain areas of a very wide spectrum of what we might narrowly call the homosexual experience. ("Cogswell, Grant (Cthulhu)")

Cthulhu takes as its essence the plot of "The Shadow over Innsmouth" (with some additional borrowing from "The Call of Cthulhu" and others), but with the major twist of making the protagonist a homosexual, which throws a shade on his relationships with various family and friends. The homosexual interpretation of some of Lovecraft's fiction, including "The Shadow over Innsmouth," is nothing new to Lovecraft studies but remained outside the purview of Cthulhu cinema until this film.

Cthulhu is an ambitious film with a lot of firsts for Cthulhu cinema: the first homosexual protagonist, and the first film to make a character's sexuality an important aspect of the narrative and the driving action behind the film, and certainly the first to include scenes of female-on-male rape and homosexual sex (neither explicit). The driving question of the story is essentially "What if a Deep One hybrid was homosexual?" and the film attempts to answer that question, which is perhaps part of where it gets stuck. Lovecraft's "The Shadow over Innsmouth" is a tale of uncovering a hidden heritage and the inevitability of biology. In the film, Russell Marsh arrives in town with no desire to reconcile with or look any deeper into his family, and finds himself embroiled in a mystery he wasn't looking for in a town he just wants to escape. In the end, the two narratives never quite reconcile; Russell finds a closet full of family skeletons, but never really discovers any greater truth about himself, which is part of the essential ending to "The Shadow over Innsmouth" that gives the story its power.

Even if the narrative runs into a bit of a paradox in that respect, as a film *Cthulhu* actually handles the subject of homosexuality rather well. The relationship between Russell Marsh and his boyfriend Mike (Scott Green) is handled with great style and some terrific dialogue, such as when Mike explains what they did as teenagers: "It was never a gay thing for me. It was just an extension of our friendship." The emphasis on reproduction, which becomes stronger as the film proceeds, echoes Lovecraft's emphasis on heredity in a very different way—not what biological horror a character might be on the receiving end of, but to what extent others will go to ensure that the line is carried on, where the pressure to produce an heir outweighs individual interests. The rape scene then is unusual but extremely Lovecraftian in that its sole purpose was for conception, rather than pleasure, but with the typical gender roles reversed.

Cthulhu is a significant film that contains the essence of weird sexuality while presenting it in a very different and (for Mythos films) novel way. In its own way, it is also a sexually restrained film, not designed to shock the straights with homosexual displays or to act as softcore homoerotica, and without the camp that often protrudes into sex in Mythos films. Even in terms of Mythos literature, *Cthulhu* is a bit of a hallmark for addressing homosexuality and the Mythos head-on, a subject that is usually ignored or left unstated, and for that at least the film deserves to be remembered.

The full range of Mythos-influenced cinema is considerably larger than the few films mentioned here. While the majority of Mythos films discussed above are adaptations of the Lovecraft Mythos or derived from his work, other non-Lovecraft Cthulhu Mythos stories have also been adapted, such as *The Shuttered Room* (1967), based on Derleth's posthumous Lovecraft collaboration of the same name; the *Night Gallery* episode *Return of the Sorcerer* (1972) and the *Theatre Bizarre* segment *Mother of Toads* (2011), which were both based on the works of the same name by Clark Ashton Smith; and *Lifeforce* (1985), based on Colin Wilson's *The Space Vampires* (1976). Among the liberties often taken by adaptations is the introduction of female characters, typically as love interests such as Barbara Crampton in *Re-Animator* (1985). Most of the sexual content in adaptations is generally constrained to female nudity and/or a few simulated sex scenes.

Other films are original works that, while based on or incorporating some material from the Mythos, are not outright adaptations, such as *The Last Lovecraft: Relic of Cthulhu* (2009), which is a cinematic outgrowth of the small body of Lovecraftian literature that assumes a) the Mythos is real, and b) Lovecraft sired children. Many of these films make nominal reference to the Mythos even if they do not otherwise use its themes or imagery. For example, director Jess Franco's X-rated *Succubus* (1967) was originally titled *Necronomicon–Geträumte Sünden* ("Dreamt Sins"), which is the sole explicit reference to the Lovecraft Mythos in the film. As Gonce put it:

> The name "*Necronomicon*" is only used to lend an atmosphere of the macabre and the forbidden to the film's pornographic surrealism. Though it is unrelat-

ed to Lovecraft's work, Franco's film still makes use of Lovecraft's fictional book in its title and, by so doing, typifies the attempts of filmmakers to eroticize the literary ideas of a man who had no use for overt eroticism. (Gonce and Harms 232)

Similar efforts include Japanese director Takao Nakano's hardcore erotic horror *ExorSister* film series (1994), where the *Necronomicon* is used to summon demons that molest their victims and the heroine with their tentacles in a live-action version of Japanese tentacle erotica anime and manga. Unconstrained by adherence to the Mythos source material, Mythos-derived films run the gamut in terms of sexual content, from nil to explicit.

An often-neglected aspect of Mythos cinema are documentaries examining Lovecraft's life and the Mythos, including *The Eldritch Influence: The Life, Vision, and Phenomenon of H. P. Lovecraft* (2004), *The Strange Case of Howard Phillips Lovecraft* (2007), and *Lovecraft: Fear of the Unknown* (2009). Some of the interviews and material in these documentaries touch on sex in Lovecraft's life and stories, but no depictions of sex are included in these films and so they are of only minor note.

Lovecraftian films are a much more ambiguous category: films that have no direct reference to elements of the Cthulhu Mythos but which are true to the spirit and style of the Mythos. Some common examples include *Caltiki, the Immortal Monster* (1959) and *Alien* (1979). Given the rather subjective nature of categorizing a film as "Lovecraftian," which could include anything up to and including Japanese Original Video Animation (OVA) adaptations of tentacle erotica manga, there is little that can definitively be said about such films in reference to sex and the Mythos except that such designations tend to reflect an individual's understanding of the Mythos and its sexual themes.

In terms of gender balance, Cthulhu cinema has primarily male protagonists and supporting casts, but often sees the inclusion of a female love interest as well, and women tend to be some of the more notable supporting characters, such as Carolyn Purdy-Gordon's brief roles in *Re-Animator* and *From Beyond*, and Macarena Gómez as Uxia in *Dagon*. A few films have female protagonists; the most notable being Dr. Katherine McMichaels (Barbara Crampton) in *From Beyond*, and Emily Ostermen (Bess Meyer) in "The Cold" and Sarah (Signey Coleman) in "Whispers" segments of the *H. P. Lovecraft's Necronomicon*. Cthulhu cinema also lays claim to a few strong female villains, such as in the title character of *Un-*

nameable, Keziah Mason (Susanna Uchatius) from *H. P. Lovecraft's The Dreams in the Witch-House* (2005), and the Mother of Toads (Catriona MacColl) from *The Theatre Bizarre*.

Cthulhu cinema only rarely includes examples of homosexuality or bisexuality, and the latter are mostly confined to certain scenes from the pornographic *Teenage Twins*. Two notable examples of Mythos films that use homosexuality are *Cast a Deadly Spell*, a cross-genre hardboiled horror film whose cast includes a homosexual thief and his cross-dressing lover; and *Cthulhu*, whose male protagonist is gay, which becomes a significant plot point in the film. Some explicitly pornographic Mythos films contain lesbian characters and scenes of lesbian sex, most notably *Teenage Twins* (1976) and *Mystery of the Necronomicon* (2001), but male homosexual encounters so far seem absent from Mythos-influenced pornographic cinema.

The Mythos and Rule 34

> If it exists, there is porn of it—no exceptions.
> —Rule 34 of the Internet

Electronic publishing is one of the most significant frontiers for the production and distribution of Cthulhu Mythos materials, from the free publication of out-of-copyright works through Project Gutenberg to original Mythos ebooks being sold through Amazon.com. Thousands of fans and professionals have published their free and commercial work through the Internet and will continue to do so. More than this, the Internet hosts major reference works and discussions that deal with nearly every aspect of the Cthulhu Mythos, serving as a medium for Mythos readers to analyze, criticize, and better understand the Mythos, its authors, and the tradition of weird fiction.

A considerable amount of the Mythos material online deals with sex, from scrutinizing academic blogposts to Mythos-themed pornography and everything in between. While rarely published in traditional journals or books, online Mythos discussion, fanfiction, and art is influential in shaping readers' knowledge and interpretation of sex and the Mythos. The popular conflation of the Mythos with tentacle erotica, for example, is probably largely due to the proliferation of such materials online. This is a brief look at some of the forms sex and the Cthulhu Mythos takes online, and their impact and influence on other Mythos media.

Discussion

> WHAT IS THIS GROUP FOR? The description of, and discussion about sex, love, and lust with beings of the Cthulhu Mythos, and other dimensional over-achievers. ("alt.sex.cthulhu FAQ")

One of the earliest online discussions of sex and the Mythos was through alt.sex.cthulhu and related newsgroups on Usenet.[5] Here, users would come together to swap fanfiction, ask questions, and generally debate and joke about all manner of things related to sex and and the Cthulhu Mythos. The tone was generally light and explicit, as evidenced by posts such as Steven Harris's "The Complete Guide to Shoggoth Sex," taking humor not just from discussing sex openly, but in combining it with the Mythos. Other early sites include the web presence of Cthulhu Sex Magazine through cthulhusex.com and myspace.com/cthulhu_sex.

Contemporary discussions of sex and the Cthulhu Mythos are focused mainly on categorization sites like tvtropes.org and wikipedia.org with pages like "Did You Just Romance Cthulhu?" and "Tentacle erotica." The tropers on tvtropes.org recognize the appearance of cosmic miscegenation in the Mythos (pages like "Interspecies Romance" and "Half-Human Hybrid") as well as various related tropes (such as "All Anime is Naughty Tentacles"). While very informal and never complete or exhaustive, these sites provide important public forums for readers to recognize and discuss love and sex in the Mythos.

Fanfiction

Fan-created fiction using the Cthulhu Mythos is prolific online, an electronic outgrowth of the same urge that drives the creation of fanzines and similar "nonprofessional" publications. Given that this fiction is often created by amateurs, fanfiction is often derided for its relative lack of quality, but it is also an honest expression of the desires and understanding of the Mythos by its fandom. With the booming popularity of the Cthulhu Mythos in popular culture, many Lovecraftian names and concepts have entered the general cultural lexicon, so that a vast amount

---

5. A partial cache of the early Usenet material is available at the alt.sex.cthulhu archive (http://www.cthulhu.org/smut/), a fuller archive is available on Google Groups (https://groups.google.com/forum/#!forum/alt.sex.cthulhu), though for several years the group has been abandoned and unmoderated, and so filled up with spam.

of fiction published online may contain references to the Mythos in nearly any context. As with the Cthulhu Mythos fiction itself, a good deal of fanfiction may be cooperative, represented in a shared universe or round-robin stories. A good example of this cooperative fiction involving the Mythos is the Whateley Academy cycle of fanfiction stories.

By contrast, Cthulhu Mythos erotic fanfiction is typically a solo effort. Mythos fan-erotica has been published online since at least the early days of alt.sex.cthulhu, and continues to be published on popular adult fanfiction sites like AdultFanFiction.net and the *Alt.Sex.Stories Text Repository* (asstr.org). While it is impossible to give a full survey of adult-oriented Mythos fanfiction, a few general statements can be made with confidence: Mythos erotic fanfic tends to be sexually explicit, follows popular tropes of the Mythos (such as cultists, virgin sacrifices, tentacle sex, etc.) rather than staying true to the "canon" of key published Mythos stories, and often features specific sexual paraphilia such as body horror, impregnation and pregnancy, size-fetish, etc. In this, there is generally little difference between Mythos fan-erotica and the commercial ebook erotica that has recently gained some prominence.

Fanart

Alongside online fanfiction, fans of the Mythos had uploaded a vast array of pictorial and video art. Again, quality varies considerably, from crude cartoons to elaborate paintings and 3D renderings as impressive as anything published professionally. Mythos fanart covers a tremendous range of styles and schools and, as with more traditionally published Mythos art, follows many of the same tropes, such as a general inclination toward nudity—although this is not always the case, as can be seen in the carefully researched Cthulhu Mythos work of Michael Bukowski (yogblogsoth.blogspot.com).

Mythos fanart online also contains adult and sexually explicit material, some of it openly pornographic. As with Mythos fanfiction, no single online location contains all this material, but various artists maintain their own pages on sites like *DeviantArt* (deviantart.com), and users post and collate collections of pornographic Mythos material on imageboards and related sites such as *Rule*34* (rule34.paheal.net). As with erotic fanfiction, no full survey of this material is possible, and most of the general assumptions given above (use of tropes, sexual paraphilia, etc.) also apply. One element that seems particularly more prominent in Mythos fanart than traditional Mythos art or Mythos fanfiction is the depiction of Mythos entities as female,[6] often with exaggerated sexual characteristics—hence the depiction of multiple images of a female Cthulhu with bare breasts and/or vagina.

Webcomics

The decline of traditional newspapers and their comic pages has also seen the rise of a webcomics, which vary from single-panel works to full comic book-style multipanel pages, from joke-a-day funnies to serious works of supernatural horror. Many webcomics make some use of the Cthulhu Mythos, particularly if their focus is fantasy or horror, and a number are focused largely or exclusively on the Mythos for their setting and characters. While print Mythos comics are still somewhat dominated by adaptations, Mythos webcomics are primarily original works. Several Mythos webcomics have been published in print form, including three volumes of *El joven Lovecraft/Young Lovecraft* (2009, 2012, and 2013) and three volumes of Goomi's *Unspeakable Vault of Doom* (2004 and 2007; rpt. 2012), but I have chosen to address them here rather than in the comics section to emphasize their origin and influences.

While much of Mythos art and fiction features more male characters than female characters, Mythos webcomics tend to have a more even mix, with more strong female characters. In Larry Latham's *Lovecraft Is Missing* (lovecraftismissing.com), for example, one of the main protagonists is Nan Mercy, a take-no-nonsense librarian out to find Lovecraft and revenge; likewise *El joven Lovecraft* ("Young Lovecraft," eljovenlovecraft.blogspot.com) by Jose Oliver and Bartolo Torres features Siouxie ("Susie"), a composite character and female counterpart for the eponymous young Lovecraft, as well as Lovecraft's aunts. The currently on-hold *Ow My Sanity* (http://owmysanity.comicgenesis.com/) has most Mythos entities manifest as human or humanoid females.

Because they address an adult audience, some of these webcomics contain more gore and references to sex than is typical for newspaper funnies. For example, François "Goomi" Launet's *The Unspeakable Vault (of Doom)* (goominet.com/unspeakable-vault/) makes references to sex, often but not

---

6. Rule 63 of the Internet: "For any given male character, there is a female version of that character."

always based around the character Shubby (Shub-Niggurath), or puns such as in "Vault 422: Delights from Beyond." Launet's work is never sexually explicit and is reminiscent in some respects of Gahan Wilson's fun-poking at the Mythos and sex, or Robert M. Price's limericks about the same in *Crypt of Cthulhu*.

Few Mythos webcomics are sexually explicit; outright pornographic webcomics using the Mythos tend to be one-shots, or pornographic single-panel images with captions. Where the Cthulhu Mythos is used in a longer pornographic webcomic work, it is generally to exploit the sexual tropes and related paraphilia that have come to be associated with the Mythos. For example, Otto Maddox/Jag27's interminable episodic serials such as the "Langsuir Chronicles" (crazyxxx3dworld.com) sometimes include references to and depictions of Lovecraftian entities such as Cthulhu, Yog-Sothoth, and the *Necronomicon;* Maddox uses the teratalogicism and cosmic miscegenation of Mythos fiction both as a plot element and to provide a vehicle for the sexual fetishes he caters to, primarily maesiophilia, incest, and body horror/size fetishes involving characters having or growing improbably exaggerated sexual characteristics.

Afterword

This is not the final word on sex and the Cthulhu Mythos. It is my hope that this work will be a guidepost for interested readers and scholars, to summarize and present what has been done in the subject up to this point, the key works and authors, and the development of certain themes and ideas. Now I would like to suggest a few paths for anyone who wishes to look a little further and dig a little deeper.

All the authors and their work discussed in this book deserve examination at greater length and from different viewpoints; and there are dozens of authors and works that by constraint of space and personal judgment I chose to mention only in passing or omit entirely. Brian McNaughton in particular is ripe for a proper biography or bibliography, particularly if anyone could track down some of the more obscure works released under his pseudonyms. Likewise, each of the individual sections of Beyond Cthulhurotica could easily be the subject of an essay or series of articles in their own right, and would benefit from the attention of those with an in-depth background in art, film, comics, manga, the occult, and history. I have also generally neglected Mythos-based and -influenced video, computer, card, board, and pen-and-paper role-playing games, sex toys,[1] as well as audiobooks and music—there is at least a substantive article or two possible on each of those subjects.

While I did touch on several works of the Cthulhu Mythos that originated in foreign languages, I chose not to attempt any concerted effort at examining sex and the non-English Mythos. The translation and dissemination of the writings of Lovecraft, his contemporaries, collaborators, and successors has passed into over a dozen or more languages, with foreign reprints in countries around the world—and these works have in turn inspired and influenced generations of writers to write new Cthulhu Mythos

---

1. Such as the squid-headed dildos in the Necronomicox line, or the tentacle dildos from Whipspider Rubberworks and Bad Dragon.

tales and incorporate Lovecraftian elements into their own native-language fiction. Sadly, relatively little of this material has passed back into English. Without the resources to do a proper review of the material, I decline to attempt saying anything definite about sex in the foreign-language Mythos save that it exists and deserves its own evaluation.

Erotica and pornography are most often overlooked or forgotten in Mythos studies; they are also often the most relevant for this particular subject. Whether because of disparagement of their explicit content or of their relative literary or aesthetic quality, it is precisely because these works have largely escaped notice (or been deliberately ignored) that makes them attractive: they are largely uncharted territories ripe for exploration. Rather than submit yet another essay on a classic story, intrepid scholars may discover the next diamond in the rough like Edward Lee.

As a final thought, I can only point to the undiscovered country. New Lovecraftian and Mythos works are likely to be produced for the foreseeable future, and while I cannot guess at their nature, at least a few of them will develop themes on sex, love, and gender and will merit examination and consideration. I look forward to reading them, and hope you do as well.

Works Cited

Several of the individual essays or articles referenced above are available in several different places—as the author and text are more important than the particular collection they might appear in, the references are sometimes given by the author of the essay first, rather than the editor of the compilation.

"Alan Moore: Unearthed and Uncut" (2010). By Bram E. Gieben. Weaponizer. Retrieved from: http://www.weaponizer.co.uk/onearticle.php?category=nonfic&articleid=181

"alt.sex.cthulhu FAQ" (23 Jan 1997). By Kevin Blackburn. alt.sex.cthulhu Archive. Retrieved from: http://www.cthulhu.org/smut/FAQ.txt

Arndt, Richard (2013). *The Star*Reach Companion*. Raleigh, NC: TwoMorrows Publishing.

Behrends, Steve (1986). "The Song of the Necromancer: 'Loss' in Clark Ashton Smith's Fiction." *Studies in Weird* Fiction No. 1 (Summer 1986): 3-12.

Blackmore, Jen, ed. (2011). *Whispers in Darkness: Lovecraftian Erotica*. Cambridge, MA: Circlect Press.

Brown University in Providence in the State of R. I. v. Kirsh, 757 F.2d 124 (7th Cir. 1985).

Bloch, Robert (1978). *Strange Eons*. 1978. Los Angeles: Pinnacle Books, 1979.

——— (2009). *Mysteries of the Worm*. Edited by Robert M. Price. Hayward, CA: Chaosium.

Brown, Steven T. (2010). *Tokyo Cyberpunk Posthumanism in Japanese Visual Culture*. New York: Palgrave Macmillan.

Bru, Ricard (2010). "Tentacles of Love and Death: From Hokusai to Picasso." In *Secret Images Picasso and the Japanese Erotic Print*. New York: Thames & Hudson.

Burleson, Donald R. (1992). "Lovecraft on Gender." *Lovecraft Studies* No. 27 (Fall 1992): 21-25.

——— (2002). "The Mythic Hero Archetype in 'The Dunwich Horror.'" In Scott Connors, ed. *A Century Less A Dream: Selected Criticism on H. P. Lovecraft*. Holikong, PA: Wildside Press.

Burroughs, Edgar Rice (1913). *The Return of Tarzan*. Retrieved from: http://www.gutenberg.org/files/81/81-h/81-h.htm.

Campbell, Ramsey (1993). *Cold Print*. London: Headline.

——— (2002). *Ramsey Campbell, Probably*. Edited by S. T. Joshi. Harrogate, UK: PS Publishing.

——— (2011). *The Inhabitant of the Lake and Other Unwelcome Tenants*. Hornsea, UK: PS Publishing.

Cannon, Peter (1997). *Long Memories: Recollections of Frank Belknap Long*. Stockport, UK: British Fantasy Society.

Carter, Lin (1982). "A Day in Derleth Country." *Crypt of Cthulhu* No. 6 (St. John's Eve 1982). Retrieved from: http://crypt-of-cthulhu.com/dayinderleth.htm.

"Cogswell, Grant (Cthulhu)" (22 January 2006). Dread Central. Retrieved from: http://www.dreadcentral.com/interviews/cogswell-grant-cthulhu.

Crawford, Gary W. (1988). *Ramsey Campbell*. Mercer Island, WA: Starmont House.

Cuinn, Catherine, ed. (2010). *Cthulhurotica*. Mercerville, NJ: Dagon Books.

de Camp, L. Sprague (1975). *Lovecraft: A Biography*. Garden City, NY: Doubleday.

——— (1996). *Time & Chance (An Autobiography)*. Hampton Falls, NH: Donald M. Grant.

de la Ree, Gerry, ed. (1973). *The Normal Lovecraft*. Saddle River, NJ: Gerry de la Ree.

Dahlquist, Joel Powell, and Lee Garth Vigilant (2004). "Way Better Than Real: Manga Sex to Tentacle Hentai." In D. D. Waskul, ed. *net.seXXX: Readings on Sex, Pornography, and the Internet*. New York: Peter Lang.

Davis, Sonia H. (1949). "Lovecraft as I Knew Him." 1949. In Peter Cannon, ed. *Lovecraft Remembered*. Sauk City, WI: Arkham House, 1998.

——— (1969). "Memories of Lovecraft: I." 1969. In Peter Cannon, ed. *Lovecraft Remembered*. Sauk City, WI: Arkham House, 1998.

——— (1992). *The Private Life of H. P. Lovecraft*. Rev. ed. Edited by S. T. Joshi. West Warwick, RI: Necronomicon Press.

Derleth, August (2003). *The Lurker at the Threshold*. 1945. Philadelphia: Carroll & Graf.

——— (2008). *The Watchers out of Time*. 1974. New York: Del Rey.

Eddy, Clifford M. (1948). "The Loved Dead." *Arkham Sampler* 1, No. 3 (Summer 1948): 21-31.

Eddy, Muriel, and Eddy, Clifford M. (2001). *The Gentleman from Angell Street: Memories of H. P. Lovecraft.* Narragansett, RI: Fernham Publishing.

Ellis, Novalyne Price (1998). *One Who Walked Alone.* West Kingston, RI: Donald M. Grant.

Eng, Steve (1984). "Robert E. Howard's Library." In Don Herron, ed. *The Dark Barbarian.* Wesport, CT: Greenwood Press.

Everts, R. Alain (1974). "Howard Phillips Lovecraft and Sex: or The Sex Life of a Gentleman." *Nyctalops* 2, No. 2 (July 1974): 19. Also printed in Everts's own fanzine *The Outsider* (c. 1975): 7-8. Available online: http://www.Lovecraftcraft.com/study/articles/hpl-sex.asp.

Faig, Kenneth W., (1991). "The Parents of Howard Phillips Lovecraft." In David E. Schultz and S. T. Joshi, ed. *An Epicure in the Terrible: A Centennial Anthology of Essays in Honor of H. P. Lovecraft.* Rutherford, NJ: Fairleigh Dickinson University Press. 45-77.

Gatto, John Taylor (1978). "Whispering in the Dark: A Peek at Lovecraft's Dirty Story." *Whispers* 3, Nos. 3-4 (October 1978): 109-13.

Geoffrey, Justine (2012). *Red Monolith Frenzy: Book 1 BLACKSTONE Erotica.* Martian Migraine Press. Amazon Digital Services.

Gonce, John Wisdom, and Harms, Daniel (2003). *The Necronomicon Files.* Boston: Weiser Books.

Grant, Kenneth (1972). *The Magical Revival.* London: Muller.

——— (1975). *Cults of the Shadow.* London: Muller.

——— (1992). *Hecate's Fountain.* London: Skoob.

Hart, Mara Kirk, and S. T. Joshi, ed. (2006). *Lovecraft's New York Circle.* New York: Hippocampus Press.

Hine, Phil (2008). "Sexual Magic: A Chaos Perspective." In Christopher S. Hyatt and Lon Milo Diloquette, ed. *Sex, Magic, Tantra and Tarot: The Way of the Secret Lover.* 3rd rev. ed. Tempe, AZ: New Falcon Publications.

——— (2009). *The Pseudonomicon.* Tempe, AZ: Original Falcon Press.

Hoffmann, Charles (2010). "Return to Xuthal." In Darrell Schweitzer, ed. *The Robert E. Howard Reader.* Rockville, MD: Borgo Press.

Houellebecq, Michel (2005). *H. P. Lovecraft: Against the World, Against Life.* Translated by Dorna Khazeni. San Francisco: Believer Books.

Howard, Robert E. (2001). *Nameless Cults The Cthulhu Mythos Fiction of Robert E. Howard.* Edited by Robert M. Price. Hayward, CA: Chaosium.

——— (2002). *The Coming of Conan: The Original Adventures of the Greatest Sword and Sorcery Hero of All Time!* Edited by Patrice Louinet and Rusty Burke. New York: Del Rey.

——— (2008). *The Collected Letters of Robert E. Howard.* Edited by Rob Roehm. Plano, TX: Robert E. Howard Foundation Press. 3 vols.

"HP Lovecraft, erotica, and why they go together." (26 October 2011) Circlet Press/Live Journal. Retrieved from: http://circletpress.livejournal.com/167685.html.

Indick, Ben P. (1976). "Lovecraft's Ladies." In Darrell Schweitzer, ed. *Essays Lovecraftian.* Baltimore: T-K Graphics.

Jaffery, Sheldon (1989). *The Arkham House Companion.* Mercer Island, WA: Starmont House.

"Jordan Krall Interviews Edward Lee" (20 April 2011). Bizzaro Central. Retrieved from: http://bizarrocentral.com/2011/04/20/jordan-krall-interviews-edward-lee/.

Joshi, S. T. (1989). *Selected Papers on Lovecraft.* West Warwick, RI: Necronomicon Press.

——— (1996). *A Subtler Magic The Writings and Philosophy of H. P. Lovecraft.* Berkeley Heights, NJ: Wildside Press.

——— (2001). *Ramsey Campbell and Modern Horror Fiction.* Liverpool: Liverpool University Press.

——— (2010). *I Am Providence The Life and Times of H. P. Lovecraft.* New York: Hippocampus Press. 2 vols.

Joshi, S. T., and Marc A. Michaud, ed. (1979). *H. P. Lovecraft in "The Eyrie."* West Warwick, RI: Necronomicon Press.

Joshi, S. T., and David E. Schultz (2001). *An H. P. Lovecraft Encyclopedia.* 2001. New York: Hippocampus Press, 2004.

Kiernan, Caitlín R. (2005). *Frog Toes and Tentacles.* Burton, MI: Subterranean Press.

——— (2007). *The Black Alphabet (A Primer).* Burton, MI: Subterranean Press.

——— (2012). *Confessions of a Five-Chambered Heart.* Burton, MI: Sub-terranean Press.

Klein, T. E. D. (1977). "Ramsey Campbell: An Appreciation." *Nyctalops* No. 13 (May 1977): 19–25.

Lee, Edward (2010). *The Innswich Horror.* Portland, OR: Deadite Press.

——— (2011). *The Dunwich Romance.* Portland, OR: Bloodletting Press.

Lévy, Maurice (1988). *Lovecraft: A Study in the Fantastic.* Translated by S. T. Joshi. Detroit: Wayne State University Press.

Works Cited

Litersky, Dorothy M. G. (1997). *Derleth: Hawk . . . and Dove*. Aurora, CO: National Writer's Press.

Locke, George, ed. (1973). *At the Mountains of Murkiness*. London: Ferret Fantasy.

Logan. (2006). *The Pornomicon*. Class Comics.

Lord, Bruce (2004). "The Genetics of Horror: Sex and Racism in H. P. Lovecraft's Fiction." Retrieved from: http://www.contrasoma.com/writing/lovecraft.html

Lovecraft, H. P. (1965-76). *Selected Letters*. Edited by August Derleth, Donald Wandrei, and James Turner. Sauk City, WI: Arkham House. 5 vols.

———— (1971). "Lovecraft on Love." *Arkham Collector* No. 8 (Winter 1971): 242-46.

———— (1986). *Uncollected Letters*. Edited by S. T. Joshi. West Warwick, RI: Necronomicon Press.

———— (1993). *Letters to Robert Bloch*. Edited by S. T. Joshi and David E. Schultz. West Warick, RI: Necronomicon Press.

———— (1994). *Letters to Samuel Loveman and Vincent Starrett*. Edited by S. T. Joshi & David E. Schultz. West Warwick, RI: Necronomicon Press.

———— (1997). *The Annotated H. P. Lovecraft*. Edited by S. T. Joshi. New York: Dell.

———— (1999). *The Call of Cthulhu and Other Weird Stories*. Edited by S. T. Joshi. New York: Penguin.

———— (2000). *The Annotated Supernatural Horror in Literature*. Edited by S. T. Joshi. New York: Hippocampus Press.

———— (2001). *The Thing on the Doorstep and Other Weird Stories*. Edited by S. T. Joshi. New York: Penguin.

———— (2004). *The Dreams in the Witch House and Other Weird Stories*. Edited by S. T. Joshi. New York: Penguin.

———— (2005). *Letters to Rheinhart Kleiner*. Edited by S. T. Joshi and David E. Schultz. New York: Hippocampus Press.

———— (2006). *Collected Essays, Volume 5: Philosophy; Autobiography and Miscellany*. Edited by S. T. Joshi. New York: Hippocampus Press.

———— (2007a). "Letters to Lee McBride White." *Lovecraft Annual* 1 (2007): 31-64.

———— (2007b). *O Fortunate Floridian: H. P. Lovecraft's Letters to R. H. Barlow*. Edited by S. T. Joshi and David E. Schultz. Tampa, FL: University of Tampa Press.

——— (2011). *Letters to James F. Morton*. Edited by S. T. Joshi and David E. Schultz. New York: Hippocampus Press.

Lovecraft, H. P., and others (1989). *The Horror in the Museum and Other Revisions*. Sauk City, WI: Arkham House.

Lovecraft, H. P., and others (2011). *The Crawling Chaos and Others*. The Annotated Revisions and Collaborations of H. P. Lovecraft, Volume 1. Edited by S. T. Joshi. Welches, OR: Arcane Wisdom.

Lovecraft, H. P., and others (2012). *Medusa's Coil and Others*. The Annotated Revisions and Collaborations of H. P. Lovecraft, Volume 2. Edited by S. T. Joshi. Welches, OR: Arcane Wisdom.

Lovecraft, H. P., and Willis Conover (2002). *Lovecraft at Last*. 1975. New York: Cooper Square Press.

Lovecraft, H. P., and Derleth, August (2008). *Essential Solitude: The Letters of H. P. Lovecraft and August Derleth*. Edited by David E. Schultz and S. T. Joshi. New York: Hippocampus Press.

Lovecraft, H. P., and Robert E. Howard (2009). *A Means to Freedom: The Letters of H. P. Lovecraft and Robert E. Howard*. Edited by S. T. Joshi, David E. Schultz, and Rusty Burke. New York: Hippocampus Press. 2 vols.

Lovett-Graff, Bennet (1995). "Lovecraft: Reproduction and Its Discontents: Degeneration and Detection in 'The Lurking Fear.'" *Para*doxa* 1, No. 3 (1995): 325-41.

——— (1997a). "Shadows over Lovecraft: Reactionary Fantasy and Immigrant Eugenics." *Extrapolation* 38, No. 2 (Fall 1997): 175-92.

——— (1997b). "'Life Is a Hideous Thing': Primate-Geniture in H. P. Lovecraft's 'Arthur Jermyn.'" *Journal of the Fantastic in the Arts* 8, No. 3 (1997): 370-88.

Lumley, Brian, and Stanley Wiater, ed. (2002). *The Brian Lumley Companion*. New York: Tor.

McCarthy, Helen, and Jonathan Clements (1998). *The Erotic Anime Movie Guide*. London: Titan.

McNamara, M. Eileen (1991). "Winfield Scott Lovecraft's Final Illness" and "Medical Record of Winfield Scott Lovecraft." *Lovecraft Studies* No. 24 (Spring 1991): 14-17.

McNaughton, Brian (1980). *Satan's Mistress*. 2nd ed. New York: Carlyle Communications.

——— (2000). *Worse Things Waiting*. Berkeley Heights, NJ: Wildside Press.

——— (30 September 2000). "Re: Has anyone read the following?" *alt.horror. cthulhu* Retrieved from: https://groups.google.com/d/msg/ alt.horror.cthulhu/wbJvVRBetkc/ipkIgmG37IoJ

Machen, Arthur (2001). *The Three Impostors and Other Stories*. Edited by S. T. Joshi. Oakland, CA: Chaosium.

——— (2003). *The White People and Other Stories*. Edited by S. T. Joshi. Oakland, CA: Chaosium.

"Manga Artist Interview Series (Part I)" (9 December 2002). Sake-Drenched Postcards. Retrieved from: http://www.bigempire.com/sake/manga1.html.

Matolcsy, Kálmán (2004). "The Innsmouth 'Thing': Monstrous Androgyny in H. P. Lovecraft's 'The Thing on the Doorstep.'" *Gender Studies* 1, No. 3 (2005); 171–79.

Miéville, China (2008). "M. R. James and the Quantum Vampire—Weird; Hauntological: Versus and/or and and/or or?" *Collapse* 4 (2008): 85–108. A revised edition (29 November 2011) appeared on *Weird Fiction Review*. Retrieved from: http://weirdfictionreview.com/2011/11/m-r-james-and-the-quantum-vampire-by-china-mieville/

Migliore, Andrew, and John Strysik (2006) *Lurker in the Lobby: A Guide to the Cinema of H. P. Lovecraft*. Rev. ed. Portland, OR: Night Shade.

Mitchell, D. M., ed. (2010). *The Starry Wisdom*. London: Creation Oneiros.

Moore, Alan (2007). *Alan Moore's Yuggoth Cultures and Other Growths*. Edited by William Christensen. Rantoul, IL: Avatar Press.

Moore, Alan; Johnston, Antony; and Burrows, Jason (2010). *Neonomicon*. Edited by William Christensen and Alan Moore. Rantoul, IL: Avatar Press.

Moore, C. L. (2009). *Shambleau: A Northwest Smith Adventure*. Lexington, KY: Wildside Press.

Moskowitz, Sam (1995) "Derleth's Lament to Love." In James P. Robert, ed. *Return to Derleth: Selected Essays, Volume Two*. Madison, WI: White Hawk Press.

Murray, Will (1984a). "An Informal History of the Spicy Pulps." *Risqué Stories* No. 1 (March 1984): 35–41.

——— (1984b). "The Dunwich Chimera and Others: Correlating the Cthulhu Mythos." *Lovecraft Studies* No. 8 (Spring 1984): 10–24.

——— (1999). "Lost Lovecraftian Pearls: The 'Tarbis' Collaboration." In James Van Hise, ed. *The Fantastic Worlds of H. P. Lovecraft*. Yucca Valley, CA: James Van Hise. 42–53.

Nelson, Dale J. (1990). "Arthur Jermyn Was a Yahoo: Swift and Modern Horror Fiction." *Studies in Weird Fiction* No. 7 (Spring 1990): 3–7.

Nelson, Victoria (2001). "H. P. Lovecraft and the Great Heresies." In *The Secret Life of Puppets*. Cambridge, MA: Harvard University Press.

O'Brien, Kevin L., ed. (2004). *Eldritch Blue: Love and Sex in the Cthulhu Mythos*. Aurora, CO: Lindsfarne Press.

Pace, Joel. (2008). "Queer Tales? Sexuality, Race, and Architecture in 'The Thing on the Doorstep.'" *Lovecraft Annual* 2 (2008): 104–38.

Pollitt, Katha (2007). *Learning to Drive and Other Life Stories*. New York: Random House.

Price, Kay (1992). *Who Was August Derleth?* Sauk City, WI: Germanium Press.

Price, Robert M. (1982). "Homosexual Panic in 'The Outsider.'" *Crypt of Cthulhu* No. 8 (Michaelmass 1982). Retrieved from: http://crypt-of-cthulhu.com/homosexualpanic.htm.

———, ed. (1983). "Mail Call of Cthulhu." *Crypt of Cthulhu* No. 17 (Hallowmas 1983). Retrieved from: http://crypt-of-cthulhu.com/ mail017.htm.

——— (1988). "Did Lovecraft Have Syphillis?" *Crypt of Cthulhu* No. 53 (Candlemass 1988): 25–27.

———, ed. (1990). *The Horror of It All: Encrusted Gems from the "Crypt of Cthulhu."* Mercer Island, WA: Starmont House.

——— (1994). "Lovecraft and Ligeia.'" *Lovecraft Studies* No. 31 (Fall 1994): 15–17.

———, ed. (1995). *The Dunwich Cycle*. Hayward, CA: Chaosium.

———, ed. (1996). *The New Lovecraft Circle*. Minneapolis, MN: Fedogan & Bremer.

———, ed. (2005). *Tsathoggua Cycle*. Hayward, CA: Chaosium.

——— (2008). *Blasphemies and Revelations*. Poplar Bluff, MO: Mythos Books.

———, ed. (2010). *The Tindalos Cycle*. New YorkY: Hippocampus Press.

Pugmire, W. H. (1990). Letter. *Crypt of Cthulhu* No. 73 (St. John's Eve 1990): 45.

——— (1999). "Lustcraft." *Tales of Lovecraftian Horror* No. 11 (Eastertide 1999): 2–3.

——— (2011). *Some Unknown Gulf of Night*. Welches, OR: Arcane Wisdom.

Punter, David (1996). *The Literature of Terror: A History of Gothic Fictions from 1765 to Present, Volume 2: The Modern Gothic*. 2nd ed. London: Longman.

Reynolds, Blair (1996). *Black Sands* 1. Room 308.

"Robert M. Price Interview" (13 March 2010). She Never Slept. Retrieved from: http://sheneverslept.com/newsandreviews/archives/1872.

Rodgers, Alan (30 May 2002). "Re: the most obscure mythos story ever published." *alt.horror.cthulhu* Retrieved from: https://groups.google.com/d/msg/alt.horror.cthulhu/J-Mx3azP1Cc/fKwje7GMfMQJ.

Rovin, Jeff (1987). *H. P. Lovecraft's Re-Animator*. Novelization of the movie, based on the screenplay by Dennis Paoli, William J. Norris, and Stuart Gordon. New York: Pocket.

Russell, Samuel D. ed. (1968). *Haunted* 1, No. (3 (June 1968).

St. Armand, Barton Levi (1977). *The Roots of Horror in the Fiction of H. P. Lovecraft*. Elizabethtown, NY: Dragon Press.

Sargent, Stanley C. (2002). *The Taint of Lovecraft*. Poplar Bluff, MO: Mythos Books.

Scott, Winfield Townley (1944). "His Own Most Fantastic Creation: Howard Phillips Lovecraft." In H. P. Lovecraft, *Marginalia*. Sauk City, WI: Arkham House. 309-31.

——— (1961). "His Own Most Fantastic Creation: Howard Phillips Lovecraft." 1961. In Peter Cannon, ed. *Lovecraft Remembered*. Sauk City, WI: Arkham House.

Shanks, Jeffrey. "Theosophy and the Thurian Age: Robert E. Howard and the Works of William Scott-Elliot." *Dark Man* 6, Nos. 1-2 (2011): 53-90.

Shea, J. Vernon (1982). *H. P. Lovecraft: The House and the Shadows*. West Warwick, RI: Necronomicon Press.

Shea, Robert, and Wilson, Robert Anton (1975). *The Illuminatus! Trilogy*. New York: Dell.

Shreffler, Phillip A. (1977). *The H. P. Lovecraft Companion*. Wesport, CT: Greenwood Press.

Sidney-Fryer, Donald (1978). *Emperor of Dreams: A Clark Ashton Smith Bibliography*. West Kingston, RI: Donald M. Grant.

——— (1988). "On the Alleged Influence of Lord Dunsany on Clark Ashton Smith." *Klarkash-Ton: The Journal of Smith Studies* No. 1 (June 1988): 9-13, 15.

Smith, Clark Ashton (1989). *Strange Shadows: The Uncollected Fiction and Essays of Clark Ashton Smith*. Edited by Steve Behrends, Donald Sidney-Fryer, and Rah Hoffman. Westport, CT: Greenwood Press.

——— (2003). *Selected Letters of Clark Ashton Smith*. Edited by David E. Schultz and Scott Connors. Sauk City, WI: Arkham House.

——— (2007-11). *The Collected Fantasies of Clark Ashton Smith*. Edited by Scott Connors and Ron Hilger. San Francisco: Night Shade. 5 vols.

"Stanley C. Sargent." (1997). "The Deep Ones Speak." Retrieved from: http://reocities.com/Athens/forum/4162/sargent.html.

Thomas, G. W. "Writing the Mythos: A Lesson in Squidgy History." Retrieved from http://www.innsmouthfreepress.com/?p=10995).

Thompson, Jason (2010, Jan. 4). "The Long Tentacle of H. P. Lovecraft in Manga (NSFW)." Retrieved from: http://io9.com/5439408/the-long-tentacle-of-hp-lovecraft-in-manga-nsfw.

Tyson, Donald (2008). *Grimoire of the Necronomicon*. Woodbury, MN: Llewellyn Publications.

——— (2010). *The Dream World of H. P. Lovecraft: His Life, His Demons, His Universe*. Woodbury, MN: Llewellyn Publications.

Urban, Hugh (2006). *Magia Sexualis: Sex, Magic, and Liberation in Modern Western Esotericism*. Berkeley: University of California Press.

Waugh, Robert H. (2011). "The Ecstasies of 'The Thing on the Doorstep,' 'Medusa's Coil,' and Other Erotic Stories." In *The Monster of Voices: Speaking for H. P. Lovecraft*. New York: Hippocampus Press.

Williams, Sara (2013). "'The Infinitude of the Shrieking Abysses': Rooms, Wombs, Tombs, and the Hysterical Female Gothic in 'The Dreams in the Witch House.'" In David Simmons, ed. *New Critical Essays on H. P. Lovecraft*. New York: Palgrave Macmillan.

Wilson, Colin (1993). "A Touch of Tragedy." In James P. Roberts, ed. *Return to Derleth: Selected Essays*. Madison, WI: White Hawk Press.

Wisker, Gina (2013). "'Spawn of the Pit': Lavinia, Merceline, Medusa, and All Things Foul: H. P. Lovecraft's Liminal Women." In David Simmons, ed. *New Critical Essays on H. P. Lovecraft*. New York: Palgrave Macmillan.

"WNW talks with Carrie Cuinn, the woman behind the Cthulhurotica anthology" (8 November 2011). Writer News Weekly. Retrieved from: http://www.writersnewsweekly.com/cthulhurotica.html.

Suggested Further Reading

In addition to the above works which I have explicitly cited throughout this book, the following is a list of additional works consulted during my research which interested readers may wish to reference.

Anderson, James Arthur (2011). *Out of the Shadows: A Structuralist Approach to Understanding the Fiction of H. P. Lovecraft.* San Bernardino, CA: Borgo Press.

Barreiro and Noé (1997). *The Convent of Hell.* New York: Nantier Beall Minoustchine.

Barret, Barbara (2011). "Letter: Howard's Escape?" *Dark Man* 6, Nos. 1-2 (2011): 8-14.

Bennet, Raine (1996). "Clark Ashton Smith, Virgin." *Studies in Weird Fiction* No. 18 (Winter 1996): 34-36. Available on *Eldritch Dark*: http://www.eldritchdark.com/articles/biographies/9/clark-ashton-smith,-virgin.

Blosser, Fred (1997). "The Sign of the Magna Mater." *Crypt of Cthulhu* No. 97 (Hallowmass 1997): 25-28.

Burleson, Mollie L. (1990). "The Outsider: A Woman?" *Lovecraft Studies* Nos. 222/23 (Fall 1990): 22-23.

Callaghan, Gavin (2013). *H. P. Lovecraft's Dark Arcadia.* Jefferson, NC: McFarland.

Cannon, Peter (1988). "Asceticism and Lust: The Greatest Lovecraft Revision." *Crypt of Cthulhu* No. 61 (Yuletide 1988): 29-31.

Danzinger, G. A. (1893). "A Sacrifice to Science." *Californian Illustrated Magazine* 3 (1893): 172-80.

Eddy, Muriel E. (1968). "Lovecraft's Marriage and Divorce." *Haunted* 1, No. 3 (June 1968): 86, 93.

Ellis, Novayne Price, and Rusty Burke (1989). *Day of the Stranger: Further Memories of Robert E. Howard.* West Warwick, RI: Necronomicon Press.

Everts, R. Alain, and Wetzel, George T. (1976). *Winifred Virginia Jackson–Lovecraft's Lost Romance.* Madison, WI: Strange Co.

Frye, Mitch. (2007). "The Refinement of 'Crude Allegory': Eugenic Themes and Genotypic Horror in the Weird Fiction of H. P. Lovecraft." *Journal of the Fantastic in the Arts* 17, No. 3 (2007): 237-55.

Gannon, Amanda (17 December 2009). "Sucker Love: Celebrating the naughty tentacle." Retrieved from: http://www.tor.com/index.php?view=blog&id=58487.

Gatto, John Taylor (1977). *The Major Works of H. P. Lovecraft: A Critical Commentary.* New York: Monarch.

Gregorak, Jean (1998). "Horror Is What a Girl Would Feel: Narrative Erotics in Depression-Era Pulp Fiction." In Ann C. Hall, ed. *Delights, Desires, and Dilemmas: Essays on Women and the Media.* Westport, CT: Praeger Publishing. 3-20.

Hoffman, Charles (1993). "Cosmic Filth: Robert E. Howard's View of Evil." Retrieved from: ttp://chuckhoffman.blogspot.com/2008/06/cosmic-filth-robert-e-howards-view-of.html.

——— (2009). "Blood Lust: Robert E. Howard's Spicy Adventures." Retrieved from: http://chuckhoffman.blogspot.com/2009/07/blood-lust-robert-e-howards-spicy.html.

——— (2009). "Elements of Sadomasochism in the Fiction and Poetry of Robert E. Howard." Retrieved from: http://chuckhoffman.blogspot.com/2010/07/elements-of-sadomasochism-in-fiction.html.

Jaxon (1972). "Tales of the Leather Nun's Grandmother." In *Tales of the Leather Nun* (23-29). Berkeley, CA: Last Gasp. Also republished in *Optimism of Youth the Underground Work of Jack Jackson* (Fantagraphics Books, 1991).

Joshi, S. T. (2008). *The Rise and Fall of the Cthulhu Mythos.* Poplar Bluff, MO: Mythos Books.

Keller, David H. (1948). "Shadows over Lovecraft." *Fantasy Commentator* 2, No. 7 (Summer 1948): 237-46. Rpt. *Fresco* 8, No. 3 (Spring 1958): 12-27.

Koki, Arthur S. (1962). "H. P. Lovecraft: An Introduction to His Life and Writings." M.A. thesis: Colombia University.

LaVine, Morgana (1982). "Lovecraft and the Male Gender Role." *Crypt of Cthulhu* No. 8 (Michaelmass 1982): 14-15.

Levenda, Peter (2013). *The Dark Lord: H. P. Lovecraft, Kenneth Grant and the Typhonian Tradition in Magic.* Lake Worth, FL: Ibis.

"Lovecraft Lives: Mike Vosburg" (1 May 2009). "Lovecraft Is Missing." Retrieved from: http://lovecraftismissing.com/?p=1232.

Marten, Robert D. (2004). "Pickman Models." *Lovecraft Studies* No. 44 (2004): 42-80.

Miller, T. S. "From Bodily Fear to Cosmic Horror (and Back Again): The Tentacle Monster from Primordial Chaos to Hello Cthulhu." *Lovecraft Annual* 5 (2011): 121-54.

North, Robert (2004). *New Flesh Palladium: Magia Erotica.* 4th ed. Minneapolis, MN: Runa Raven Press.

Price, Robert M. (1982). "Legacy of the Lurker." *Crypt of Cthulhu* No. 6 (St. John's Eve 1982). Retrieved from: http://crypt-of-cthulhu.com/ legacyoflurker.htm.

———— (1988). "Mildew from Shaggai." *Crypt of Cthulhu* No. 61 (Yuletide 1988): 26-28.

Ralickas, Vivian (2008). "Art, Cosmic Horror, and the Fetishizing Gaze in the Fiction of H. P. Lovecraft." *Journal of the Fantastic in the Arts* 19, No. 3 (2008): 297-316.

Sterling, Kenneth (1951). "A Reply to Keller's Article on Lovecraft." *Fantasy Commentator* 3, No. 5 (Winter 1951-52): 153-54. Rpt. *Fresco* 8, No. 3 (Spring 1958): 27-29.

Tompkins, Steve (24 January 2009). "The Conscience, and the Kisses, of a King." *Cimmerian.* Retrieved from: http://www.thecimmerian.com/the-conscience-and-the-kisses-of-a-king/.

Wilson, Robert Anton (1973). *The Sex Magicians.* Chatworth, CA: GX, Inc.

For more general background on the history, use, and development of sex in science fiction and fantasy fiction in general, Joseph W. Slade has a good listing under the heading "Science Fiction and Fantasy Erotica" in *Pornography and Sexual Representation: A Reference Guide* (2001, Greenwood Press, 3 vols.)

Index

Adultery 41, 171, 207
Alcestis (Davis-Lovecraft) 56
Aleister Crowley and the Hidden God (Grant) 249, 251
Amatory Experiences of a Surgeon, The 60
Androgyny 175, 254
Arabian Nights, The 18, 58, 64, 138
"Rendezvous in Averoigne, A" (Smith) 171
Ars Amatoria (Ovid) 18
"Arthur Jermyn" (Lovecraft). *See* "Facts concerning the Late Arthur Jermyn and His Family"
"Asceticism and Lust: The Greatest Lovecraft Revision" (Cannon) 158
Asexuality 67, 90, 124-28, 129, 157-58, 167, 169, 175-76, 186, 212, 224, 226
Atlantean Necronomicon, The (Warlock Asylum) 254
"At the Gate of Deeper Slumber" (Kiernan) 214
At the Mountains of Madness (Lovecraft) 108, 124, 126, 147, 151; parody, 158

Barlow, R. H. 21, 31, 39, 42, 43, 44, 45, 46, 55, 128, 157, 161, 173, 174, 175
Barreiro, Ricardo 139, 150, 267, 270
BDSM 29, 35, 143, 144, 147, 149, 152, 163, 165, 166, 167, 168, 191, 192, 195, 219, 230, 242, 262
Beardsley, Aubrey 60, 144, 146
"Behold, I Stand at the Door and Knock" (Price) 207, 209
"Beneath the Tombstone" (Price) 138
Berkeley, Elizabeth. *See* Jackson, Winifred Virginia
Bertiaux, Michael 252-53
Bestiality 31, 66, 70, 71, 77-78, 177, 219
Best Little Witch-House in Arkham, The (McLaughlin) 235

Beyond, The (film) 267
"Beyond the Wall of Sleep" (Lovecraft) 74, 107
Beyond Re-Animator (film) 277-78
"Beyond the Threshold" (Derleth) 187
"Beyond the Wall of Time" (McNaughton) 200
Beyond Tickling (film) 280
Birth control 20-21, 22
Bisexuality 68, 96, 124-25, 157, 161, 175, 181, 182, 211, 232, 241, 270
Bishop, Zealia Brown Reed 47, 69, 99, 102, 103, 104, 160
Black Alphabet, The (Kiernan) 215, 217
"Black Brat of Dunwich, The" (Sargent) 45, 235
Black Goat of the Woods with a Thousand Young. *See* Shub-Niggurath
Blackburn, John 267, 270
Blackmore, Jen 233
Black Sands (Reynolds) 269
"Black Stone, The" (Howard) 166, 168, 195, 241-42
Bloch, Robert 49, 131, 132, 138, 157, 176-79, 202
"Bloom of Sacrifice, The" (Pugmire) 212
Blue Girl, La 150
Boccaccio, Giovanni 18, 138
Bondage. *See* BDSM
"Born in Strange Shadow" (Pugmire) 125, 212-13
"Bothon" (Whitehead) 99
"Boy with the Bloodstained Mouth, The" (Pugmire) 212
Bradbury, Ray 55
Bride of Re-Animator (film) 276, 277
Brite, Poppy Z. 161, 235
Broers, Jim 263
"Brood of Bubastis" (Bloch) 177
Brown, Kirsten 261

305

Brundage, Margaret 30, 132, 164, 168, 262
Bukowski, Michael 261
Burroughs, Edgar Rice 72-73, 103, 234
Bush, David Van 17, 26

Caigan, Khem 145
"Cairn on the Headland, The" (Howard) 168
"Call of Cthulhu, The" (Lovecraft) 145, 147, 153, 166, 168, 255, 261, 281
Call of Cthulhu (RPG) 160, 205, 229, 230, 268, 273
Campbell, Ramsey 123, 132, 134, 138, 139, 163, 179-81, 183, 188-95, 199, 201, 202, 206, 207, 208, 209, 213, 217, 231, 234, 242, 258
Cannon, Peter 42, 54, 91, 97, 156, 158-59, 196-98, 207
Carter, Lin 135, 163, 171, 175, 181, 206, 234, 238, 262
Carter, Margaret L. 142, 237
Case of Charles Dexter Ward, The (Lovecraft) 65, 80, 117, 124, 193, 201, 203, 274
Catullus 77
Censorship 21-22, 32-35, 43, 132, 144, 149, 165, 167, 189, 191, 223, 234, 264-66, 271
"Challenge from Beyond, The" (Lovecraft et al.) 148, 160
Chambers, Robert W. 97, 106, 173, 263
Chappell, Fred 236
"Child of Dark Mania, The" (Pugmire) 212
"Children of the Night, The" (Howard) 125, 138, 169
City of the Living Dead (film) 267
Clayton, Sheena 202-3, 204
Clore, Dan 229
Cobb, Irvin S. 79, 97
"Cold Print" (Campbell) 134, 138, 180, 189, 191-92, 207, 209, 213, 217, 231
Coley (comic) 270
Collins, Nancy A. 235
Collrin, Paul M. 229
Colour out of Darkness, The (Pelan) 236
"Colour out of Space, The" (Lovecraft) 124-25, 274
Conan the Barbarian 149, 266

Confessions of a Five-Chambered Heart (Kiernan) 214
Convent of Hell, The (Barreiro-Noé) 139, 150, 267, 270
Corben, Richard 264, 269
Corman, Roger 149, 275
"Courtyard, The" (Moore) 224-25, 269
Crane, Hart 41, 42, 46
"Crawling Chaos, The" (Lovecraft-Jackson) 27
Crofts, Anna Helen 99-100, 160
Crowley, Aleister 207, 245, 246-47, 248, 250, 251, 252, 253, 254, 255, 256, 259, 260
Cthulhu 57, 84, 121, 122, 123, 124, 126, 127, 134, 135, 145, 147, 148, 150, 153, 162, 167, 176, 178, 226, 228, 229, 234, 236, 240, 250, 261, 262, 263, 264, 265, 266, 267, 270, 285, 287, 288
Cthulhu (film) 274, 280-82
Cthulhu on Lesbos (Jalajel) 239
Cthulhurotica 132, 155, 160, 231-33, 261, 262, 278
Cthulhu Senryu (Mamatas) 239
Cthulhu Sex Magazine 228-29, 235, 239, 261, 273, 285
Cuckoldry 163, 171, 207
Cuinn, Carrie 111, 117, 132, 160, 231-32
Cults of the Shadow (Grant) 249, 252
"Curate of Temphill, The" (Cannon-Price) 207, 208
Curse of the Crimson Altar (film) 274
"Curse of Yig, The" (Lovecraft-Bishop) 62, 63, 64, 69, 72, 84, 86, 87, 91, 102, 104, 110, 112, 115, 117, 118, 119, 120, 131, 134, 141, 153, 154, 259
Cybele 76-77, 165

de Camp, L. Sprague 13-14, 34, 44, 100, 108, 113-14, 164, 181, 186, 200, 244
de Castro, Adolphe 99, 101-2
Dagger of Blood (comic) 267, 270
"Dagon" (Lovecraft) 50, 121
Dagon (Chappell) 236-37
Dagon (film) 274, 276, 283
Damned Highway: Fear and Loathing in Arkham, The (Keene-Mamatas) 236

"Dark Brotherhood, The" (Derleth) 186
Darkest Part of the Woods (Campbell) 190, 193-94, 195
"Daughters of Feud" (Howard) 168
Davis, Sonia H. 14-15, 16, 17, 18, 19, 21, 23, 24, 26-28, 31, 32, 35, 36, 38, 40, 53-56, 69, 92, 94-95, 109, 157, 158, 160, 179
"Dawn of Discord" (Smith) 172-73
Dead Will Cuckold You, The (Smith) 171
Decameron, The (Boccaccio) 18, 138
"Demoiselle d'Ys, The" (Chambers) 173
Demonbane 272
Demon Beast Invasion 149
Demons by Daylight (Campbell) 189-90, 195, 208
Derleth, August 18, 20, 31, 32, 36, 41, 54-55, 56, 70, 99, 101, 131, 132, 135, 148, 157, 161, 162, 163, 171, 172, 179-88, 189, 193, 195, 200, 202, 205, 207, 209, 213, 236, 238, 244, 245, 249, 253, 258, 282
"Derma Sutra" (Kiernan) 214, 217
"Devil's Hop Yard, The" (Lupoff) 196
Die, Monster, Die! (film) 274, 275
"Discovery of the Ghooric Zone" (Lupoff) 196, 238
Diver and Two Octopi (Hokusai) 144-45
Doc Savage: His Apocalyptic Life (Farmer) 135
"Documents in the Case of Elizabeth Akeley" (Lupoff) 186
"Dolls" (Campbell) 195
Donnel, Jean Ann 229
"Doom That Came to Dunwich, The" (Lupoff) 196
"Doom That Came to Innsmouth, The" (McNaughton) 200, 203, 204
"Door to Saturn, The" (Smith) 175
Downward to Darkness (McNaughton) 198, 199, 200, 201, 203, 205
Dracula (Stoker) 58, 134
Dream of the Fisherman's Wife (Hokusai). See *Diver and Two Octopi*
Dream-Quest of Unknown Kadath, The (Lovecraft) 79, 84, 88, 108, 125, 134; comic, 158
Dreams from R'lyeh (Carter) 238

"Dreams in the Witch House, The" (Lovecraft) 65, 90-91, 114, 115, 117, 119, 120, 274; film, 276
"Dreams of Flesh and Stone" (Collrin) 229
Dubisch, Mike 261
Dunsany, Lord 61, 79, 97, 99-100, 248
"Dunwich Horror, The" (Lovecraft) 59, 61, 62, 63, 64, 66, 67, 68, 69, 72, 78, 81-85, 86, 87, 91, 98, 102, 108, 110, 112, 114, 115, 118, 119, 120-21, 133, 134, 135, 136, 141, 142, 144, 148, 150, 153, 169, 173-74, 176, 178, 179, 184, 193, 201, 207, 209, 222, 226, 231, 232, 235, 251, 258, 262, 276
Dunwich Horror, The (film) 149, 262, 274-75
"Dunwich Lodger, The" (McNaughton) 204, 221
Dunwich Romance, The (Lee) 143, 219, 221-22
"Dweller in Darkness, The" (Derleth) 253
Dwellers in the Mirage (Merritt) 148

Eddy, Clifford M., Jr. 32, 56, 58, 99, 100-101, 136, 195
Eddy, Muriel E. 28, 56, 101
Eldritch Blue: Love & Sex in the Cthulhu Mythos 132, 206, 209, 229-31
Ellis, Havelock 17, 25, 43, 92, 246
Ellis, Novalyne Price 164-65, 170
"Enchanted Fruit, The" (Campbell) 208
"End of the Story, The" (Smith) 138
Erotic Spectacles, The (Cohen) 204
Esoterika Biblion Society 30
Everts, R. Alain 15, 16, 19, 27, 56
"Exham Priory" (Price) 206
"Ex Libris" (Kiernan) 214

"Faces at Pine Dunes, The" (Campbell) 139, 190, 192-93, 195, 201, 231
"Facts concerning the Late Arthur Jermyn and His Family" (Lovecraft) 59, 70-73, 76, 77, 80, 82, 84, 85, 87, 88, 98, 105, 106, 110, 111, 112, 113, 115, 116, 121, 131, 135, 140, 177, 178, 193
"Fall of the House of Usher, The" (Poe) 59, 74, 75, 82

Falstaff Press 30, 166
"Family Tree of the Gods" (Smith) 135, 174-76
Farmer, Philip José 135, 149
"Fat Face" (Shea) 235
"Feery's Original Notes" (Price) 208, 245, 252
Fetish. *See* Paraphilia
Finlay, Virgil 261
"Fish Bride" (Kiernan) 214
"Fishhead" (Cobb) 79, 97
"Fisherman of Falcon Point, The" (Derleth) 185, 188
Flagellation. *See* BDSM
Franco, Jess 282-83
Frankenstein (Shelley) 58, 98, 126, 277
Frazer, Sir James George 77, 248
Freud, Sigmund 17, 22, 24, 107-8, 201, 246; theories of, 37, 213
"From Beyond" (Lovecraft) 278, 280
From Beyond (film) 276, 278, 283
Fulci, Lucio 267
"Fungal Stain, The" (Pugmire) 212
Fungi from Yuggoth (Lovecraft) 212, 224, 238, 264

Galpin, Alfred 41, 42, 58
Gamwell, Annie E. P. 35, 36
Gemini Rising (McNaughton) 198, 199, 200, 202
Geoffrey, Justine 241-42
"Ghoulmaster" (McNaughton) 200
Giger, H. R. 150, 263, 283
Gilman, Charlotte Perkins 99, 177
Girl Meets Tentacles (comic) 267, 271
Golden Bough, The (Frazer) 77, 248
Goodfellow, Cody 278
Gordon, Stuart 276, 278, 280
Gorman, Herbert 97
Grant, Kenneth 244, 245, 247, 248-52, 253, 254, 255, 256, 257, 258, 259, 260
"Great God Pan, The" (Machen) 59, 60, 61-63, 65, 67-68, 79, 81, 82, 83, 84, 85, 102, 109, 110, 111, 122, 136, 144, 146, 173-74, 191, 193, 203, 226
"Green Decay, The" (Price) 207
"Green Meadow, The" (Lovecraft-Jackson) 27
Greene, Sonia H. *See* Davis, Sonia H.

H. P. Lovecraft 1890-1937 (Kuchar) 158
Haeckel, Ernst 51, 87, 151
Haldeman-Julius, Emanuel 43
Haller, Daniel 275
"Harbor-Master, The" (Chambers) 97
Hatfield, Gordon 41-42
Haunted Palace, The (film) 274, 275
Haunter at the Threshold (Lee) 198, 219, 220, 221
Haiyore! Nyaruko-san 272-73
Heald, Hazel 28, 69, 99, 106, 160, 234
Heavy Metal: magazine 150, 265; film: 271
Hentai 148, 152, 239, 271, 279
"Herbert West—Reanimator" (Lovecraft) 126, 156-57, 241
"Herbert West—Reincarnated" (McNaughton) 204
"Herburt East: Refuckinator" (Lisbon/Lustcraft) 156-57, 241
Hermaphrodite 123, 256
Hewetson, Al 265
Hine, Phil 245, 247, 254-56, 258, 260
"His Mouth Shall Taste of Wormwood" (Brite) 235
Hokusai, Katsushika 144-45
"Holiness of Azédarac, The" (Smith) 173
Holly, David 241
Home Brew 75, 171, 261
Homosexuality 14, 15, 38-48, 68, 73, 96, 97, 128-29, 139, 151, 152, 156-57, 161, 170, 181, 182, 183, 187, 189, 191, 192, 199, 204, 205, 207, 208-9, 211, 219, 221, 224, 232, 235, 239, 240-41, 246, 251, 255, 257, 260, 262, 265, 270, 273, 274, 281-82, 284. *See also* Lesbianism
"Horror at Martin's Beach, The" (Lovecraft-Greene) 18, 108
"Horror at Red Hook, The" (Lovecraft) 78-79, 80, 112, 120, 166, 168; parody, 158
Horror Between the Sheets (Morel) 132, 228
"Horror from the Bridge, The" (Campbell) 190
"Horror from the Middle Span, The" (Derleth) 185, 187, 188
"Horror in the Burying-Ground, The" (Lovecraft-Heald) 98, 106-7, 114, 118

"Horror in the Museum, The" (Lovecraft-Heald) 121, 147
"Horror under Warrendown, The" (Campbell) 190, 193
Houdini, Harry 19
Houellebecq, Michel 67, 107, 108, 133
"Hound, The" (Lovecraft) 101, 110, 207, 213, 235
"Hound of the Partridgevilles, The" (Cannon) 156, 198
"Hounds of Tindalos, The" (Long) 197
House Across the Way, The (McNaughton) 199, 200-201
House by the Cemetery, The (film) 267
"House of the Monoceros" (Smith) 172-73
Howard, Robert E. 18, 39, 49, 125, 131, 132, 135, 138, 147, 148, 158, 160, 163, 164-70, 172, 173, 175, 195, 200, 206, 234, 238, 241, 242, 274, 276
Huxley, Thomas Henry 50, 51
Hymen 18

"I Wore the Brassiere of Doom" (Price) 207
Image of the Beast (Farmer) 149
"Imp of Aether, The" (Pugmire) 212, 213
In Flagrant Delight (McNaughton) 199
"In His Darkling Daughter's Womb" (Jens) 234
"In the Walls of Eryx" (Lovecraft-Sterling) 36
In the Yaddith Time (Schwader) 238
Incest 18, 31, 38, 48, 73-75, 81-82, 83, 86, 133, 163, 176, 193, 194, 201, 203, 213, 235, 242, 277, 288
"Incubus of Atlantis, The" (Price) 207
Indick, Ben P. 113-14, 115
"Infernal Attractors" (Goodfellow) 278
Inhabitant of the Lake and Less Welcome Tenants, The (Campbell) 180, 188, 190, 191
"Ink" (Mojzes) 143
"Innsmouth Clay" (Derleth) 185, 188
Innswich Horror, The (Lee) 142, 159, 219, 220, 221
Interbreeding. *See* Miscegenation

"It Was the Day of the Deep One" (Cannon) 198

Jaccoma, Richard 275
Jackson, Winifred Virginia 27-28, 160
Jalajel, David 239
James, M. R. 146, 147, 218-19
Jaxon 265, 266
Jens, Tina L. 234
Joshi, S. T. 18, 27, 30-31, 35, 38, 41, 42, 49, 50, 53, 71, 72, 75, 77, 81, 93, 94-95, 96, 99-100, 101, 127, 128, 159, 195, 200
Joven Lovecraft, El 287

Kalem Club 14-15, 17, 198
Kama Sutra 138
Keene, Brian 236
Keller, David H. 35-36
Khai of Khem (Lumley) 234
Kiernan, Caitlín R. 109, 129, 139, 161, 214-18
King, Stephen 107-8
Kirk, George W. 15, 17, 30, 44
Kleiner, Rheinhart 16, 28, 34, 44, 45, 47, 49
"Kraken, The" (Tennyson) 145
Krafft-Ebing, Richard von 17
Krall, Jordan 219

Last Lovecraft: Relic of Cthulhu, The (film) 159, 282
Last Revelation of Gla'aki, The (Campbell) 190
"Last Test, The" (Lovecraft-de Castro) 63, 104, 106-7
Launet, François 287
LaVey, Anton 251
Lee, Edward 132, 142, 143, 158, 159, 198-99, 204, 218-23, 235, 242, 277, 290
Leiber, Fritz 30, 131
Lesbianism 43-44, 161, 170, 204, 208, 214, 241, 257, 273, 279, 280, 281, 284
Letters from an Old Gent (Pugmire) 157
Lévy, Maurice 37, 71-72
Lifeforce (film) 282
"Ligeia" (Poe) 59, 92, 117

"Lights! Camera! Shub-Niggurath!" (Lupoff) 196
Litersky, Dorothy 54–55, 182, 183
Long, Frank Belknap 13–14, 15, 27, 28, 34, 38, 42, 49, 50, 101, 128, 135, 148, 196–97, 198
Lopez, Zesar 265
Lord, Bruce 67, 113, 125–26, 128–29
Lovecraft, H. P.: and chastity, 20–21; as a fictional character, 157–59; on gender and homosexuality, 38–44; gender identity and sexuality of, 44–48; honeymoon of, 19; on love, 23–27; marriage of, 14, 16, 17, 18, 19, 21, 23, 24–25, 26–27, 34, 43, 44, 45, 47, 53–54, 55, 67, 69–70, 92, 94–95; on miscegenation, 48–53; and Oedipus complex myth, 37–38; on pornography and censorship, 28–34; on sex, 14–15, 21–23; relationships with women, 19, 21, 27–28, 69; sexual education of, 15–18; sexual experience of, 19–21; sex in his weird fiction, 65–70, 107–28; and syphilis myth, 34–37
Lovecraft, Linda: Michel Parry as, 190; comic character, 266, 268
Lovecraft, Lori 268
Lovecraft, Sarah Susan ("Susie") 37–38, 40, 45, 109, 117, 287
Lovecraft, Sonia. *See* Davis, Sonia H.
Lovecraft, Winfield Scott 34–35, 36, 159, 228
Lovecraft Chronicles, The (Cannon) 159, 197, 198
"Lovecraft in Heaven" (Morrison) 109, 158, 159
Lovecraft's Book (Lupoff) 158, 196, 198
"Loved Dead, The" (Lovecraft-Eddy) 32, 66, 100–101, 129, 131, 136, 195
Lovelace, Linda 266
Loveman, Samuel 15, 17, 31, 42, 44, 46, 55, 146, 157
Lovett-Graff, Bennet 50–51, 66, 88–89, 108
Lumley, Brian 135, 180, 206, 234, 258, 261
Lupoff, Richard 158, 195–96, 238

Lurker at the Threshold, The (Derleth) 163, 183, 184, 185, 187, 193, 207, 209, 237
"Lurking Fear, The" (Lovecraft) 59, 73–75, 76, 82, 85, 87, 101, 108, 110, 115, 131, 168–69, 178, 261

Machen, Arthur 43, 59–65, 67, 81, 97, 98, 102, 125, 128, 144, 146, 147, 168–69, 171, 173, 191, 192, 209, 228, 245, 248, 249, 265
McLaughlin, Mark 235
McNaughton, Brian 124, 125, 132, 163, 198–205, 210, 219, 221, 239, 271, 289
"Made in Goatswood" (Campbell) 190, 195, 208
Maeda, Toshio 144, 149, 150
Magical Revival, The (Grant) 244, 248, 249
Magick of Atlantis: Sauthenerom, The (Ripel) 247, 254
Mamatas, Nick 236, 238, 239
"Mannikin, The" (Bloch) 176
"Man of Stone, The" (Lovecraft-Heald) 65, 98, 106, 114, 118, 119
Marblehead (Lupoff). *See Lovecraft's Book*
Marten, Robert D. 117
"Mask, The" (Chambers) 106
Masochism. *See* BDSM
Mason, Asenath 258–60
Masterson, Graham 237
Masturbation 126, 246, 260, 262
"Mate for the Mutilator, A" (Price) 209, 245
"Medusa's Coil" (Lovecraft-Bishop) 91, 98, 104–6, 109, 114, 115, 117, 119, 173
Merritt, A. 58, 103, 148
"Merry May" (Campbell) 195
"Meryphillia" (McNaughton) 200
Métal Hurlant 149, 150
Miéville, China 143–44
Miller, Henry 158–59, 180, 181
Miscegenation 48–53, 63–64, 70, 71, 72, 74, 75, 76, 82
Mistry, Charlotte 241
Moe, Maurice W. 30, 32–34
Mojzes, Bernie 143

"Moon Lens, The" (Campbell) 123, 180, 191
"Moon of Skulls, The" (Howard) 170
Moon Pool, The (Merritt) 58, 103
Moonchild (Crowley) 207, 246, 251
Moore, Alan 159, 223-28, 242, 245, 269
Moore, Catherine L. 148, 160
Morbus Gravis 149
Moreno-Garcia, Silvia 160
Morrison, Grant 109, 158, 159, 256
Morton, James F. 15, 16-17, 23, 44, 48, 104
Mother Hydra 121-24
"Mother of Serpents" (Bloch) 177
"Mother of Toads" (Smith) 133, 173, 282
"Mound, The" (Lovecraft-Bishop) 98, 102, 103-4, 115, 117, 118, 119, 121, 122, 126, 127, 128, 131, 173, 175
Move Under Ground (Mamatas) 236
"Mud" (McNaughton) 124, 204
Murray, Margaret 65, 90, 168, 248
Mystery of the Necronomicon (anime) 279, 284

"Nameless Offspring, The" (Smith) 125, 136, 173-74
Necronomicon (film) 276, 278, 283
Necronomicon (Giger) 263
Necronomicon: The Book of Dead Names (Hay) 200, 245, 252, 258
Necronomicon (Simon) 244, 245, 252, 253-54, 255, 256, 257, 258, 260
Necronomicon Gnosis (Mason) 258-60
Necrophilia 18, 100-101, 129, 163, 172, 178, 182, 193, 217
Nelson, Victoria 36, 65-66, 88
Neonomicon (Moore) 225-27, 242, 245, 269
Nightmare's Disciple (Pulver) 235
Noé, Ignacio 139, 150, 267, 270
"Nothing Personal" (Lupoff) 196
"Novel of the Black Seal" (Machen) 59, 63-64, 65, 79, 83, 84, 88, 102, 121, 125, 141, 146, 150, 168, 169, 174, 210, 251
Nudity 30, 33, 105, 132, 133, 145, 150, 166, 170, 182, 207, 217, 218, 226, 229, 261, 263, 264, 265, 266, 273, 274, 275, 277, 278, 279, 282, 286, 287

O'Brien, Kevin L. 112, 141, 229-30, 231
"Old Horns, The" (Campbell) 190, 195
Oliver, Jose 287
Olympia Press 180, 192, 199, 204
120 Days of Sodom (Sade) 138
Orgone 225, 245, 252
"Out of the Aeons" (Lovecraft-Heald) 123, 234
"Outsider, The" (Lovecraft) 48, 73, 108, 111

"Paedomorphosis" (Kiernan) 214
"Pages Found among the Effects of Miss Edith M. Tiller" (Kiernan) 214, 217
Pages Torn from a Travel Journal (Lee) 219, 220, 223
Paraphilia 15, 120, 136, 141, 154, 192, 194, 199, 207, 219, 220, 230, 239, 255, 280, 286, 288
Parody 61, 100, 103, 146, 156-57, 158-59, 197, 233, 238, 241, 271, 275, 277, 280
"pas-en-arrière" (Kiernan) 217-18
"Pathetic History of Sir Wilful Wildrake, The" (Lovecraft) 29, 58
Pedophilia 18, 41, 189, 191, 192, 195, 207, 208, 219
Pelan, John 219, 235, 236
"Perils of Liberated Objects, or, The Voyeur's Seduction, The" (Kiernan) 139, 217
"Philtre Tip" (Bloch) 138, 177
Picasso, Pablo 145, 146
"Pickman Models, The" (Marten) 117
"Pickman's Model" (Lovecraft) 125, 178, 218, 225, 255
"Pickman's Other Model" (Kiernan) 217-18
"Picture in the House, The" (Lovecraft) 192
Place Called Dagon, The (Gorman) 97
Playboy 176, 263, 278
Poe, Edgar Allan 18, 59, 66, 75, 92, 97, 171, 186, 210
Pornomicon, The (Logan) 139, 262, 270
Pretty Little Mouth, A (Tanzer) 161
"Prey of the Goat, The" (Carter) 142, 237
Priapus 18

Price, E. Hoffmann 91–92, 99, 167, 172, 274
Price, Robert M. 36–37, 45, 48, 81, 93, 125, 129, 138, 162, 184, 197, 205–9, 210, 212, 229, 238, 245, 252, 261, 288
Prime Chaos (Hine) 255
Prostitution 29, 35, 91, 139, 155, 168, 170, 217, 221, 226, 227, 230, 235
Pseudonomicon (Hine) 255, 258
Psycho (Bloch) 177
"Psychopompos" (Lovecraft) 114
Pugmire, W. H. 125, 157, 161, 163, 209, 210–13, 216, 238, 239
Pulptime (Cannon) 159, 198
Pulver, Joseph S., Sr. 236

Ramba (comic) 267
Rape 39, 59, 64, 78–79, 85, 92, 115, 120–21, 125, 136, 141, 143, 152, 154, 155, 166, 169, 170, 190, 192, 193, 199, 207, 219, 225, 226, 227, 228, 232, 234, 235, 268, 275, 278, 279, 280, 281, 282
"Rats in the Walls, The" (Lovecraft) 50, 59, 75–77, 85, 103, 113, 115, 123, 131, 136, 177, 178, 191, 202, 206; comic, 265
Re-Animator (film) 274, 276–77, 278, 280, 282, 283
"Recognition" (Moore) 159, 228
"Red Hand, The" (Machen) 122, 128, 168
Reich, Wilhelm 225, 245, 252
Re-Penetrator (film) 157, 277, 280
"Return of Hastur, The" (Derleth) 185, 187
Rimel, Duane W. 122
Ripel, Frank G. 247, 254
R'lyeh Sutra (chonzz) 239
R'lyeh Text, The (Hay) 252
"Round Tower, The" (Price) 207
Russ, Joana 160

Sacher-Masoch, Leopold von 29
"Sacrifice to Science, A" (de Castro) 101–2
Sade, Donatien Alphonse François, marquis de 29, 138, 176, 219, 222
Sadism. *See* BDSM

"Sandwin Compact, The" (Derleth) 187
Sappho 77
Sargent, Stanley C. 38, 45, 115–16, 161, 210, 235, 238
Satanic Rituals, The (LaVey) 251
Satan's Love Child (McNaughton). *See Gemini Rising*
Satan's Mistress (McNaughton). *See Downward to Darkness*
Satan's Seductress (McNaughton). *See Worse Things Waiting*
Satan's Surrogate (McNaughton). *See The House Across the Way*
"Scarlet Succubus, The" (Lee-Pelan) 219, 235
Schwader, Ann K. 238
Scott, Winfield Townley 14, 18, 34, 35, 37–38, 48, 53–54, 179, 200
"Scream for Jeeves" (Cannon) 197–98
"Seal of R'lyeh, The" (Derleth) 188
"Second Staircase, The" (Campbell) 195
"Secret of Sebek, The" (Bloch) 177
Sennitt, Stephen 109, 245, 256
Serpieri, Paolo 149, 150
Sesqua Valley and Other Haunts (Pugmire) 211, 239
"Seven Geases, The" (Smith) 176
Sex: anal, 129, 152, 205, 241, 246, 258, 260; oral, 143, 241, 248, 260, 267n2; with animals: *see* Bestiality; with the dead: *see* Necrophilia; with Mythos entities: *see* Xenophilia; with tentacles: *see* Tentacle sex. *See also* Adultery, Androgyny, BDSM, Cuckoldry, Hermaphrodite, Incest, Masturbation, Miscegenation, Nudity, Paraphilia, Pedophilia, Prostitution, Rape, Sex toys, Sexuality, Sexually transmitted disease, Sexual symbols, Tantra, Voyeurism
Sex toys 204n4, 227, 279, 289n1
Sexual Inversions (Ellis-Symonds) 43, 92
Sexuality: of August Derleth, 182–83; of H. P. Lovecraft, 44–48; of Mythos writers, 159–61. *See also* Asexuality, Bisexuality, Homosexuality, Transsexuality
Sexually transmitted disease 22, 34–38, 57, 88, 89–90, 129, 141, 159, 205, 228
Sexual symbols 33, 45, 84, 104, 107–9, 124–25, 142–53, 166, 191, 246, 250, 255, 261–62, 278

"Shadow in the Attic, The" (Derleth) 187–88
"Shadow Kingdom, The" (Howard) 276
"Shadow out of Time, The" (Lovecraft) 124, 126, 147, 186
"Shadow over Innsmouth, The" (Lovecraft) 59, 64, 69, 72, 77, 80, 85–90, 92, 97, 98, 105, 110, 111, 112, 113, 114, 115, 121, 122, 129, 131, 135, 136, 140, 141, 142, 153, 154, 178, 191, 193, 220, 231, 261, 262, 28
"Shambleau" (Moore) 148, 160
"She Devil" (Howard) 167
Shea, J. Vernon 16, 20, 25, 31, 42, 46, 48, 65, 69, 98, 108, 109
Shea, Michael 235
Shelley, Mary Wollstonecraft 58, 98, 126, 277
"Shining Pyramid, The" (Machen) 128, 168
"Ship in Mutiny, The" (Howard) 170
"Shoggoth Makes Three" (Donnel) 229
Shub-Niggurath 59, 63, 74, 104, 110, 121–24, 126, 134, 191, 196, 237, 242n6, 253, 254, 256–57, 259, 263, 288
"Shunned House, The" (Lovecraft) 114
"Shuttered Room, The" (Derleth) 135, 185, 282
Simon 244, 245, 252, 253–54, 255, 256, 257, 258, 260
Skull (comic) 265–66
Smith, Clark Ashton 31, 39, 75, 123, 125, 131, 132, 133, 134, 135, 136, 138, 145–46, 147, 151, 160, 163, 167, 171–76, 207, 210, 219. 235, 238, 261, 272
Smith, Tevis Clyde 167, 170
"Some Distant, Baying Sound" (Kiernan) 129, 213
"Sound and the Fungi, The" (Cannon) 197
"Space-Eaters, The" (Long) 197
Space Vampires, The (Wilson) 282
Spare, Austin Osman 247–48, 249, 250, 255, 259, 260
"Spawn of the Green Abyss" (Thompson) 235

Spicy pulps 92, 133, 159, 163–64, 165, 167, 168, 170, 172–73, 274; *Snappy Stories,* 29
Star*Reach (comic) 266
Starry Wisdom: A Tribute to H. P. Lovecraft, The 224, 256
Sterling, Kenneth 35
Stevens, Carter 275
Stoker, Bram 58, 134
Strange Eons (Bloch) 177–79, 202
Succubus (film) 282–83
"Supernatural Horror in Literature" (Lovecraft) 39, 60, 64, 75, 97–99, 109, 153
Swift, Jonathan 18, 58, 90, 104

Tales from the Leather Nun (comic) 265
Tales of Sex and Sorcery (Whitechapel) 235
Tales of the Cthulhu Mythos (Derleth) 180, 189, 261
Tantra 208, 246, 249, 254, 257, 258, 259, 260
Tanzer, Molly 160
"Tarbis of the Lake" (Price) 91–92
Tarzan Alive (Farmer) 135
Teenage Twins (film) 275–76, 280, 284
Tennyson, Alfred, Lord 145
Tentacles of Love (Carter) 236
Tentacle sex 139, 142–53, 209, 217, 222, 231, 232, 233, 236, 240, 241, 250, 261–62, 267, 270, 271, 272, 275, 283, 285, 286
"Terror from the Depths, The" (Leiber) 30
"Terror of Cut-Throat Cove, The" (Bloch) 177
"Testament of Athammaus, The" (Smith) 175
Theobald, Sally 207
"Thing from Lover's Lane, The" (Collins) 235
"Thing on the Doorstep, The" (Lovecraft) 38, 68, 69, 91–97, 98, 111, 113, 114, 115, 117, 124, 126, 128, 135, 137, 153, 195, 197, 201, 231, 232
Thompson, C. Hall 235
Thompson, Jason Bradley 158
"Thousand Young, A" (Price) 138, 207, 209, 230

Throne of Bones, The (McNaughton) 199, 200
"Through the Gates of the Silver Key" (Lovecraft-Price) 64, 91
Tide of Desire (McNaughton) 202, 203, 271
"To My Dear Friend, Hommy-Beg" (McNaughton) 200
Toldridge, Elizabeth 24
Torres, Bartolo 287
"Tower of the Elephant, The" (Howard) 170
Trail of Cthulhu, The (Derleth) 187, 261
Transexuality 96, 151, 161, 213, 214
Transition of Titus Crow, The (Lumley) 234
"Trap, The" (Lovecraft-Whitehead) 129
"Treasure of Abbot Thomas, The" (James) 146
"Tree House, The" (Price-Pugmire) 212
Trolley No. 1852 (Lee) 158, 159, 219, 220, 223
Tsathoggua 134, 135, 171, 173, 174, 175, 176, 207
Turner, James 195-96
Tyson, Donald 256-58, 260

"Ubbo-Sathla" (Smith) 151, 175, 176
"Under the Pyramids" (Lovecraft-Houdini) 19, 114
"Unnamable, The" (Lovecraft) 77-78, 184
Unnameable, The (film) 274, 278
"Unspeakable Betrothal, The" (Bloch) 177
Unspeakable Vault (of Doom), The 287
Urotsukidōji 149

vagina dentata 108
Vosburg, Mike 266, 268
Voudon-Gnostic Workbook (Bertiaux) 252
Voyeurism 139, 217

"Walker in the Cemetery, The" (Watson) 235
Wandrei, Donald 54, 195
Warlock Asylum 254
Watson, Ian 235
Weird Sex-Fantasy 149
Weird Tales 30-31, 92, 100, 132, 133, 147, 164, 167, 171, 179, 187, 188, 193, 200, 202, 236, 238, 262

"Whippoorwills in the Hills, The" (Derleth) 185
"Whisperer in Darkness, The" (Lovecraft) 123
Whispers in Darkness: Lovecraftian Erotica (Blackmore) 233-34, 262
White, Tim 261
"White People, The" (Machen) 59, 64-65, 81, 98, 111, 168, 192, 193, 209, 269
Whitechapel, Simon 235
Whitehead, Henry S. 99, 129
"Why I Want to Fuck Cthulhu" (Clore) 229
Wicked Walter 204
"Wilbur Whateley Waiting" 207, 245
Wilde, Oscar 42, 55, 60, 210
Wilson, Colin 36n2, 66, 133, 179, 180, 200, 220, 227, 245, 251
Wilson, Gahan 263, 288
"Witchcraft of Ulua, The" (Smith) 132
Wood, Wally 149
"Worms of the Earth" (Howard) 169, 170, 173
Worse Things Waiting (McNaughton) 198, 199, 200, 202, 203
"Woven Offspring, The" (Pugmire) 212
Wright, Farnsworth 30, 132, 150, 205

Xenophilia 63-64, 75, 76, 82, 83, 86, 105, 106, 112-13, 114, 125, 131, 135, 136, 156, 170, 178, 198, 206, 212, 217, 220, 225, 230, 234, 251, 263, 264, 265, 266, 274, 275, 285, 288. *See also* Tentacle sex
"Xuthal of the Dusk" (Howard) 148, 168

Yellow Book 60, 144
"Yellow Wall Paper, The" (Gilman) 99, 177
Yog-Sothoth 63, 66, 84, 85, 98, 123, 124, 126, 133, 134, 135, 141, 153, 154, 178, 212, 234, 270, 288
Yuzna, Brian 276, 277-78, 280

"Zaman's Hill" (Moore) 224, 228

www.ingramcontent.com/pod-product-compliance
Lightning Source LLC
Chambersburg PA
CBHW060110170426
43198CB00010B/836